SPIES
IN THE
CONGO

SPIES
IN THE
CONGO

AMERICA'S ATOMIC MISSION
IN WORLD WAR II

Susan Williams

PublicAffairs
New York

Published by PublicAffairs, an imprint of Perseus Books, a division
of PBG Publishing, LLC, a subsidiary of Hachette Book Group, Inc.

A CIP catalog record for this book is available from the Library of
Congress.
LCCN: 2016936154
ISBN 978-1-61039-654-7 (hardcover)
ISBN 978-1-61039-655-4 (e-book)
First published in the United Kingdom in 2016 by C. Hurst & Co.
(Publishers) Ltd.
UK ISBN 9781849046381

First Edition

10 9 8 7 6 5 4 3 2 1

For Tendi

CONTENTS

CONTENTS

Photographs follow page 200.

ABBREVIATIONS AND CODEWORDS

A-2	Intelligence Section of Air Staff, US
Abwehr	Intelligence Service, Germany
AEF	Afrique Equatoriale Française
AHEC	Army Heritage and Education Center, US Army War College
ALSOS	US mission investigating Germany's atomic project in Europe
AMEW	Africa-Middle East Wing Headquarters
ATC	Air Transport Command, US
AZUSA	OSS atomic intelligence mission in Europe
BCK	Compagnie du Chemin de Fer du Bas-Congo au Katanga
BCRA	Bureau Central de Renseignements et d'Action
BEW	Bureau of Economic Warfare, US
BOAC	British Overseas Airways Corporation
C	Chief of SIS
Caltex	California Texas Oil Company (see also Texaco below)
CDT	Combined Development Trust
CFL	Compagnie des Chemins de Fer du Congo Supérieur aux Grands Lacs Africains
CIA	Central Intelligence Agency, US, successor to OSS
CIC	Counter Intelligence Corps, US Army

ABBREVIATIONS AND CODEWORDS

CIG	Centre d'Information Gouvernemental
CIG	Central Intelligence Group
COI	Office of the Coordinator of Information, US, predecessor of OSS
CSK	Comité Spécial du Katanga
DNI	Director of Naval Intelligence, US
ETC	Études et Traitements Chimiques
Eville	Elisabethville
FBI	Federal Bureau of Investigation, US
FEA	Foreign Economic Administration, US, successor to BEW
FOI	Freedom of Information, UK
FOIA	Freedom of Information Act, USA
FRUS	Foreign Relations of the United States
G-2	Army Intelligence, US
G-5	Civil Affairs division of SHAEF
HEU	Highly Enriched Uranium
HMG	His Majesty's Government, UK
HMSO	Her Majesty's Stationery Office
IAEA	International Atomic Energy Authority
IDB	Illicit Diamond Buying
IDSO	International Diamond Security Organization
Leo	Léopoldville
M	Head of MI5
MALPAS	British intelligence network to monitor Axis shipping
MED	Manhattan Engineer District
MEW	Ministry of Economic Warfare, UK
MI5	Security Service, UK
MI6	Secret Intelligence Service, UK, also known as SIS
MIS	Military Intelligence Service, US
MO	Morale Operations, OSS
NARA	National Archives and Records Administration, US

ABBREVIATIONS AND CODEWORDS

ONI	Office of Naval Intelligence, US
OSS	Office of Strategic Services, US
OWI	Office of War Information, US
Pan Am	Pan American Airways
R&A	Research and Analysis Division, OSS
RG	Record Group
SAPE	Société des Ambianceurs et des Personnes Élégantes, Congo
SEDEC	Société d'Entreprises Commerciales au Congo Belge
SI	Secret Intelligence, OSS
SIS	Secret Intelligence Service, UK, also known as MI6
SO	Special Operations branch, OSS
SOE	Special Operations Executive, UK
SOGEDEX	Rubber company serving as a cover for British agents
Tanks	Tanganyika Concessions
Texaco	California Texas Oil Company (see also Caltex above)
TNA	The National Archives, UK
TORCH	Allied invasion of North Africa in 1942
Tube Alloys	British atomic project
UKCC	United Kingdom Commercial Corps
UN	United Nations
UNRRA	United Nations Relief and Rehabilitation Administration
USG	US Government
W/T	Wireless/Telegraphy
X-2	Counter-intelligence branch, OSS

CAST OF CHARACTERS

Key OSS personnel are emboldened

ANGELLA, see Chidsey, Shirley Armitage

Bascom, William (former OSS agent), Chief of US Foreign Economic Administration, Accra, Gold Coast, codename PSYCHE in British B-2 PROTECT

Basehart, Harry W., OSS agent and head of mission Accra, Gold Coast, codename OJIBWA, under military cover

Beaudinet, Jean N., Chef de Sûreté, Léopoldville, Belgian Congo

Beecher, Willard, OSS Africa Section personnel and training officer, Washington

Benton, J. Webb, US Consul General, Léopoldville, Belgian Congo, as of 26 April 1944

Berg, Morris 'Moe', OSS agent, Europe, codename REMUS

Binney, Alexander 'Alec', Major, SOE official, Accra, Gold Coast, codename JUNO in B-2 PROTECT, code symbol W/M, codenumber 2324

Bonner, Douglas Griswold 'Doug', Major, OSS agent, Accra, Gold Coast, codename first WELSH, then CRUMB, codenumber 371, under military cover

Boulton, Wolfrid Rudyerd 'Rud', Divisional Deputy of Secret Intelligence, OSS, Africa Section, Washington, codename NYANZA, **codenumber first 951, later 178**

Bruce, David K. E., Head of Secret Intelligence, OSS, Washington

Buell, Robert L., US Consul General, Léopoldville, Belgian Congo, as of 24 January 1945

Bunche, Ralph, OSS officer, Research and Analysis Section, Washington

CARL WEST, **see Hogue, Wilbur Owings 'Dock'**

Chapin, James 'Jim', Dr, OSS agent Belgian Congo, codename CRISP, **under cover of Special Assistant to US Consul in Léopoldville (an ornithologist)**

Chidsey, Shirley Armitage, OSS agent and administrator, Léopoldville, Belgian Congo, codename ANGELLA, **codenumber first 1080, later 987/50**

CIGAR, see Starcher, H. Watson

Clark, Corporal, OSS agent Accra, Gold Coast, codename HANLY

CLOCK, **see Kirkland, John W.**

COACH, **see Luther, Duane D.**

Cousin, Jules, administrative director of Union Minière, Katanga

CRISP, **see Chapin, James**

Crocker, C. I., Major, SOE official, West Africa, codename VULCAN

Cromie, Leonard J., US Vice Consul, Léopoldville, Belgian Congo, as of 3 December 1941

CRUMB, **see Bonner, Douglas Griswold**

Cunliffe-Lister, Philip, Viscount Swinton, British Cabinet Minister, Resident in West Africa, Accra, Gold Coast, codename MARS

CAST OF CHARACTERS

D'Albertanson, Noel Ildefouse, SOE official, Accra, Gold Coast, code symbol W15

Davis, Leonard R., OSS agent and communications officer, Accra, Gold Coast, codename TRUCK, codenumber 979, under military cover

De Gesnot, Justin, Comptroller of Customs in Albertville, an information source of Hogue

De Gesnot, [first name unknown], Comptroller of Customs in Matadi, an information source of Hogue

Dean, Howard Brush, Vice President of Pan Am Africa

Decoster, Jean, OSS cutout, Belgian Congo, codenumber 253/25

Denis, Armand, OSS agent, Léopoldville, Belgian Congo, under cover as naturalist and photographer, collecting live gorillas

Donovan, General William J. 'Wild Bill', Director of OSS, codenumber 109

EBERT, see Harris, Huntington

Einstein, Albert, German-born American physicist

FLARE, see Schmidt, Adolph W.

Gerard, A. S., assistant to Van Bree. See Van Bree, Firmin

Greer, Thomas N., OSS cutout, Léopoldville, Belgian Congo, under cover of US Bureau of Economic Warfare, which became Foreign Economic Administration

Groves, General Leslie R., Military Commander of the Manhattan Project

Hahn, Otto, German chemist

HANLY, see Clark, Corporal

CAST OF CHARACTERS

Harris, Huntington 'Hunt', OSS agent Lourenço Marques under cover of War Shipping Department; then OSS head of station, Accra, Gold Coast; codename EBERT, codenumber 185

Heisenberg, Werner, German atomic theoretician

Hemptinne, Félix de, Monseigneur, Roman Catholic Vicar Apostolic of Katanga

Hogue, Ruth Regina (maiden name West), wife of Dock Hogue

Hogue, Wilbur Owings 'Dock', OSS agent Liberia, codename CARL WEST or WEST; then head of station, Léopoldville, Belgian Congo, codename TETON, under cover of Special Assistant to US Consul, Léopoldville; codenumber 253

HOMER, see Violett, Lanier

Hunt, Mary Winifred (maiden name Hutchinson), British Secret Intelligence Service official in Lourenço Marques, then wife of Huntington Harris, Accra.

Ingle, Edward M., US Vice Consul, Léopoldville, Belgian Congo, as of 22 September 1942

Jacobs, Leon P., Chief of Police at Matadi

Jaubert [erroneously called Joubert in some documents], OSS cutout, Elisabethville, Belgian Congo, under cover of US Bureau of Economic Warfare, which became Foreign Economic Administration

JUNO, see Binney, Alexander

Kirkland, John W., OSS agent Ivory Coast, later Belgian Congo, codename CLOCK, under cover of Texas Oil Co; codenumber 953 in Ivory Coast, 1060 in Congo

Laxalt, Robert 'Bob', Code Officer, US Consulate General, Léopoldville, Belgian Congo, June 1944–April 1945

Liddell, Guy, MI5 Official

CAST OF CHARACTERS

Llerena, Eduardo D., OSS agent, Portuguese Guinea, codename RUFUS, codenumber 555, under cover of Pan American Airways

LOCUST, see Stehli, Henry Emil

Luther, Duane D., OSS agent, Accra, Gold Coast, codename COACH, codenumber 946

Magruder, John, Deputy Director, OSS, Washington

Mallon, Patrick, US Consul, Léopoldville, Belgian Congo, as of 16 October 1940

MARS, see Cunliffe-Lister, Philip

Marthoz, Aimé, Managing Director of Union Minière

Martin, Edwin W., Vice Consul, Léopoldville, Belgian Congo, as of 21 March 1944

Menzies, Sir Stewart Graham, 'C', Head of MI6

Muggeridge, Malcolm, British Secret Intelligence Service official, Lourenço Marques, Mozambique

NORTH, see Weaver, Johnny

NYANZA, see Boulton, Wolfrid Rudyerd

OJIBWA, see Basehart, Harry W.

Oppenheimer, J. Robert, American physicist, Technical Director of the Manhattan Project

Pash, Lt.-Col. Boris T., Head of Intelligence and Security Division, Manhattan Project

Price, Hickman, Head of US Bureau of Economic Warfare, which became Foreign Economic Administration, Belgian Congo

PSYCHE, see Bascom, William

REMUS, see Berg, Morris

Russell, Peter, SOE official in Accra, Gold Coast, codename PLUTO, code symbol W15

CAST OF CHARACTERS

Ryckmans, Pierre, Governor General of the Belgian Congo (1934–1946)

Scheerlinck, François, provincial head of the Sûreté, Katanga

Schmidt, Adolph W. 'Schmitty'/'Dolph', Major, OSS head of station Accra, Gold Coast, codename FLARE, under military cover

Schwartz, Harry H., US Vice Consul, Léopoldville, Belgian Congo, as of 8 December 1943

Sengier, Edgar, Managing Director of Union Minière, based in New York

Shepardson, W. H., Chief of Secret Intelligence OSS, Washington

Shepherd, Francis, British Consul General in Léopoldville, Belgian Congo

SILVA (codename), OSS agent, Lobito, Angola

Starcher, H. Watson, OSS agent Ivory Coast, codename CIGAR, under cover of Pan Am

Stehli, Henry Emil, OSS agent Léopoldville, Belgian Congo, codename LOCUST, codenumber 923, under cover of business interest in silk textiles

Stephens, Peter, British consul in Elisabethville, Belgian Congo

Stimson, Henry L., US Secretary of War

TETON, see Hogue, Wilbur Owings

TRUCK, see Davis, Leonard R.

Turk, Lieutenant James, US Army finance officer, Accra, Gold Coast

Van Bree, Firmin, Director of Union Minière, Société Générale, and other appointments

CAST OF CHARACTERS

Van Weyenbergh, Maurice, Senior Executive at Union Minière, Elisabethville, Belgian Congo

Violett, Lanier 'Vic', OSS agent Luanda, Angola, codename HOMER, codenumber 397, under cover of Texas Oil Co.

VULCAN, see Crocker, C. I.

Weaver, Johnny, OSS agent Accra, Gold Coast, codename NORTH

WELSH, see Bonner, Douglas Griswold

Williams, Alan, British Consul General in Léopoldville, Belgian Congo

Withers, Charles D., US Economic Analyst, Léopoldville, Belgian Congo, as of 2 September 1943

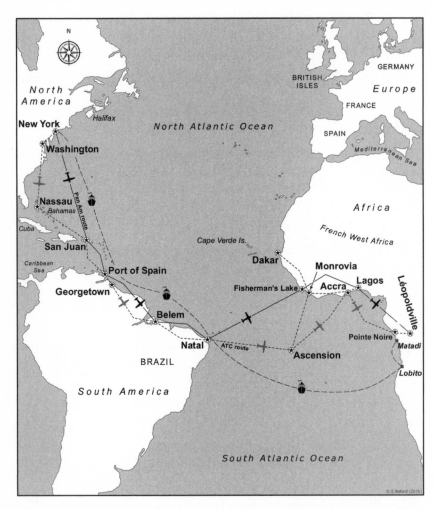

Map 1. Transport routes between the Belgian Congo and the US in 1943-45: flight routes between New York and Léopoldville used by the Pan American Airways clipper service and by US Air Transport Command (ATC); and a sea lane between Matadi and New York.

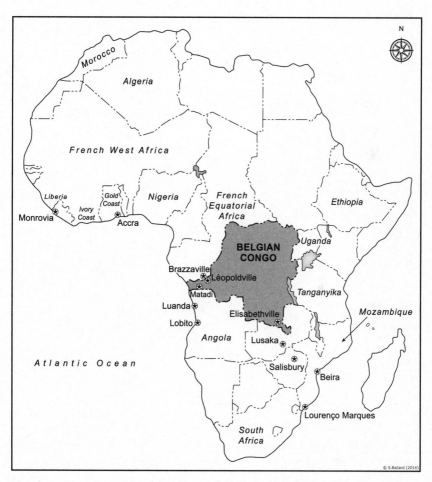

Map 2. The continent of Africa in the years of the Second World War.

Map 3. The routes used to deliver uranium from Shinkolobwe to the coast, on its way to the US. Shipments in 1942 were dispatched via rail to Lobito in Angola. From early 1943 they were freighted to Matadi, to avoid travel through a colony of Portugal, a neutral country. This was a long, complicated route: by train to the railhead at Port-Francqui; by barge on the Kasai River to where it joins the Congo River and on to Léopoldville; and from there by rail to Matadi.

LETTER FROM ALBERT EINSTEIN TO PRESIDENT ROOSEVELT, 2 AUGUST 1939

Albert Einstein
Old Grove Rd.
Nassau Point
Peconic, Long Island

August 2nd, 1939

F.D. Roosevelt,
President of the United States,
White House
Washington, D.C.

Sir:

Some recent work by E.Fermi and L. Szilard, which has been communicated to me in manuscript, leads me to expect that the element uranium may be turned into a new and important source of energy in the immediate future. Certain aspects of the situation which has arisen seem to call for watchfulness and, if necessary, quick action on the part of the Administration. I believe therefore that it is my duty to bring to your attention the following facts and recommendations:

In the course of the last four months it has been made probable - through the work of Joliot in France as well as Fermi and Szilard in America - that it may become possible to set up a nuclear chain reaction in a large mass of uranium,by which vast amounts of power and large quantities of new radium-like elements would be generated. Now it appears almost certain that this could be achieved in the immediate future.

This new phenomenon would also lead to the construction of bombs, and it is conceivable - though much less certain - that extremely powerful bombs of a new type may thus be constructed. A single bomb of this type, carried by boat and exploded in a port, might very well destroy the whole port together with some of the surrounding territory. However, such bombs might very well prove to be too heavy for transportation by air.

The United States has only very poor ores of uranium in moderate quantities. There is some good ore in Canada and the former Czechoslovakia, while the most important source of uranium is Belgian Congo.

In view of this situation you may think it desirable to have some permanent contact maintained between the Administration and the group of physicists working on chain reactions in America. One possible way of achieving this might be for you to entrust with this task a person who has your confidence and who could perhaps serve in an inofficial capacity. His task might comprise the following:

a) to approach Government Departments, keep them informed of the further development, and put forward recommendations for Government action, giving particular attention to the problem of securing a supply of uranium ore for the United States;

b) to speed up the experimental work,which is at present being carried on within the limits of the budgets of University laboratories, by providing funds, if such funds be required, through his contacts with private persons who are willing to make contributions for this cause, and perhaps also by obtaining the co-operation of industrial laboratories which have the necessary equipment.

I understand that Germany has actually stopped the sale of uranium from the Czechoslovakian mines which she has taken over. That she should have taken such early action might perhaps be understood on the ground that the son of the German Under-Secretary of State, von Weizsäcker, is attached to the Kaiser-Wilhelm-Institut in Berlin where some of the American work on uranium is now being repeated.

Yours very truly,

A. Einstein

(Albert Einstein)

1

INTRODUCTION

THE MANHATTAN PROJECT AND SHINKOLOBWE

'*La prochaine guerre sera gagnée par le pays qui aura le contrôle de l'urane*'.

(The next war will be won by the country which has control of uranium.)

Minister in Winston Churchill's Cabinet to Edgar Sengier,
Director of Union Minière, May 1939[1]

On 2 August 1939, Albert Einstein, the Nobel Prize winning physicist, signed a letter to President Franklin D. Roosevelt, warning of the potential of Hitler's Nazi regime to develop an atomic bomb.[2] Some recent research, he told Roosevelt, 'leads me to expect that the element uranium may be turned into a new and important source of energy in the immediate future', which would make it possible to set up a nuclear chain reaction generating vast amounts of power. This new phenomenon, he said, would lead to the construction of 'extremely powerful bombs of a new type'. He added that Germany had stopped selling the uranium from the Czechoslovakian mines it had taken over and he recommended giving 'particular attention to the problem of securing a supply of uranium ore for the United States'. Einstein

1

was a pacifist, but he wanted to prevent Nazi Germany from having sole possession of this new destructive power.[3]

Einstein's letter fired the starting-pistol for America to enter a kind of race that the world had never known before: the race to develop the atomic bomb before Germany.

Since it was impossible to build an atomic bomb without uranium ore, it was essential to obtain sufficient ore of high quality. The United States, Einstein told Roosevelt, 'has only very poor ores of uranium in moderate quantities'. There was some good ore in Canada and the former Czechoslovakia but 'the most important source of uranium', he said, was in Africa—in the Belgian Congo (now known as the Democratic Republic of Congo). This source was the Shinkolobwe mine in Katanga, the southernmost province of the Congo, and was owned by a huge Belgian mining company called the Union Minière du Haut Katanga. Shinkolobwe, which is near the town of Jadotville (now known as Likasi) and nearly ninety miles northwest of Elisabethville (now Lubumbashi), the capital of Katanga, had been used to produce radium, a by-product of uranium. The mine was a huge, open gash about a half-mile square, with terraced sides that went down about 225 feet.[4] It had been closed in 1937, fell into disrepair and became flooded. However, a large stock of mined uranium ore was still piled up there.[5]

The uranium from the Shinkolobwe mine was remarkable. It assayed as high as 75 per cent uranium oxide, with an average of over 65 per cent.[6] This was exceptional in comparison with the other ores that were available: from the Eldorado mine in the Northwest Territory of Canada and from the Colorado Plateau, which contained 0.02 per cent uranium oxide; or from the South African uranium ores derived from gold-mine operations, which had a uranium oxide content of the order of 0.03 per cent.[7] The unique richness of the Katanga ore was essential at that time for any physicist hoping to build an atomic weapon. 'You have to have a relatively rich source of ore,' noted Lorna Arnold, a nuclear historian, looking back from the perspective of the twenty-first century, 'to be able to quickly amass sufficient amounts of uranium metal, from which you might either separate out the rare fissionable isotope or manufacture fissionable plutonium—and Shinkolobwe is by far the richest known source of uranium in the world.'[8]

In response to Einstein's initiative, President Roosevelt in October 1939 set up a Uranium Committee as an advisory body, which was chaired by Lyman J. Briggs, director of the National Bureau of Standards. Then, when it was discovered in April 1940 that the Kaiser Wilhelm Institute of Physics in Berlin had started an extensive research programme involving uranium, the committee's work took on a new urgency: it recommended the funding of significant research in the US, especially work at Columbia University in New York on nuclear chain reactions.[9]

In June 1940, shortly after Belgium's defeat and occupation by Germany, the Uranium Committee encouraged Edgar Sengier, the Managing Director of Union Minière, to move its mined supplies of Congolese uranium to the US for safekeeping.[10] There was serious concern at this time that the Congo might be invaded by Nazi Germany. Sengier later noted having serious reservations about security in Katanga—'la sécurité au Katanga était mal garantie'.[11] Before the war, the ore had been shipped to a Union Minière refinery in Belgium; but now that Belgium was occupied by the Nazis, it was decided to ship the ore directly from the Congo to America.[12]

Towards the end of 1940, 1,200 tons of the stockpiled uranium ore at Shinkolobwe—of approximately 70 per cent uranium oxide—were shipped to New York.[13] A commercial arm of Union Minière was specially set up in New York to arrange for the transport of the ore. This was the African Metals Corporation, also known as Afrimet, which became the sole agent for the sale of Union Minière products in the US. During September and October 1940, the ore was shipped from the Congo and was stored on arrival on Staten Island in New York.[14]

Edgar Sengier, a qualified engineer, had worked for Union Minière since 1911; he was appointed director of the company in

1932.[15] He later claimed that it was entirely his own idea to send the uranium to New York. 'I did this,' he told the writer John Gunther in the mid-1950s, 'without telling anything to anybody.'[16] This was evidently not the case, since the initiative had been taken by Roosevelt's Uranium Committee. However, Sengier did move to New York to liaise with the US government, staying in central Manhattan. Sengier—who turned 60 towards the end of 1939—was 'a polished man, somewhat stout, with pale skin, white hands, a fringe of white hair, and a short silver moustache', who, according to Gunther, seemed to convey 'a pleasant sense of benevolence and good will.'[17] But he had nerves of steel—and he was presiding over a unique supply of a mineral that had the power to change history.

On 9 October 1941, two months before Japan's attack on Pearl Harbor, Roosevelt gave the go-ahead to the atomic project. This involved the setting-up of 'a separate secret state', notes Richard Rhodes in *The Making of the Atomic Bomb*, 'with separate sovereignty linked to the public state through the person and by the sole authority of the President.'[18] The 'Manhattan Engineering District' was formed within the Army Corps of Engineers, to be known as the Manhattan Project. Secrecy was already the watchword of the whole enterprise and this name was chosen as a way of avoiding giving any clues about its concerns. The Project was authorised formally a few weeks after Pearl Harbor, which led to America's entry into the Second World War.

In January 1942, Roosevelt approved the top secret development of an atomic bomb.[19] The project now received full support from the army, in order to meet the emerging need for large-scale construction and design.[20] In September that year, the President gave military command of the Manhattan Project to General Leslie R. Groves, a West Point graduate, who was described by Kenneth Nichols, his second-in-command, as 'the biggest sonovabitch I've ever met in my life, but also one of the most capable individuals'.[21] The civilian head of the Project was Henry Lewis Stimson, the Secretary of War. Groves and Stimson were responsible for what the war historian Max Hastings has described as 'the most ambitious military project in history', in which 'the stakes were as high as the world has ever known'.[22]

The initial funding for the Project, which was in excess of $37 million—worth about $597 million in 2015—was channelled into a secret dummy account, so as to avoid detection by any foreign spy. An additional reason for channelling the funds in this way was to avoid the legal requirement of obtaining the approval of Congress.[23] Seeking such approval would have been very awkward in the case of what became a huge disbursement, reaching $2 billion—worth about $27 billion in 2015.[24] Because of Groves's position at the head of the 'top-secret, unlimited-budget project', states Patrick Marnham in *Snake Dance*, a study of the nuclear age, he was 'without any question from November 1942, for three years, one of the most powerful men in the world'.[25]

Under Groves's leadership, the Manhattan Project developed at breakneck speed. He sent Nichols to negotiate with Edgar Sengier over the purchase of the 1,200 tons of Congolese uranium ore stored on Staten Island, and also to acquire the 1,000 tons of mined ore that was still stockpiled at Shinkolobwe. Nichols was astonished by the richness of Congolese ore, which he emphasised in an interview after the war:

> *Nichols:* They were hand sorting this damn stuff, because it came out of Shinkolobwe to 65% U3O8 [uranium oxide]. To give you an idea of it, we think we have got a good mine out in the west if it is three-tenths of one percent.
>
> *Interviewer:* My God.
>
> *Nichols:* They were hand sorting it to 65% and their waste piles were 20% uranium, U3O8. They had that stored just outdoors over in Shinkolobwe. They had hand sorted this stuff, and that was the waste that went by.[26]

The ore stored on Staten Island was transferred immediately to the Corps of Engineers. Arrangements were also made to ship to the US the stock of ore remaining in the Congo: 950 further tons of approximately 70 per cent ore; and about 160 tons of 20 per cent ore.[27] To make this possible, Union Minière ran three round-the-clock shifts at Shinkolobwe, where the miners worked in the open pit under searchlights.[28]

The miners sorted and packed up the uranium ore by hand and, according to estimates, they could have been exposed to a year's worth of radiation in about two weeks.[29] Some of their Belgian overseers believed that the miners did not know what they were handling.[30] The mine polluted the entire area, affecting the ground and the water supply, and many of the miners' homes were constructed from radioactive materials.[31]

By December 1942, about half of the ore from the Congo had arrived in the US safely. Shipments in 1942 were dispatched via the port of Lobito Bay in Angola, on the southern border of the Congo. But Angola was seething with Nazi spies: it was a colony of Portugal, which was a neutral country under the semi-fascist dictatorship of Antonio Salazar, flirting with Hitler and giving Germany economic assistance. As a result, the port of Lobito was a busy mix of Allied, German, and neutral activity—and so an unsafe place for the shipping of uranium. It was decided instead to send the uranium to the US via the port of Matadi, the Congo's single outlet to the sea. It involved a much longer and, from a logistics point of view, far more difficult route—two journeys by train and one by barge—with repeated loading and unloading. But it was more secure than the straightforward rail journey to Lobito: shipping the ore via Matadi meant that it would never leave the Congo before sailing.

From the last week of January 1943, all uranium transported by sea went through Matadi. Now the uranium—in sealed barrels marked 'Special Cobalt'—was sent north by train from Shinkolobwe to the railhead at Port-Francqui (now Ilebo) on the Kasai River, in the province of Kasai. From there, the barrels were loaded on to barges, which sailed downstream to where the Kasai River joins the Congo River and then onward to Léopoldville (now known as Kinshasa), the capital of the Congo; at that point they were taken by train to Matadi.[32] The Manhattan Project sent skilled personnel and equipment to the Congo to improve the railroads.[33]

INTRODUCTION

This was a journey of epic proportions, crossing about 1,500 miles. Although it was a safer route than the journey to Lobito, its length and its complexity generated other risks, as Major John Lansdale of the Manhattan Project warned General Groves. 'There is a possibility,' he pointed out in a memorandum, 'that part of the shipments dispatched from the mine are not received at Matadi, since the shipments arrive at Matadi by railroad, then river boat, and again by railroad.'[34]

From Matadi, the barrels of uranium were shipped to the US. The carriage of large shipments of uranium necessitated extreme care in scheduling operations and shipments, because of the risk from German submarines in the South Atlantic. After consultation with the Transportation Corps of the US Army, it was decided that the safest method of shipment was by fast motor vessels, travelling out of convoy. It was decided to ship the ore by 16-knot boats managed by the American West African Line, known as the Barber Line, which ran a service between New York and Matadi.[35] Two shipments of ore were lost at sea: one late in 1942, through enemy action; and one early in 1943, through a marine accident. Approximately 200 tons of ore were lost through sinking.[36]

Uranium for the Manhattan Project was also transported by air on the Pan American Airways clipper service. The Brazil–West Africa air link was expanded to include a route through central Africa, 'primarily to tap a supply of uranium from what was then the Belgian Congo', notes a study of the trans-South Atlantic air link during the war.[37] Captain Marius Lodeesen, the pilot of the Pan Am China Clipper, later recalled that he was called to the chief pilot's office and his boss, Horace Brock, said he was to fly the China Clipper to Léopoldville 'on a top secret flight'. When he asked why he had been chosen for this special flight, he was told it was because he was the only pilot who had been there before. 'On the return flight,' he was instructed, 'stop only for fuel. No overnights. I'll give you a double crew and Captain George Duff as co-captain.' Howard Brush Dean, who was the Manager for Pan Am Africa, 'will be your only passenger. No questions, no answers. Dean knows what to do.'[38]

To make these flights reliable, the US needed to improve landing facilities. A US Army Air Force intelligence officer reported in 1942 on the progress of work to build an aerodrome in Elisabethville, the capital of Katanga. It was 'an excellent field,' he said, with 'very extensive gasoline facilities'. He added that an airport was also being built at Léopoldville:

> they were also putting in a concrete landing strip that is as good as you will find anywhere on the African Continent. They are working day and night there. That was the only project in Africa in which they were working 24 hours a day.

Both airports were ready for operation by July 1942.[39]

General Groves set up a special office in New York called the Murray Hill Area (named after the area in which it was located, like the Manhattan Project) to locate and assess the world's supply of uranium—and to find more. The work was done in great secrecy by the office's mining and geology experts, who had to rely on published data for much of their findings; in the case of the Soviet Union and Germany, this task ranged from difficult to impossible. Despite these obstacles, they felt able to estimate that the Shinkolobwe ore, together with known sources of uranium on the North American continent, made up over 90 per cent of the world's potential supply of uranium.[40]

With the enormous budget at Groves's disposal and the backing of the White House, explains Tom Zoellner in *Uranium*, he made deals with some of the largest chemical and engineering corporations in America: Bechtel, DuPont, Raytheon, Eastman Kodak, and Union Carbide, who were hired to erect the apparatus necessary to build a bomb. 'But,' adds Zoellner, 'raw uranium was the first concern.'[41]

The US should 'allow nothing to stand in the way of achieving as complete control as possible of world uranium supplies,' insisted Groves.[42] The need for control, stated an internal report written for him, 'cannot be over-emphasised'—and this meant control of Congolese ore. It would not necessarily mean the ownership of the Belgian Congo, added the report, nor the ownership of the uranium-bearing regions or deposits in the Belgian Congo. But it would certainly mean the right to control the rate of flow of supplies from that region and the right to determine who was to receive the ores.[43]

In August 1943 the Manhattan Project moved from its headquarters in New York to Oak Ridge Tennessee, which became the development centre of the bomb and its headquarters for the rest of the war. Laboratory and engineering work was done at more than thirty sites all over the nation and in Canada. But, despite this massive development, it remained a secret. This was especially important to Groves, given the possibility that the Germans were developing a bomb programme. He adopted a worst-case scenario: that unless and until it was confirmed otherwise, they should assume that Germany was working on a bomb at full capacity. This position was shared by President Roosevelt and Winston Churchill, who had agreed that Britain should cooperate with the US on the construction of the bomb; British scientists working on Britain's secret atomic bomb project—Tube Alloys—were sent to the US to join the Manhattan Project.

When Roosevelt met Churchill for talks on 19 June 1942 in Hyde Park, New York—where the atom bomb was 'the most complex and, as it proved, overwhelmingly most important subject' on the agenda—they speculated on German progress. 'We both,' wrote Churchill in his memoirs, 'felt painfully the dangers of doing nothing. We knew what efforts the Germans were making to procure supplies of "heavy water"—a sinister term, eerie, unnatural, which began to creep into our secret papers.' What, he exclaimed in horror,

> if the enemy should get an atomic bomb before we did! However sceptical one might feel about the assertions of scientists, much disputed among themselves and expressed in jargon incomprehensible to laymen, we could not run the moral risk of being outstripped in this awful sphere.[44]

In the summer of 1943, Roosevelt told James Byrnes, then Director of the Office of War Mobilization, about the Manhattan Project, asserting that the Germans were ahead of the US in the atomic race. The President's belief, wrote Byrnes years later, stimulated the 'extraordinary efforts put forth on the Manhattan Project', which at its peak claimed the labour of 125,000 men.[45]

The safeguarding of information was secured by a strict 'need to know' policy: not one of the laboratories, universities, plants or contractors was given any information about the overall structure of the Project. 'The majority of workers did not know what the Project was doing, or what other plants at their own site were doing, or what the other departments in their own plant were doing,' records an institutional history of the Counter-Intelligence Corps, an intelligence organisation within the American military that was given responsibility for the Project's security. 'All the sites, materials and special items of equipment were given code names. So were many of the scientists. And since the top scientists were the few people who did know what the Project was about, they were given bodyguards from a special group of CIC agents—who were really spying on them.'[46]

'Only about six men in the U. S. Army,' commented the physicist Arthur Compton, a Nobel Prize-winner who was involved in the Manhattan Project, 'are permitted to know what is going on, including Secretary of War Stimson!'[47] James Byrnes described the resounding silence on the topic in the corridors of power:

> After the first discussion, neither the President nor I mentioned the atomic project to each other for many months. In fact, no one ever talked about it unless it was absolutely necessary. I remember once mentioning it to Secretary of War Stimson who, from its very inception, personally supervised the Manhattan Project. His reaction indicated surprise that I knew about it.

Even by April 1945, adds Byrnes, only four members of Congress had been given any concrete information about the Project.[48] Harry Truman was not informed of the Project before assuming the presidency after Roosevelt's death in April 1945.

This secrecy extended firmly to everything related to Congolese uranium and the Shinkolobwe mine. The Belgian uranium deals were 'one of the most tightly kept secrets' of the war, notes Jonathan Helmreich in a detailed study of America's relations with Belgium and the Congo between 1940 and 1960.[49] 'The most important deposit of uranium yet discovered in the world,' stated a top secret American intelligence report in November 1943, 'is in the Shinkolobwe Mine in the Belgian Congo.'[50] The Congo's 'known resources of uranium, which are the world's largest,' added the report, 'are vital to the welfare of the United States ... Definite steps should be taken to insure access to the resources for the United States.'[51]

It was a matter of great urgency to the US to persuade Sengier and Union Minière to reopen the Shinkolobwe mine as soon as possible, in order to acquire all its uranium ore. Negotiations were held with Union Minière, Belgium and Britain; meanwhile, careful plans were drawn up regarding logistics, methods and costs.[52]

The only major deposit under Nazi Germany's control was at Joachimsthal, in Czechoslovakia. But the production of the Joachimsthal deposits was small, when compared to that of the Belgian Congo, or even to that of Canada and the United States.[53] Groves was assured by his intelligence and security aides that Germany was not getting any uranium from the Congo. 'There is no evidence,' he was told, 'that any concentrates or ores are reaching destinations other than the US.'[54]

But Groves was not willing to take any chances—he was determined at all costs to stop Hitler's forces from obtaining Congolese uranium ore. It was possible, though difficult, to try to ensure that Germany did not obtain the ore through legitimate channels. Much more challenging was the threat of smuggling: there were already well established smuggling routes from the Belgian Congo to Germany, which could be used to transport the ore.

To deal with this threat, Groves turned to the Office of Strategic Services, a wartime intelligence service which had been newly set up by President Roosevelt. In late 1943, OSS sent a top agent to Africa to tackle the problem of smuggling; this was Wilbur Owings Hogue, a sombre and very clever civil engineer with a self-deprecating sense of humour, who became OSS chief of station in the Belgian Congo. Hogue, who went by the name of 'Dock' because he disliked 'Wilbur' so much, nursed a dream of becoming a full-time author—but, like so many of the men and women who served in the Second World War, had to put his ambitions on hold. He was joined in 1944 by Henry Stehli, a sophisticated but easygoing and gentle man who worked in peacetime in the family business—the famous Stehli Silks Corporation. The OSS station office in Léopoldville was managed by Shirley Chidsey, a petite woman whose size belied her adventurous spirit and lively nature.

Other OSS agents stationed in West Africa—Douglas Bonner, Adolph Schmidt, Duane Luther, Lanier Violett, Huntington Harris, and John Kirkland—also participated in the mission in significant and covert ways. From Washington, this network of agents was directed by the Africa Section of OSS Secret Intelligence; its chief was Rudyerd Boulton, an ornithologist in peacetime, whose commitment to his new post led him at times to be tough, even ruthless. His task was made all the more difficult by the obstacles in the field, such as poor channels of communication, erratic means of travel, lack of adequate information, and frequent severe illness.

For over seventy years, this mission has been unknown to the world, and not one of the men—and one woman—who carried it out has received due recognition. Their service was concealed by the total secrecy that blanketed everything to do with the Manhattan Project—and especially its reliance on the uranium ore from the Shinkolobwe mine in the Congo. But now, thanks in large part to recent releases of OSS and other records, it has been possible to uncover this extraordinary story. The courage of OSS agents in the Belgian Congo, and their singular contribution to the war against fascism, are the subject of this book.

2

TETON

On 7 November 1943, Dock Hogue flew into Léopoldville, the capital of the Belgian Congo. He was on a mission for the Secret Intelligence Branch of the Office of Strategic Services, with the cover of 'Special Assistant' to the American Consul stationed in the Belgian colony. Just short of six feet three, Dock Hogue was thirty-four years old and a qualified civil engineer.[1] He was well-built and athletic—a boxer and high diver in college—and strikingly good-looking, with a narrow moustache. His brown eyes were intense: 'the most piercing eyes,' observed a US Army officer who met him in the Congo, 'I had ever encountered. When I was introduced to him, I felt he was reading my mind.' His face sometimes seemed to close down into an unrevealing 'sphinx cast', which was emphasised by the premature balding of his dark hair.[2]

The heat was baking when Hogue arrived in the Congo: up to 30 degrees Celsius, with the highest humidity of the year, when the air 'pressed down like a smothering blanket', in Hogue's own words.[3] But he was fully prepared for this sharp contrast with the more temperate climate of Idaho, his home state: for although he had not yet been to the Belgian Congo, he had already spent seven years in tropical Africa. Between 1936 and 1941, he had worked as an engineer for the Firestone Rubber Company in

13

Liberia, the republic established on the west coast of Africa in 1847 by former slaves from America. He had then joined OSS in 1942 and carried out a counter-espionage assignment in Liberia and Ivory Coast.

Hogue was a man whose life had taught him the techniques of survival. His mother Carrie had hanged herself when he was just fifteen, and it was he who found her body. After that, he grew up in a cheerless home with his undemonstrative father—who was also an engineer—and two brothers. The household was always short of money, which cast a shadow over his childhood and education. After enrolling at the University of Idaho at Moscow, it took him eight years of hard work—alternating semesters of study with semesters of paid work for the Reclamation Service—to graduate as a civil engineer. But he had a special advantage: a gift for writing gripping stories, ranging from detective fiction to true romance, which he sold to pulp fiction magazines such as *Adventure*, *True Confessions* and *Fight Stories*. Running through his fiction was the theme of goodness and decency, oiled by a bottle of Scotch, triumphing over dishonesty and evil. Few authors of popular stories wrote so well and fluently as Hogue, and this extra income helped to ease his financial difficulties.

He was clever and his marks were high. But he would not have managed to qualify if he had not been driven by ambition and an unusual capacity for concentration and hard work. He enjoyed good company and played 'a mean jazz and honky tonk piano'.[4] But he rarely socialised—not because he was a loner, but because he simply didn't have the time.

Hogue gained important experience as a professional engineer with the building of the Idaho state highway from Galena summit to Salmon City from 1931 to 1936. But he was not solely an engineer—he had other dreams too. After obtaining his first degree, he went on to obtain a Master of Arts in English literature, also at the University of Idaho. He nourished fond hopes of becoming a full-time writer some day and was on the editorial staff of the *Blue Bucket*, a quarterly campus magazine with student literary pieces; he was also an active member of the English Club. Other modes of communication interested him as well, and he had his own 8 mm movie camera, which he took with him to Africa. Some of the films he made there were in colour, which had only become possible in the late 1930s and was still a novelty—a mark of his fascination with modern gadgets.

While at university, he fell in love with another student: Ruth Regina West, a slim and dazzling beauty who was also from Idaho. Dark-eyed and elegant, Ruth had hair down to her waist, which she wore in a bun on the nape of her neck. Her father was a railroad conductor and she was the first in her family to obtain a college degree. Like Dock, she relished travel and adventure and went on a grand tour of Europe with her mother and a sister after graduation. Writing to her from Liberia in 1938, Hogue exploited this shared interest to beat off a rival. 'Please don't marry Bill Baggs,' he implored her, 'or I won't take you to Europe and Egypt and Africa with me.'

His suit was eventually successful and he flew back to the US to marry Ruth. They tied the knot on 14 January 1940 and six days later they left America for a three-week journey to Liberia on the ancient, battered SS *Zarembo*, a freighter with accommodations for eight passengers; Ruth was the only woman on board.[5] 'They are honeymooning on a freighter bound for Liberia, Africa', observed a college newspaper in admiration.[6]

Ruth settled happily into the small community of Americans living on Firestone's plantation near the capital city of Monrovia,[7] and Dock started to enjoy life in a new way. Before his marriage, he had brought his work problems home to an empty bungalow, where he tried 'to beat them senseless with a whiskey bottle'. But now he shared them with Ruth, who was sympathetic and genuinely interested in the massive hydro-electric project he was supervising.[8] She came from a warm and loving family—very different from Dock's—and was expressive, readily showing emotion. This made him feel awkward and uncomfortable at times. In a 'home movie' shot by Dock in Liberia, she is sparkling and lively, while his own countenance is stern and buttoned-up, lightened only by the glint of humour in his eyes. But in several scenes, they are touching each other with a natural warmth and physical affection.

Their new life together did not last for long: war between the US and Japan was starting to appear inevitable, wrote Hogue later, which meant war with Italy and Germany at a time when 'Italians and Nazis were rampant in North Africa'.[9] They decided that Ruth should go back to the US—after just one year and ten months. Ruth's diary records their wait at the port for a passage home. Dock rowed through the surf with her to the ship; they said goodbye and then, completely miserable, she watched her husband row back to shore. 'Hope you miss me half as much as I do you,' wrote Hogue after she had gone. 'I love you. Dock.'[10]

Ruth arrived in New York five days before Japan's attack on Pearl Harbor on 7 December 1941.[11] The United States of America now entered the war. Like other American men at this time, Dock expected to go into national service—and he was eager to join up. But before he had any opportunity to take this forward, he was recruited by OSS to use his experience of working in Liberia to spy for America in Africa. It was a 'neat little assignment', thought Hogue, and he welcomed it.[12] He returned to the US a few months after Ruth, to get 'lined up' for this new responsibility.

Spying for OSS required elaborate training. At first, little train-ing had been given to new agents. But it was not long before intensive training camps—such as 'the Farm' in Maryland—were set up for men and women about to go overseas. They learned about explosives, weapons, sabotage techniques, clandestine radio procedure, coding and encryption. Those who were destined for intelligence work, like Hogue, took special courses in espionage, ciphers, communications, concealment, and the handling of agents, as well as weapons and martial arts.[13] 'When the end of the world comes, if I am still around,' observed one agent drily, 'it will represent no change from what I have been used to. However, thanks to my very thorough OSS training, I hope to take it in my stride.'[14]

Hogue took easily to the special work of OSS. During his train-ing, he and another trainee were sent to retrieve some documents from a room. When they entered the room, the lights went out and they were jumped upon by a large number of men intent on beat-ing them up. Hogue 'took off like a shot and got the hell out'—and passed the test. The other trainee stayed to fight, so failed.[15]

The trainees were given practical advice. Agents going to Africa were instructed to take 100 tablets of Atebrin, to help prevent and treat malaria, as well as baby powder, a 'J & J Utility Medical Kit', and antiseptic mouth wash. Required clothing included two sun helmets, a terry cloth sports jacket, a light trench coat, a strong leather belt, two pairs of good sunglasses, and one white dinner jacket, 'preferably sharkskin'—a lightweight fabric favoured by British diplomats in Africa.[16]

Once he had completed his training, Dock met Ruth in New York, staying near Times Square. Then he set off again for Liberia, in his new role. For this first OSS mission, his codename was 'CARL WEST', a combination of his middle brother's first name and his wife's maiden name; sometimes this was abbreviated sim-ply to 'WEST'. He was acutely aware of his double role: 'To all concerned, I was again in Liberia as a Firestone engineer. Actually—and the word be damned—I was a spy.'[17]

At this time, Liberia had diplomatic and strong trade ties with Nazi Germany, a relationship which Hogue captured on film. Walking slowly up and down past the Executive Mansion in Monrovia, the residence and offices of President Edwin Barclay, he carefully filmed a flag with a swastika—the emblem of Hitler's Third Reich—flying from the building, as well as a German flag prominently displayed.[18] Despite pressure from the US, Barclay sustained his reluctance to issue a declaration of war against the Nazi regime and Japan. It was only after the end of his term, when William Tubman was inaugurated in January 1944 as the new President, that war was declared.[19]

Hogue's mission was dangerous but successful. Under the cover of counting rubber trees, he set up secret networks of contacts and informants in Liberia and in adjacent Ivory Coast, which was under the control of the Nazi-allied Vichy government in France. This helped to prepare the region for the Allies' invasion of North Africa. A generous sharing of American cigarettes—'good old Camels'—facilitated the process.[20]

Ruth, alone and missing her new husband, gave birth to their son, Gilbert, on 9 January 1943. A few months later, Dock returned home and was able to see his baby son. In the late summer of 1943 the family went on holiday to the Grand Teton National Park of Wyoming, which bordered the place where he had grown up in Idaho. Here Dock made a colour film, which shows him standing in front of Grand Teton, the highest mountain of the Teton Range. For generations, the Tetons had been important to the Hogue family—and it was after this visit that Dock changed his OSS codename from WEST to TETON. It would remind him of the home he loved and perhaps he hoped it would bring him the strength of the mountains for his next posting.

Before leaving for the Congo, Hogue went to Washington to be briefed on his mission by the head of the Africa Section in the Secret Intelligence branch of OSS. This was Wolfrid Rudyerd—'Rud'—Boulton, whose official title was Divisional Deputy of Secret Intelligence.[21] He was responsible for planning, organising, and operating intelligence activities in Africa and was one of just seven executive members of the Secret Intelligence division who were authorised to see and to handle Top Secret material.[22]

Boulton was a distinguished ornithologist in his early forties, who had been the Curator of Birds at the Field Museum of Natural History in Chicago since 1937; he had been given an indefinite leave of absence, to take up his post in Washington.[23] He had made many extensive expeditions to central and southern Africa and on one of them, in 1930, he had stayed in Africa for fifteen months, collecting birds.[24] Such a background was not unusual for OSS personnel—'everything from psychologists, anthropologists, linguists, and mathematicians to ornithologists'.[25] And like many of them, Boulton chose a codename reflecting his career interests—NYANZA, the name of a province in south-western Kenya around Lake Victoria, where he had conducted some research.

With greying temples and thick rimless spectacles, Boulton looked more schoolmaster than spymaster. He had a cleft chin, a high forehead, and brown hair and eyes.[26] But this nondescript appearance belied a strong personality; in later years, some colleagues said he drove people 'dotty with detail'.[27]

The shift from ornithology to intelligence coincided with another dramatic change in Boulton's life. The previous year, he had divorced his first wife (after whom Mrs Boulton's Woodland Warbler, *Seicercus laurae*, is named),[28] an ethnomusicologist who had made a number of trips to Africa as a music collector—some with Rud. Then, on 9 April 1942, just days before moving to Washington, Boulton married Inez Travers (after whom the Evergreen Forest Warbler is named *Satrocercus mariae boultoni*),[29] an unconventional woman with pre-Raphaelite red hair who was well known in art and poetry circles and had served as President of the Renaissance Society at the University of Chicago.[30] While Boulton was rooted firmly in the real world, she was deeply interested in spiritual concerns and was preparing to write *Beyond Doubt, A Record of Psychic Experience*.[31]

Rud Boulton and Dock Hogue were among the very first people to work for America's wartime intelligence service. For it was a brand new organisation: whereas other major global powers had had espionage systems for some time, the USA had no central intelligence and covert operations agency until the Second World War. In July 1941, William J.—'Wild Bill'—Donovan had set up the Office of the Coordinator of Information (COI) on the instruction of President Roosevelt, who believed that the US needed information and intelligence. Donovan, in his late fifties, was a millionaire New York lawyer and a much-decorated hero of the 1914–18 war; a handsome, well-built man with blue eyes, he exerted a compelling personality and presence, with boundless energy and ambition. He had spent time in Britain studying the operation of the British Secret Intelligence Service (SIS), also known as MI6, and had persuaded Roosevelt—a personal friend—that the US needed a similar agency.[32]

America's entry into the war in December 1941 gave an urgency to the aims of this new organisation. Six months later, the COI was divided into the Office of Strategic Services (OSS) and the Office of War Information (OWI). The OSS was established as a branch under the US Joint Chiefs of Staff and General Donovan, who was rarely out of army uniform, reported directly to the President.[33] In March 1943, a presidential executive order stated that OWI would be responsible for official propaganda, leaving OSS in charge of covert activities—collecting and analysing strategic intelligence and executing operations overseas.[34]

Donovan was later to describe OSS as a kind of experiment—'a group of Americans constituting a cross section of racial origins, of abilities, temperaments and talents'.[35] It was a 'most un-military military', with a highly informal atmosphere, few distinctions between officers, and no saluting or drill. Initiative and individual responsibility were encouraged. 'I'd rather have a young lieutenant with guts enough to disobey an order,' said Donovan, 'than a colonel too regimented to think and act for himself.'[36] Dock Hogue fitted the bill perfectly.

Where Hogue differed from many other OSS personnel, however, was his tough upbringing and lack of social status. For OSS overwhelmingly recruited staff from the privileged worlds of the Ivy League—elite universities such as Yale, Princeton and Harvard. They came from the same social circles and many of them already knew each other when they joined.[37] This contributed to the glamour that was associated with the service. It also led to objections outside the organisation and some onlookers joked that the initials OSS stood for 'Oh So Secret', 'Oh So Social', 'Oh Shush Shush', or even 'Oh So Silly'.[38]

One British intelligence official, Malcolm Muggeridge, who was stationed in Lourenço Marques (now Maputo) in Mozambique (also known at the time as Portuguese East Africa) by the Special Operations Executive—the British counterpart of OSS, which was set up in July 1940—was struck by the patrician backgrounds of the OSS men he met. 'They came among us, these aspiring American spymasters,' he sneered in his memoirs, 'like innocent girls from a finishing-school anxious to learn the seasoned demi-mondaine ways of old practitioners—in this case, the legendary British Secret Service.' He noted that most of the early arrivals:

> were Yale or Harvard dons, who imagined themselves writing Ashenden-type stories when the war was over; in the case of the chestier ones, Hemingway-esque ones. Or they might be the offspring of Senators or Congressmen, adept at looking after their own. Or unsoldierly sons of generals, or the un-nautical sons of admirals. Or advantageously connected in some way with the State Department or the New York Times.

'Indubitably,' he added, they were 'an elite corps.'[39]

Some 21,643 men and women were to serve in OSS during its three-year existence.[40] They included a range of remarkable people: Julia Child, later a famous chef and television personality, who worked in the Chungking office in China; New Yorker cartoonist Saul Steinberg, who taught Chinese guerrillas how to blow up bridges; and Kermit Roosevelt, grandson of the former President Theodore Roosevelt. Many of them, judged Muggeridge, were extremely good at their job and often better than their British counterparts. 'The first feeling of awe and respect,' he noted, 'soon evaporated; and it turned out that the finishing school products had learnt all the tricks and devices of the old practitioners in no time at all, and were operating on their own.' They had an advantage over British agents, he added enviously, because they were given 'lavish supplies of money' to use for bribes. Their 'reckless dispensing,' he complained:

> sent up the accepted tariff of bribes to astronomical proportions everywhere, making even the cost of trivial services like getting charladies to go through wastepaper baskets quite exorbitant. As for the police—once the OSS appeared on the scene, it cost as much to suborn an assistant inspector, or even a mere sergeant, as would once have sufficed to buy up the whole force.[41]

The operational divisions of OSS were headquartered in Washington. These were Secret Intelligence (SI); Special Operations (SO), which carried out commando-type combat operations; Research and Analysis (R&A), which was largely staffed by academics; and X-2, which dealt with counter-intelligence. Secret Intelligence, where Rud Boulton had his office, was based in Temporary Building 'Que' on 25th and E Streets, on top of Navy Hill, and was a sprawling, low structure at the end of Constitution Avenue, not far from the Lincoln Memorial and overlooking the Potomac River. It had previously been used by the Public Health Service for animal research and was ridiculed by Berlin radio as the home of '50 professors, 10 goats, 12 guinea pigs, a sheep, and a staff of Jewish scribblers'.[42]

The activities of SI, SO, and X-2 mostly took place in the field, reporting to Washington. R&A largely worked in Washington, which provoked some agents to mock it as the 'Chairborne Division'. But these 'eggheads', observes Max Hastings in *The Secret War*, 'produced an extraordinary range of reports, most of them interesting, a few outstanding'. Nothing comparable was produced in London; the only drawback was that few of R&A's reports were read by the decision-makers prosecuting the war.[43]

One of R&A's analysts was Ralph Bunche, a brilliant scholar specialising in African affairs, who went on after the war to become a senior UN diplomat; in 1950 he was awarded the Nobel Peace Prize for his mediation in Palestine. Bunche, one of the few black personnel in OSS, was brought from Howard University to handle 'the subjects of colonial policy and administration, native problems, and race relations.' He became a key member of the 'flamboyant and happy-go-lucky outfit' of self-trained Africa specialists, organised by Rudolph Winnacker, who came from Harvard.[44] Bunche and William Bascom, an anthropologist, wrote *A Pocket Guide to West Africa* for army and navy personnel. It urged them to leave American racial views at home when they travelled to Africa. 'Though darker than most people you know,' advised the *Guide*:

and differing considerably in the way they eat, dress, and live, the West Africans are pretty much like people all over the world. In town, there are officials, clerks, artisans, laborers, and hired help; in the country-side, peasant farmers. They marry, raise families, drink the native brews, enjoy their ceremonies and parties, react to hardship as you do.

'Like white folks,' added the *Guide*, 'the West Africans have upper and lower classes and it would be a serious mistake to assume that all Africans are alike or that they all think and act alike.' Their gods, it stated firmly, 'are as real to them as ours is to us'.[45]

Up until the Second World War, the US had viewed Africa as functioning within the European sphere of influence and most Americans knew little about this vast continent. 'The level of intelligence knowledge and operations in the US was very low,' stated one OSS agent stationed in Accra. 'I recall Ralph Bunche telling me at that time the files at US Army Intelligence on West Africa were composed almost completely of clippings from the *New York Times*.'[46] When another agent, Adolph Schmidt, was told that he would be joining the Africa Section, he was puzzled. 'I don't know anything about Africa,' he pointed out to David K. E. Bruce, the head of Secret Intelligence. But Bruce simply replied by asking: 'Who does?'[47]

Schmidt went with Bunche to restaurants and bars in Washington and was surprised at the level of racism they encoun-tered. 'Ralph Bunche and I hit it off well,' said Schmidt, 'even after I made the foolish mistake of inviting him to lunch at the Mayflower and getting us both unceremoniously thrown out.'[48] This reflected the racial inequalities of the US at that time—as well as some attitudes at OSS. An organisational report on work in Africa complained that because the 'total number of white inhabitants on the entire continent is so small', it was 'next to impossible' to infiltrate agents under real cover. 'Every new arrival,' asserted the report, 'was suspect from the start.'[49] This might have been less of a problem if OSS had recruited agents for overseas from the African American community.

All European colonies in Africa had been drawn into the war in some way—and when the Germans occupied North Africa, it became a theatre in the conflict. It was feared that major parts of Africa could fall swiftly under Nazi domination—and a German invasion of the whole continent was considered a real possibility, with the risk of even greater threats. If Nazi forces were able to establish bases in West Africa, they would be only about 1,800 miles from the lightly defended Brazilian coast. To protect against this danger, the US Army made careful surveys of all roads and river routes and began to construct a chain of air bases 'right smack across Africa's midriff, through the French and Belgian territory', in the words of one American working in central Africa for the Office of War Information.[50]

In the event of Africa becoming a major battleground, it was thought that every kind of military, naval, economic, political and psychological intelligence would be required. This need was all the more pressing because State Department coverage across Africa was thin and there were few consulates. This was the rationale that led OSS to set up the Africa Section in the division of Secret Intelligence, under the leadership of Boulton.

As Field Marshal Rommel pushed into Egypt in the summer of 1942, threatening British control of the Suez Canal, the Africa Section was ordered to cover the continent 'as thoroughly as possible'. It initiated a large-scale operation, using undercover agents to gather information for a Strategic Survey; this was used in the planning for Operation Torch, the successful invasion of French North Africa by the Allies in November 1942.[51] Typical requests from Ralph Bunche to agents in the field were: 'What is the diameter of the telephone wires between Casablanca and Oran? What is the gauge of the railway track between Casablanca and Oran?'[52] OSS also prepared sabotage units and sought to influence military groups in preparation for the invasion. This was a considerable achievement for an organisation that was still new and feeling its way forward.

Operation Torch eliminated the threat to Africa from Germany, and there was no immediate threat from Japan. Nonetheless, the Africa Section grew in size. By the end of the war, a total of 93 agents had been placed in Africa, of whom 45 were covert personnel, 36 were semi-covert, and 12 were overt. Examples of covert personnel were the men sent to West Africa as employees of the California Texas Oil Company (also known as Caltex and Texaco), and of Pan American Airways.[53] Pan Am loaned to OSS its employees at its hubs throughout Africa; one of them, codenamed CIGAR, reported on German U-boats prowling off the Ivory Coast.[54] Dock Hogue's role in the Congo would be of a semi-covert nature: he would be acting under cover, but with his presence known to the Belgian Governor General of the colony.

The headquarters of the Africa Section in Washington ran three field bases: Accra in the Gold Coast, which was a British colony (now independent Ghana);[55] Cape Town in South Africa;[56] and Addis Ababa in Ethiopia.[57] Its activities involved maintaining and extending secret intelligence networks to gather political, economic, military, psychological, medical, and social information, which was then processed for dissemination to the appropriate American authorities. These included R&A and X-2 within OSS; and the Military Intelligence Service (MIS), the Director of Naval Intelligence (DNI), the Intelligence Section of Air Staff (A-2), the Foreign Economic Administration (FEA), and the State Department.[58] Secret Intelligence handled the direction of missions and back office functions.

Rud Boulton—whose codenumber for use in pouch letters and cables was 951—would be the chief point of contact for Dock Hogue in the Congo, whose codenumber was 253. He carefully briefed Hogue on the demands of his mission, which resembled that of other OSS officers in Africa: to spy on enemy agents and their activities; to devise ways and means of expanding American intelligence operations to meet future developments on the African continent; and to obtain secret military and economic information.

Hogue, however, was given an additional mission: to protect the export of uranium to the USA from the Shinkolobwe mine in the province of Katanga, in the south of the Congo, and to ensure that the uranium did not end up in enemy hands. One important means of achieving this, he was told, would be an investigation into the smuggling of strategic war materials, such as copper, tin, and industrial diamonds, as a way of revealing the smuggling channels and agents used by the Axis powers—the nations fighting the Allied forces. This mission, he was instructed, was an absolute priority and of paramount importance to the security of America. It was also top secret: his operation would be completely clandestine and should not be mentioned explicitly in any cable or letter, even if enciphered. If it was necessary to report on matters relating to uranium, he was told, then he should use a cover to refer to the mineral, such as diamonds.

But Hogue was not told *why* uranium mattered to the US. 'I don't know what it's for,' he explained to an American code officer during his posting in the Congo. 'We're not supposed to know. I doubt whether the German agents here know, either.' He explained that the US had been buying and importing the stuff 'in carloads' since 1940, 'which was sent to enrichment plants to make it purer.' But, added Hogue, 'Don't ask me "purer for what".'[59]

Hogue's ignorance about the purpose of the uranium was no different from that of most of the people who were involved in some way in the transport of the ore, such as Edwin Webb Martin, one of the American vice consuls in Léopoldville. Martin, a highly regarded diplomat, discovered on his arrival in March 1944 that it was his special responsibility to organise the shipment of uranium to the USA. 'Our particular work there, aside from the routine consular duties,' he explained some time afterwards, 'was to expedite the shipment of raw materials, and particularly uranium. We used to ship uranium—that is we used to issue consular invoices for commercial shipments of uranium by air.' At the time, he thought it was a 'very expensive' thing to do. 'It wasn't until the explosion of the first atomic bomb,' he recalled, 'that I realized what the significance of it was, because in those days I think this was the primary source of uranium, that part of

Africa.'[60] Another American vice consul, Harry H. Schwartz, also signed invoices for uranium which he later learned was destined for the Manhattan Project.[61]

From the very start, Hogue had misgivings about the special mission he was given, which he expressed to Boulton during his indoctrination in Washington. Possibly the lack of clear information contributed to his doubts, as did his concern that such a mission would lead to difficulties with the Belgian Congo administration. He also thought it might provoke a conflict with the Consul General, Patrick Mallon, who—as the Department of State's representative—would be unlikely to support an OSS investigation of which he had not been informed.[62]

But Boulton brushed Hogue's doubts aside. It is unclear whether Boulton himself knew why uranium was of such key importance. As always on the secret topic of the atomic project, nothing was written down unless absolutely necessary, and was only shared within the tiny circle of those who needed to know. There is no direct record, for example, of Hogue's indoctrination by Boulton into his Congo mission—only a later commentary by Hogue, which described his immediate reaction.

In any case, Boulton's orders had come from the very highest levels of the US government—and he was determined to follow them through. It was a comfort to him that Hogue was such a professional spy. 'He is one of the most capable and experienced of all our men,' observed Boulton with satisfaction, 'and should be able to clarify the "enigma of the Congo" for once and for all.'[63]

3

CRISP

Dock Hogue was not the first spy to be sent to the Belgian Congo by William J. Donovan's new outfit. As early as November 1941, the month before Japan's attack on Pearl Harbor, Donovan wrote a letter to President Roosevelt, asking him to authorise the expenditure of $5,000 (about $80,000 today) to send an intelligence agent to the Congo.[1] This was Armand Denis, a friend of David K. E. Bruce, the head of OSS Secret Intelligence. Denis was a naturalised American originally from Belgium, who had already established a reputation in the Congo as a photographer, motion picture producer and expert on African wild life.

Roosevelt readily agreed. It is not surprising that powerful American figures wanted a close eye kept on the Belgian Congo, given Einstein's warning to Roosevelt in August 1939. Einstein had urged the US to obtain Congolese uranium in order to build a fission bomb—and to keep it out of German hands. His warning took on a new urgency just nine months later, when the Germans invaded Belgium, the Congo's colonising power. Belgium surrendered at the end of May 1940 and became an occupied country. A question mark now hung over its colony in Africa: would it be neutral in the war or would it support one of the two sides? If the Congo—a territory of about 1 million square miles, roughly eighty times the size of Belgium—were to support one of the sides, which one? And if it chose to support Germany, would it give its uranium to the Axis powers?

The Governor General of the colony, Pierre Ryckmans, a former law professor who had held this position since 1934, was given contradictory instructions. On the one hand, he was ordered by the Belgian Minister of Colonies, Baron Albert de Vleeschauwer, and the rest of the government-in-exile, to keep the Congo in the war on the British side, along with Ruanda-Urundi, which had been entrusted to Belgium by the League of Nations.[2] On the other hand, he was instructed by the king of Belgium, Léopold III, to resume neutrality.[3]

But Ryckmans swiftly made a decision. On 28 May 1940—the date of Belgium's surrender—he publicly and firmly rejected calls for neutrality, declaring the Congo's complete support for Britain against Hitler.[4] The capitulation of the home army, he asserted, did not involve the colonial army, either in fact or intent.[5]

Ryckmans was in a strong position: he held extensive executive powers and had the support of the colonial army. He made a commitment to the Allies to provide them with strategic minerals and other products, such as rubber, that were seen as necessary to the fight against Germany. He also ordered the internment of every male German national of military age, and the surveillance of all other German subjects in the colony.[6]

But allegiances in both Belgium and its colony were far from clear. The Belgian Prime Minister, Hubert Pierlot, and his cabinet chose to continue fighting against Germany, alongside Britain. First they moved to France, forming a government-in-exile; then, when France signed the armistice with Germany the following month, they went to London. But King Léopold III 'bowed to the German victory': even when Pierlot and the Foreign Affairs Minister, Paul-Henri Spaak, tried to persuade him to join them in exile, he refused.[7] Officially he was a prisoner-of-war, but his decision to stay was seen as a sign that he planned to collaborate with the Germans and to establish a new government under German control. On 28 June 1940, Pierlot publicly called Léopold a traitor, on the radio.

Several Belgian political groups openly collaborated with the Nazis—such as the fascist Rexist movement in francophone Belgium, which had been founded by Catholic intellectuals and was led by Léon Degrelle; the Flemish Nationalists of the Vlaams Nationaal Verbond; and their National Socialist and pan-Germanist rivals in Flanders, DeVlag (the Duits-Vlaamse Arbeidsgemeenschap).[8]

Those who knew of Einstein's warning were acutely worried by the behaviour of Société Générale, the mammoth Belgian financial concern of which Union Minière du Haut Katanga—the huge mining company producing the uranium at Shinkolobwe in the Congo—was a part. Initially Société Générale withdrew to the French city of Bordeaux and intended to return to Belgium, and not—as urged by the government-in-exile—to go to Portugal, Britain, Canada or the USA. 'As soon as we return to Belgium,' observed an internal note of Société Générale, 'we must endeavour to ensure the links with the colony, in agreement with the occupying forces. This need will be especially felt if the war lasts.' Some business leaders stated that acting otherwise 'would not be loyal towards Germany'.[9]

A report produced by the American Bureau of Economic Warfare stated that just before Pearl Harbor, 'we heard from a generally well informed source, that at a meeting held in Brussels on the premises of Union Minière, it was decided that they [that is, Société Générale] would play on both sides in this war, and thus divide risks, stocks and funds.'[10]

In Brussels, the German occupying forces set up a Kolonial Politisches Büro, which sought to establish links with the services of the Ministry of Colonies, which had remained in Belgium. 'Perhaps it was someone from this office,' speculated the historian Guy Vanthemsche, 'who contacted an official at the Union Minière to say that Germany was especially interested in Katanga: The big mining companies could remain, but German influence over it would have to be increased.'[11]

In the Congo itself, there was evidence of support for the Nazis at this time. Monseigneur Félix de Hemptinne, the Roman Catholic Vicar Apostolic of Katanga, took the side of the Germans in their defeat of Belgium. Now in his mid-sixties, de Hemptinne had a distinctive appearance: very tall and with an extremely long white beard.[12] A loyal follower of Léopold II and arch conservative, he was a powerful man in the province of Katanga; he and his Benedictine Order had supplanted all other Roman Catholic, as well as Protestant, competition. Monseigneur de Hemptinne and two other men—Aimé Marthoz, the Managing Director of Union Minière, and Amour Maron, the provincial commissioner—met frequently for talks at the Cercle Albert, an exclusive private club in Elisabethville, the capital of Katanga and the centre of its mining interests. Each of these three men, explains David Van Reybrouck in his book, *Congo: The Epic History of a People*, 'stood at the head of one of the pillars of colonial power: government, finance/industry, and church'—a kind of 'colonial trinity'.[13]

An official of the US Office of War Information who visited the colony in 1942 noted 'a lot of sentiment favouring doing business with Hitler' and it was reported that cheers went up in some quarters when an Allied boat had been sunk.[14] When Jews in Belgium were forced to wear yellow stars in 1942, and the first convoys of Jews were being deported from the country, anti-Semitism was appearing in the Congo too, especially in Elisabethville, the home of the Congo's first synagogue. Here, the shop windows of Jewish merchants were daubed with swastikas and insults.[15]

As early as December 1940, the *New York Times* had observed that Nazi Germany had its eyes on the Congo. 'If the Germans succeed in their conquest of England and France,' it had warned, 'there is no doubt that the whole of the Belgian Congo will be swallowed up, just as surely as will the empires of France and Great Britain. Meanwhile the Congo joins that growing list of colonies without motherlands, and waits [sic] the answer of its final disposition.'[16]

These were worrying developments and had a special relevance for those who were concerned about the possibility of Hitler building an atomic bomb with uranium from the Congo. The US was badly in need of reliable information about the colony that was not available through normal channels: on German espionage, the attitude of 'native chiefs', industrial production and development, and the movement of Congolese products. This was the kind of intelligence that Bill Donovan wanted Armand Denis to gather—'with a view', explained Donovan to Roosevelt, 'to testing German intention in Central and South Africa'.[17]

Denis assumed a convincing cover for his mission: that he was collecting live gorillas.[18] Given this, as well as his familiarity with the Congo and the fact that French was his first language, he was expected to perform well as a spy in the Belgian colony. But it was a very challenging role to take on, not least because Donovan's intelligence outfit was still in its infancy and unlikely to give Denis adequate support. When he arrived in Africa in February 1942, there were still four months to go before the Office of the Coordinator of Information was divided into the Office of War Information and OSS, and the infrastructure was weak. No one in Washington had even sorted out channels of communication for Denis to send his reports back home.

As it turned out, Denis was a disappointment as a spy. He wrote long reports, but they were little more than travelogues, with scant military or political intelligence. Some of the information he gave was worrying, such as rumours about the smuggling of industrial diamonds and rare minerals, especially across the Angola border, to the enemy; he also reported that it would be 'relatively simple' to blow up numerous bridges or the railroad. But all the information he sent was too vague to be of any real use.

Instead, he devoted most of his time to the acquisition of live apes, his cover work. This was proving to be disastrous, in any case, chiefly because of the diseases affecting the gorillas and himself. He suffered from hookworm and a recurrence of an old kidney infection, and his feet became so infected that he was unable to walk for nearly a month. The four gorilla groups he captured were all 'heavily, horribly infected with [a] peculiar flesh-destroying disease', and on one hunt seven 'disfigured beasts' had to be killed, because they were 'so awful'. He acted 'as nurse' to gorillas he captured, of whom twenty-nine died; and after that, he looked after the survivors 'day and night'. A positive result of this, he reported, was that he had been able to study the gorillas' disease and believed he now understood its cause and how to treat it. 'For my part,' he wrote to David Bruce, the head of Secret Intelligence, on 17 September 1942, 'I think we have solved the gorilla secret.'[19]

But he was unable to shed light on any other kind of secret—the secrets that his superiors in Washington had sent him to discover. He readily acknowledged his failure as a spy in the conclusion to a long report on the gorillas. 'I cannot,' he said, 'see the forest for the trees.'[20] He was starting to think that it was time to abandon his espionage role—a view that was growing in Washington. He stayed for a while longer in central Africa, working with gorillas, and finally returned to the US in March 1943.

Halfway through 1942, Donovan's Office of the Coordinator of Information had been divided into OSS and the Office of War Information. A month later, in July, the establishment of an OSS station in the Belgian Congo had been approved. It took its place within the OSS structure on 28 October 1942—as Project Africa #4B.[21] And by now, Donovan had a new agent in the Congo: Dr James ('Jim') Chapin, who left Washington on 30 August 1942. OSS was quickly developing into a fully fledged intelligence and special operations organisation, which gave Chapin a clear advantage over Denis. Codenames were starting to be used and Chapin had the codename of CRISP.[22] His cover was that of 'Special Assistant' to the American Consul, based in Léopoldville.

Like Boulton, CRISP was an ornithologist—indeed, he was one of the most highly regarded ornithologists of the twentieth century. He was based at the American Museum of Natural History in New York and had spent a considerable amount of time in the Congo before the war, researching birds and writing *The Birds of the Belgian Congo*. En route to the Congo in September 1942, he was ordered by OSS Secret Intelligence to stop at Ascension Island in the South Atlantic to solve 'a menace' to the new airfield of the American Air Force—namely, too many birds.[23] The airbase, from which patrol planes could cover thousands of miles of open sea, was of strategic importance to Air Transport Command. However, sooty terns—known locally as 'wideawakes'— had long been coming annually to Ascension to lay their eggs. Shortly after the base opened, the wideawakes started to arrive and lay their eggs just beyond the end of the runway; and every time a plane started down the runway, the birds would rise up in a great cloud, enveloping the plane and causing damage.

Many solutions were tried, but with no success: smoke candles, dynamite blasts, and a planeload of cats to kill the birds (but instead the cats were killed, by a different species of bird). Dr Chapin, however, solved the problem. He advised destroying the eggs, so that the birds would leave and not nest again in the same area. After about 40,000 eggs had been smashed, the wideawakes left the runway area to join colonies on other parts of the island.[24] The airbase was widely known as 'Wideawake Airfield'.[25]

Chapin was confident, authoritative, and highly skilled as an ornithologist. When he arrived in the Belgian Congo, he hoped that this expertise and experience would stand him in good stead as a spy. 'My ornithological interests,' he reported to Boulton, 'have been put to work opening as many doors as possible for me, so that I may know the people at the tops of the ladders and get their expressions of opinion as frankly as possible. All this takes a great deal of time...'. He would try, he said, to 'speak to anyone I meet, whether Belgian, British, American, or native, on any subject that may seem of interest to me—or to you.'[26]

Chapin's orders were much the same as those given to Denis: to investigate the presence and activities of enemy agents in the Belgian Congo; to devise ways and means of expanding American intelligence operations to meet possible future developments on the African continent; and to obtain military and economic information from the Belgian Congo that was not available through existing channels. He was also expected to watch developments in neighbouring territories and to liaise with OSS agents stationed there. It is possible that he was told to monitor the transportation of uranium, but there is no document recording this.

Secret Intelligence in Washington had great hopes of Chapin. But it was not long before he showed signs of stress: he was evidently more comfortable bird-watching than spy-watching. He longed for his wife Ruth to be sent out to help him. 'I am getting swamped with typing and ciphering,' he wrote in frustration in December 1942. 'For Heaven's sake, send me Ruth!'[27] He felt overwhelmed. 'It takes me about two hours,' he complained irritably, 'to encipher a cable of 200 letters and then test it by deciphering it before I send it off.'[28]

He thought it would be a good idea for OSS to send an additional agent to the Congo—as well as Ruth. 'When I start on longer travels, with Ruth with me I hope,' he suggested to Boulton, 'there should be a man in Léopoldville, not a skulking, secret agent who might only make trouble for me, but a naturalist, preferably from the American Museum.' He recommended that 'a mammalogist, herpetologist, ichthyologist, or entomologist would be better than another ornithologist'.[29] 'Ornithology,' he concluded, 'is a wonderful camouflage, even though I may really not need it.'[30] Ornithology was also work he enjoyed more than espionage, trying to obtain live Congo peacocks for the Léopoldville zoo, for example.

Chapin felt snubbed by Lt.-Col. Cunningham, the American Army Intelligence Officer, who had left Léopoldville to go with the Fighting French towards Libya. 'Of course he left without saying a word to me,' grumbled Chapin resentfully, 'but that is not surprising, for Cunningham told me from the very start that he regarded the Office of Strategic Services as thoroughly superfluous.'[31] Chapin was also annoyed with Major Douglas Street of

British Secret Intelligence—'the one most apt to be critical of anything not British'.[32] The difficulty with Street, mused Chapin, was that 'he is a fighting man, a fine one, extraordinarily young to be a Major. He is highly educated too, but largely by Jesuits in France and probably Oxford too. He is a patriot and a killer.' Such men, thought Chapin, were 'wonderful for winning wars', but 'cannot put themselves in another fellow's shoes, and grasp his side of the argument'.[33]

In Chapin's view, 'military people are so cocky, and feel sure they know everything'. On one occasion, when Chapin was meeting a contact off a flying boat, Major Street also turned up at the dock—'and he didn't want to recognise and shake hands with me'. Presumably, Street did not want to blow Chapin's cover—or his own. When Chapin insisted and continued to hold out his hand, Street exclaimed in irritation: 'Some people don't know there's a war on!' 'Military men,' complained Chapin crossly, 'don't realise that the war must be won behind the front, as well.'[34]

In December 1942, the US Air Transport Board refused to grant flight priority for Dr Paul Brutsaert, the chief medical researcher for the Belgian Congo government in Léopoldville, to transport four guinea pigs carrying *Trypanosoma gambiense* to the Harvard Medical School. Chapin was furious about this and took action. 'There was only one thing to do,' he reported to Boulton, 'since the Army does not appreciate the importance of teaching tropical medicine properly.' That 'only thing' was to send Boulton a cable, insisting on Dr Brutsaert's priority. But since there was no time to put the cable into cipher, he sent it uncoded.[35] This ran counter to the firm instructions to agents in the field: to maintain secrecy at all costs and to function on a strict 'need to know' basis.[36]

In Washington, the Africa Section staff were becoming increasingly impatient with Chapin's reports, many sections of which were routinely crossed out on arrival as useless. Boulton was frank with Chapin. He was convinced, he told him, that 'the training and indoctrination you received before your departure either was too hurried or you have forgotten it'. He tried to impress upon him the need to send objective information, not gossip, and to forgo ornithological activity.[37]

This was a worrying situation: it was becoming clear that Chapin was not only inadequate, but also a threat to the security of others and the organisation, because of his blithe lack of concern for cipher and secrecy. 'How little of your material has been of value,' wrote Howard Chapin (a senior OSS official, who was no relation despite having the same surname) bluntly to CRISP. 'So far, we are disappointed in the results produced by the Congo mission.' He insisted that any cable should be written in cipher, not in clear text. In a further letter, Howard Chapin expressed particular regret that when CRISP sent some information that *was* important—about the sinking of a ship convoy by a submarine—it arrived too late to be useful.[38] Finally, the Africa Division had had enough. Boulton wrote to tell Chapin that he had failed and was going to be withdrawn from the Congo.[39]

This pushed Chapin to the point of emotional collapse. Whereas Denis had been perfectly happy to acknowledge his lack of ability as a spy, his successor took it personally. 'Chapin was sent away from here on an Army plane,' wrote Leonard J. Cromie, the US Vice Consul, in an official OSS dispatch in early April 1943. 'He is not rational; he is suffering from a nervous depression.' His personal belongings were gathered together to be sent after him and his secret papers were left stored in the OSS safe at the Consulate.[40]

If Chapin had been able to return immediately to his wife Ruth, to the quiet comfort of life at home, and a proper rest, he may have had a good chance of recovery. But as soon as he returned to the US, Boulton arranged for him to be admitted to the Henry Phipps Psychiatric Clinic at the Johns Hopkins Hospital in Baltimore.

'I thought everything was going so well,' wrote Chapin bleakly to Ruth. 'Keep in touch with Rud. He is our best friend ... it seems as though everything went wrong with me in the Congo, and I understood nothing.'[41] He gave way to frequent attacks of despair and his doctor decided to use an aggressive treatment. Chapin's frame of mind, said the doctor to Ruth, was 'just the sort we have found is most likely to respond well to [electric] shock therapy'.[42] He warned her that occasionally 'the patient sustains a fracture of the vertebra or a long bone. There may also be a memory disturbance.' But the result in many cases, he added, 'has been extremely gratifying'.[43]

This was not the case with Chapin. Once the treatment had started in June, he was left 'weak and miserable'. 'I do feel so sorry that he must be so tortured,' wrote Ruth miserably to Boulton. 'It seems so unfair.'[44] A little later, she discovered that— just as she had been warned—the shock treatments had caused a severe injury and had been discontinued. 'No doubt', she wrote to Boulton:

> you know of the injury to his right arm during one of the treatments—chipped off a bit of bone in the upper arm. The arm has been bandaged, so that explains the absence of letters for two weeks now. The doctor said the arm was coming along and hoped that the bandage could soon be removed. I hope so.[45]

Chapin was finally discharged on 30 September 1943 and went home. Willard Beecher, the personnel and training officer of the OSS Africa Section, wrote to the director of Secret Intelligence to explain the doctor's diagnosis: 'a "Manic-Depressive" psychosis', with a poor prognosis of a cure. He predicted that Chapin was likely to fall ill again, in which case he would be faced with suicide or a recurrence of symptoms, with subsequent confinement. 'In the light of this fact,' he commented, 'the tragedy of suicide may appear the kinder fate.'[46]

But Chapin returned successfully to his previous life. In less than a week after his release, on 4 October, he went back to his position at the American Museum of Natural History. At the very end of December 1943, he sent Boulton a summary of his work for OSS. He included, with evident and possibly mischievous pleasure, the fact that Dr Brutsaert—who had moved to the US in early 1943—had 'succeeded in taking guinea pigs with him by air!'[47]

4

CRUMB

OSS Africa Project #4B in the Belgian Congo had been 'crippled' by Jim Chapin's illness, noted Secret Intelligence with concern.[1] This called for an immediate intervention by Africa Project #7— the OSS station in Accra, the capital of the Gold Coast. This station, which had been established in November 1942, served three separate territories: the Gold Coast itself, the Republic of Liberia and the Belgian Congo.[2] It was under the direct command of Rudyerd Boulton, Divisional Deputy of the Africa Section in Secret Intelligence.

Accra's station chief was Major Douglas—'Doug'—Griswold Bonner, a Princeton-educated stockbroker and partner of the firm Bonner and Gregory in New York City. He had been appointed a Major in the US Army in April 1943, on Donovan's orders, on the grounds that a military status would be essential for this 'extremely hazardous' mission.[3] Now in his early forties, Bonner cut a dash in his army uniform—six foot tall and fair, with a wiry build, ruddy complexion, and trim moustache. Bonner was described approvingly by his superiors in Washington as 'a man of the world, traveller with knowledge of French, good conversationalist with upper class manners. ... Fairly intelligent, gets along well with others (with British, French), gives himself a good time. Excellent liaison officer, agreeable and courteous.'[4]

41

Bonner's OSS codename was CRUMB. Initially, he had used the codename WELSH. But when he suspected that he had compromised its secrecy by not deleting it from a report he showed to the British, he changed it to SNAFU. 'Snafu' was an acronym in military parlance for 'Situation Normal All Fucked Up'—or, in more sedate circles, 'Situation Normal All Fouled Up'. It was also the name of a character in a number of short animated training films made by the US Army: Private Snafu was the 'US Army's worst soldier ... sloppy, lazy and prone to shooting off his mouth to Nazi agents'.[5] Bonner, who had a keen sense of humour, was evidently having fun when he proposed this new codename. 'We figured that no one would be foolish enough to take the name of SNAFU,' he wrote playfully, 'so that from a point of view of duplication it would probably be safe.'[6] Boulton picked up on the joke. 'Just about everybody in OSS has tried to take "Snafu" as a code name,' he retorted, 'and the lucky holder got it about six months ago. Realising, however, that every consideration required our Chief of Mission to have a dignified, distinctive name, the entire Africa Section went into deep meditation; and as a result CRUMB was born.'[7]

A small staff of OSS men ran the station under Bonner's command. Johnny Weaver—codenamed NORTH—had been at Princeton with CRUMB. 'Perhaps you think that when two Princeton men meet in the field they begin to praise each other to the home office,' he wrote to Washington. 'The fact is that if I slip one inch Bonner will give me the "sack" and the reverse is true and we both know it.'[8] The Communications Officer was Ensign Leonard R. Davis, codenamed TRUCK, an experienced cipher man in his late thirties. He joined the station in May 1943, to operate the Message Center, bringing with him a range of items requested by Bonner, such as air mail stationery, two narrow 'ace' combs, and two dozen assorted lipsticks. 'The last item is not for ourselves,' explained Bonner, 'but to endear us to some of our British friends. Lipsticks are quite unobtainable here.'[9]

TRUCK was much liked by his colleagues because of his jocular nature and readiness to help out. 'TRUCK who came out of the hospital late this week,' reported another member of staff, 'arrived to help with a backlog of work which could have easily resembled the Que building. But do we complain, hell no, on charged the light brigade!'[10] But TRUCK did have one complaint. 'The social life here,' he said despondently, 'is nil.'[11] This was difficult for Bonner, too, who was missing his wife Kathleen—his second wife, whom he had only recently married. He was grateful to Rud and his wife Inez for staying in touch with her. 'I do want to thank you and Inez for your kindness to Kay,' he wrote from Accra. 'You have both been a great help to her to say nothing of the fact that she has become devoted to you.'[12]

One US officer observed that the chiefs of OSS headquarters 'had a spectacular talent for living in style. The Cairo villa looked like a bastard version of the Taj Mahal.'[13] But this could not be said of Bonner's HQ in Accra: a small house, which combined both office and residence, with a kitchen in a separate building. Upstairs were two bedrooms and a bathroom with cold running water. There was also a store room which TRUCK planned to use as a 'cryptographic hideout', to increase security. The household staff consisted of men who were described in correspondence to Washington as 'Number One and Number Two boy, a cook and a laundry boy'—using the British colonial practice of referring to servants as if they were children. The house was three blocks from the main artery between Accra and the US Africa-Middle East Wing (AMEW) Headquarters, which OSS staff called the 'Eagles' Nest' owing to the number of high-ranking officials, with whom Bonner was in daily contact. It was 4½ miles from AMEW, about 1½ miles from Accra, and four blocks away from the house of the US Theater Commander, Brigadier General Hoag.[14] The seat of British intelligence was 6 miles away at Achimota College, a prestigious colonial boarding school in the Achimota Forest, within the metropolitan area of Accra.

'Keeping the house running, keeping the cars functioning, and running back and forth to AMEW and Achimota take almost all day,' complained Bonner wearily. 'It then means that Davis and I have to spend the evening hours on cables and reports, to the extent that we are often up until two and three in the morning. This is no good in this climate.' They also had to deal with endless streams of people coming through—Military Observers and Naval Observers—and to entertain British and American officers and civilians. They asked for a stenographer to come and help— 'preferably a young good looking one'.[15]

Jim Chapin's breakdown had left a vacuum in the Belgian Congo, which created yet more demands for the Accra team. Less than a month after Chapin's sudden departure from the Congo, Major Bonner flew to Léopoldville to tidy up his papers in the OSS safe at the Consulate and to see what was going on in the colony.[16] No document is available to show whether or not Bonner was aware of the uranium issue, but it is likely that, as head of the West Africa mission, he was informed of it. He was certainly aware of the importance of the Congo's resources to the war effort.

At this stage in the war, the threat of Nazi domination of Africa had virtually disappeared as a result of Operation Torch, the Allied landing in North Africa in November 1942. By mid-1943, the Allies had ejected Rommel's Afrika Korps from Egypt, Libya and Tunisia, and the Axis powers were losing to increased Allied power on every front. French colonies that had previously backed the Vichy regime shifted their loyalty to Charles de Gaulle, the leader of the Free French.

But despite these positive developments for the Allies in Africa, America was increasing its presence in the Congo and American forces were posted to different parts of the colony. This was not always successful. A report produced at OSS in January 1943 stated that although American troops in the Congo had been 'very well received' by the Belgians, the arrival of 'American Negro troops' was much resented. These troops were quickly withdrawn, suggesting that it was a priority for the US not to alienate the Belgian administration. There had also been an incident of riotous behaviour by American soldiers, when a group of engineering troops went on a spree after landing at the port of Matadi.[17]

Several weeks later, it was reported that a native village had been moved wholesale to protect the health of an American encampment, which had been beset by malaria and dysentery. 'The site of the American encampment,' it stated, 'was rather near a swamp and a native village. The native village has been moved and the swamp has been drained.'[18]

Bonner's first action on arrival in Léopoldville was to pay his respects to the American Consul, Patrick Mallon, who presided over the large new Consulate that had been built earlier that year, replacing the smaller one which had operated since 1929. The next priority for Bonner was to make contact with officials in the US Bureau of Economic Warfare, known as BEW, which had been established by the US government to procure strategic resources for the war effort. In the Congo, these resources were many—and most importantly, uranium. By April 1943, a considerable amount of Congolese ore had been delivered to the Corps of Engineers: the initial shipments of over 1,200 tons of approximately 70 per cent ore, which had been stored on Staten Island; 950 further tons of approximately 70 per cent ore; and about 160 tons of 20 per cent ore.[19]

But more was wanted—and it was estimated that 2,220 tons of low grade material, in the form of tailing dumps, were still at the Shinkolobwe Mine. In Léopoldville in April 1943, Hickman Price, the burly Texan who was head of the Congo office of the Bureau of Economic Warfare received an urgent telegram from the Secretary of State, Cordell Hull. The message was straightforward: to buy and ship to the USA all the Congolese uranium that was available. This instruction was the outcome of a decision reached on 8 March 1943 by the American Combined Policy Committee—that 'the deposits in the Belgian Congo should be exploited as rapidly as possible and the material, both high grade and low grade, removed to safe territory.'[20]

As soon as Price received the telegram, he rushed off to find Maurice Sluys, the Belgian Colonial Minister in charge of the Congo's mines. Together, they went to inform Governor General

Ryckmans of their mission and then left the same day in a chartered plane for Elisabethville. There they were met by Jules Cousin, the administrative director of Union Minière in Katanga, who told them that the Shinkolobwe mine was closed. At the men's request, Cousin arranged for them to visit the mine quarry, where they saw a huge shed containing heaps of leftover tailings, as well as tailings piled up around the quarry.

'In the name of my government,' announced Price, 'I am buying everything and want you to ship it to America.' Cousin tried to explain that in the case of the tailings, only a milligram of radium could be extracted, but he was interrupted by Sluys. Price, he said, would not take no for an answer. General Groves later commented on the value of these tailings and the availability of another large amount of ore. 'It was not as rich,' he said, 'as that which we had previously obtained from the Congo, but the Congo's poorest was much better than the best from Canada or the Colorado Plateau. These dumps had been built up during the years as a result of hand-sorting the richer ores. Their uranium content varied widely from 3 per cent to 20 per cent.'[21]

Price also asked for mining to be re-started, to which Cousin replied that he would consult Sengier in London or New York within a few days. Cousin appeared curious. 'Why,' he asked, 'does your government, which already has at its disposal 60 grams of radium, which is enormous, want these minerals and why does it insist that the deliveries should be made in the shortest possible time?' Price was non-committal. 'I have no idea!' he said. 'My government cabled me: make the purchase and get it shipped urgently ... and I obey!'

According to Sluys, some time later, not one of the three men was in any doubt 'about the immense importance of sending this mineral to the USA!' But he also said that they did not know what the uranium was for—and that he and Price were unaware of the earlier shipments of uranium from Katanga to the USA.[22] It is unclear whether Sluys was telling the truth about himself and Price, but he was certainly wrong about Jules Cousin. According to an intelligence memorandum prepared for General Groves on uranium in Katanga, Cousin had earlier voiced a personal belief that American interest in uranium was due to experimentation to build the world's most powerful bomb. 'He didn't say where he got the idea,' reported the memorandum, 'but predicted that the "radium bomb" will soon put in an appearance and blast the Axis off the map.'[23]

Arrangements were made for the transportation of the additional uranium to the USA. Since March 1943, none had been sent through Lobito in Angola—all shipments were leaving via the Congolese port of Matadi. In late May 1943 it was reported to General Groves that 400 tons would sail to the US at the end of the month on the *Talisman*; and 305 tons had been allotted to the *Titania*, leaving on 1 June. Still more was on the way to Matadi from Katanga.[24]

Governor Ryckmans, with whom Price and Sluys had conferred before their trip to Elisabethville, evidently had his own suspicions about the eventual purpose of the uranium. In his journal on 23 May 1943, he wrote: '*L'Union Minière exporte du "special crude ore". Aurons-nous des surprises un jour?*'—'Union Minière is exporting "special crude ore". Will we have some surprises one day?'[25]

The Bureau of Economic Warfare provided Bonner with a place to stay in the former US Military Headquarters in Léopoldville—a very large room with a proportionally large bath.[26] Bonner had no complaints about his living arrangements, but for the most part he was finding the Congo even more frustrating than the Gold Coast. A particular irritation was the 'lack of graph paper for ciphering', since he had forgotten to bring some with him.[27]

Bonner was not impressed by the Belgians in the Congo and the colonial administration. 'The Congo is not in the war effort,' he reported bluntly to Washington. 'My distinct impression is that any contributions that they are making are nominal.' The stores, he said, were far better stocked with necessities and luxuries than those of the Gold Coast, Dakar, or Lagos, and even gasoline rationing was a loose arrangement which vaguely restricted people to 75 per cent of their previous year's consumption. 'From what I can gather,' he added, 'these people just don't know that there is a war on. All they know is that business is good. They want airplanes, trucks, refrigerators from us and are willing to pay cash for them. Why not. They are making money.' But it caused him concern. 'How much of this apathetic attitude is due to basic sympathy with the Axis cause and how much to an acquisitive nature,' he wondered, 'remains to be determined.'[28]

Many Belgian settlers, in Bonner's view, were doubtful about the Allies' ability to resist the Germans and would have preferred Ryckmans to wait a while to see what happened, before deciding to support the Allies against the Axis powers.[29] This was particularly true, he thought, of the big business interests of the colony and he was concerned to hear about a meeting held shortly after the invasion of Belgium at the home in Elisabethville of Jules Cousin, the administrative head of Union Minière, where ways of supporting Hitler and Léopold III were discussed. Cousin was a close friend of Edgar Sengier: they had trained in engineering at the same university and were both from southern Belgium.[30]

The meeting was attended by a number of Belgians who were very influential in the Congo: Odon Jadot, the Managing Director of the Belgian railway company Compagnie du Chemin de Fer du Bas-Congo au Katanga, which was known as BCK and was based in Elisabethville; by Félix de Hemptinne, the Roman Catholic Vicar Apostolic of Katanga; by Delannoy, the head of the local Court of Appeals; and by a director of one of the Katangan railroads, possibly Firmin Van Bree. Everyone at the meeting was sworn to secrecy. Under pressure from Cousin, it was decided at the meeting to send a message to Governor General Ryckmans, urging him to refrain from anti-German statements or acts. They were to insist that the Congo stay neutral and trade with Germany, Britain or America, as any neutral would trade.

But at the last moment, Jadot, who was apparently supposed to take the message, pulled out. He announced at the meeting that his brother was a prisoner of war in Germany and it was his view that sending such a message to Ryckmans would be unpatriotic. As a result, so far as was known, nothing was done.

Jadot, in fact, came out wholeheartedly on Ryckmans's side after this episode.[31] His company was essential for the transport of uranium to America: for BCK was the railway line which took the barrels of ore from Katanga to Port-Francqui, where they were loaded on to barges to Léopoldville, before being put on a train to Matadi—and then shipped to the US. The BCK company was benefiting from new equipment, such as cranes, sidings and wagons, and repairs, which were paid for at least in part by the US and facilitated by the US War Production Board, in conjunction with BCK itself and with the Belgian Embassy on Fifth Avenue in New York.[32]

Jadot had chosen to support Governor General Ryckmans against Hitler. But he was the only one of the powerful men at the meeting to make that choice. There was evidently friction, reported Major Bonner to OSS, between the key men in Société Générale, based in Elisabethville, and Ryckmans, based in Léopoldville. Bonner added that Jules Cousin had told the British Vice Consul that Ryckmans 'would be out soon'.[33]

Bonner also reported on suspicions that Aimé Marthoz, the Managing Director of Union Minière, was pro-German. Marthoz was a slight, wiry man in his fifties, who had escaped from Belgium with his wife and two children in December 1941. Some people, said Bonner, had wondered how Marthoz had managed to travel without problems through France, Spain and Portugal. Marthoz had given the impression that he received passports and other assistance from members of the French underground; and that in Lisbon he did not say he was going to the Congo, but simply asked for a visa to Angola. But even if that were true, thought Bonner, it would have been difficult to obtain a visa for the Congo in Luanda, without the connivance of the Germans. Marthoz was quoted shortly after his arrival in Elisabethville as saying that he preferred to see the Germans in Paris, because they were more efficient and intelligent than the French.[34]

49

There were rumours of collaboration by other Belgian industrialists, too. One man who was being very carefully watched was Firmin Van Bree, a Director of Société Générale, Union Minière, Société International Forestière et Minière du Congo (Forminière), a lumber and mining company, including diamonds, and Vice President of the Compagnie des Chemins de Fer du Congo Superieur aux Grands Lacs Africains (CFL).[35] Van Bree was well known for his reactionary views and was dubbed 'God the Father' by his senior subordinates.[36] But OSS and British intelligence feared worse—that he was actively working with the Germans.[37] A newly released SOE file reveals very real concern, especially in 1940–1941 and then in December 1943–January 1944, that Van Bree (also referred to in the file as Van Brae) was pro-Nazi.[38] David Bruce, head of OSS Secret Intelligence, took a personal interest in the findings. A range of allegations was put forward to indicate collaboration with the Nazis, but no conclusions were drawn beyond the fact that Van Bree was 'entirely out for his own interests, and is more concerned with his commercial advancement than with helping the war effort.'[39]

Félicien Cattier, a leading personality of Société Générale, the president of Union Minière in Brussels (in 1932–39 and then in 1944) and the president of the Compagnie Maritime Belge, had apparently been seen dining publicly with Hermann Goering, the commander in chief of the Luftwaffe and confidant of Hitler, shortly before a meeting in Lisbon with Firmin Van Bree. Another rumour involved Celestin Camus, Director General of CFL, who was reported in late 1940 to have received from an unknown sender in Lisbon a telegram urging that no anti-German statements should be made by the executives of Société Générale or its subsidiaries.

Bonner consulted the British Consul General in Léopoldville, Francis Shepherd, who gave him a similar account—that in his opinion, there was a 'considerable prevalence of neutralism', along with 'timidity, doubt, hedging and selfishness', in the Belgian Congo's official and big business circles. Even the victory of the Allies over the Germans at the battle of El Alamein, believed Shepherd, had done little to engender a war spirit, but had fostered resistance to self-sacrifice in the support of the war.[40]

An urgent priority for Bonner was to establish a network of 'cutouts'—sub-agents who could provide information, but would not otherwise be involved in the espionage process. But recruiting American cutouts in the Belgian Congo was extremely difficult, complained Bonner to Boulton:

> You have very limited supplies of material. Cunningham, one of the Pan-Am men there, is strictly an adolescent, the OWI [US Office of War Information] men with the one exception of Iams, who I do not know well enough, I would not give the time of day to. Mallon has a Vice Consul, and an assistant, neither of whom, being career men in the Foreign Service, have the hardboiled mentality that it takes for our type of work.

'You don't have to be a thug,' added Bonner, 'but you certainly need to be from Missouri.'[41]

Nor could he hire 'a Britisher'. If he *had* hired a British man, he told Boulton, he would have assumed he was 'doing work for both sides'. He was also doubtful about hiring someone from Portugal or a Belgian:

> As far as the Portuguese go, they might work out as sub-agents, but I am not sure enough of my ground there to trust any of them as the head man. And as for the Belgians, you have to be damn sure of your ground when you ask a man to work for another country or at least you have to be willing to spend quite a bit of money unless you just want simple bank-robbing done.[42]

After considerable searching, Bonner was able to find an American in Léopoldville who agreed to serve as a cutout. This was Thomas N. Greer, who worked for the Bureau of Economic Warfare; before being sent to the Congo, he had worked for the Lend-Lease Administration in Washington, liaising with the Belgian Embassy in relation to the Congo. The job of BEW was to estimate the needs of the Congo in terms of its imports, and also to control on the spot the shipping of Congolese products. This meant that the cover needed for Greer's work for OSS was easily established, which was an advantage. All the same, Bonner was not entirely happy about Greer, who expected a salary of $200 per month: 'If the wage is less than that I do not believe that he will have enough interest in OSS to do a job.'[43] Greer's first report, he commented drily, was 'far from being an epic-making document'.

Bonner also recruited a cutout in Katanga: an engineer named Jaubert, who was attached to BEW as an advisor; Jaubert was Belgian, but had been living in California before the war. 'The mission is stationing a man named Joubert [sic] permanently in Elizabethville [sic],' reported Bonner to Boulton in May 1943, 'who will be able to keep Greer posted on what transpires up there.'[44]

Major Bonner returned to Accra once he had established Greer and Jaubert as cutouts. He then returned to the Congo for two weeks in mid June, during which time he went to Katanga and picked up information relating to Jules Cousin, uranium and Union Minière, which was passed on to the Manhattan Project.[45]

At the end of his visit to the colony, Bonner sent a formal report to Washington on the situation he had found, but made no reference to Katanga.[46] This would be consistent with the overall pattern relating to the Manhattan Project, where records were not kept unless absolutely essential and where potential evidence was effaced (in maps of the Belgian Congo, the name of Shinkolobwe was removed).

Bonner's visit was regarded as a great success. 'We cannot overemphasise how productive we think your trip there has been,' wrote Rud Boulton to Bonner. 'It is a territory about which we knew virtually nothing until you went there.'[47] Dr Bunche, he added, 'considers your report a most accurate analysis of the Congo state of mind.'[48] Some of Bonner's remarks, noted Boulton with evident pride, 'were quoted verbatim in R & A's weekly Psychological Warfare Geographical round-up.'[49]

The Congo was of central importance to America. And it was clear to Bonner that after the failures of Denis and Chapin, an agent of the highest calibre was needed to represent OSS in the

Belgian colony. 'As the "affaire Crisp" is still commented upon locally', he warned Boulton, 'I believe that it would be a great mistake for OSS to send any man here who was not considered seriously.'[50] There was also concern about relations between OSS and British intelligence—'our opposites'. The British, reported OSS agent NORTH in Accra, were 'a bit leary of American Anthropologists and Bird Experts'.[51]

Boulton's office worked hard to find someone suitable for the role. This was not easy: the candidate needed to be cool-headed and professional in his approach. He also needed to speak French and have some experience of living in Africa. Finally, in July 1943, several months after Chapin's sudden departure from the Congo, Boulton was able to report to Bonner that this important mission had been given to the ideal man—Wilbur Owings Hogue, who had just returned from a Secret Intelligence mission for OSS in Liberia.

5

CHIEF OF STATION, CONGO

On 18 September 1943, Dock Hogue left Washington DC for central Africa on his way to the Belgian Congo.[1] Throughout August he had prepared for his next mission in Africa, carefully studying a list of intelligence contacts provided by Bonner, with the names of Allied military and naval observers, helpful consular officials, cooperative local officials and citizens.[2] 'The Congo list,' wrote Boulton to Bonner, 'was exactly what we wanted and TETON joins us in expressing heartfelt thanks. While en route to his post he will have further opportunity to discuss with you the individuals involved.'[3]

Hogue's journey to the Congo took over six weeks, with two important stops. The first was in Accra, where he arrived on 28 September 1943 after a long week of flying on the Pan Am clipper service—via Miami, over Belem and Natal in Brazil and then via the Ascension Islands.

He was expected to work closely with the OSS station in the Gold Coast, under the leadership of Major Bonner. But Hogue's superiors had made it clear to him and to the Accra station that his mission was special and different. It carried an autonomy that OSS missions in Liberia and the Portuguese African colonies, for example, did not have. 'In so far as your relationship with the Congo is concerned,' Boulton had informed Bonner:

> the situation is somewhat different. While nominally and on an organizational chart this territory will be technically under your jurisdiction, in view of the fact it falls within the Theater Command, nevertheless, from the standpoint of actual operation it will be, to all intents and purposes, autonomous.

All Theater Command requests pertaining to the Congo would continue to pass through Bonner, and copies of all cables and reports sent to Washington would be forwarded to him. 'But WEST, whose new name is TETON,' explained Boulton, 'may conduct operations separately and independently as his judgement sees fit. There will also be direct communications between Léopoldville and Washington.'

TETON, added Boulton, 'is one of our most reliable and experienced agents and is fully competent to operate independently,' but was 'more than anxious' to consult with Bonner on all problems of major importance and 'can always be counted on for complete cooperation'.[4]

Boulton sent Bonner important information to pass on to Hogue: that his gun had been sent to the US Consulate in Léopoldville, without the knowledge of the Consul, Patrick Mallon. 'State Department pouch contains TETON's pistol,' he told Bonner. 'Inform TETON, but Mallon should not have this information.'[5] Hogue's pistol was a thin, flat, single-shot 45, known as a 'Liberator';[6] its low accuracy and useful range of about 25 yards limited it to close-proximity anti-personnel work.[7] It was a 'crude little toy', which had 'killed more spies than any machine pistol... The shooter has one chance to hit. At close range, the impact is devastating.'[8]

On orders from Washington, Bonner made arrangements for Hogue to visit Liberia first, before going on to Léopoldville. Recent coverage of OSS activity in Liberia had been inadequate, worried Boulton, and Hogue was 'the man best qualified to assess things up there on a more effective basis'.[9] He was also asked to assess whether the undercover organisation he had earlier set up in Ivory Coast would function effectively under the new OSS representative.

Hogue gave a positive report on the reliability of the cutouts being used in Liberia. One of these was Dr Arthur G. Hyde, a young company physician employed by the Firestone Plantation at Cape Palmas, who worked for OSS without remuneration. Another good cutout was David Embree, who had had 'perhaps more experience with Liberian affairs than any other American living', as the head of the Booker T. Washington Institute in Kakata and of the College of West Africa in Monrovia.[10] But overall, Hogue believed that the current coverage of Liberia through a few cutouts was not sufficient, and that one well-trained OSS representative was needed there.[11] He also recommended strengthening the operation in Ivory Coast.

Bonner was enthusiastic about Hogue's visit to the Accra station. 'We have had several very satisfactory chats with TETON in regard to Liberia,' he reported to Washington, 'and have benefited greatly from his wide experience there. Meeting him has been a real opportunity for us to learn something and we have been listening avidly.'[12]

The two men planned to travel together to the Belgian Congo on 25 October, on an Air Transport Command plane—'if things go according to schedule', Bonner warned Boulton darkly, 'which as you know is most unlikely.'[13] Bonner did not enjoy flying with the ATC, bouncing around in a metal bucket seat. 'I want you to know,' he grumbled to Boulton, 'that I am giving my derriere for my country. These bucket seats on the ATC ships have made a permanent change in the contours of my anatomy.'[14]

As Bonner had predicted, there was indeed a delay and they had to catch a later plane. But finally, on 7 November 1943, they left Accra and flew to Léopoldville's airport—a 'long, uncertain rectangle cut out of the jungle'.[15] Close by was the colonial city, which was set on the bank of the mighty Congo River—the deepest river in the world and the ninth longest, with a volume second only to the Amazon.

Léopoldville was a commercial hub: products for trade from elsewhere in the colony were transported there by the Congo River, and then transported further on by the railway connecting Léopoldville with the Atlantic port of Matadi. An American visitor described it as a modern city situated on Stanley Pool (now known as Pool Malebo):

> a lake 30 miles wide through which the Congo River flows. The rapids at the lower end are a breathtaking sight. The volume of water is tremendous, about twice that of the Mississippi I believe and the fall is rapid from Léopoldville to Matadi.[16]

Hogue was immediately fascinated by the Congo—a vast, diverse, multilingual territory. The Congolese people numbered 15 million and between them spoke 242 languages, of which Kikongo (also known as Kituba), Lingala, Swahili and Tshiluba were the most common; many of those in the cities also spoke French or Flemish, the languages of the colonisers. The white population at the start of the war was less than 30,000, of which two thirds were Belgian and spoke French or Flemish as their first language.[17]

Hogue was always intrigued by the lives of others—which was an important quality for a spy. But he was not only interested in the individuals who were the focus of his work. He was also aware of, and interested in, the people living in the countries he visited. When he made his amateur films in Liberia, he had sought to record people's daily lives, filming their homes and visits to the market. Now, in the Belgian Congo, he regretted that he spoke none of the indigenous languages. He quickly started to learn Swahili, which was also spoken in other parts of Africa. Using a book called 'Basic Swahili', he prepared a list of important words and phrases, which he sent to Washington.[18] 'I suggest that anyone leaving the office for any part of Africa from Matadi to Mombasa to Capetown,' he wrote to the Secret Intelligence office, 'learn these if said person does not already know them. They'll be a big help with the natives.'[19]

Bonner, like Hogue, was conscious of the difficulties caused by knowing none of the languages spoken by the Congolese. 'It was difficult to get much information from the natives,' he reported to Boulton in June 1943, 'as few of them speak French well enough to permit much interrogation.'[20]

For the most part, the 'natives' were not easily visible to a foreigner, as a result of the enforced segregation and inequalities between the colonised and their rulers. 'Even the most casual visitor to the colonial Congo', commented one observer, 'could not fail' to observe the racism: in the cities and towns, there were separate living areas for blacks and whites, and many so-called 'European' shops had separate counters for Congolese customers. There were also a 'thousand petty vexations': Africans, whatever their status, were almost invariably addressed by the familiar '*tu*' form, as a 'patronizing expression of vague contempt'. They were also referred to by some Belgians as *macaques*—'monkeys living in trees'.[21]

In Léopoldville, the 'European city' of Kalina (now known as Gombe) was separated from the rest of the city by a cordon sanitaire comprising a golf course, a botanical garden, and a zoo. Matters relating to the civilian population in the city were supervised by two separate offices: the Bureau de la Population Blanche and the Bureau de la Population Noire. The Congolese were required to live in the *cité indigène*—the 'native city'—and had to be back in that area each night by 9 o'clock, unless a special permit had been issued. Congolese caught outside the 'native' city after 9 o'clock without a special permit were often arrested and imprisoned, sometimes for as long as two weeks. For repeated offences, recorded an American consul in the mid-1940s, lashings with a cat o'nine tails were not infrequent.[22]

An American code officer who joined the US consulate during the war was horrified by the racial inequalities in the Belgian Congo. On his first day, he was faced with the sight of a Congolese man in ragged shorts, kneeling on the ground, with a Belgian officer standing over him with a *chicotte*, a whip made of leather thongs tipped with metal at the ends. 'The whip whistled,' recorded the code officer, 'and the air seemed filled with a bloody haze. Every lash was followed by a scream of agony. When the prescribed number of lashes had been delivered, the black's skin from neck to waist was a mass of blood with ribs shining through.' The code officer was informed that this brutal attack was a punishment for stealing a pack of cigarettes from a Belgian. He learned, too, that blacks were clubbed off the sidewalk for not stepping aside for a white; and that it was common practice for a driver who had run over a black person to turn back and run him over again. 'Welcome to the Congo,' commented the code officer's companion drily.[23]

In 1885, King Léopold II had turned the territory into the Congo Free State—his own personal fiefdom. He exploited it to produce vast wealth from rubber and cotton plantations, through the forced labour of the Congolese. The *chicotte*, which at this time was made from hippopotamus hide with razor-sharp edges, was instrumental in this process; a hundred lashes of the *chicotte*, records Adam Hochschild, the author of the pathbreaking *King Leopold's Ghost*, was a common punishment and could be fatal.[24] Murder and amputation were regular punishments and in the 23 years Léopold 'owned' the Congo, an estimated 10 million people died as a result of the routine brutality and executions—50 per cent of the population.[25]

In 1908, Léopold was forced to relinquish control to the Belgian Parliament, which introduced some measures to curb the excesses. But the changes did not bring the exploitation and inequality to an end. Instead, it was now Belgian companies, rather than the King, which extracted the colony's valuable minerals and raw materials, making huge profits; and the Congolese were still subjected to forced labour and treated as second-class citizens. The *chicotte* remained a 'key tool of control, now often in the hands of private corporations', notes Hochschild. At the gold mines of Moto, '26,579 lashes were administered to miners in the first half of 1920 alone'.[26]

During the Second World War, the African workforce of men, women and children was put at the disposal of European employers—and suffered terribly.[27] The legal maximum for forced labour was increased from 60 to 120 days per man per year and the penalty for evasion was six months in prison. Heavy quotas were introduced for agricultural and other goods, especially for palm fruit and wild rubber, forcing people to work excessive hours to achieve the required output. Congolese workers laboured at everything, records Hochschild, 'from the railways to rubber plantations to the heavily guarded uranium mine of Shinkolobwe'.[28]

Pay was very low. According to an American missionary in October 1942, unskilled labourers were paid 2½ francs a day by the Belgians; mine workers were paid 1 or 1½ francs a day plus a quantity of food such as rice, fish and oil. He believed that this labour was 'tremendously underpaid', especially since the miners had to account for 12 cubic metres of excavation a day.[29] In certain regions, such as Kivu province, no wage at all was paid at the start of the war. Jules Marchal records that in Kivu, the governor waited until August 1944 before ordering a wage to be paid; even then he did not specify the amount, 'in order to avoid publishing a figure which might seem derisory'. The wage had to reach half a franc before the employer could ask the administration to assist him with a supply of workers.[30]

The collection of wild rubber in the forest, abandoned after the days of the Congo Free State, was forcibly resumed.[31] The directive to harvest rubber in the area of Equateur, close to Lake Léopold, writes David Van Reybrouck, 'caused the population to shudder'—for it was in this region that the atrocities in the Free State had left the deepest scars. The younger generation had heard stories from their parents or grandparents about the enforcement of rubber quotas, which involved the amputation of hands and limbs, flogging, and murder.[32] Now, the Allies wanted:

> ever more rubber for the tires of hundreds of thousands of military trucks, Jeeps, and warplanes. Some of the rubber came from the Congo's new plantations of cultivated rubber trees. But in the villages Africans were forced to go into the rain forest, sometimes for weeks at a time, to search for wild vines once again.[33]

In 1939, the Congo had produced just over 1,256 tons of rubber; but by 1944, that had risen to nearly 12,475 tons.

An agronomist called Vladimir Drachoussoff worked for the colonial civil service, going from village to village to boost the war effort. 'In the Lopori and close to Lake Léopold,' he wrote in his diaries, under the pen name of Vladi Souchard, 'I personally saw two old blacks who had lost their right hands [in the days of the Congo Free State] and who had not forgotten those days.' Many of the villagers tried to avoid the collection of rubber, insisting there were no rubber vines in the area, that they had never seen them, or that the vines had been exhausted. 'What right,' Drachoussoff asked himself in his diaries, 'do we have to drag the Congolese into our war? None whatsoever. Yet necessity knows no law ... and Hitler's victory here would install a racist tyranny that would make the abuses of colonialism look good.'[34]

'Increased Allied demands for African raw materials,' comments the historian Bruce Fetter, 'poisoned relations between Belgian officials and their colonial subjects'.[35] The demand for rubber drove terrified people into the jungle, despite the tsetse flies and predators, with the result that as much as 20 per cent of the population of the forest became infected with sleeping sickness, which had previously been vanquished.[36] People also streamed out of the rural areas into the cities to escape the rubber and other quotas. Between 1940 and 1945, Elisabethville's African population rose from 26,000 to 65,000, a growth rate of 18 per cent a year—the highest in the city's history.

Many men were recruited to the mines, in some cases forcibly, to hew out the minerals and raw materials required for the war. In Manono, the railroad siding was stacked high with piles of tin ingots, waiting to be transported to the ports. 'When I was there,' wrote a visitor:

> planes were arriving daily to fly back to America supplies of Tantolite, an alloy requisite found in tin ore, whose function is still a military secret. Twenty-four hours a day the natives work in the mines and foundries, producing essentials of war for allies they have never seen. By day, they toil in the dazzling white surface mines, sweat pouring over their tattooed bodies, dripping over perforated lips and ear-lobes pierced with bone.

By night, he added, 'the furnaces flare red tongues of flame out into the still Katanga dark. The ingots of tin mount up, white in the sunlight. The trains come and go, wailing across the lonely plains: sirens scream a reply. Day workers replace night workers. The mines do not sleep.'[37] Between 1938 and 1944, the Union Minière workforce almost doubled: from 25,000 to 49,000; so did the number of fatal accidents at Union Minière plants.[38]

The movement of men to the mines made it even more difficult for the women, children and old people left behind in the villages to achieve the production quotas set for vegetable products, such as palm oil and cotton.[39] Many thousands of Congolese men also saw active service: they were conscripted as soldiers and porters by the Force Publique, the Belgian colonial army, and served in Ethiopia (also known at the time as Abyssinia), Nigeria, Egypt and Palestine. Louis Ngumbi later recalled his induction into the army in 1940, after being arrested and beaten, on the orders of a Belgian. He only realised he had to join the army when he was given a uniform to wear of khaki shorts, shirts and white socks. The Belgian authorities used one of the tricks used by Léopold II to force him not to escape, by threatening to arrest his parents and mistreat them. At that time, said Ngumbi, 'You couldn't shake hands with a white. You couldn't sit with a white. We were thinking maybe white people were not human.' When Ngumbi found out about the Nazis, he wanted to fight against them: 'During that period, Hitler wanted to colonize the world, and we were trying to stop him.'[40]

Starting in February 1941, the Allied troops sent to free Ethiopia were reinforced by the 11th battalion of the Force Publique: some 3,000 Congolese soldiers and 2,000 bearers, with one Belgian officer to every fifty Africans. Thanks in part to their efforts, Ethiopia was liberated from Italian occupation. 'Here, for the first time in history,' notes David Van Reybrouck in Congo, 'an African country had been decolonized by African soldiers.'[41] Congolese also served in the Belgian field hospital, which operated in Somalia, Madagascar and Burma, and which became known as the tenth Belgian Congo Clearing Station; it had two operating tents, a radio tent, and other tents for patients. 'The fact that Congolese paramedics cared for Burmese civilians and British soldiers in the Asian jungle,' comments Van Reybrouck, 'is a completely unknown chapter in colonial history, and one that will soon vanish altogether.'[42]

Doug Bonner stayed in Léopoldville for ten days and his company was much appreciated by Hogue.[43] There were still a number of outstanding matters to clear up as a result of Chapin's departure, such as returning a gun and cartridges to their owner.[44] It was also helpful to have a personal introduction to the Belgian colony, which had a very different history from Liberia, where Hogue had worked for six years, and a long history of association with the USA.

On the one hand, there was a growing American presence in the Congo and good radio reception in Léopoldville, so that—as one American businessman put it—'the United States comes in clearly between 9 and 10 pm'.[45] News about the war came in regularly. 'We get it about as often as you do on the radio,' wrote the representative for General Motors to his family—'two or three times a day. I have a little portable which does me well, and listen in to Lowell Thomas now and then at 12.45 just as you do. It comes short wave from Boston...'[46]

But at the same time, Hogue felt somewhat isolated, especially once Bonner had flown back to Accra. Unlike Jim Chapin and Armand Denis, who had numerous friends and contacts at the Léopoldville zoo and in scientific circles, Hogue did not know anybody in the Congo when he arrived. Nor was it easy for him to meet and talk to people: there was no natural community of Americans, as there was in Liberia at the Firestone Harbel Plantation. There, Hogue had had a natural circle of friends with whom to fish and enjoy a beer late at night. 'Peter Farley caught a 35 pound barracuda last Saturday which is the biggest this season,' he reported from Harbel in a letter to Ruth in 1942. 'Leave it to Peter. I lost two nice ones the other night. Worked them up to the boat and let them away while Dee was making up his mind to gaff them.'[47]

Like Jim Chapin, Hogue's cover in the Congo was that of 'Special Assistant' to the American Consul, Patrick Mallon, who had agreed to this, as had the State Department. Hogue had therefore expected to be given an office at the US Consulate, which would be in keeping with his cover. But there was apparently no space available—which seemed odd, given that the Consulate had so recently moved into a large new building. Hogue wondered if this reflected a lack of support for his posting. Many American diplomats had little patience with OSS, and the relationship between OSS and the State Department was often tense, especially in postings overseas.

Such tension was all the more likely to occur when OSS asked the State Department for diplomatic cover. The US Ambassador in Ankara, for example, vigorously opposed such a request. 'He feels very *strongly*,' wrote his office to Washington, 'that the Embassy must *not* be used to give cover to OSS ... he himself believes that the entire idea of "cover" for OSS is ridiculous.'[48] OSS agents themselves were not always keen: they did not want to be scrutinised or to have their communications read by the Consul and his staff.

In a non-military territory such as the Congo, Hogue was in the awkward situation of having to serve two masters: the Joint Chiefs of Staff and the State Department representative. This could prove difficult to manage, he thought, since any OSS agent in the field knew that secret information is information which a government or organisation does not wish to become known—'that to obtain such, certain risks are assumed and certain activity undertaken which would not be condoned by the Department of State'.[49] In Liberia, he had already experienced this kind of difficulty.

But Boulton was hopeful that things would be different in Léopoldville. It was possible, he wrote, that the State Department's representatives 'will allow us more latitude and be less suspicious of our activities since we have explained the facts to them'. He planned to monitor the situation carefully:

> How this works out remains to be seen. We want TETON to keep us well informed regarding the supervision exercised over his activities, but using the Army Courier would be resented by the State Department if discovered. Consequently it will be well to keep the cards above the table as long as possible and resort to other devices only if the former proves impossible.

'As you know,' Boulton wrote to Bonner, 'Mallon has the right to inspect our letters to TETON as well as his letters to us. We hope he won't exercise either right. If, however, TETON finds that Mallon is reading our letters to him, instruct him to inform us right away lest we express views that might be unwelcome.'[50]

The protection from scrutiny of secret communications was of paramount importance—hence Boulton's concern. Paper communications for OSS agents were brought in the diplomatic pouch by the courier from the State Department in Washington. CRUMB's station in Accra, however, was critical of common practice. 'May we suggest that the mere sealing with wax [of a pouch letter] adds little if any security to a letter in our humble opinion,' wrote Bonner to Washington. 'What,' he asked, 'is to prevent someone removing your wax, reading the contents and putting another blob of wax on using elementary care to see that the old stains are covered?' He suggested that using 'some odd coin or seal for the purpose, something that could not be easily duplicated, would help. We are using a Saint Christopher medal. I think that all your Pouch Letters should be sealed this way.'[51]

The arrival of a diplomatic courier at the Léopoldville consulate was a dramatic affair and was described by a member of the consular staff. A manacle, he said, linked the diplomatic pouch to the courier's wrist and the pouch itself was a sturdy leather and canvas affair. One particular courier opened the pouch with an 'impressive' key attached to a silver chain he wore around his neck. The key was accompanied on the same chain by a Saint Christopher's medal. He wore a tight-fitting shoulder holster, 'with the thinnest and flattest automatic pistol I had ever seen'. He also carried a double-edged knife strapped to the underside of his left arm. 'If a man knows how to use it,' the courier had explained, 'a knife can save him at close quarters better than a gun ever could.'[52]

Hogue was a highly disciplined agent and, unlike Chapin, ready to follow procedure regarding cipher, regardless of the time it needed. But this proved challenging at first. 'While I was in Accra,' he reported to Washington, 'TRUCK and I fixed up a communications system for Accra–Leo. He changed this after I left there, and our tests did not work out—at least on this end.' Hogue wired the Message Center in Accra to inform TRUCK (Leonard Davis, the Communications Officer) that he could not break his first five messages. But in his spare time, he was able to crack them all; and on 22 December, he wired the good news to Davis. He then sent a report to OSS headquarters. 'The error was mine, not TRUCK's,' he reported, with disarming frankness. 'I simply cannot spell—.'[53]

With Bonner's assistance, an office was found for Hogue by the large mission of the US Foreign Economic Administration, in their own offices. The FEA had been created by President Roosevelt on 25 September 1943 to unify and consolidate governmental activities relating to foreign economic affairs. It absorbed the Office of Economic Warfare, which had been set up just a couple of months earlier on 15 July 1943, to replace the Bureau of Economic Warfare.[54]

The FEA also supplied him with a place to stay—the same large room and bath where Bonner had stayed on his visit to Léopoldville earlier that year. It was arranged that Hogue would 'mess' with the FEA and their staff would take care of his cleaning and laundry.[55] This arrangement afforded none of the luxury of the Consulate. But it provided Hogue with everything he needed and had the advantage of easy contact with FEA officials. These included Greer and Jaubert, the cutouts established by Bonner, who had initially worked for the Bureau of Economic Warfare and were absorbed by the Foreign Economic Administration.

In May and June 1943, Bonner had created the basis of an OSS infrastructure in the Congo and it was now Hogue's responsibility to take it over and run it himself. Very quickly, this heightened his visibility in the Congo. He was followed by 'numerous individuals for days', after starting to investigate the addressee, Colette Finale, of a letter intercepted by censorship in Lisbon. His investigation in Léopoldville, he reported, revealed several channels pointing to Axis sympathisers or agents and had 'stirred up a nest of hornets'.[56]

He was also becoming visible to British intelligence in the Gold Coast. Major Bonner, who had returned to Accra from Léopoldville in the middle of November, was holding discussions with the British concerning illicit diamond buying, known as IDB. On 14 December 1943, he reported to Washington that he and British intelligence officials had 'today decided upon an arrangement to hold a comprehensive conference concerning IDB in Accra'.[57] Next day, a Most Secret report was sent to London from British intelligence in Accra, stating that SOE and OSS in West Africa would pool their resources, both intelligence and operational, in the pursuit of diamond smugglers. The IDB operation, it said, would be coordinated in Accra and would involve the Belgian Congo and Liberia, which would be specifically American spheres of activity, and Angola, which would be a British sphere. In the Congo, added the report, 'OSS have H an excellent man, planted'.[58] This 'excellent man' was Hogue.

6

'ATTENTION! BLOC RADIOACTIF!'

A priority for TETON was to liaise with the OSS agent in Angola, the Portuguese colony on the southern side of the Congo's border. Like Mozambique on the other side of the African continent, Angola was neutral in the war, under the direction of its colonial ruler. But Portugal—which was one of the neutral powers in Europe—took a cynical position: it supplied both the Allies and the Axis with strategic raw materials, including wolfram, which was vital for producing war munitions, to Germany.[1] Its regime was similar to that of Spain, under General Franco, in terms of its internal policies and antipathy to Russia. But it was not an open associate of the Axis nations, as was Spain under Franco, who had been helped into power by Hitler and Mussolini. It also wanted the support of the British fleet to maintain its colonial empire. In October 1943, Portugal granted the Allies an important military concession, in the use of naval and air bases in the Azores.[2] In effect, Portugal was on both sides and was regarded as untrustworthy by America.

It was for this reason that the Manhattan Project had ended all shipments of uranium ore to the US through the Angolan port of Lobito, sending them instead via the Congolese port of Matadi, or by air. But this would not prevent the smuggling of the ore from the Congo to Angola, from there to Portugal, and finally from Portugal to Germany. This was a real risk, since the border between the Congo and Angola was very long and very porous.

The OSS agent in Angola was Lanier John Violett, a handsome and strapping man who was even taller than Hogue at six foot six inches. He was stationed in the capital city of Luanda on the Atlantic coast, a deepwater port that had once been a major cen-tre of the slave trade. Violett came from an old American family, with roots in the cotton world of Louisiana, members of which were now prominent in Manhattan's 'smart set'. His elder broth-ers went to Yale but he opted for a more adventurous pathway in life: first he enlisted in the New York National Guard, and then in the 101st Cavalry. When America entered the war, he joined the ranks of OSS and was sent to Angola in 1942 by the Special Operations division, under cover of inspector for the Texas oil company (also known as Texaco).

Violett reported to Special Operations that there were 343 Germans in Angola and that, according to rumour, they had caches of machine guns.[3] He also sent details about the German Consulate at Luanda and the Italian Consulate at Lobito, which were passed on to the Research and Analysis Division. 'Between the two of them,' observed a report by R&A on Angola, in alarm, 'the coun-try is well covered.' Several Nazi leaders owned large plantations and the most important German in the colony was the German shipping supervisor, in residence at Luanda.[4] The Roman Catholic Bishop in Luanda, like de Hemptinne in Elisabethville, was known to be sympathetic to fascism.

Major Len Manderstam, the British intelligence officer who set up and ran SOE in Angola—under cover of working for a com-pany called General Mining—frequently came across Violett.[5] 'Now at that time,' wrote Manderstam in his memoirs of the war:

> the American OSS had in Angola an agent called Vic Violet [sic], a most unlikely name for a six feet six inches tall former New York mounted policeman. Violet, known to his friends as "the Oil King", was in charge of the Texaco office in Luanda.

When Violett was asked by Manderstam if he had an American cheque book, he replied: 'Of course, but I haven't got a bean in the account.' Then he produced the cheque book. When Manderstam tore a blank cheque from the book and made it out for $40,000, Violett thought it was 'a huge joke' and 'signed it with a flourish'.[6] Gestures like this were typical of 'Vic' Violett, who earned a reputation for maverick behaviour.

In August 1943, a few months before Dock Hogue's arrival in the Congo, Violett was transferred to Boulton's team in Secret Intelligence; his codename was HOMER and his codenumber was 397. His codename may have been a tribute to the ancient Greek poet; or possibly it was a reference to a minor character called Homer Simpson in Nathaneal West's *The Day of the Locust*, a bleak novel of modern American life published a few years earlier, in 1939.[7] Homer Simpson was a deadweight and ineffectual; but Violett was expected to be an asset to Secret Intelligence because of his cover of working for Texaco, which enabled him to move about freely in Angola, without provoking suspicion. In addition, he was familiar with the smuggler trails across the border with the Congo.[8]

Dock Hogue was anxious to make contact with Violett. But flying to Luanda was complicated to arrange and the drive between Luanda and Léopoldville was a difficult one: a three-day journey covering hundreds of miles of hazardous dirt roads through jungle and scrubland, by way of Matadi, Ambrizete and along the coast road.[9] Fortunately for Hogue, Violett came to Léopoldville in November to meet with him. He had an easy pretext: for Léopoldville was the headquarters of Texaco in West Africa and an oil conference was being held there.

'We got together several times,' reported Hogue to Washington, 'and through him I was able to become fairly well acquainted with Mogardo, one of the leading Portuguese merchants in the Congo. CRUMB will be interested to know this as he was anxious for me to meet Mogardo.' Violett, mused Hogue, 'is quite a lad—.'[10]

Violett had engaged a man by the name of Diaz to represent the Texas Company in Léopoldville, which surprised Hogue.

71

Little was known about Diaz. But a British intelligence officer, who noticed Diaz and Violett together at Luanda airport awaiting departure for Léopoldville, observed that a messenger told Diaz that Romao, the Angolan Chief of Police, wished to see him, to give him some final instructions. Diaz then rushed off to see Romao.[11] This worried the British officer, since Romao had been suspected for some time of being pro-Nazi and was known to have favoured local Germans through his position. Furthermore, operations against the Angolan smuggling traffic had been made extremely difficult by the fact that Romao protected the smugglers and was possibly involved in smuggling himself.[12]

The British officer, who was based in Accra, wrote to Major Bonner to share his concerns. This led Bonner to start having doubts about HOMER's judgement. Why, he wondered, had Violett picked Diaz for this job? Perhaps, he speculated, Romao had planted Diaz on Violett, in an effort to get Diaz into the Belgian Congo under the cover of working for the Texas Company—or perhaps Violett had taken on Diaz for Romao, in return for reciprocal favours. It was also possible that Diaz had gone to the Congo with the knowledge and connivance of the Chief of Police in Léopoldville, for the purpose of having a Portuguese man keep an eye on the Belgian Portuguese.[13] Bonner sent a worried cable to Washington. 'To be perfectly honest,' he warned, 'Diaz stinks from Angola to Liberia and our prestige in East Africa is suffering tremendously because of him ... Find out from HOMER why Diaz was employed in Congo as Texas man. He is under suspicion having got in touch with the local Chief of Police whose name is Romao.'[14]

It is possible that Bonner was having concerns generally about the role of Texaco in the Congo. As a man who was extremely well-informed, he would have known about an article in the *New York Herald Tribune* in 1940, which revealed that the then President of Texaco, Torkild Rieber, had been an active supporter of fascism. In 1937, Texaco tankers taking oil consigned for Belgium changed direction to Franco's ports in Spain; shipments continued after the outbreak of the European war in 1939. Rieber also had plans for shipping oil to the German Navy, which he discussed with Hermann Goering, the head of the Luftwaffe and close associate of Hitler. He brought to the US a German lawyer, whose salary was paid by Texaco and who was given an office in Texaco's headquarters in the Chrysler building in Manhattan. The lawyer's mission was to dissuade American businessmen from supplying arms to Britain, on the grounds that Britain was close to defeat and America should develop good relations with Germany. When these details were revealed in the press, the law-yer quickly returned to Germany and Rieber was compelled to resign at a meeting of Texaco shareholders.[15]

Marcellino—'Marcy'—Da Costa, the US consul in Luanda, does not appear to have shared Bonner's concerns about Violett, and recommended to Hogue that he use Diaz as a cutout. But when Hogue asked Violett for his opinion, he advised against using Diaz—even though he himself had engaged Diaz to work for Texaco. Hogue decided that Diaz was too much of a risk. 'I have met Diaz,' he reported. 'He is a young, flamboyant type very much in the public eye around Léopoldville. I have a feeling the Belgians are watching him closely, so I will let him ride along.'

Hogue would not have been surprised to learn that Romao, Angola's Chief of Police, was collaborating with the Nazis, given the complicated position of Portugal and its colonies in the war. In the Congo, however, where the Governor General had made a clear commitment to the Allied cause, it would be reasonable to expect the Chief of Police to support the Allies. But this appeared not to be the case, as Hogue discovered when he went on a fact-finding trip to the port of Matadi, 368 km from Léopoldville. He went there on the daily train, which left in the morning at 7.00 a.m., arriving in Matadi at 6:00 p.m. He would have travelled in the coach combining first and second class passengers, which was exclusively for whites; the Congolese had to travel in the third class coaches.[16]

Matadi, on the bank of the Congo River, was a very large and busy port. As soon as Hogue arrived, he went directly to see

Monsieur De Gesnot, the Comptroller of Customs, who told him that Léon P. Jacobs, the former Police Commissioner, whose job was to look out for Nazi spies operating at the port, was involved in diamond smuggling. In 1942, said De Gesnot, Jacobs had smuggled the equivalent of a small typewriter case of industrial diamonds out of the Congo in Red Cross parcels. These parcels were usually shipped to Lobito, from where they went by Portuguese ship to Lisbon. Jacobs always insisted upon placing the Red Cross parcels aboard ship himself, in order to avoid detection; and, in any case, Red Cross parcels usually escaped examination by customs officials. De Gesnot also suspected that Jacobs collaborated with Sa Carneiro, the Angolan Customs chief, in smuggling various products across the Congo-Angola border.

But effective action against Jacobs was impossible, warned De Gesnot, because he was protected by Jean Nicholas Beaudinet, the Chef de Sûreté in Léopoldville.[17] Jacobs, he added, furnished Beaudinet with narcotics, which he got from Portuguese ships.[18]

Hogue was alarmed by these allegations. Taking his leave of De Gesnot, he rushed off to see Monsieur Dom, the head at Matadi of the Société d'Entreprises Commerciales au Congo Belge, known as SEDEC, to ask him what he knew about Beaudinet. Dom gave him the same account.[19]

This was a worrying development—especially since Beaudinet was in effect Hogue's Belgian Congo 'opposite' and had formerly been Ryckmans's private secretary. But, noted Hogue, Beaudinet was on the list of suspicious people drawn up by Bonner. He had also been distrusted by former OSS agent Chapin. 'That man,' Chapin had said dismissively, 'is like a stone wall with a sugary smile painted on it.'[20] The British didn't like him either. 'Very amiable, talkative and superficially helpful,' commented a British intelligence report on key figures in the Congo, 'but is also tricky and untrustworthy and inspires little confidence. Is known to have on one occasion most improperly revealed this consulate-general as the source of confidential information.' He also had a reputation of being 'unduly influenced by the ladies'.[21]

Hogue's reports to Washington were focused and highly perti-
nent, in contrast to the efforts of Armand Denis and Jim Chapin.
So when Hogue cabled a report to Washington on the allegations
against Beaudinet, Boulton took it very seriously. For not only
was Beaudinet an important individual in the Congo, but he was
a government official. It was becoming increasingly important,
thought Boulton, that Hogue maintain maximum independence
from the US Consul and his staff.[22]

Once Hogue had returned to Léopoldville from Matadi, he
made plans to see other parts of the Congo. By now, he had been
in the Congo for nearly a month, and he was especially keen to
visit Elisabethville in Katanga—the Congolese headquarters of
Union Minière, which supplied the Manhattan Project with uranium. Hogue left the capital on 6 December 1943. In terms of
the weather, this was not the best time to travel: hot, with the
rains of November still ongoing, often every day. He packed the
outfit that had been issued to him to protect against malaria,
including his black mosquito boots.[23]

Hogue's particular cover for this trip was the registration for
the draft of all American males in the Congo, a task which had
initially been given to the Consul, Patrick Mallon, by the State
Department. This was a plausible cloak for Hogue's trip, given
that his overall cover in the Congo was that of 'Special Assistant'
to the Consul. It also, as the Africa Division in Secret Intelligence
noted with satisfaction, would put him in contact with individuals who might be useful.[24] The consulate staff were pleased, too,
to have this painstaking job taken off their hands. Mallon, as well
as Vice Consuls Mark Ingle and Leonard Cromie, reported
Hogue, 'continue to give me every possible assistance. I feel a bit
guilty in the amount of time I consume as they have their own
jobs to do. They were all extremely helpful in getting this trip laid
out for me.'[25] So far, he thought with relief, Boulton's fear that
the Consulate would interfere in the work of OSS was not being
borne out.

It was a long way from Léopoldville to Katanga, even by air—a
flight of 960 miles over the Belgian Congo and a corner of

Angola.[26] Hogue was surprised by Elisabethville, which was different from any other city he had visited in Africa and was European in style—at least, in the central areas designated for whites. 'Its broad avenues and modernistic architecture,' noted one American visitor, 'give the impression of a sumptuous metropolis. The shops are elegant, furnished with luxuries from all over the world, and the European quarter is handsomely organised ... with an ease and graciousness among its inhabitants.'[27]

'One of my assignments here in the Congo, as you well know,' Hogue reported to Washington, 'is to find out just how the Société Générale dovetails with other corporations outside of the colony ... I beg to report that the opening wedge has been driven as the result of this trip. Details will come...'[28]

Hogue had done his homework on Union Minière du Haut Katanga. He knew that it was a huge concern, which was tightly controlled by the Belgian finance company Société Générale de Belgique;[29] the other major financial interests in Belgium were Empain, Banque de Bruxelles, and Cominière. By the outbreak of the Second World War, comments André Mommen, Société Générale controlled directly or indirectly 70 per cent of the Congolese economy and its influence was 'practically total' in certain mining areas, notably Katanga and Kasai, and in maritime and rail transportation. Société Générale was also involved with the Diamond Company of Angola (known as DIAMANG).[30] In effect, adds Mommen, the mining companies 'constituted a state within the Belgian Congo because they produced 22 per cent of the colony's GDP and 60 per cent of its export. Of this production, 75 per cent came from Katanga.'[31]

Belgian corporate law had no 'arm's length' provisions and interlocking directorships were common.[32] The relationship between Société Générale and Union Minière was close.[33] Société Générale also participated in the Compagnie du Chemin de Fer du Bas-Congo au Katanga (BCK) and in Forminière.[34] A large slice in Union Minière was also held by the British company Tanganyika Concessions ('Tanks' for short), which was entitled to substantial royalties on the minerals produced. British directors of Tanks also sat on the board of Union Minière and the Vice-President of Union Minière was the British Lord Stonehaven. One of the directors of Tanks was the South African magnate Harry Oppenheimer, who was chairman of De Beers Consolidated Mines and director of numerous other companies. He was also a director of Société Minière du Bécéca, known as Sibéka, a diamond mining company. The interlinking of Oppenheimer's business interests illustrates well the relationship between the minerals mined by different companies—between, for example, the uranium mined by Union Minière, and diamonds mined by Sibéka.[35] Union Minière had procured a concession in Katanga covering 7,700 square miles, more than half the size of Belgium itself.[36] It mined not only uranium, but also copper, cobalt, radium, zinc, cadmium, germanium, manganese, silver, gold and tin, which were exported out of the Congo by two different routes. One of these routes was provided by the BCK, based in Elisabethville, which after January 1943 transported uranium to Port-Francqui, en route to the port of Matadi. The other route was provided by the Benguela railway, which was owned by the British company Tanks and which went to the port of Lobito and the port of Beira in Mozambique.

No record is available of Hogue's visit to Katanga, beyond the bare facts of his travel and a brief film he took showing the post office in Elisabethville and the centre of the city. In the same way, there was no detailed record of Doug Bonner's visit to Katanga in June 1943.

Presumably, Hogue met with Jaubert, the cutout established by Bonner, and spoke to various sources about Union Minière's activities. He may also have visited the company's offices in Elisabethville and Jadotville, the Shinkolobwe mine, and the railway hubs used to transport uranium. He had briefed himself to carry out such visits and had a report on the mining activities at Shinkolobwe in his possession. It was also reported later that while in the Congo, he worked not only in Léopoldville but also 'at some mine neither he nor anybody else in authority wants to talk about'.[37] But all such investigations in Katanga were clandestine and top secret.

If Hogue did visit the Union Minière headquarters in Elisabethville, he may have seen its museum, which proudly displayed 'extraordinarily beautiful specimens of, *inter alia*, malachite and uranium', according to Sir Evelyn Baring, the governor of the British colony of Southern Rhodesia (now Zimbabwe), who visited the museum in 1944.[38] An American writer, John Gunther, went to this museum after the war. At its entrance, he saw 'a block of pitchblende, uranium ore, as big as a pig. It was coloured black and gold, and looked as if it were covered with a green scum, or moss made of stone. It came from Shinkolobwe ... a small sign says "*Attention! Bloc Radioactif!*"' Inside the museum, Gunther saw 'lumps of other uranium ore, a characteristic of which is their savage, morbid colour', as well as ores that were brightly coloured—yellow-green and silver, yellow-red, a brilliant marbled orange, fawn and gold, lettuce green, and dull black mixed with pea green. 'Most extraordinary of all,' he thought, was 'vandenbrandeite, which is greenish-grey, yellow, black, and orange, in tiger stripes.' In the office of Maurice Van Weyenbergh, a senior executive at Union Minière, he saw yet more samples of this 'brilliant, hideous ore':

> One chunk looked like a metal watermelon, pink and green, but it also had flaming veins of gamboges, lemon, and orange. The reflection was trite, but difficult not to summon—rocks like these have fire in them not only figuratively but literally.

Gunther wondered if there might be any health risks associated with uranium. 'I even touched a piece of ore loaded with it,' he wrote, 'then wanted to wash my hands quickly, out of the silly fear that it might be radioactive enough to hurt.'[39]

Joseph Volpe Jr, who was one of General Groves's right-hand men and who visited the Shinkolobwe mine during the war, was also concerned about the health risks of uranium. When he went to Union Minière headquarters in Elisabethville, according to Gunther, he saw a large lump of high-grade pitchblende in a geologist's office. Laughing, he called out to the Belgians working there: 'Don't you boys know that this stuff makes you sterile?' They said they weren't worried—that they had all had several children. But then Volpe told them about research that had just taken place in the United States, showing how dangerous uranium could be. The next time he visited the geologist's office, he noticed that the uranium had disappeared.

Volpe then asked about the water in the area—'Do you drink the water around here?' Again, the answer was dismissive: 'Of course! The radium content is infinitesimal.' But Volpe's question had touched a nerve. 'No one,' recorded Gunther, 'drank water from that particular area from that day on.'[40] In this respect, Gunther's account is revealing: clearly he meant that no *Belgian* drank water from that particular area from then on. Presumably Africans in the vicinity were not informed and in any case had few, if any, alternatives sources of water.

From Elisabethville, Hogue travelled up into the north-central territory of the Congo and filmed some of the journey with his 8 mm movie camera. This film indicates that he took a major part of the same journey that was used to transport the barrels of uranium from Katanga to Matadi. It shows a BCK train reaching the railhead at Port-Francqui, and then the loading of goods on to ferries on the Kasai River; the boats, full of cargo, can be seen sailing slowly down the Kasai River to the Congo River.

Hogue was grateful for the plausible cover supplied by Mallon. 'It is impossible to travel in the Belgian Congo,' he reported, 'without it being quite well known who you are, where you are going, and why. You cannot walk into the railroad station and buy yourself a ticket to such and such a place without ... giving your name as one can do in the States.' Even travel in your own car, he added, 'is subject to scrutiny, and it is wise to get yourself organised through the touring Club du Congo Belge of which yours truly is a member'. He was mentioning these things, he said, 'so that should we ever operate in the Congo under real cover, it *must be good*'.[41]

After more than a month, on 10 January 1944, Hogue's tour around the Congo came to an end. 'I hope to make another trip soon across the north part and down into the central area,' he reported to headquarters. 'After this jaunt (if it can be arranged) I will make my recommendations to you as to just what should be done with regard to American intelligence activity in the Belgian Congo.'[42]

In the meantime, he was able to report that South African liaison in the Congo was handled by Major John Quarry, while British liaison was taken care of by Major Birch and his assistant, Captain Best. Major Kenyon Bolton, Chief of the US Military Intelligence Mission in Brazzaville, French Equatorial Africa, frequently crossed the Congo River to visit Léopoldville. 'With such an assembly of rank in Léopoldville,' observed Hogue drily to the Africa Section training officer, 'I am more than ever glad that Rud and you did not send me here as *Lieutenant* Hogue.'[43]

He regretted that he had not had a good camera on his journey. 'I would like to suggest,' he recommended to the Secret Intelligence training office, 'that more stress be placed on the use of a very small, inconspicuous camera, i.e. the Minox in connection with the preparation of dossiers. It is very easy to grab a picture of a desired personality at a gathering. A photograph attached to a dossier would be of great help to the next person taking over.'[44] The Minox was a miniature stainless steel camera, small enough to be concealed within the palm of the hand; although ideally suited for photographing documents, it could also be used for general photography and its small size made it easy to conceal and operate with one hand.[45]

Hogue was pleased, though, that he had taken some 'home movies' of his travels, which he sent by pouch to OSS Secret Intelligence in Washington. He also knew that Ruth, back home, would be eager to watch the movies. 'If you, Rud, or someone in the office has an 8 mm projector, and you wish to see them,' he wrote to Willard Beecher, the personnel and training officer for the OSS Africa Section, 'please put your name and address in the spot for same.' But otherwise, 'kindly fill that space in with my wife's name and address, and the films will be returned to her'.[46] The films reached Ruth safely—and are still in the possession of Dock Hogue's family.

7

ANGELLA

On the other side of the Congo River from Léopoldville, just 2½ miles away, was Brazzaville, the capital of the French colonial territories known as the AEF or l'Afrique Equatoriale Française (French Equatorial Africa). There was no OSS representative in Brazzaville, so AEF was included in Hogue's beat. However, the American Office of War Information—effectively OSS's sister organisation, since they were both spawned from the COI—had an office in the city, which gave Hogue a base there.

Visitors flying into the area on the Pan Am clipper service were surprised by the contrast between these two cities facing each other. 'As the plane hovered over the Congo, and settled into Stanley Pool,' observed one American, 'I was struck by a dramatic double image. On one side of this historic stretch of water I could make out the dusty roads and primitive roofs of Brazzaville, capital of the French Congo. Facing it, as New York faces Brooklyn, was the sprawling expanse of a modern city, complete with smokestacks, electric lights and asphalt avenues.'[1]

There was a regular ferry service between the two colonial capitals: two launches, leaving from opposite points on the river at the same time. This schedule was adopted because it was just 20 minutes' floating time from the crossing point to the start of the rapids known as the Livingstone Falls. But if one of the boats became disabled, the other one could try to rescue the passengers.[2] A special speedboat across the river was provided by Pan American Airways for American official personnel, which was helpful to Hogue.

French Africa was a cause for concern to the US and Britain, since many French African colonies sided initially with the pro-German Vichy regime of Marshal Pétain, following the fall of France. But this was a complicated picture, especially since the US considered the Vichy regime to be the legal government of France right up to June 1944, when the Allies successfully invaded German-occupied Europe. Unlike Britain, the US chose not to support the Free French because of de Gaulle's colonial policies, especially in relation to Southeast Asia.

French Equatorial Africa consisted of four provinces: Chad, Ubangi-Chari, Middle Congo and Gabon. Brazzaville was the capital both of Middle Congo, which was widely known as 'French Congo', and of the AEF as a whole. The AEF was the only territory in the world from 1940 until 1943 that was controlled by the Free French. On 22 October 1940, de Gaulle established the Council for Defence of the Empire in Brazzaville and the African city assumed an enormous symbolic importance.[3] Félix Eboué, a black man born in French Guyana, was made Governor General of the AEF in 1941. As the former governor of Chad, he had taken a lead in French Africa in the support of de Gaulle. By June 1943, anti-Vichyism had been declared in French West Africa—and the AEF had helped to show the way.[4]

Because the US recognised the Vichy regime as the legal government of France, there was widespread resentment in the AEF against America and Americans and, very often, stilted, unfriendly relations. This was 'the condition that coloured all US-French relations', commented an American working for the Office of War Information—'the fact that our government did not recognise de Gaulle'.[5]

This created a tense situation for Hogue on his visits to Brazzaville; he was not seen as an enemy, but he wasn't on the right side either. Moreover, it was difficult in the AEF to work out who supported the Allies, and who supported the Axis. One example of this, he thought, was Commander Jean-Jacques Rechenmann, the head of the Free French intelligence operation in Brazzaville. Rechenmann was reputed to have in his possession papers of the French Deuxième Bureau, the French intelligence agency, which was now associated with Vichy France. Rechenmann was believed to be open to financial inducements, and 'in case this method failed, information could be obtained by more aggressive means. [He is] well known in French circles but his loyalty to the cause has been questioned as he is suspected of working for the Germans.'[6]

The importance of Brazzaville in the war effort was underlined by the installation in June 1943 of a powerful 50 kWh short-wave transmitter at Radio Brazzaville. It had developed out of a small radio club started up by amateurs and then became a medium for propaganda on behalf of Free France and the Allied cause. The opening of the new transmitter is shown at the beginning of L'Amitié Noire, a film that was shot in 1943 and narrated by Jean Cocteau.[7] 'Un nouveau monstre,' intones Cocteau at the start of the film, 'vient de naître en Afrique. C'est un animal merveilleux, hérissé d'antennes et parcouru d'ondes. C'est Radio-Brazzaville'–'A new monster has just been born in Africa. It's a wondrous animal, bristling with antennae and pulsating with airwaves. It is Radio Brazzaville.'[8] In the film there are close-up shots of Radio Brazzaville—the staff, the machinery, the workshop, the tickertape machine, and other offices. From here, daily programmes went out to countries in different parts of the world.

One of the people shown in the film, working hard at a desk with modern equipment, is a young woman—who may have been an American called Shirley Armitage Chidsey.[9] The features of the woman cannot be clearly seen, but it is certainly the case that a woman called Shirley Chidsey worked for Radio Brazzaville as a transcriber. Before coming to Africa, Chidsey had worked in the New York OSS office as a stenographer specialising in French from October 1942 until February 1943.[10] But she had been anxious to serve overseas—even if this meant she had to leave the OSS office, where she was 'very highly thought of for her work, her conduct, and general attitude'. When the opportunity came up of a job at Radio Brazzaville, she jumped at it.[11] This, she thought, would be an ideal way of doing her bit for the war.

Shirley Chidsey, who was born Elinor Shirley Stewart, was in her mid-thirties when she went to Brazzaville. Her features were plain, but she had an intelligent, independent, and lively air which made her almost beautiful. Her OSS personnel file records that she had grey eyes, brown hair, a fair complexion, and petite build: just five foot one inch tall, weighing 52 kg. Her father had died when she was a toddler and when her mother married again to Percival Armitage, he formally adopted her. She grew up in a gracious home in Swarthmore, Pennsylvania, where two more daughters were born. Mother and daughters were frequently seen in the society pages of the local newspapers. But the daughters wanted more out of their lives than a busy calendar with the smart set, and developed independent minds and lives. Shirley spent time as a student in New York at Barnard College and then at Columbia University, and took 'numerous writing and lit. courses', as well as French.[12] Her younger sister Peggy worked as a volunteer for the Swarthmore fire department during the war and was photographed in uniform helping to quench a huge blaze near Philadelphia.[13] Frannie, her other sister, became an airline stewardess.

Shirley had an appetite for travel and adventure. By the time the US entered the war, she had already lived for three years in Haiti, three months in Hawaii, a month in France, and a month in Germany, and had visited China. In 1935 she had married Donald Barr Chidsey, an author of fiction, mostly sea adventures, and biographies. She went with him to Tahiti, where she sailed in his boat and helped to manage a coconut plantation; she also learnt to speak Tahitian. While there she made friends with a number of writers, including F. Scott Fitzgerald, who later inscribed a copy one of his books to her. She also worked as the editor of *Mutiny on the Bounty* and the rest of the *Bounty Trilogy*, written by Charles Nordhoff and James Norman Hall; they wrote alternating chapters and it was her task to integrate them into a coherent narrative.[14]

Tahiti has often been described as paradise. But the same could not be said of the Chidseys' marriage: she separated from him in February 1940. The separation was not legal until 1944, but the break-up was permanent. Shirley then went to New York and placed an advertisement in November 1940 in the *Saturday Review of Literature* for a 'Girl Friday'—doing typing, research, and stenography.[15] She then worked in Santa Barbara, California, as secretary to Charles Nordhoff. But when the US entered the war, she wanted to serve—and joined OSS.

Shirley Chidsey had patience, initiative and courage. But despite these qualities, she soon became miserable in Brazzaville. She was painfully aware of the anti-American sentiment in the colony, which was particularly strong at work, as a result of America's support for the Vichy regime. She regretted her decision to leave OSS and commented sadly: 'Thought I would be of more vital use to [Radio Brazzaville] (mistakenly).' In a postcard to her mother, she reported that she had been invited on dates for dinner and was going to a dance, but wondered if it would have been a better idea to join the Women's Army Auxiliary Corps. 'Rather wish,' she wrote with feeling, 'I had joined the WAACS tho' and perhaps got to North Africa with them.'[16]

She met Dock Hogue on one of his early visits to the French colonial capital. They had much to talk about: not only an interest in literature and writing, but even the field of engineering, since Chidsey's stepfather was a civil engineer. They were also both isolated and lonely.

Shirley told Dock about her 'urgent desire to escape Brazzaville' and her 'extremely disagreeable living and working conditions'. He suggested that she leave Radio Brazzaville and cross the river to Léopoldville, to become his stenographer and assistant. No doubt he felt sorry for her and her predicament appealed to his sense of chivalry. But he was also overburdened with work and badly needed help. She seemed ideal: she spoke French fluently and she had even worked in the past for OSS.

Hogue sent a pouch letter to Boulton to ask for permission to hire Chidsey. He needed secretarial help, he said, but the only woman he could find was 'an Egyptian girl' who could not be trusted or utilised to any degree, for security reasons.[17] It was particularly important that he had 'a loyal and competent person' he could trust, he pointed out, since he was the only OSS representative in the Congo. When he was absent from his post:

> there is no one to take care of emergency situations. For this reason, it is essential that the secretary in Léopoldville be herself of 'agent stature' ... [and] she must have complete loyalty to OSS and the proper feeling for the security of operations.[18]

Moreover, he added, there was not a single American woman in the Congo who was capable of taking dictation—unlike Shirley Chidsey.

Boulton was sympathetic to Hogue's request and was impressed with Chidsey's record and capabilities. By 8 December 1943, he had started the process to hire her formally, such as investigations into her background and references.[19] She was asked to fill out a number of forms, which were sent to the Congo by pouch. A question about sports and hobbies elicited an arch response: 'None particularly'. When asked if she had ever used intoxicants, she responded: 'The usual "occasional cocktail".'[20]

In Hogue's view, the vetting process was not moving fast enough. The paperwork was growing: he was now buying a Dodge truck for the OSS station, which involved countless documents. He was also making short trips out of Léopoldville, such as to Luanda in the middle of January, to see HOMER, which meant that the office was left unsupervised. He therefore increased the pressure on Boulton. 'Considering Shirley Chidsey's satisfactory record with the OSS,' he cabled on 19 January 1944, 'is it possible for me to employ her as full time assistant and secretary should the situation require it? She is unhappy with the Brazzaville position and will resign shortly. If I may hire her, what salary may I pay? This is only for my knowledge.'[21]

By 25 January 1944, all the checks on Chidsey in Washington had been made and security approval was given for her to start work for the African Section of OSS.[22] Hogue came to a formal arrangement with her: that she would leave Brazzaville and start working for him at the beginning of April.[23] Her codename would be ANGELLA and her codenumber would be 1080. For now, she made plans for the move to the Congo and arranged to stay at the Pension Paula, a small hotel in the centre of Léopoldville, which was not far from the railway station.[24]

As a woman, Chidsey was in a minority in OSS, which was dominated by men and male attitudes. The Ivy League universities that most of them had attended 'were all male, and the OSS was very heavily so'.[25] One successful woman agent, Elizabeth MacDonald, wrote a memoir after the war entitled *Undercover Girl*, which gives a colourful picture of the sexism of the organisation. 'Women have no place in the war,' one Colonel told her dismissively. 'All the time I've put in overseas—and that's four years—I've only come across one who was worth her salt. And she was a Czech, at that.'[26] When Donovan told Margaret Griggs, who was placed in charge of hiring women, to get the 'right types' for COI, the fore-runner of OSS, one definition of right type was a Smith graduate who could pass a filing exam.[27] Most of the 26,000 women who joined OSS worked in the secretarial field and only a small percentage—some 700—served overseas.[28]

This led to difficulties in the field. For one thing, it meant the agents were short of secretarial help. In Accra, the OSS mission had no choice but to turn for help to a Mrs Miller, who did short-hand and typing. But because she was British, they could only give her work they had in common with the British. She also complained a lot. 'On arrival each morning Mrs Millar [sic] threatens to resign because of the volume of work,' wrote TRUCK to Boulton, 'but we pay no attention to it.'[29]

The men also felt lonely at times without women. 'Please give my kindest regards to Inez and also to Walter, Smitty, and that rascal Mrs Callivet,' wrote Bonner to Boulton on one occasion, referring to Ruth Caillavet, Boulton's assistant, who had previously served in the White House on Mrs Eleanor Roosevelt's staff. 'Please tell her for me,' he added good-humouredly, 'that I sleep in a single bed out here and I don't like it.'[30] TRUCK was less bothered. His only complaint, he said, was 'the lack of blondes—there are many deep brunettes'.[31]

John W. Kirkland, the OSS agent in Ivory Coast, who was code-named CLOCK, suffered badly when waiting to hear from America if his wife had given birth safely to their first child in November 1943. A couple of days before the due date, he sent an anxious cable: 'Due to the complications which have been reported I am especially desirous of hearing about my wife.'[32] Being so far away and at the mercy of unreliable communications, his relief and joy at the news of a baby daughter were intense. 'Give my love to my wife,' he cabled Boulton, 'and say that the father is both proud and thrilled. A baby girl was exactly what was wanted.'[33]

One OSS agent posted to sub-Saharan Africa worked out an ideal situation regarding women and companionship—by marrying the assistant of a British intelligence official working in the same city. This OSS agent was the tall and very thin Huntington Harris, known as Hunt, who came from a prominent banking family in Chicago. Codenamed EBERT by OSS, he was sent in 1942 as chief of station to Lourenço Marques, the capital of Mozambique, under cover of working for the War Shipping Administration.[34] His British 'opposite' there was Malcolm Muggeridge, who worked for the Secret Intelligence Service and whose boss was Kim Philby, the head of the Iberian section of Counter-Espionage (and a double agent who was covertly relaying information to the Soviet Union).

From the very start of the war, Lourenço Marques was a hotbed of intrigue and intelligence-gathering.[35] A number of spies, both Allied and Axis, were stationed there, to obtain information on shipping traffic and U-boats in Mozambican and South African waters. Lourenço Marques was close to the border of South Africa, which had entered the war on the Allied side with only the slimmest vote in favour, when a vote was taken in parliament.[36]

Muggeridge and Harris moved into a property together on the outskirts of Lourenço Marques, with a garage that had a door into the house, through which sub-agents could slip without being noticed. Harris was 'an enormously tall American', commented Muggeridge, adding that he was typical of OSS spies—'unmilitary by temperament, while belonging to rich patrician families'. He was also 'a pleasant companion, with a dry drawling wit' and his extra supplies of cash were helpful—especially with a policeman mysteriously referred to as 'Inspector Y'.[37] The two men ran cutouts together and set up two secret radio transmitters, in case diplomatic cable and pouch facilities inside Mozambique were disrupted. Harris sent to Washington a table of the German and Italian intelligence organisations with about a hundred photos and descriptions of people, obtained from the files of the Portuguese Security Police.[38]

Muggeridge was a known philanderer, whose harassment of grown women and girls led to the nickname of 'The Pouncer' when he worked in later years at the BBC. Now, in Lourenço Marques, he was involved in a heady affair with a Portuguese woman known as Bibla.[39] While this was going on, Harris was quietly getting to know Muggeridge's assistant, Mary Winifred Hutchison, who was employed by SIS, the British secret service. She was born in Shanghai, China, the daughter of John Colville Hutchinson, the commercial counsellor of the British Consulate in Chungking. She was sent to boarding school in England and then returned to Shanghai when the Second World War began. After the Japanese occupation of Shanghai, she was interned there and then exchanged for Japanese diplomats at a neutral point in Africa.[40]

Hunt and Mary's working relationship flowered swiftly into love—and eventually marriage. He was 29; she was just 22, but had already lived through some remarkable events and shown great courage. They were married by the American Consul in Lourenço Marques on 9 October 1943 and their union was also solemnised at the English Church in the city on the same day. Afterwards the British Consul hosted a reception for them in his home. This was the 'latest war romance', commented the *Chicago Tribune* with pleasure.[41]

OSS benefited from the marriage in practical ways. When Harris broke his leg, Mary helped him to carry on working. 'I am doing my work at home as a result of a broken leg', he wrote from Lourenço Marques to Washington in January 1944. 'With wife's assistance, however, I can carry on.'[42] But British intelligence lost a valuable member of staff: after her wedding she stopped working for SIS, in accordance with the social mores of the time.

8

'BORN SECRET'

On 17 November 1943, Doug Bonner had returned to the Gold Coast from his trip to the Congo with Dock Hogue. Almost a month later, he was joined in Accra on 13 December by Major Adolph–'Dolph'–W. Schmidt who, like himself, was an OSS agent with military status. Schmidt, a good friend and distant relative of David Bruce, the head of OSS Secret Intelligence, was one of the first members of OSS and had contributed to the Strategic Survey in readiness for the North African invasion in November 1942. In August 1943 he went to West Africa to support OSS men in the field. Nearly forty years of age, Schmidt had a mature and pragmatic approach to life and work. He had studied at some of the best universities in Europe and America and was a graduate of Princeton University and Harvard Business School. In peacetime he was a successful banker and philanthropist in Pittsburgh and had married Patricia Mellon, a member of the wealthy and influential Mellon family, who was serving in the Navy as a cryptographer.

Schmidt's OSS codename was FLARE. He may have chosen this name in memory of his childhood in McKeesport, Pennsylvania, which at that time was a centre of the steel industry. As a boy, he had looked out of his bedroom window at night and watched the huge flares that lit up the sky over the steel mills, when buckets tipped the molten metal into moulds. He thought the flares were beautiful, like fireworks, and he recollected them with pleasure for the rest of his life.[1]

Bonner and Schmidt went together to Cairo in the middle of December for talks with the OSS station in Egypt. The main topic on their agenda was whether or not there should be a permanent office in Cairo; but they decided against it, on the grounds that the work of OSS in Egypt was of little immediate concern to the Middle East Theater Command. The main field headquarters would therefore remain in Accra, as before; when special needs arose, the Chief of the Accra office would go to Cairo, 24 hours away by plane.

After the talks, Bonner returned to Accra. Schmidt remained in Cairo, waiting for orders from Washington. He had been promised he could return home by Christmas 1943 and was looking forward to seeing his wife and children.

Orders finally arrived on 25 January 1944—but not what he was expecting. The head of the Cairo Message Center contacted him to say he had a telegram for Schmidt. But he was unable to read it, as it was written in the secret code used by OSS to communicate only with Schmidt. At first Schmidt could not read it either, since it was based on a poem he had chosen for this purpose—but he couldn't remember the verses. At last he found a way to decipher the message: 'Proceed at once Accra. Take charge main Field Base. Further instructions will await you there.' He left as quickly as he could on a DC-3 flight, dubbed the Sahara Desert Express.

He arrived in Accra on 9 February. Here he found another cable, with instructions to go to the Congo:

> Proceed at once to Léopoldville. Arrange to have all shipments of uranium ore from Katanga mines checked for possible diversions to areas other than port of Matadi. This must be done without disclosure to the British (your hosts), to the Belgians (who are captives of the Germans in Brussels and Antwerp), or to the American Consul General in Léopoldville (who has been uncooperative and unfriendly with OSS to date).

Schmidt was astonished. When he read this telegram, he thought headquarters 'had really gone wacky. I knew nothing about uranium except that it was a radioactive element.' What, he wondered, 'has this got to do with World War II?' But he took the mission seriously when his plane approached the mouth of the Congo River and, looking down, he saw two freighters lying off the port of Matadi. 'Now one freighter anywhere on the west coast of Africa at that time was an event,' he thought to himself, 'but two freighters, one loading and the other waiting—something important was really going on. So I put my doubts away.'[2]

Years later, Schmidt described this episode in his life to Richard Dunlop, Bill Donovan's biographer, who took notes of what he said. These abbreviated notes give a sense of what was going through Schmidt's mind at the time:

> Accra, W Africa, field base—next sent there, secret instructions await me there—try and find uranium—orders from Que Bldg. go to Léopoldville in Congo—see 2 ships waiting to be loaded. Rumors in Wash—uranium being diverted to Europe—Germans working on bomb?[3]

This was a top secret assignment. Outside the Pentagon, stated the cable waiting for Schmidt in Accra, 'only three people in Washington know of this message'.[4]

Though Schmidt was startled when his superiors at OSS ordered him in January 1944 to investigate uranium smuggling in the Congo, he was even more surprised at the cover he was given to use: 'Use as your cover investigation of diamond smuggling.'[5] He recalled this instruction when interviewed by Dunlop, who wrote in his notes:

> Own job, under cover of trying to look for ind. diamonds, getting illegally to Germany, was to find uranium sources ... diamonds going to Addis Ababa to Italians to Germany. Not to tell Belgians.[6]

Uranium was such a tightly guarded secret in the years of the Second World War that it was essential to use a plausible cover. This applied to all those who—whether on the Allied or the Axis side—were seeking to build an atomic bomb; and it required a way to refer to uranium, without actually using the word. In one case involving the German atomic effort, gems were used as a cover: the making of synthetic rubies and sapphires for the watch industry was used to cover atomic research done by Degussa in Frankfurt.[7]

The Americans used a range of covers. One of these was to give the mineral a label that would be accurate but sufficiently vague as to shroud its identity, such as 'raw materials'. In one variation on this, Arthur D. Storke, a British mining engineer working on a major study for General Groves to estimate the world's total uranium resources, was described as working in 'the crucial field of raw material procurement'.[8] Sometimes the label was a mouthful, such as the official codename for the Manhattan Project: 'Development of Substitute Materials'.

Jules Cousin, the administrative director of Union Minière in the Congo, received an explicit order from Washington, via the African Metals Corporation in New York—the American arm of Union Minière—not to mention uranium by name in any documents. Instead, he was told that the label 'crude minerals substance' should be used. Privately, according to information collected by Major Bonner during his visit to Katanga in June 1943, Cousin thought this rather foolish, since it would still call attention to uranium, albeit indirectly. Nonetheless, he told all those involved in the production of uranium in Katanga to obey the order.[9]

Sometimes cover was provided by means of omission. In the first report of the Foreign Economic Administration, detailing the first year of its existence, the word 'uranium' does not appear at all—even though the objectives of the FEA were to obtain all the raw materials needed for the war. The 'phenomenal success of America's war industry in turning out ... vital war materials needed to overcome the Axis,' stated the report, 'has been the ability of our war industry to get strategic and critical raw materials.' But despite the rich endowments in the US of natural resources, it added, 'many of the critical raw materials essential to the success of our war program are produced in insufficient quantities, or not at all, in this country'. The report then proceeded to list the raw materials that were imported, through the facilitation of the FEA: copper, lead, mercury, platinum, tin, nickel, industrial diamonds, tungsten—and even loofa sponges. But nowhere was uranium mentioned. The Belgian Congo was mentioned only once and very briefly, in connection with tantalite.[10]

All imports of material for the Project were rendered invisible.[11] In September 1943, the Military Intelligence Service of the War Department sent instructions to the Collector of Customs that 'certain shipments' arriving at the port from the African Metals Corporation, the American arm of Union Minière, should be admitted free of duty and import tax. These shipments would be identified on arrival by an authorised representative of the US Engineer Office, Manhattan District.[12] In this way the shipments avoided the notice and scrutiny of customs officials.

Records and documents relating to the Project were listed as 'born classified' and 'born secret'.[13] In April 1943 plans were drawn up to prevent the publication and circulation of any statistics concerning importations and exportations of uranium ore. 'That a necessity exists for this policy, in the interest of safeguarding information concerning this project,' wrote Colonel J. C. Marshall, the District Engineer of the Corps of Engineers, to General Groves, 'is I believe quite evident and of primary importance.'[14]

In the autumn of 1943 General Groves took command of all atomic intelligence responsibilities. Before this, the various intelligence agencies—OSS, army intelligence, navy intelligence, and lesser units—had been operating independently of one another in atomic spying.[15] This job was now given to the Counter-Intelligence Corps or CIC (known by their colleagues as the Creeps),[16] an intelligence organisation of the American military, and was 'by far the biggest assignment in CIC's history'.[17] The Project's Intelligence and Security Division was under the direction of Lt.-Col. Boris T. Pash, a US Army military intelligence officer.[18]

Documents coming into the Corps of Engineers from academics working for the Manhattan Project, such as physicists at the

University of Chicago, were stamped with a clear warning: 'This document contains information affecting the National Defense of the United States within the meaning of the Espionage Act ... Its transmission or the revelation of its contents in any manner by an unauthorised person is prohibited by law.'[19]

At Oak Ridge, the development centre of the bomb, and its headquarters, there was a special Manhattan District CIC detachment, which by the end of the war had 148 officers and 161 enlisted men. From January 1944, John Lansdale of the CIC was made a special assistant to General Groves, with full responsibility for all intelligence and security matters affecting the detachment. Its work was conducted by 6,000 guards and Military Police, who checked the credentials of personnel seeking to enter the various sites.

The physicist J. Robert Oppenheimer, who directed the Los Alamos National Laboratory in New Mexico, where the bombs were designed, fell under suspicion because of his pre-war Communist sympathies. He was kept under careful surveillance by the CIC, at the instigation of Colonel Pash.[20] But Oppenheimer was also the target of other attempts to spy on him. Anne Wilson, who had been one of Groves's personal assistants and moved to Los Alamos to be Oppenheimer's secretary, was asked by John Lansdale to send him a letter each month reporting on what she saw in Oppenheimer's office—for $200 a month. She was only twenty years old but had strong moral convictions according to which such snooping would be unacceptable. She flatly refused. After the war, she learned that Groves had ordered that she be covered by surveillance whenever she left Los Alamos.[21]

All the incoming and outgoing mail of the Manhattan Project was screened for leaks and newspapers were scanned by the censorship section for violations of the censorship code. Extreme efforts were made to prevent any spotlight on uranium. 'When one CIC agent noticed that pages concerning uranium in new reference books in a library were showing signs of use,' records the history of the CIC, 'agents were set to reproduce similar signs of wear in other sections of hundreds of other library volumes.' Between September

1943 and the end of 1945, CIC agents investigated more than 1,500 cases of loose talk and leakage of information. A CIC undercover office was set up in the area of Oak Ridge, ostensibly the office of a magazine subscription company, and later an insurance agency. Agents masqueraded as gamblers, contractors, pest controllers, electricians, hotel clerks and bell hops.[22]

The OSS carefully masked its concern with atomic matters. Chemical and bacteriological warfare was codenamed TOLEDO and used as a cloak 'because the two subjects were always handled together—partly in an attempt to disguise the overriding American interest in the German bomb program'.[23] Moe Berg, an OSS agent who was sent to Europe to investigate this programme, was informed that the words 'radioactive' and 'atomic' were 'taboo'.[24]

Illicit diamond buying (IDB) was an ideal cover to cloak an investigation into uranium smuggling, since watching out for the smuggling of one product would be likely to reveal the smuggling of others. The OSS agents in West Africa were all told to look out for diamond smuggling. But in a cable to Hunt Harris in Lourenço Marques, Rud Boulton made it clear that it was not the diamonds themselves that were the target of such investigations, but rather the information they smoked out about smuggling methods. 'In preclusive purchasing operations,' he explained, 'diamonds are given a [A1] priority, but of even greater urgency is to ascertain how the smuggling is carried on and the names of the persons in the smuggling gang, from the estimation back to the source.'[25]

Diamonds were a particularly good cover for uranium, since they were mined in similar areas of the world, such as the Belgian Congo. The Congo had been an important source of diamonds ever since the setting up in 1906 of the Société Internationale Forestière du Congo-Forminière. This was a Belgian corporation of which at least half the capitalisation was American and which had about fifty mines in the province of Kasai.[26] Diamonds were a highly profitable business and tales of diamond smuggling in the Congo were legion. One of the best known was Hergé's Tintin *in the Congo*, first published in 1931, in which Tintin and his dog Snowy unearth a diamond smuggling ring in the Congo, run by the American gangster Al Capone.

Furthermore, diamonds and industrial diamonds were both regarded during the Second World War as strategic war materials that were at risk of being smuggled to the Axis powers. The diamonds were used for a range of purposes, such as cutting tools, producing precision instruments, and as abrasives.[27] However, they were perhaps not as essential as has been generally assumed. According to one expert, 'diamonds for general industrial use are very much over-rated, as even the most junior engineer must know'; he adds that they 'are not essential to the armament industry'.[28]

Germany was thought to be running short of industrial diamonds and to be smuggling them in from Africa and elsewhere, which alarmed the Allies. The British SOE decided to investigate. They set up a rubber company called SOGEDEX as a front to form dedicated intelligence networks and to monitor and seize Axis shipping; these operations were known generally as MALPAS. One of the networks set up by SOE was the 'S' organisation, a group of pro-British Portuguese with key positions in the Angolan railways, army and post office, who acted as unpaid volunteers to monitor Axis activity.[29]

OSS agents collaborated on occasion with the British investigations into IDB. This was an ideal means of monitoring the smuggling of uranium: investigations could simply be grafted onto IDB inquiries, without attracting notice. As Major Bonner wrote to Boulton, his station in Accra was assisting SIS and SOE, 'with the sole view of identifying Axis channels and agents'.[30]

But illicit diamond buying was difficult to investigate. The entire monthly requirement of German industry could be carried on one agent's person, because the bulk was so small. Using certificates—known as navicerts—to control the passage of ships served as an effective way for the Allies to prevent bulk cargoes reaching the Nazis. 'During the war some neutral ships operating out of Angola were given so-called Navy Certs, enabling them to go on their way without being searched by the Royal Navy.'[31] But bulk cargoes were measured in tons and shiploads. It was far more difficult for a contraband official to check whether a ship carrying a legitimate cargo of, say, wheat or hides from the Argentine to Spain, did not also carry a few carats of industrial diamonds.

As well, the security services in the countries involved might resent any outside interference and even collude in the traffic themselves. And there were a number of potential channels. From the Congo, for example, they could be sent by rail, boat, or air to Angola and thence by ship, submarine, or diplomatic pouch to Europe.[32] Smuggling rings were organised, sometimes of Nazi agents, and sometimes of adventurers simply out for monetary gain. The temptation to engage in smuggling was great, because the prices paid were high. There were well-defined routes in South America down to Buenos Aires or another important seaport. In Africa and the Middle East, there were routes to Vichy-controlled territory or to Turkey. The possibilities of evasion were endless, sometimes involving the use of local police or officials who were lax or corrupt.[33]

One way to detect smuggling was to plant intelligence operatives inside the illegal rings running the underground markets. These operatives could spot the contraband before it reached shipboard. This undertaking, commented two Chiefs of the Blockade Division in the FEA during the war, led to 'a few of those rare situations in which the intelligence industry—usually as dull and prosaic as double-entry bookkeeping—actually began to resemble the spy thrillers of popular fiction'.[34] Allied agents bought and sold strategic minerals on the illegal market, and followed the progress of individual packets through various intermediaries to the ships intended to carry them. This relied upon good intelligence. The US used FBI agents in Latin America and OSS operatives in the Iberian Peninsula. Leads and clues emerging at the ports from the Office of Naval Intelligence, as well as from US Army intelligence and from consular officials, were brought together in Washington and explored.

Many searches drew a complete blank. But there were some successes. On the basis of a report from an Allied intelligence agent, a shabby fibreboard trunk, which was being shipped by a dock worker in a Latin American port to a relative in Spain, was investigated. It looked innocent on first inspection—no false bottom, and no contents except old clothes and family photographs. The trunk was reinforced with black-painted straps, made of what appeared to be ordinary iron. But when it was scraped off, it turned out to be pure platinum—many thousand dollars' worth, and enough to supply Germany's needs for months. Another search on a ship revealed that the toothpaste tube a passenger squeezed seemed to be unusually lumpy; the lumps were industrial diamonds.[35]

The British author Graham Greene was instructed to investigate IDB when he served during the Second World War as an MI5 official in Sierra Leone. He drew on this experience to write his novel, *The Heart of the Matter*—in which the hero, Major Scobie, a colonial policeman based in an unidentified West African colony, has to inspect passenger ships to look for diamonds smuggled by Lebanese. He discovers that diamonds are being smuggled in the stomachs of live parrots. Yusef, a Syrian merchant he suspects of smuggling, mocks his efforts: 'You want to stop industrial diamonds going to Portugal and then to Germany, or across the border to the Vichy French. But all the time you are chasing people who are not interested in industrial diamonds, people who just want to get a few gem stones in a safe place for when peace comes again.' He argues that it is a futile business. 'Only small men,' he says, 'are interested in industrial diamonds. Why, for a whole matchbox full of them, you would only get two hundred pounds. I call them gravel collectors.'[36]

It was also the case that although the Axis powers were thought to be in acute need of diamonds, the Allies were not. There were 20 million carats in the United States and Canada at that time, which amounted to more than two years' world consumption;[37] and by the end of 1943 Britain was 90 per cent self-sufficient.[38]

The situation regarding uranium was altogether different. The United States, insisted Groves, would 'allow nothing to stand in the way of achieving as complete control as possible of world uranium supplies'.[39]

Hogue was dealing with a situation that was far more dangerous than that of Yusef's gravel collectors. He did not know the purpose intended for uranium—and the fact that even a matchbox full of this rare mineral could contribute to the building of a bomb with unprecedented explosive powers. But it had been made clear to him that the need to stop the smuggling of uranium was a matter of the highest priority in the war against fascism.

9

THE MISSION

Some decades after the war, Schmidt recalled that after receiving instructions in Accra to initiate investigations of uranium smuggling, he had departed immediately for Léopoldville. However, it appears that with the passing of time, the details of events became blurred in his mind, since there is no suggestion in OSS cables or pouch letters from the period that he visited the Congo before early April 1944. Instead, having reached Accra on 9 February 1944, he threw himself into the duties of station chief in Accra. This had become a very important station: as well as working with the OSS station in the Belgian Congo, it was responsible for Secret Intelligence activities in British West Africa, Portuguese Guinea (now known as Guinea-Bissau), Liberia, and those parts of French colonial Africa which could be handled effectively from Accra. There was also a network of informants and cutouts, numbering nearly fifty people.

The task of the OSS station was, as before, to uncover enemy activities of any nature in West Africa.[1] But the priority for Schmidt, on instructions from OSS Secret Intelligence in Washington, was the investigation of uranium smuggling to Germany from the Congo. Furthermore, he had to use diamond smuggling as a cover, so needed to take careful note of investigations into IDB. This required discussions with Major Alexander 'Alec' Binney, an SOE intelligence officer stationed in Accra who was the head of MALPAS—the British intelligence network designed to monitor and seize Axis shipping. 'The entire situation,' reported Schmidt to Boulton, 'is in good shape. I will meet Binney tomorrow.'[2]

Alec Binney, now in his mid-thirties, was liked by most people as a genial and hard-working colleague. He had earned an adequate degree at Oxford and then worked as a schoolmaster at the public schools of Westminster and Shrewsbury, where he enjoyed his hobbies of shooting, fishing, riding and music. He did well enough at most things, but did not show much promise for leadership. 'I cannot,' said one of his superiors at SOE, 'recommend him to take command of anything for I feel that his abilities and inclinations do not lie on these lines.' Nonetheless, Binney had been promoted swiftly and was now head of the SOE/SIS combined Mission West Africa. 'Our West Africa Mission was, I think, unique,' observed one of its officials:

> in that since July 1942 it was a joint SIS/SOE Mission with the Head of the Mission—who happened to be an SOE Officer—being representative of both bodies on the West Coast, and empowered to employ SOE bodies in SIS work. The Mission also worked far more closely with MI5 than any other SOE Mission of which I have knowledge.

Within the intelligence structure, Binney's code symbol was W/M and his code number 2324.[3]

Binney's American opposite on IDB was a new OSS agent in Accra—Duane D. Luther. Previously Luther had been in Beira in Mozambique, where, like Violett in Angola, he had been working under the cover of employment by Texaco. Boulton sent instructions on his mission in Accra. 'Your major job at the beginning,' he wrote to Luther on 20 December, 'will be the coordination of the IDB investigation, which we are glad to say now appears to be getting started on a sound footing, after a long period of frustration in trying to work out some satisfactory arrangement for cooperating with the British.'[4]

Luther and Binney got on well together. Binney was 'a nice chap', reported Luther to Boulton, 'and, naturally, has a good background on the whole show from Angola to Dakar'. But he didn't entirely trust him. 'I have noted,' he added, 'that while Binney ostensibly offers all the information he has, he is making certain reservations which often come into the open during subsequent conversations.' This didn't bother him in the slightest. 'Nothing new,' he said confidently, 'and two usually play at that game.'[5]

Now in his early thirties, Luther had grown up in San Francisco and studied mathematics at the University of Berkeley. But, bullish by nature, rather than an intellectual, he then followed his instinct for physical fitness and stayed on at Berkeley to take an MA in physical education. He did not come from a military background—his father was a salesman and his mother a nurse—but his marriage had brought him into military circles. His father-in-law (who happened to be a Mayflower descendant) had been military attaché to the American Embassy in Rio de Janeiro, Brazil; after Pearl Harbor, he commanded the 601st Anti-aircraft Brigade and then the New York Anti-aircraft Region.[6]

While at Berkeley, the burly Luther had coached the 145-pound basketball team; and when he joined OSS, he chose the codename COACH. Now he was in charge of a very different sort of team: the OSS Accra station. This was a temporary responsibility, which was required because of the gap between Bonner's departure for Washington and Schmidt's forthcoming arrival. 'It is a pleasure and a compliment,' wrote COACH cheerfully to Boulton on 19 December 1943, 'to be able to take over this post from CRUMB and I appreciate the responsibility and assure you that I will do my level best to make a success of it.'[7]

It was a demanding job. 'As CRUMB has probably told you,' wrote Luther, 'we work here anywhere from 12 to 15 hours per day. The office being also our home lessens our possibility of getting away from work, even at night.' The pace was much faster in Accra than in Mozambique. 'Oh for the life of East Africa! Where things are only complicated by great discomfort and a few wild animals,' he joked to Boulton. 'I sometimes feel that someone has transplanted the Grand Central Station and all trains leave via our front door. Outside of that we lead a very quiet and sober life (hic).' They were grateful to get copies of *Time Magazine* and asked for two extra copies, to trade in Accra with friends.[8]

Boulton sent Luther instructions for the IDB investigation. 'The first step,' he wrote in a pouch letter, 'will be to arrange a conference in Accra.'[9] This was planned for early February, when OSS and 'our British opposites'[10] would work out a strategy.[11]

At the centre of the IDB operation was the Congo—and TETON. 'Only from the standpoint of what is leaking into Angola from the Congo will the two territories be associated,' wrote Luther to Boulton. 'It is felt this matter can be coordinated later but in the meantime we get going on the Congo study.'[12] He suggested that instead of waiting for the conference, 'we call TETON up here whenever he is ready, and can leave Leo, to study that matter with our opposites'.[13]

Preparations for the conference triggered fresh concerns about Firmin Van Bree and OSS sent requests to British intelligence for further information on him. 'No concrete evidence here on Van Brae,'observed an anxious cable sent from Washington to London on 13 February 1944, 'but much suspicion.'[14] 'C', the head of British SIS, took the view that Van Bree was in the clear, but some British consular staff in the Congo and OSS were strongly suspicious.[15] A report was drawn up listing a range of doubts expressed by senior officials about Van Bree's loyalties and behaviour, including the concerns of one Mr Pedler, the former head of the British Economic Mission in the Congo. Pedler had said that Van Bree was in contact with many important Germans in Lisbon and he believed that it would be a simple matter for Van Bree to sell diamonds through this channel.[16] There was some discussion in London about a plan to ask the Belgians for their view of Van Bree, but it was agreed that 'this course is most undesirable'.[17]

Hogue returned to Léopoldville from his fact-finding tour of the Congo on 10 January 1944. He was now living in more comfortable conditions: a bungalow on Avenue Olsen (now Avenue Kabasele Tshamala), the long road linking the city's airport with the downtown area.[18] But not very long after his return, he fell victim to a debilitating illness, which was diagnosed as a bad case of amoebic dysentery. For a time, he was so ill and weak that he was laid low, just staying in bed. This meant that he was out of contact with OSS in Washington and Accra for a period of time. 'I know that he only just returned from the bush,' commented Luther, 'and in all probability has not had time to get caught up on his backlog.' He felt sympathetic towards his fellow agent, even though he was unaware of his illness. 'Believe me,' he added with a sigh, 'I know how it is.'[19]

Once Hogue had started to recover, he wrote to Boulton to ask if medical care in the field was the responsibility of the individual, or an operational expense. But he didn't want news of his illness to get back to his wife, Ruth, and worry her. 'Please,' he asked Boulton, 'don't tell my wife.'[20]

It was not at all unusual for OSS agents in West Africa to fall ill. NORTH in Accra suffered four attacks of malaria in four months in 1943 and was in 'rather bad shape'.[21] John Kirkland, the OSS agent in Ivory Coast, who used the codename CLOCK, suffered from dysentery, malaria, inexplicable swellings, and a range of other diseases, relying on alcohol as prevention and cure. 'My health is good,' he reported, 'thanks, no doubt, to the possibility of having a couple of drinks a night. I mean that seriously. A couple of whiskeys do no end of good to one's morale and general outlook.'[22] Hogue would have known about the risk of tropical disease in West Africa. All the same, he must have been dismayed by the severity of his illness: he was an amateur boxer, accomplished swimmer and high diver, and had until now prided himself on his high level of fitness.

Now that Hogue was well enough to make contact with Accra, he arranged to fly there on 1 February. But then news emerged of a forthcoming conference in Brazzaville, which had been organised by General de Gaulle's French Committee of National

Liberation, now installed in Algeria. This was a significant development for the region, as Luther realised as soon as he heard of it. 'Kindly give us full information on the Brazzaville conference,' he wrote to Boulton. 'We know nothing about it.'[23]

But the OSS Africa Division also knew nothing. And since Hogue was the only agent with the means of finding out about it, his plans had to be changed. 'It is essential for us to receive a play by play account of the Brazzaville conference,' wrote Secret Intelligence to Accra. 'In one way or another, therefore, TETON must supply complete coverage of it.'[24] To Hogue in the Congo, Secret Intelligence sent new orders: 'with regard to the forthcoming Brazzaville conference, send us by cable the most complete possible summary, now and while it is being held, of everything relating to it, including plans'.[25] Hogue duly rescheduled his trip to Accra and crossed the Congo River to Brazzaville, to attend the conference. This wasn't simply a matter of catching a ferry; he also had to ensure that as well as Belgian Congo francs to use in the Congo and British pounds for his forthcoming trip to the Gold Coast, he had sufficient French colonial francs to use in AEF. Careful track of all these funds had to be maintained, since OSS headquarters demanded full and accurate accounts.

The Brazzaville Conference, as it came to be known, was opened by de Gaulle on 30 January 1944 and lasted until 8 February. It was attended by French politicians, high-ranking colonial officials from the French African colonies, and military men, who unanimously rejected the Vichy regime in favour of the Free French. Governor Ryckmans attended the conference and emphasis was placed on Belgian-French unity.[26]

Hogue's movie camera offered him the best way of gathering intelligence about the conference and sharing it with Washington. He filmed the opening ceremony in colour: General de Gaulle, accompanied by an aide, wore a light khaki uniform with a pith helmet; Governor General Éboué was dressed in a white uniform with a red sash; and the Belgian Governor General, Pierre Ryckmans, wore an all-white uniform with a white pith helmet. At the start of the ceremony, after some photographs of the Governor Generals have been taken, the camera also cuts to show a black Congolese soldier wearing a dark blue uniform and a fez.[27]

Using his cover as Special Assistant to the Consul, he was able to attend a number of discussions. He noted that although attention was paid to the need for colonial reform in postwar French Africa, there were no black representatives apart from Governor General Éboué. The conference set out an explicit principle of commitment to colonisation:

> The aims of the work of colonisation accomplished by France in the colonies exclude any idea of autonomy, any possibility of evolution outside the French Empire: the constitution of self-government in the colonies, even in the distant future, is to be excluded.[28]

The only offer in support of self-government was a weak proposal to endow the colonies with a federal assembly. A resolution was adopted by the conference which stated that French Indo-China must be reunited with the Empire after liberation. Like the Belgian government-in-exile, the Free French appeared not to see any parallel between the trauma of occupation as suffered by their own nation under the Nazis, and the colonisation of African territories by the French.[29] The true motive of the conference, assessed Hogue, was to make the French colonial empire appear a powerful force.[30]

After the conference Hogue left Brazzaville and returned to Léopoldville, leaving almost immediately for the Gold Coast. But he was still unwell and arrived shaken and ill. It was quickly decided that Luther should accompany Hogue to Liberia, to seek medical care from the American doctors at Harbel.

'We were greatly disturbed to hear of TETON's dysentery,' Boulton wrote to Luther, on 11 February 1944, 'and we are crossing our fingers in the hope that his Liberian friends will clear it up.' But the fact that Hogue would have an opportunity to check up once more on OSS activities in Liberia, was some compensation for Boulton. 'While we were disappointed that his efforts in IDB and other Congo matters will be delayed for a while,' he told

Luther, 'we were glad to hear that he will have an opportunity to look into the Liberian picture again.'[31]

Hogue responded well to treatment in Liberia. On 14 February 1944, he and COACH had lunch in Cape Palmas with Charles Ramus, an old chum of Hogue's. They then went to the Firestone plantation, where Hogue was able to introduce Luther to Chancellor, a cutout he had set up on his mission there. 'I am very much impressed with this man,' observed Luther, 'and TETON must be congratulated for having chosen him.'[32]

On 15 February, they both returned to the Roberts Field airfield in the 'duck'–the Pan American Airways clipper. Luther then flew to Accra, but TETON was unable to hitch a ride on the same plane. He had to wait for a week before he could get a flight back to Accra.[33]

The arrival of Hogue, restored to a modicum of health, provided Schmidt with an opportunity to discuss with him the use of IDB as a cover to investigate the possible diversions of uranium. There is no record of any discussions between them at this time. As always on the secret topic of the atomic project, nothing was written down unless absolutely necessary, and only within the small circle of those who were in the know. It is also unclear whether Luther or Lanier Violett, who had arrived in Accra from Angola for the IDB conference, were included in these preparatory discussions.

The IDB conference finally took place toward the end of February 1944: a meeting of OSS and SOE, under the guise of MEW–the British Ministry of Economic Warfare. The attendant officials included FLARE, TETON, COACH and HOMER on the American side, and Major Binney and Major C. I. Crocker–codenamed VULCAN–on the British side. No minutes of the meeting are available, but references to discussions were made in some cables and other documentation.

It was noted that several channels were being used for smuggling: carriers on neutral ships or aircraft, the German diplomatic pouch, Belgian Congo Relief Fund parcels, and German submarines landing at isolated points on the African coast. The normal routes went from West Africa or central Africa either through the Iberian Peninsula or through the Near East, where the smuggled goods could readily be picked up by German or Japanese agents. The Germans, it was reported, were paying prices seven to eight times the London value for industrial diamonds on the underground market in Spain and Portugal, and the Japanese were also willing to pay these prices.[34]

TETON was instructed at the IDB conference to investigate the methods by which the Axis powers were obtaining industrial diamonds from the Congo; to obtain a list of all employees of Forminière; to check the possible use of Red Cross parcels as a means of moving industrial diamonds to Europe; to determine if industrial diamonds were being forwarded to Europe through diplomatic pouches; and to contact smugglers and buy industrial diamonds from them.

Hogue's main task, however, was to investigate smuggling through purchases on the illegal market. Luther had already cabled Washington with a request for $25,000 for Hogue to use, in order to carry out this mission. This was a great deal of money, worth over a third of a million US dollars in 2015.[35] But as Schmidt pointed out to Hogue, no dealer in his right mind was going 'to talk samples and the only way his interest can be aroused to come out in the open is to hear a substantial sum. The one I have requested is small enough in this business.'[36]

There was disunity among the British about the plan for Hogue to contact smugglers directly and to buy from them. In London, MEW officials were insisting that diamonds should be purchased on the illegal market so as to provide evidence of leakage, while SOE in Accra believed that buying contraband stones would provide no information on any 'safe' channel of major supply.[37] But the senior men of OSS Secret Intelligence in Washington as well as in West Africa were united in their support for Hogue's mission. This would be the best way, they believed, of achieving Schmidt's objective: checking all shipments of uranium ore from

Katanga mines 'for possible diversions to areas other than the port of Matadi'.[38]

'Mr Hogue,' observed OSS in Washington, 'was assigned the most difficult part of the investigative problem on the smuggling of industrial diamonds to Germany.'[39] Any reference to his most dangerous assignment—the tracking of uranium smuggling—was left unsaid.

10

THE BRITISH OPPOSITES

The OSS agents posted to West Africa relied on espionage coop-eration with their British 'opposites' in a variety of ways. The British, 'with a long tradition of intelligence activities,' observed OSS agent Jack Harris, an anthropologist stationed in Accra in its early months, 'had been in West Africa for some 80 years with a network of informants in place reporting to trained agents ... It would have been foolish for us to undertake setting-up parallel sources of intelligence in the field and we did not.'[1]

Accra was one of the two main centres of British SIS and SOE intelligence in West Africa; the other was Lagos in Nigeria. But the British did not have intelligence structures only in their own colonies. In addition, notes the historian Kevin Yelvington, they placed clandestine agents throughout the French territories, such as French Togo and Dahomey, which surrounded both the Gold Coast and Nigeria.[2] An agreement between SOE and OSS prohib-ited OSS from engaging in undercover and surveillance opera-tions in British territory. In return, the British were expected to supply OSS with information from their own sources.[3]

General Sir Harold Alexander, a British military commander who was popular with both British and American officers, offered some guidance on how to handle Americans to General Alan

Brooke, chief of the imperial general staff. 'We must tread very warily,' he warned. 'If they think we are sneering at them—and God forbid that—or that we are being superior, they will take it very badly, as they are a proud people.' The line to take, he advised, was 'that we are comrades and brothers in arms, and our only wish is for them to share the horrors of war (and the handicaps) and reap the fruits of victory together'.

According to M. R. D. Foot, the official historian of SOE, this was the approach that SOE sought to follow in its dealings with OSS, but 'not always with success'.[4] In Foot's view, it was a marvel that the two organisations managed to work together at all. British society, he said:

> was still closed and formal, even more class-ridden than American; more hostile to self-made, self-advertising men; still aware, particularly in the officer class, of the importance of the monarch; and fully aware that on the empire, which then covered a quarter of the globe's land surface, the sun never set.

The United States, by contrast, 'provided a wide open society, aggressively republican, full of enthusiasm for those who had come up from nowhere, and profoundly anti-imperial—hostile to the British empire, at any rate'.[5]

SOE, like OSS, was a new organisation that had been set up for the purpose and the duration of the war. According to Major Len Manderstam, who ran the SOE outfit in Angola, it was loathed in the upper echelons of the Foreign Office, who looked upon the organisation 'rather as a maiden aunt might regard a niece who had become a successful callgirl'.[6] But although it was new, it was less new than OSS: it had been set up in July 1940, so had had a two years' head start. Initially, it attempted to mentor OSS.

But OSS insisted on making its own mistakes. 'As time passed,' noted Foot, 'the OSS grew more and more competent' and a balance point was reached at which the OSS was recognisably no longer the weaker partner. In December 1943, a senior SOE official observed that OSS had now 'definitely established themselves ... and we must resist the temptation to continue to treat them as an inexperienced younger brother.' Thereafter, wrote Foot, the OSS 'moved on from strength to strength, and SOE began to lag behind. By the end of the war there was no doubt that it was SOE that was the weaker partner.'[7]

But resentment of OSS smouldered among some members of SOE, such as Major Manderstam. His own antipathy first developed in Morocco when OSS men took over the work he had started and then, as far as he was concerned, took the credit. 'If we had been given the facilities they enjoyed,' he complained, 'we would have been able to achieve much more. They received greater financial backing, they had the best equipment and they had more personnel.' He was 'staggered by their indiscipline', which he found especially annoying. 'God knows,' he said, 'we in SOE were not slaves to the military manuals, but we were paragons compared with them. It made my hair curl to see a sergeant sitting on the edge of his commanding officer's desk and addressing the colonel by his first name.'[8] No doubt Manderstam would have been horrified by the last stanza of the 'OSS Hymn':

> The brass hats don't know 'F' all, the rest are snafu too,
> It takes a damned magician to know just what to do.
> An order here, an order there, it's anybody's guess.
> You too can be a fubar if you join the OSS.

'Snafu' was the wartime acronym for 'Situation Normal All Fucked Up', which Bonner had playfully proposed as a codename; and 'fubar' stood for 'Fucked Up Beyond All Repair'. The lyrics were certainly irreverent—but did not offend the top brass of OSS in any way. According to Douglas Waller in his biography of General Donovan, 'Wild Bill' relished listening to songs like these.[9]

The OSS staff in Accra had frequent cause to spend time with British military and intelligence officials. The governor of the Gold Coast was Sir Alan Burns. But to meet the demands of war, a special organisation was set up in Accra in 1942: the West African War Council, which coordinated a Military Division and a Civil Division. This was headed by Philip Cunliffe-Lister, otherwise known as Viscount Swinton, a prominent Conservative politician and former Colonial Secretary.[10] Before coming to Africa, Swinton had been at the helm of British intelligence, in the role of 'executive control' of MI5, with responsibility for its reorganisation. He had not been popular with the staff, one of whom complained that he acted as if MI5 was 'a large detective agency carrying out frequent raids in fast cars'.[11]

Lord Swinton's posting in Accra was that of 'Cabinet Minister, Resident in West Africa' (frequently abbreviated to 'Resmin'), with responsibility for the four British West African colonies: Nigeria, the Gold Coast, Sierra Leone and Gambia. His headquarters were at Achimota College.

Not long after his arrival, Swinton believed he could notice a growing American influence in the Gold Coast, which he didn't like. In December 1942, he protested at the 'apparent subordination of British interests to American control', and reported to London on rumours that after the war the Americans were planning to take over the West African colonial empires.[12]

Douglas Bonner, as head of the OSS station in Accra, tried hard to be friendly to the British. 'It might amuse you to know that at the request of Mr McKenzie, British Consul in Brazza,' he wrote to Boulton, 'I have undertaken to play nursemaid to a small chimpanzee on the trip from Leopoldville to Lagos, provided he can get passage for it from the ATC. It is going to Major Allen, aide to Lord Swinton.' A successful agent, he added drily, 'has to be ready to do anything'.[13] When Bonner asked Boulton for a new secretary, he specified that he or she must be 'a presentable person who can dine here with such high ranking British officials as may from time to time come here for dinner'. This person, he added, 'should not eat peas with his knife nor talk out of turn on a dozen controversial matters with our opposites. If he does not measure up to these rather peculiar requirements he had best be billeted at camp instead of living here in the house.'[14]

Douglas Bonner's opposite was Major Noel Ildefouse D'Albertanson, an SOE official with the code symbol W15, who was based at Achimota. He had been employed in Lisbon before the war by the New York-based Socony Vacuum Oil Company and kept the post while working for SOE; this provided an ideal cover to travel around West Africa.[15] D'Albertanson was a 'good running mate' and opposite for Major Bonner, decided Johnny Weaver, who was on Bonner's staff:

> They should each be able to teach the other a thing or two! DA as he is called is a very able man in all ways pertaining to intelligence and economics and you will note that he is now in charge of the Belgian Congo.[16]

Bonner, too, was impressed by D'Albertanson. 'I have had several talks with DA,' he reported to Washington, 'who will no doubt be one of the head men for the British here. I consider him to be the smartest, coldest agent that I have ever met. He could well be a model in one of our area schools. I have run into him first in Accra, next in Leopoldville and last in Dakar. Finally, we seem to approach a friendly basis.'[17]

TETON's opposite in Accra was Peter Russell, a major in MI5, who was posted to Accra in 1943 as head of defence security. Russell's duties included counter-espionage and security operations against German spies who were tracking convoys. Unlike Binney, he had excelled as a student at Oxford and was known for his 'razor-sharp intelligence'.[18]

Swinton's structure of officials in Accra and Lagos was given the name of 'B-2 PROTECT'. These twenty-six officials were given the codenames of Roman deities and Swinton himself was MARS—the god of war. Hogue's opposite, Peter Russell, was given the codename of PLUTO—the god of death. Luther's opposite, Alec Binney, was JUNO—queen of the gods. One Military Intelligence Liaison Officer was JUPITER, the king of the gods; the other—Major Crocker, based in Angola—was VULCAN, the blacksmith of the gods and god of the underworld. B-2 PROTECT also had a sub-structure: a further twenty-six men whose codenames were the names of trees.[19] These were junior intelligence agents and sub-agents operating across the region, not just the Gold Coast and Nigeria.

The purpose of B-2 PROTECT is unclear. One of the twenty-six men was an American, who was chief of the FEA office in Accra—William Bascom, who had previously been in OSS. Possibly Bascom was the US liaison officer in B-2 PROTECT. His codename was that of a Greek, rather than of a Roman, deity—PSYCHE, the goddess of the soul and the wife of Eros.

Johnny Weaver found the British hard going. 'You know,' he grumbled to Boulton wearily, 'that the British are very slow to warm up to anyone and no person can expect to become bosom pals with them in one week.' He drew the Washington office's notice to the fact that 'our British opposites almost to the man were educated at either Oxford or Cambridge'.[20] He relied on Bonner's boundless charm to impress the British. 'After TROUT left,' he reported, 'other opposites appeared and I shoved all of them down [Bonner's] throat as quickly as possible and each fellow has remarked in a very favourable manner as to Bonner's personality and brains and energy.'

Swinton 'said in a moment of elation that all these Americans out here are great fellows,' reported Weaver. But, he added, 'We know he doesn't think that.'[21] One MI5 official suggested to Bonner the idea of getting some of the senior British and American officers together over a drink, to smooth out some of the petty differences. Bonner was pleased: 'We volunteered to be of any assistance we could in this praiseworthy endeavour.'[22] It had some success. Five days later, Bonner reported on a further meeting with the Resident Minister. He was 'happy to relate,' he told Washington, that 'we are getting quite chummy with the loyal royalty. He came up and put his arm around us and we chatted very pleasantly for fifteen or twenty minutes.'[23]

Outside West Africa, too, there was often tension between American and British officials operating abroad. This was the result of various factors, local and national—and, not least, a different perspective on colonialism. Most of Donovan's men were anticolonialist, writes Max Hastings, which led to chronic difficulties with the British and French.[24] The contrast in attitude was reflected in the functioning of the intelligence services. In the late summer of 1943, General Donovan introduced a new training programme for OSS agents going abroad on active service, which mentioned colonialism as an explicit OSS target along with Nazism, fascism and militarism.[25] After a visit to India towards the end of 1943, Donovan sent a detailed report to Washington on the grinding poverty he had seen. British colonial rule, he had concluded, 'stands in the way of any immediate economic development'.[26]

On 14 August 1941, Roosevelt and Churchill had jointly announced the Atlantic Charter, which made a commitment to self-government: to 'respect the right of all peoples to choose the form of government under which they will live'. Roosevelt made it clear that in his view, the Charter's principles applied to all peoples. But this was not Churchill's position. The Charter was not, he stated firmly in the House of Commons on 9 September 1941, applicable to the British Empire; rather, it referred only to 'the restoration of the sovereignty, self-government and national life of the States and nations of Europe now under the Nazi yoke.'[27] Over a year after the Charter was signed, he insisted: 'We mean to hold our own. I have not become the King's first minister in order to preside over the liquidation of the British Empire.'[28]

In Washington, the Africa Section of OSS wanted to know more about Swinton. 'We all follow with interest your forays into high society with Lord Swinton et al,' wrote Rud Boulton to Bonner on 27 October 1943. Then he suggested a possible topic for after dinner conversation: Swinton's economic interests. Swinton, he said, was Chairman of the Board of Directors of the United Kingdom Commercial Corps.[29] The UKCC had been set up in 1940 as an arm of the Ministry of Economic Warfare, to keep important commodities out of German hands.[30] The only effective way of depriving Germany of supplies, asserted Swinton, was 'to act at the source, and to buy as much as we could of the most important materials ourselves, a process known as "pre-emptive purchase"'.[31]

The Board of UKCC were hand-picked by Swinton. One key member was Alfred Chester Beatty, a wealthy and successful American mining entrepreneur who had moved to Britain and who has been described as 'one of Winston Churchill's backroom advisers on raw materials supply'.[32] To what extent the work of the UKCC may have involved uranium is unclear.

On the one hand, the atomic bomb project was such a tightly guarded secret in Britain, even in the most elevated circles, that 'C'—Sir Stewart Graham Menzies, the head of MI6—believed that 'only about three or four people were supposed to know anything about it in this country'.[33] (Menzies was 'shocked', according to MI5 official Guy Liddell, 'that large number of people in US, inc. FBI, knew about uranium bomb').[34] But Menzies may well have under-estimated the number of 'three or four'—of whom Liddell was one, since he occasionally heard about it from C, 'very confidentially'.[35] This means that only about two or three other people were supposed to know, which is unlikely. In any case, it is possible that a few key figures in relevant departments, such as Swinton, were aware of the importance of uranium and the necessity to keep the matter secret, but did not know why.

Swinton visited the Belgian Congo on several occasions. On his first visit to the Congo, in September 1942, he was accompanied by Roger Makins—'a good man from the Foreign Office', who had been assigned to him by Anthony Eden, the British Foreign Secretary.[36] Makins was to become the chief British negotiator on atomic energy collaboration after the war and was dubbed 'Mr Atom' in the White House and the State Department.[37] Swinton visited the Congo again in 1943, going to Katanga. 'Here are all the minerals, the vast copper mines of the Union Minière, tin mines and diamond workings,' he commented in his memoirs—but without mentioning uranium, Union Minière's chief attraction at that time to British and American interests.[38]

On yet another trip to Katanga in 1943, Swinton was taken by Jules Cousin of Union Minière to stay at Jadotville, 'the centre of the copper mines'—and the closest town to the Shinkolobwe mine. 'I believe,' recalled Swinton later, that 'someone once called the Katanga minefield a geological scandal, because every known mineral was found mixed up in the most irregular manner. This presents many difficult technical problems, but the ores are so rich that the results are highly satisfactory.'[39]

It is unclear whether or not US authorities knew about Swinton's visit to Cousin in 1943. But it *is* clear that the British did not know about the visit to Cousin in April that year by Hickman Price, the American head of the Bureau of Economic Warfare. Nor does Price's visit appear in Groves's history of the Manhattan Project, *Now It Can Be Told*. Instead, Groves's history gives a different account. It records that Captain Phillip L. Merritt, the geologist at the Murray Hill Area who was in charge of raw ore procurement, went to the Belgian Congo in the autumn of 1943 to make certain that there were no other easily exploitable ores in the area. As a cover story, wrote Groves, Merritt's visit was cloaked as an interest in radium to illuminate gauges. And as expected, added Groves, there were no new sources, so Merritt also checked to see whether there were any tailing dumps that contained a substantial amount of ore—which proved positive.[40] But there is a discrepancy between the date given by Groves for the alleged acquisition through Merritt of these uranium tailings, and the date of the actual acquisition through Price.

This discrepancy may have been a deliberate move by Groves to remove from the historical record the secret cooperation with the US of Belgian Congo officials, all the way up to the Governor General.

Groves may also have wanted to conceal from the record the fact that the US was secretly and proactively seeking Belgian uranium during the period of negotiations leading up the Québec Conference on 19 August 1943, when Roosevelt, Churchill and Mackenzie King, the prime minister of Canada, signed the Québec Agreement (and also agreed on the 1944 invasion of Europe across the beaches of Normandy). The Québec Agreement arranged for British atomic research and materials to be subsumed into the Manhattan Project and for British and Canadian scientists to move to the US, to work at Oak Ridge, Los Alamos, and other atomic research and development sites. The Agreement also established the Combined Policy Committee to coordinate weapons development: a committee of two representatives from Britain, one from Canada, and three Americans, chaired by the US Secretary of War, Henry L. Stimson.

Under the terms of the Québec Agreement, it was clear that Britain and Canada would be junior partners in the atomic project. Nonetheless, the rhetoric underpinning it was one of partnership and shared aims between the three countries. In this context, unilateral efforts by America to obtain and control all the uranium in the Congo—if they had become known—might have been treated by Britain and Canada with suspicion and mistrust.

11

FLARE

While in Accra for the IDB conference with the British, TETON had been instructed to investigate smuggling through purchases on the illegal market. This required careful preparation not only by himself in the Belgian Congo, but also by the OSS station in the Gold Coast. Duane Luther, the new arrival in Accra with responsibility for IDB, had already cabled Washington with a request for $25,000 for this purpose. Adolph Schmidt, the station head—codenamed FLARE—sent Hogue a pouch letter to explain developments. 'I suggested that they collect as many Belgian Congo francs as were available in New York and Washington,' he reported, 'and pouch them to you at Leo and that the balance be sent here to Accra in dollars where we would attempt further conversion with the help of our friends.' He advised Hogue to procure a simple balance scale, such as the kind used by gold-smiths and jewellers.[1]

Then Schmidt raised the issue of Edgar Sengier's African Metals Corporation, which was the organisation specifically set up in the USA to purchase uranium in the Congo, as the American arm of Union Minière. 'I have also asked the boys at home,' said Schmidt, 'to do some snooping around New York to see if some financial intelligence could be unearthed through the

125

banks regarding possible payments in New York to Sengier's African Metals.'

Since Schmidt made mention of 'Sengier's African Metals', he was clearly referring to uranium. But because he was using diamonds as a cover, he carefully cloaked his concerns in a diamond framework: 'This may be remote for it would be most simple for the Germans to pay for the diamonds in Antwerp or Brussels.' He also told Hogue that he had asked Washington to find out about Société Générale's connections in South Africa and in South America, and to send this information 'to both of us for that also may provide some clues'.[2] Schmidt evidently harboured suspicions that Union Minière was selling some uranium from Shinkolobwe to the Axis powers.

Schmidt also had reason to believe that in Germany and Norway, carborundum factories served as a cover for atomic research and production—as was in fact the case in the Niagara Valley in New York. 'Try to find out, by means of A-2 Liaison,' he advised Washington, 'if Norwegian and German carborundum factories have been bombed, and whether their production has been lessened or halted.' If they had not been bombed, he 'strongly' suggested that these plants should be 'continuous targets', and that Frank J. Tone, the chairman of the Carborundum Company in Niagara Falls, should be asked to supply their precise locations.[3] The Carborundum Company—along with other companies in the Niagara Falls region—was engaged in various phases of the Manhattan Project; in 1943 and 1944, it developed methods for engineering and shaping uranium rods.[4] But since the company's original product in the 1890s had been carborundum—a kind of abrasive, with qualities similar to those of diamonds—it was a straightforward matter to avoid revealing any details of its work on uranium. Here too, diamonds—or, at least, artificial diamonds, in the form of carborundum abrasives—were used as a plausible cover for uranium.

Groves was determined to exert total control over the Shinkolobwe mine. 'The Army hopes to get the Belgians to open up the mines, which are now full of water,' noted a Manhattan Project internal memo in January 1944; the Army, it added, planned 'to get as much as possible of the African ore into this country at the earliest possible time.'[5] In February 1944, Groves recommended to the President that the mine be reopened and that the USA and Britain should take whatever steps were necessary to ensure 'joint control' of the uranium in the Congo.[6] However it appears that he was more interested in sole, than in joint, control.

But before Hogue started to organise the purchase of smuggled goods, Schmidt wanted him to arrange for two cutouts to check that all the uranium from Shinkolobwe had arrived safely in Matadi, ready for shipping to the USA. One cutout, he instructed Hogue, should obtain the weigh-bills of the ore being loaded onto the freighters in Matadi; and the other should get the weigh-bills for barrels of ore being loaded at the mine in Katanga (1,500 miles away) for rail transportation to Matadi. In this way, it would be possible to check for any discrepancy between the quantity of uranium leaving the mines and the quantity reaching the port. Both men were to listen 'for any clues to previous or future such shipments' and were to be supplied with adequate cash and trade goods. Steps were to be taken to enhance their covers and they were to make monthly reports—or more frequently, if necessary—through their normal communications.[7]

Schmidt told Hogue to give the job in Katanga to Jaubert, the cutout established by Bonner the year before. This meant that Hogue had to change his plans: he had expected to fly to Elisabethville soon after his return from Accra, but Schmidt wanted him to induct Jaubert in Léopoldville. Schmidt was adamant that he didn't want Thomas Greer to conduct the indoctrination. Greer, who by now had replaced Hickman Price as head of the FEA in the Congo, had also been a cutout set up by Bonner—but Bonner had had misgivings about Greer from the start, and these misgivings were shared by Schmidt. Once Jaubert had left Léopoldville for Katanga, said Schmidt, Hogue could then go on to Elisabethville himself; and once there, Jaubert should report to him. After that, Jaubert should not return to Léopoldville directly, in order to maintain his cover.[8]

As well as being Dock Hogue's superior officer, Adolph Schmidt was about ten years older and took an avuncular interest in his welfare. He also liked him. On the one hand, they came from very different backgrounds: he was Ivy League, with a supportive and affluent family behind him, while Hogue had struggled to pay to study at the University of Idaho. But on the other hand, they had much to share: they were both clever, had courage and an appetite for adventure, and they both enjoyed fishing and relaxing over a beer. Schmidt was therefore pleased to receive a cheerful communication from Hogue. 'It was good news,' he wrote, 'to learn that you are feeling well and that the combination of the yellow fever shot with everything else did not get you down.' He was relieved, too, that a letter from Hogue had arrived in Accra within four days, which was a significant improvement over past communications.

Under Schmidt's instructions, Hogue made arrangements for checking that the weigh-bills for uranium loaded in Katanga matched the weigh-bills for the uranium that reached Matadi. The initial results of the check were reassuring: there was no discrepancy. But this was not Hogue's chief task: for Schmidt had been told to check 'for possible diversions to areas *other* than port of Matadi'. This meant searching out the smuggling of uranium though other likely routes: via Angola; via the British colonies of Northern Rhodesia (now Zambia) and Southern Rhodesia (now Zimbabwe), which were linked to the Congo by the Benguela Railway; and by air.

In early March, to follow up the Angola angle, Hogue met with Lanier Violett in Léopoldville. 'Next week,' announced OSS agent SILVA from Luanda on 26 February 1944, 'HOMER will drive to the Belgian Congo, where he will pursue loads regarding IDB.'[9] It appears, however, that there were some doubts about Violett's trustworthiness at around this time at OSS headquarters. In late January, OSS Secret Intelligence had tried to find out how long the Texas Company planned to keep Violett in his post at Luanda, on the grounds that it was 'rather important for us to know now the possibilities of his removal within the next six months'.[10] Arguably, this may have reflected their wish to keep a man in the capital of Angola. But it is more likely that they were unhappy about having Violett working for them, given a document written on 25 April 1944, recording a telephone conversation between Boulton and E. K. Merrill, a senior OSS colleague. Merill told Boulton that he had arranged with a Mr Borie at Texaco headquarters in New York to replace Violett:

> I discussed the question of arrangements to be made with T [sic], who is to take the place of Violett. Mr Borie agreed that the same arrangements that had been in effect with Violett would be entirely acceptable to them.[11]

Since Violett had not said he was planning to leave, this conversation reveals that discussions about getting rid of him, or at least moving him, were taking place between OSS and Texaco. As it turned out, 'T' was not sent to Angola and Violett stayed in post, but was carefully watched. It is unclear whether Hogue was informed of the concerns about Violett.

To follow up the Rhodesian angle, Hogue crossed the southern border of the Congo into Northern Rhodesia, and then went on to Southern Rhodesia.[12] There he obtained information that Bulawayo in Southern Rhodesia was a major collecting centre for smuggling from the Congo, Angola and South Africa. This was because Bulawayo was a stop on the South African Airways route to Cairo, and an important rail centre linked to Beira, Lourenço Marques, Lobito, Luanda and Matadi. Its central location and 'the laxity of customs control', he reported to Washington, 'made it an ideal point for the collection of supplies from various sources and their distribution to different outlets'. Parcels of diamonds, he discovered, dribbled in from many sources in small quantities, to be purchased by a central collector and then dispatched by rail through couriers under good cover.[13]

In terms of the risk of diversion by air, Schmidt relied on British efforts to get airport security under control, which seemed to be successful. 'The British must bear the major share of the control burden across the Central Africa band,' wrote Schmidt to Boulton, 'but Russell informs me MI5 already have it well in hand.'[14] The monitoring of aircraft was unpopular—but producing unexpected finds. On 18 March Lord Swinton reported to London that seven civilian planes passing through Lagos had been searched, but that the Belgian and French crews and passengers had been surprised and resentful. A number of them were found to be carrying compromising documents, some of them relating to illicit gold transactions in Lagos.[15]

On 3 April 1944, Schmidt flew to Léopoldville on a 'special mission'. He needed to see Hogue in person: to give him the Belgian Congo francs which would be needed to make a purchase on the contraband market. But first he had to get a large set of cheques converted into francs at the Banque du Congo Belge in Léopoldville, the bank's headquarters. 'I had misgivings all the way down on the plane,' he reported to Boulton. 'Everything clicked so well, something must be wrong.'

As it turned out, something *was* wrong. When Schmidt landed, he asked for Major Marable, the finance officer with the War Area Service Corps, who was supposed to have brought the cash from Accra to Léopoldville, but was told he had left on the British airline flying boat (BOAC) that morning. Marable's name had even 'been omitted from the cable which had been handed to Snowden, ATC Operations officer at Leo, and no one could make any sense of it'. Major Marable had been chosen for this job because his face was known to the staff at the Banque du Congo Belge, so his appearance at the bank would be less likely to trigger suspicion when converting large amounts of money.

Once again, communications in West Africa had broken down. 'It might be well for you to be acquainted with the difficulties of this communication system to the Congo,' reported Schmidt wearily to Boulton. He had rewritten the message twice, he said, and it was perfectly clear. He had then passed it on to the Signal Corps in Accra, who enciphered it. The Signal Corps radioed it to Major Bolton, Chief of the US Military Intelligence Mission in Brazzaville, in Army cipher, which was the only cipher available to them from Accra. Major Bolton's Warrant Officer had deciphered the message and paraphrased it. Then, however, it was necessary:

> to carry the message from Brazzaville across the Congo River to Leopoldville and deliver it to the addressee, in this case Lt. Snowden. There is sometimes a delay of two days if no one is leaving Brazzaville on the day of receipt. This accounts somewhat for the fact that TETON did not receive four of our cables from Accra until three weeks after being sent out—in this case Bolton had forgotten the indicator. Snowden showed the message to Marable to see if he could make sense out of it, but of course without his name on it, he could offer no solution.

These were the only code facilities in the Congo, apart from commercial facilities available at the Consulate, 'which incidentally we are now using exclusively with TETON, although expensive'.[16]

Because Major Marable didn't get the message in time, it looked as if Hogue would not get the Belgian Congo francs he needed. But 'the day was saved' by one Lt. James Turk in Army finance. Turk was 'dumbstruck' when Major Marable walked into the WASC Accra office on the night of 3 April, reported Schmidt, and was told what had happened. He immediately obtained permission to rewrite the cheques in his own name; he then hopped on to the mission ship that was leaving that night, arriving in Léopoldville on 5 April.[17]

Next day, Turk went to the Banque du Congo Belge, an imposing white building with long covered balconies on the Avenue Hauzeur (now Avenue Wagenia), not far from the Léopoldville Zoo and the Botanical Gardens. As he had expected, he did not have any difficulty converting the cheques into cash, because most cheques from Accra were signed by him and his signature was known to the bank tellers. 'But still we were not through,' reported Schmidt to Boulton:

> They insisted on giving him one million francs in 10,000 note denomi-
> nations. I shook my head because I knew they were all marked. So on
> the morning of 7 April Turk went back to the bank and told them that
> on second thoughts, they were too large for his purposes.

TURK's 'cashier friend' asked no questions and agreed to change the bills. However, he did not have sufficient 1,000 franc notes on hand, he explained apologetically, so would have to give him smaller notes. As a result, reported Schmidt, 'Turk returned triumphantly with a tremendous package of 500 franc notes.' Turk had not been told what these funds were for, and asked no questions. Schmidt innocently remarked to him that this would mean a heavy load to carry back in the suitcase to Accra—'and then quietly that evening turned over the whole batch to TETON'.[18]

Hogue was in good spirits. For one thing, he was now living in a bungalow, which was far more comfortable than the room provided by the FEA. And just three days before Schmidt's arrival in the Congo, Shirley Chidsey (ANGELLA) had started working for him on a formal basis. This gave him the administrative and secretarial support he badly needed and she had many fresh, good ideas for the management of the office. In addition he now had the regular company of a smart, funny, woman, who was quite different from many other American women of the time. Not only was she happy to travel in Africa on her own, but she was an enthusiastic railfan, like the rest of her family; her stepfather took his daughters on trips just to see different steam engines.[19] As a result, Shirley had become an avid reader of *Railroad Magazine*, an American journal devoted to trains and railways. This interest in railroads was a useful resource, given the importance of the Congo's rail networks to the colony and to the export of Congolese war materials, including uranium, to America.

Fluent in French, Schmidt was able to move around Léopoldville discreetly. He stayed in the Sabena Guest House, a comfortable small hotel which had been built about ten minutes' drive from the airport by Sabena Airlines, the national airline of Belgium. The Guest House was near the offices of the FEA, where Hogue—

and now Shirley Chidsey—were based. Schmidt and Hogue met in secret. 'TETON and I did our talking in his rooms and were not seen together in public or by the American staff in his building,' he assured Washington. Evidently he was not telling the FEA officials what he was up to.

The chief focus of their discussions was the purchase of uranium on the contraband market, to smoke out smugglers. Schmidt counselled Hogue not to do this himself, but to use a specially chosen cutout. He was concerned that Hogue's activities should not be visible to Belgian Congo officials, since this was not something that would be appreciated by Governor General Ryckmans. 'It will be a delicate business at best,' commented Schmidt to Boulton, 'which Belgian Surety should not have too much trouble in tracing, and in my opinion it is not worth his expulsion from the colony.'[20] By 'Surety', Schmidt meant the Sûreté d'État—and the Chef de Sûreté in Léopoldville was Jean Beaudinet, who had already been pinpointed by Hogue as protecting diamond smuggling through Matadi. Secret Intelligence had noted this bluntly in a situation report: 'Mr. Hogue discovered that Beaudinet, Chef de Sûreté at Leopoldville and his Belgian Congo opposite, was plainly mixed up in this racket.'[21]

On 5 April 1944, in the course of Schmidt's visit to the Congo, Hogue contacted Beaudinet directly. He sent him a list of four people living in, or planning to visit, the Belgian Congo, and he asked if Belgian Intelligence had any information on them. Beaudinet replied just over a week later. The only help he offered related to two men living in the coastal region of Mayumbe. 'We have never had any unfavourable report on them,' he said, adding, 'In view of the information you have given, a closer watch will be kept on them.' The letter was grudging; but he signed it with the utmost courtesy, as required of a formal letter in French (though it was written in English): 'With kindest regards, my dear Mr Hogue, believe me, Yours very truly, Beaudinet.'[22]

The provincial head of the Sûreté in Katanga was François Scheerlinck—another name on the list of suspicious people that had been drawn up by Doug Bonner the previous year. While travelling around the Elisabethville region, Bonner had been accompanied by Scheerlinck, 'a rather short, round-headed Teutonic appearing man' in his early forties, and had been suspicious of his allegiances. He reported that Scheerlinck was seen in the company not only of his wife, but also of Mrs Evelyn Fitch, a British woman who worked for Belgian censorship and was reported to be his mistress; a tall, rather heavy woman in her late thirties or early forties, she was the wife of a British captain stationed in Cairo, while her two children were in England. 'She is frequently seen talking and dining with young British officers who pass through,' reported Boulton to his colleagues. Several high ranking British officers had tried to have her sent home on the grounds that she was a menace to British morale and local goodwill, but she had stayed on, living at the plush Hotel Léopold II in Elisabethville. 'Mrs Evelyn Fitch, working for the Belgian censorship in Elizabethville [sic],' assessed Boulton, 'is either a German, Belgian, or British agent.'[23]

It was clear to Schmidt that the mission in the Congo was extremely dangerous to TETON personally. It was also at risk of making public America's involvement with Congolese uranium. It was therefore essential to maintain absolute secrecy—and to help with this, Schmidt recommended that all other IDB investigations should be suspended for the time being. This was agreed by Secret Intelligence in Washington, who also wanted to ensure that the US Consul in Léopoldville, Patrick Mallon, did not find out about TETON's activities.

Schmidt caught the first Sabena plane back to Accra on 10 April, arriving the following morning. Hogue, he told Boulton, 'looked well and reported he was feeling fit', though was still worried about his amoebic dysentery. But it had been a productive trip: 'We were able to cover a lot of ground on IDB and other problems and it was good to see him.'[24]

12

THE CUTOUT

After Schmidt had left the Congo and gone back to Accra, Hogue prepared to fly to Elisabethville at the start of May, to find a way of making some approaches to smugglers. He expected to stay there for the rest of the month. 'TETON,' he reported to Washington, 'finds it necessary to be at Elizabethville pushing diamond purchases from the 3rd of May to the 1st of June.'[1] It would be a demanding trip and take nearly a month. But for the first time since he had become head of the OSS station in the Congo, he did not have to worry about leaving the office unattended, which was a serious security risk. This time, he was able to leave the station and its affairs in ANGELLA's capable hands.

He agreed fully with Schmidt's advice to use a cutout to purchase smuggled goods, rather than attempt it himself. But it would be hard to know how or where to find the right person to do this. Before going down to Elisabethville, he consulted a man whom he had grown to trust—George M. Saks, who had been one of the largest coffee roasters in France but, being a Jew, had been forced to leave in 1940. Now in the Congo, he was working for a company called Bunge Co., an international food company.[2] He also consulted Jaubert and Greer, his informants in the US Foreign Economic Association. He then drew up a list of three candidates.

But almost as soon as he arrived in Katanga, he had to discount two of the candidates, for practical reasons. This left him with only one option—Jean Decoster, a retired journalist now in his sixties. Decoster seemed to Hogue to be reassuringly 'pro-American and pro-Allied', as well as knowing a great deal about smuggling—'like most newspaper men, they are pretty well informed'. When Hogue offered him the role of cutout, he 'jumped at the chance to be of service'.[3]

Decoster was a prominent left-wing figure in Katanga, who had left Belgium for the Congo at the age of thirty and, after varied employment, had set up a new daily newspaper in Elisabethville in 1931—*L'Echo du Katanga*.[4] *L'Echo* was avowedly socialist and intended as a direct challenge to the right-wing *L'Essor du Congo*, which expressed the attitudes of the elite and of the Roman Catholic Church in Katanga, led by Archbishop de Hemptinne.[5]

Decoster had been active in the trade union movement throughout his working life, but over time had developed a strong disapproval of the fact that union members in the Congo—who were all white—were only concerned with white workers' demands and ignored the needs of Africans. This, he thought was not only racist but extremely unfair in material terms, since the working and living conditions of white workers far surpassed those of the Congolese. White workers, he pointed out, had the benefit of cheap labour and servants and 'perpetrate all the injustices, of which they accuse their capitalistic employers, on their own native servants'. Decoster was now chiefly interested in the improvement of African workers' conditions and used *L'Echo* to advance his views.[6]

In this respect *L'Echo* was different from the third newspaper in Katanga: *L'Informateur*, which had begun in 1934. It was also consciously left-leaning but represented the European unions.

Decoster's paper was vigorously anti-fascist and anti-neutralist. It took a pro-Soviet stance and encouraged people to join *Les Amis de l'Union Soviétique au Katanga*—the Friends of the Soviet Union in Katanga. The local authorities suspected him of getting subsidies from a communist organisation in South Africa, but

Peter Stephens, the British consul in Elisabethville, dismissed such an idea. Decoster, he believed, was neither a communist nor a subversive—simply a working man who admired Russia and also had friendly sentiments towards the British and Americans. In his view, neither Decoster nor *L'Echo du Katanga* should be taken very seriously.

In 1938, Decoster had started a 'Saturday Swahili' page in *L'Echo*, publishing letters written in Swahili. This was an immediate success, records Bruce Fetter: the letters revealed that many hard-working Africans badly wanted lessons in business French and in accounting, so that they could get better jobs. Decoster, who was a self-taught accountant, decided that he would immediately start classes in these subjects and teach them himself, with the help of his son Albert. The classes were well attended and hugely popular, but were regarded as 'highly suspicious' by government officials and by Archbishop de Hemptinne and other senior members of the Catholic Church. This was partly because the classes were outside the control of the Benedictine mission, which dominated the provision of education in Katanga. But it was also because they were organised by Decoster, whose activism to promote the rights of the Congolese made him an enemy of the Belgian administration, the Catholic Church, and the mining companies.

Most of the Belgian elite in the southern province loathed any idea of 'native' rights. A list of key figures drawn up by the British Consulate described Jules Cousin as being 'of a vindictive nature, and will certainly try to punish the originators of the labour movement. Fears the Bolshevist Bogey in the Congo.' The same, it observed, could be said of his wife, Madame Cousin. It added that Cousin was:

> small, autocratic, reactionary, determined to look after his own interests and the interests of Union Minière, come what may. Was quite prepared to collaborate in producing copper for the Germans when it seemed obvious that they had won the war, but has since decided on which side his bread is buttered.[7]

A similar picture was painted of Monseigneur de Hemptinne: as a man who 'hates "communism," syndicalism, trade unionism and anything which savours of the right of the workers to dictate the terms on which they shall work'.[8] This description was consistent with a letter addressed by de Hemptinne to the prime minister of Belgium, the minister of colonies, and the Governor General, in which he wrote with deep anxiety about the change in attitude he saw around him in the Congo. 'A spirit of antipathy and defiance,' he warned in December 1943, 'is spreading everywhere. The native is detaching himself from our authority. More and more, he seeks refuge from our influence and prestige. The face of the Congo is changing.' Belgium, he feared, was 'on the way to losing its crowning achievement in Africa'.[9]

Once war was declared, the Katanga authorities had seized the opportunity to suppress Decoster's classes and to put some of the students in detention. The Sûreté, which had been keeping a careful eye on him, now shadowed him routinely. But despite this, Decoster managed to maintain contact with his students and encouraged them to unite peacefully in a demand for better jobs and wages. He advised trying to bring the soldiers of the Force Publique on their side. He made explicit references to the Atlantic Charter and called for 'freedom of speech and of the press' and 'individual freedom, with the abolition of the chain and the whip, which reduce us to the condition of beasts of burden'.[10]

Decoster gave up the editorship of *L'Echo* in 1942, handing it over to his son Albert. He now concentrated on his extensive forest concessions in the Kasai, which involved him in travelling and exporting timber to South Africa.[11] But he also used this as an opportunity to intensify his political work. 'By the last quarter of 1943,' notes Bruce Fetter, 'Decoster and the Africans had formulated concrete plans for a strike.'[12] Decoster's public role was a small one. But behind the scenes he was busy: writing editorials favouring salary increases; giving the strikers small sums of money to feed their families; and writing to the leader of the Belgian socialists in London, Camille Huysmans, asking for support for the strike.

Decoster's efforts were part of a larger picture of resistance by workers and intellectuals in the Congo. In 1941, employees of Union Minière had struck in protest against the gradual decline in their standard of living; by 9 December, workers at all the main Union Minière sites were out. At its peak, the strike had brought together workers in Elisabethville, Jadotville and Kipushi, including factory workers, railwaymen, night soilers, watchmen and food peddlers.[13] The company brought in the colonial army to deal with it.

In Elisabethville, the response to the strikers was brutal. On the town's soccer pitch, the strikers refused to go back to work and demanded a raise in wages. Mine workers later recalled that Amour Maron, the provincial governor of Katanga, pointblank shot Léonard Mpoyi, who was trying to negotiate with him:

> Maron demanded that the workers return home. Mpoyi responded 'I refuse. You must give us some proof that the company has agreed to raise our salaries.' So Maron said, 'I have already demanded that you go to the office to check.' Then he pulled a gun out of his pocket and shot Léonard.[14]

Maron then ordered the Force Publique to fire on the strikers; about seventy were killed and one hundred wounded.[15] 'It was a year deep in the war of 1940–45,' wrote André Yav, a resident of Elisabethville. 'Many, many people died. They died for a higher monthly wage. That day there was great sorrow in Elisabethville, because of that *bwana* governor.'[16] In the view of David Van Reybrouck, this was 'the first, open expression of open protest' in the social history of the Congo.[17]

On 20 February 1944, a major mutiny by Congolese soldiers of the Force Publique broke out in the barracks at Luluabourg (now Kananga), the capital of Kasai province. Luluabourg was an important administrative and commercial centre, with gracious and wide avenues, and good hotels; but these advantages were reserved for whites only. As in other Congolese cities, the living areas of blacks and whites were segregated and there were deep racial inequalities.

The mutiny was savagely crushed. Eighteen of the soldiers who had taken part in the mutiny were executed—one hanged, and seventeen shot; another man committed suicide. Many others received brutal corporal punishments and there were numerous dismissals.[18]

Some of the mutineers escaped to the southern province of Katanga and the central province of Sankuru where, records one historian, 'they planted the seeds of further insurrection'. Another mutiny broke out at almost the same time in Jadotville, near Shinkolobwe, while at Elisabethville the colonial administration managed 'only just in time' to get wind of some 'plotting among intellectuals'—an accusation that pinpointed Decoster. According to Bruce Fetter, officials were relatively restrained in the suppression of the mutiny at Elisabethville, but the soldiers who had participated were punished, as well as the most active conspirators. These included Decoster, who was sent to do war work in Equateur Province, 'a well-known site of semi-official punishment'.[19]

There was also an uprising in Kivu province in spring 1944 by followers of the Watchtower movement, which was influenced by Jehovah's Witnesses in South Africa and known in the Congo as Kitawala, many of whom worked in the gold mines. This led to a bitter showdown with the ruling administration, in the course of which hundreds of blacks and three whites were killed; the leader of the revolt was hanged.[20]

Major Bonner, on his visits to the Congo in 1943, had been aware of dissatisfaction among Congolese people. But he drew a mistaken conclusion. 'The Belgian Congo native,' he said, 'is very well subdued and I should strongly doubt that this dissatisfaction would ever amount to anything.'[21] Presumably he was unaware of the strike of 1941.

Hogue did not make this mistake. He was far more aware than Bonner of the deep undercurrents of unhappiness and resistance. And as one strand of his job was to supply OSS with a steady flow of information that was not available through official channels, he sent Secret Intelligence an account of the Luluabourg Mutiny and of the harsh conditions that had led to it. 'Taxation runs about 10 per cent of gross income, payable in cash,' he noted with disapproval, 'and non-payment is punishable by imprisonment with forced labor. Native unions are not tolerated.'[22]

Hogue was particularly concerned about the apparent growing disaffection in Katanga. This, he feared, was providing a fertile ground for enemy activities. There was also a problem in British-ruled Northern Rhodesia, over the border from Katanga, where there were 'subversive elements among the native mineworkers'. In Hogue's view, this generated an unacceptable risk—that workers at the Shinkolobwe mine and on the railroads transporting the uranium were potentially vulnerable to persuasion by the enemy. In any case, the very fact that Shinkolobwe was in Katanga, as was Elisabethville, the city housing the headquarters of Union Minière, made it crucially important that the province was watched at all times. But it was impossible for him to do this from Léopoldville, which was so far away. He therefore sent a strong recommendation to Washington that a second US consulate should be opened—in Elisabethville.

Boulton needed no persuasion. As soon as he received this communication from Hogue, he presented a powerful case for an Elisabethville consulate to Whitney Shepardson, the Chief of OSS Secret Intelligence. There was a 'most urgent need', he insisted, for OSS to expand into Katanga: 'Effective intelligence work in this area requires that a US consulate be opened in Elizabethville.' He pointed out that the area was too remote from Léopoldville to be covered effectively by an OSS representative stationed there, especially because of the endless problem of communications. This could only be solved, he said, 'by opening a consulate through which the intelligence obtained can be transmitted safely to Léopoldville and to furnish the necessary cover for an OSS representative'. This plan, he urged, should be implemented as soon as possible.[23]

Within just a few hours of sending this memo to Shepardson, Boulton sent him another one, telling him that Perry Jester, a

Foreign Service officer on the African Desk in the State Department, had been pushing for such a move for some time. 'We need,' he said, 'the cover and communications available only through a consulate located at that point.' Boulton added that it was the specific recommendation of 'Mr Hogue, the OSS Chief of Mission in the Congo'.[24]

The US government was deepening its hooks into the Belgian Congo. Plans had been made to raise the Consulate in Léopoldville to Consulate General in July 1944 and on 26 April 1944, J. Webb Benton arrived from New York to replace Patrick Mallon and prepare to take up the post of Consul General. Benton was a high-ranking diplomat and his salary was almost double that of Mallon.[25]

Hogue instructed Decoster to travel to Luluabourg. This arrangement had nothing to do with the recent mutiny which had taken place in that city. Instead, it was because Luluabourg was an important commercial and transport hub, which offered prime conditions for smuggling. It was also a stop on the BCK railway line from Katanga to Port-Francqui, the route used to transport uranium ore part of the way to Matadi; Luluabourg was two stops from Port-Francqui, about 240 miles south.

Decoster's mission was to try to pick up information about smuggling, through the assistance of a local resident and friend. Then, if at all possible, he was to buy diamonds on the illegal market and use that purchase to uncover important smuggling channels. Hogue gave Decoster 100,000 francs for expenses. For the purposes of his communications with Washington, he allocated Decoster a codenumber: since his own was 253, Decoster became 253/25.

Hogue had met with Decoster in secret. But even so, he was sailing close to the wind with his choice of Decoster as a cutout in Katanga. For Decoster represented everything that was loathed by the Katanga elite and he was being followed by the Sécurité. From the point of view of being 'with us', as Hogue put it,

Decoster was unimpeachable. But from the point of view of his support for African workers, he was a huge risk.

Unaware of the risks surrounding his new cutout, Hogue was pleased with the arrangements he had made. He also set up an investigation in Angola along the Benguela Railway, which was the other route to the coast from Katanga. 'Attempts are being made at present to buy diamonds from Eville [Elisabethville] to Vila Luso through a good cutout,' he reported with satisfaction to Washington.[26] Vila Luso (now known as Luena) was a stop on the Benguela Railway in Angola, en route to Lobito Bay.

Before leaving Elisabethville to return to Léopoldville, Hogue took some 8 mm film of some white men looking at local merchandise outside the post office—the white-painted *Palais du Poste*. Their clothes suggest they are American or British officials, one of whom is sitting on some steps talking to African traders who are showing him a set of large striped rugs. The trader then shows him some other objects, including a watch and an ornate tasselled mat. Soon after this, Hogue himself is filmed, presumably by one of his colleagues, and we see him being shown a selection of small and large metal masks. Evidently enjoying the encounter, Hogue picks up a mask and holds it up to his face, before deciding to purchase one, and the episode ends with a rather enigmatic close-up of Hogue's eyes in shadow under the rim of his helmet, with his lower face concealed. It is as if Hogue is playing with the image of a spy—the kind of image that informs some of the popular fiction that Hogue liked to write. The difference here, though, is that it wasn't fiction: he really *was* a spy.[27]

Hogue was able to return to Léopoldville nearly three weeks earlier than he had expected, now that he had set up his important cutout in Katanga. 'On the 11th of this month,' he cabled on 12 May, 'TETON went back to Leo.'[28] This was valuable, as there were a number of clues he wanted to follow up. At the start of June he sent information to FLARE which was then forwarded to Washington: 'TETON in contact Diamond carrier Leo. Cabled [that] he now knows Diamond parcels are collected at Bulawayo and pass through Congo to Jacobs at Matadi.'[29]

Then Hogue fell ill yet again, with a severe bout of malaria.[30] But as soon as he was well enough, he flew to Luanda in Angola on the weekly plane from Léopoldville, to check out possible smuggling in the Portuguese colony. On 10 July he sent 'Schmitty' in Accra an account of the customs setup he had found in Luanda. 'People who were well known,' he reported, 'were apparently subject to no examination—for example, Sabeck, Klein's assistant at Sabena.' He himself was passed through at both ends without examination, because he had semi-diplomatic immunity. 'It was evident to me,' he said,

> that any person with whom the officials on both ends were familiar would have no trouble carrying diamonds since the chances of being examined are very small. You know, perhaps, that a Belgian Congo Customs officer cannot search the person of an individual. He is limited to baggage only.

Only the Sûreté, he added, 'conducts the search of the person of an individual'.[31] This was worrying, since Hogue was now certain that Jean Beaudinet, the Chef de Sûreté in Léopoldville, and François Scheerlinck, the provincial head of the Sûreté in Katanga, were mixed up in the smuggling racket.

The OSS network of West Africa was in the midst of a change in personnel. In February, Corporal Clark, codenamed HANLY, had replaced Leonard Davis (TRUCK) as Communications Officer in Accra, with responsibility for the operation of the Message Center. On 2 March 1944, Luther (COACH) went to Washington; and it was planned that Schmidt would follow him in early July.[32]

On 14 June, Captain Harry W. Basehart joined the team in Accra.[33] Basehart offered a range of skills: he was an anthropologist, had newspaper experience, and was a graduate of army administration school. His military status was an important qualification, felt Boulton, because it was desirable to have an officer at all times at the Accra station.[34] Basehart, like Hogue, was an unusual recruit for OSS, in that his background was far from privileged and his family had suffered badly in the Great Depression. Now in his early thirties, he had attended the University of Chicago as a mature student and then did fieldwork researching the Oneida people of Wisconsin. This was interrupted by the outbreak of war, when he was drafted into the army.[35] But he chose a codename which reflected the subject of his academic research—OJIBWA, the name of a large group of Native Americans in the USA and Canada

The next expected arrival in Accra was Hunt Harris—EBERT. Harris was coming from Lourenço Marques, where he had been Chief of Station since November 1942, to take over the helm in Accra.[36] He would be coming with his wife Mary, whom he had married the previous year in Mozambique. On 30 May 1944, Schmidt wrote to Boulton to report on the arrangements that were being made. 'Since no other bungalows are available,' he wrote, 'Basehart and I will move to Camp when the Eberts arrive, since we have only one large bedroom and one bath here. After consultation with Hunt, I believe the permanent arrangement can be worked out satisfactorily.' A note of annoyance crept into his account of these domestic arrangements: 'Little did I think that I would be concerned with parlor, bedroom and bath in Africa.'[37]

EBERT arrived at Accra on 23 June; his wife was expected a few days later.[38] To the frustration of the OSS officers tasked with making their travel plans, Air Transport Command refused to carry women and so an alternative route had to be found. The ATC, cabled HANLY, 'will not carry wife. Have wired [EBERT] take first BOAC or Sabena plane.'[39]

While these changes were taking place at the Accra station, efforts were being made to increase security in communications across OSS in West Africa. Boulton sent instructions in a pouch letter on 27 June to 'use only code numbers in pouch letters, pouch reports and on the innermost envelope containing pouch material'.[40] Codenames would still be used where appropriate, he said, but codenumbers should replace them as the primary identifier of an agent. This would not lead to any change in Hogue's own practice: nearly all his pouch letters were signed, in a tidy but elegant hand, with his own number written in words— 'Two Five Three'.

13

LOCUST

In Léopoldville, Hogue and Chidsey were preparing for the arrival on 13 July 1944 of Henry Emil Stehli, who would join them as a new member of the OSS station in the Congo. Stehli was an attractive man, with open and friendly features, fair hair and blue eyes—and though not quite reaching the lofty heights of Hogue, Violett and Harris, at about five foot eleven he was taller than average and of sturdy build. Now 41 years old, he was easygoing and very sociable, with a good-natured sense of humour—well liked by both men and women, who sought out his company. He was related to Doug Bonner: his wife Grace was the sister of Doug's first wife; and his sister Lilly had married Doug's brother.[1] This meant that he was connected with another OSS officer involved in some way in the Congo mission.[2]

Henry Stehli was a fourth-generation member of the 'Stehlis of Zurich'—the family that had created the Stehli Silks Corporation, which was famous for its distinctive and sophisticated silk fabric designs. He was born in Switzerland and brought to the USA as a child, where he studied at St Paul's, a prestigious boarding school in New Hampshire, and then at Yale; throughout his years of study, he was popular and a successful all-rounder. After college he went on a trip round the world and then joined the family company with enthusiasm, always carrying with him a Stehli and Company pencil, in a distinctive green and engraved in gold with the firm's name. But he enjoyed social life too and played many gentleman's sports, all to a respectable club level.

Stehli's OSS codename was LOCUST—a happy reminder of his family estate in Locust Valley, Long Island (though his wife, Grace, and two children moved to an apartment on Park Avenue in Manhattan for the duration of the war). His codenumber was 923; and his cover was that of a businessman with a manufacturing interest in silk, which was highly plausible. Hogue gave information about Stehli's arrival to the local press, as a way of reinforcing his cover. Stehli was also completely fluent in French, since he had spent his early years in Switzerland and his family still spoke French at home and at dinner parties. He would be 'ideal', judged Boulton, 'for work in the Congo'.[3]

According to an obituary published after Henry Stehli's death, he was sent to the Congo 'principally to divert shipments of uranium from Europe to the United States'.[4] He was temporarily assigned by Hogue to assist Charles Dudley Withers, the American economic attaché, who was taking an instrumental role in the export of Congolese uranium to the US. 'Withers, whom you know,' wrote Hogue to Boulton, 'has agreed to take Stehli under his wing, and see that he gets around town in the proper manner.'[5] Hogue, who tended to sympathise with the underdog, had a soft spot for the 28-year-old Withers. 'The poor economic attaché here,' he wrote to Boulton, 'gets reminded at least once a day that four men in the Consulate General outrank him.'[6]

It had been arranged that Stehli would have an office in the American legation, which was raised in July from the rank of Consulate to that of Consulate General. By working in the same building as Benton, hoped Hogue, Stehli 'will have many ins which I have not had'.[7] He would also need a car, since the Dodge truck could not be used by all three members of the growing OSS station. Hogue was therefore arranging to buy a car from George Saks—a 'brand new Ford, super deluxe sedan coupe'.[8]

It had been over nine months since Hogue had first arrived in the Congo—a period of intense difficulty, sickness, excessive travel, and loneliness. But, little by little, the situation had grown easier. For one thing, he was no longer working as a one-man band, but had the intelligent support of ANGELLA, who also kept things going when he was away. Hogue was pleased when Washington reported receipt of information which he and ANGELLA had gathered. 'How does our little office stack up for volume?' he inquired. 'I won't ask about quality,' he commented with his characteristic self-effacing humour, 'because that is always a problem.'[9]

In a short film organised by Hogue at the American legation in Léopoldville, he looks happy and relaxed. So too does a woman who resembles Shirley Chidsey, who is shown photographing two superbly dressed *Sapeurs*—members of the SAPE (*Société des Ambianceurs et des Personnes Élégantes*), which represented a tradition that had evolved in the Congo as a means of resistance to the colonial system, through fashion and dress. The *Sapeurs* proudly show off their outfits, from their fashionable round spectacles all the way down to their elegant shoes. The woman in the frame laughs cheerfully and with good will as the men trying to use the large camera scratch their heads, baffled.

One of Hogue's achievements in the previous nine months had been to establish a number of 'dependable' contacts across the region, including American missionaries and Rabbi Levy, the leader of the Jewish community in Elisabethville. At Albertville (now Kalemie), he relied on Justin De Gesnot, the brother of the De Gesnot who was his contact in Matadi.[10] The fact that his list of contacts did not contain any Congolese people is hardly surprising given that the majority of the population were excluded from the government of their country and had no influence.

The OSS station in the Congo was now well established and was ready, believed Hogue, to benefit a great deal from the addition of Henry Stehli. But just three days before Stehli's arrival, there was an unexpected and shocking development. Hogue received a letter from Peter Stephens in Elisabethville, which stated: 'A mutual friend of ours has been blown wide open in no uncertain manner.' There were no details in the letter, because the British were having 'pouch trouble' and Stephens had had to resort to the open mail. But there was enough to suggest that something had gone wrong regarding Decoster. 'That's all I've had to go on so far,' reported Hogue worriedly to Boulton.

Stephens had also written a full account of what he knew for Alan Williams at the British Consulate General in Léopoldville. In a 'Secret and Personal' letter, he reported that according to information he had received, Hogue had arranged with Decoster to discover the source of smuggling by purchasing a diamond. Decoster, wrote Stephens, had been shadowed by one of the agents working for François Scheerlinck, the head of the Sûreté in Katanga, who denounced him a few days after his arrival in Luluabourg as 'being in the employ of a foreign power'. This scared Decoster, who sought to establish his innocence by saying this was in Belgium's own best interests and revealing Hogue's part in the affair—thus compromising Hogue's cover in the colony. 'I do not know,' commented Stephens, 'how Decoster gave himself away in the first place.' Decoster asked Stephens not to tell Hogue what had happened, but Stephens felt he ought to know—so sent Hogue the cryptic, but instructive, letter which alerted him to the new development.[11]

Then Hogue heard that at a big party on Saturday night, A. S. Gerard, the right-hand man of Firmin Van Bree, had asked the American Vice Consul, Leonard Cromie, some questions about Hogue: 'Who is this man, Dock Hogue? What does he do?' Since Gerard knew Hogue perfectly well, this was odd, to say the least. Hogue put it down to the fact that Jules Cousin had just arrived from Katanga in Léopoldville—'hence I assume that Cousin is digging for information'. But why, he wondered, had Cousin suddenly arrived in the capital, all the way from Elisabethville? Cromie told Gerard that Hogue was a consular official working mostly with the FEA.[12]

Putting these scraps of information together, it was evident to Hogue that some of the leading Belgian industrialists in the

Congo—some of whom were strongly suspected of working with Nazi Germany—were watching him very carefully. It also looked as if the secret arrangements he had made in May with Jean Decoster had been exposed. If so, this was a very serious development, although Boulton sought to reassure him. 'Why worry about your exposure?' he wrote from Washington. 'You are right, they are wrong. Do you think that you are in danger? Is there anything that they can do that will injure you?'[13]

Hogue's immediate concern, he reported to Adolph Schmidt in Accra, was to keep Stehli 'from being connected with me'.[14] But he planned to continue with the local diamond buying operation. 'The chap running it is in this thing for patriotic purposes,' he pointed out, referring to Decoster, 'and I don't think he will be upset by anything that might happen. If I have to fade out, Stehli can simply act as an anchor for him, and give him the money if he gets a parcel.' In the meantime, Hogue was getting a visa for French Equatorial Africa. 'If things should turn disagreeable here,' he said, 'I'll transfer operations across the river.'[15]

He told Major Crocker, the British SIS official working on IDB, of his concerns and encouraged him to expedite his activities. 'I have advised VULCAN,' he reported to Schmidt, 'of the uncertainty of my position here at the moment, and urged him to push Rodrigues into the Eville country. There is no use to mark time.'[16] His conversation with Crocker had led to some interesting fresh information about British intelligence in the Congo:

> I have wondered for some months just whom the British had as intelligence here. It did not seem natural that they would not have someone. VULCAN told me openly, apparently assuming that I knew, that Kitts, the British Rubber director for French Equatorial Africa, keeps an eye on many things in this part of the world. Since Kitts and VULCAN work together, he is probably SIS.[17]

Kitts worked in Brazzaville, the capital of the AEF, but he lived in Léopoldville. Further investigation revealed that he was placing agents in Cabinda, an exclave province of Angola, as 'rubber men'.[18]

Hogue went down to Matadi to consult Monsieur De Gesnot, the Comptroller of Customs, to see if he had picked up any news—and he had. De Gesnot believed that the Governor General had discovered that Hogue was trying to get evidence on IDB by actual purchase, and this was causing worry among the 'higher-ups'. A rumour was also circulating that Léon P. Jacobs, the former Police Commissioner working at Matadi, was being watched. If Hogue's activities in Elisabethville *had* been exposed, warned De Gesnot, Lieutenant General Paul Ermens, the Commander-in-Chief of the Force Publique—who was now in Katanga—would have heard of it. He would then have notified Ryckmans that the American Government suspected diamond smuggling in the Congo. De Gesnot said he had been offered an attractive promotion, which he believed was 'simply to get him to keep his mouth shut'.[19]

It was always possible, speculated Hogue, that Decoster had become frustrated in his efforts to buy industrial stones and staged a 'one man propaganda campaign to bring the thing out in the open'. This, he reflected, would tie in with the fact that Arthur Brenez, the founder of *L'Avenir Colonial Belge*, a left-of-centre news-paper, had started talking in Léopoldville about diamond smuggling—because Brenez was a personal friend of Decoster.[20]

ANGELLA had another idea: that Decoster had not blown Hogue at all, but someone else had done it. 'There seem to be a lot of possible angles,' he told Schmidt, 'and I'm still in the dark.' He was going to get in touch with Peter Stephens at Elisabethville for 'all the gory details that he can rake up'. In fact, reflected Hogue hopefully, the situation might not be so bad after all. For if the Governor suspected industrial diamonds were reaching the enemy from the Belgian Congo, he would presumably try to do something about it. 'That,' he commented, 'goes back to one of the angles we discussed at Accra about bringing the thing out in the open. Of course, this is an unfortunate way to have it come out—.'[21]

Then Hogue sent a full report to Washington. 'My IDB work at Eville,' he announced, 'has been revealed. Have notified Accra I am going to keep LOCUST covered, even if it means leaving the Congo to do it. I will not be able to leave for Eville until I feel certain about the conditions here.'[22]

In the midst of this developing crisis, in the afternoon of 13 July 1944, Henry Stehli arrived on an ATC plane in the Congo, after a stop in Accra en route. He was immediately alerted to the new difficulties, but kept his cool. 'Everything,' he reported to Washington calmly, 'is going well.'[23] Hogue was delighted to see him. 'I feel a sudden decline in ambition,' he reported to Washington, 'and am sincerely glad that 923 is here full of vim, vigor, and vitality. I think you got him here at the proper time.'[24] Stehli also brought some comforting reminders of home, such as a suit for Hogue, sent by his wife.

It was essential, believed Hogue, that Stehli remain under cover until he was firmly entrenched and had many friends—'That's why I insist he go slowly now, and build up that cover. The textile idea is excellent.'[25]

Stehli quickly settled in at the American legation and took over the use of the truck. 'Until our staff increases, or something unforeseen happens,' reported Hogue, 'the two vehicles will be adequate.' It was planned that Stehli would take over the sedan when Hogue was out of the city. It would be a challenge, though, if the two men were going to share the vehicles in this way, to ensure that nobody guessed that they were working for the same outfit.

Meanwhile, Hogue was trying to find out what role Jean Beaudinet, the Chef de Sûreté in Léopoldville, had taken in recent events. He told OSS headquarters he would send material on this soon. 'Incidentally,' he added, 'Colette Finale has a very nice pair of legs, and is no mean dancer. You should meet her—.'[26] There is no way of interpreting this statement, since the identity of Colette Finale is unknown. However, an earlier report by Hogue to OSS shortly after his arrival in the Congo had referred to a letter to Colette Finale, which had been intercepted by censorship in Lisbon, revealing Axis sympathisers or agents—which had led to Hogue being followed by 'numerous individuals for days'.

Hogue was interested to learn that soon after Decoster was arrested, Harry Oppenheimer—the South African magnate and chairman of De Beers, who was also a director of Sibéka and Tanks—made a hurried visit to the Congo.[27]

Rudyerd Boulton wondered if there had been a 'double cross' by the British in the IDB investigation. This made sense to Hogue. 'I am wondering, as I sit and wait for news from Elisabethville,' he wrote four days after Stehli's arrival, 'if perhaps my "reported" exposure as an IDB agent might not be more of this same "double cross". Your para. 3 about "turning us in" may be just what has happened to me.' If this should prove to be true, he added, 'I'll shoot the first man who ever suggests again that I work "with the British".'[28]

His annoyance was not limited to the British, however. He was increasingly conscious of the difficulties created for OSS by the American Consul General. Vice Consul Cromie had complained in front of Benton that the Consul General was not getting to see paraphrases of the cables that he, Hogue, received from Washington. But, as Hogue was quick to point out to Cromie, his instructions did not allow him to reveal information received from Washington, and the same was true for LOCUST. 'It's a continual matter of standing your ground against Foreign Service penetration,' fumed Hogue, 'and I'm getting damned tired of it. We don't ask how they do their business, so why can't they leave us alone?'[29] Then he answered his own question:

> The root of evil is the 'Caste System' of the Foreign Service. If I am the Acting Consul, Consul, or Consul General, all Government employees here are under me. I'll stand no nonsense. You don't even have a grade—but me, I'm Rank 5. Frankly, 951, talk about a caste system in a democracy, just inspect the Foreign Service.

'To get my stuff out of here the past few months,' he added, 'I have used subterfuge—phony paraphrases, the Army pouch to Accra, the British pouch without going through our Consulate.' In his experience, he had met in the field only two Foreign Service officials who had expressed confidence in what OSS was trying to do. Most of them, he believed, 'are scared stiff that we're going to pull something that is going to reflect on them as individuals attached to the Consulate. I have tried to build up a feeling of confidence here in me personally. Am afraid I have not gotten very far.'[30]

Years later, in an interview, Adolph Schmidt echoed Hogue's description of the festering mistrust between State officials and OSS in the Congo. 'We have [consul general] in Léopoldville—fights us—we have separate [communications] which makes him believe we're reporting on him.'[31] The bad relations between the two groups were especially awkward, now that Hogue's position had become so unclear and precarious.

But Hogue, as always, wished to be fair. When Boulton expressed doubts about some of the information Hogue had provided, which had come from a source at the American legation, he defended its authenticity. 'You are wrong, old sock,' he told Boulton. 'The bulk of those opinions came from one of the best informed members of our Foreign Service here. He has reported very similarly to the State Department. Notice the underlining.'[32]

At around this time there was an attempt on Hogue's life with a bomb.[33] The source of this information is reliable, but no details are available in any documents that have been released.[34] Nonetheless, it is clear that this marked a watershed moment in Hogue's mission in the Congo.

At the start of July, the OSS station in Léopoldville had looked set to grow in size and strength. But now Hogue realised that he might need to leave the Congo at short notice and return to the US. He was willing to take a trip up through Liberia first, 'to see what is cooking there'; but his preference, he told Boulton, would be to take the boat directly from the port of Matadi to New York—a trip of about seventeen days.[35] Whatever happened, he was adamant that he would not leave Stehli until he was firmly entrenched. It is clear that Stehli was fully briefed on the uranium issue. But, Hogue told Boulton, he would not allow him to get involved in the diamond buying operation, because of the danger involved—unless Washington sent instructions to the contrary.

'Let me repeat,' he told Boulton, 'I think you made a good choice in 923, and I'm happy to have him here. He thinks you're tops, and I know you'll make a good team.' Then Hogue made a wry comment on his own predicament: 'This isn't a benediction even if it sounds like one. I'm still around—and out of jail.'[36]

Stehli's arrival had been a godsend, not least because of his steady, sensible approach to problems, which calmed the feverish atmosphere. Despite the fact that he had been accustomed throughout his life to a large household of servants, he found it easy to fit in and to defer to Hogue as chief of station.[37] The three members of the OSS team were already cooperating well together and Hogue parried Boulton's instructions to provide Stehli with mentorship. 'As far as my imparting much to him', he wrote:

> that's limited. Like life, much of what little I know can be learned only by experience. 923 will have to get that experience. I get what you mean, however, although you express it like a college professor. Why not just say, 'be a father to him'?[38]

A note of irritation entered into his letter to Boulton, who was sending so many orders, from so far away. 'All our work here is coordinated,' he wrote firmly. 'Do not concern yourselves with us.'[39]

Boulton fully agreed with Hogue that Stehli should not engage in the IDB operation. On 25 July he sent Stehli an urgent cable, instructing him to terminate immediately 'all questions or references relative to the industrial diamond program to anyone in the Congo. Stop IDB purchase program and investigation until you are notified further.'[40]

Hogue was starting to suspect that Decoster had not, after all, been a good choice of cutout. It looked increasingly as if Decoster had decided to bear the brunt of the work himself, instead of getting an organisation together, as he and Hogue had agreed. Decoster owned property at Dilolo and also at Luluabourg, which gave him an excuse to travel. But Luluabourg was now a hotbed, having been the scene of the mutiny, and was also right on the edge of the diamond fields. As soon as Decoster had arrived there, he was followed continually by the Sûreté, who then picked him up after five days; presumably he had been hot on the trail of something. 'Just how I was blown,' wondered Hogue, 'I don't know. The old man has plenty of guts, but he was undoubtedly pressured pretty hard.'[41]

Decoster faced a possible jail sentence of five years if convicted of being an agent of a foreign intelligence officer. He was fighting mad at the Sûreté, reported Hogue, and was not in jail. The public prosecutor's department, the Parquet, was investigating his finances of the past few years; 'He is a rabid Socialist, and they would naturally like to hang something serious on him.' But Decoster had not appealed to Hogue for any help and there was no evidence connecting the two men except his word, which Hogue guessed had been dragged out of him under pressure. The whole story seemed to have circulated widely and Hogue heard that Beaudinet had been making fun of him. But, suspected Hogue, Beaudinet was worried about how much he, Hogue, knew about his role in IDB and the big cut he got from protecting Jacobs, the former Police Commissioner—who was supposed to be looking out for Nazi spies at Matadi, but was actually involved in smuggling.

In Liberia, Hogue had gained a reputation for selecting and indoctrinating excellent cutouts, which had ensured the success of his mission there. But he felt he had failed in the Congo. 'Now, for the sake of people who will come after me,' he mused to Boulton with his usual candour, reflecting on what he had been taught at the OSS training school, 'let us remember this, and point it out to fellows at school. My man was unimpeachable from the standpoint of being *with us*. He got caught because he was *too prominent*. Everybody knew him—especially the Sûreté.' But also, he added, no one should have to attempt a job as delicate as selecting a cutout and setting up something like an IDB outfit, without at least months of residence in that part of the country—'I had ten days. This is not an effort to excuse my blundering. I muffed the job, and will take the responsibility. The point is—we must not have it repeated somewhere else.'

He had decided to make Beaudinet think he knew a lot—'I can weather the storm better on that basis than any other.' Formerly, he commented to Boulton in a long pouch letter, a strategy like that 'would have been a sure way to cut my throat. Now that it is cut, it doesn't make much difference.'[42] What he didn't tell Boulton was that someone had tried to kill him. 'Think I'd better wind this up, 951,' he wrote, with feeling. 'Good luck to you, although I need it most. Two Five Three.'[43]

14

'HOTBED OF SPIES'

Three days after Hogue's activities in Elisabethville were blown open in the Congo, Adolph Schmidt left Accra for Washington, as planned, to serve as Rud Boulton's second-in-command—Assistant Deputy Chief of the Africa Division.[1] Before leaving, he reported to OSS headquarters that no uranium ore had been diverted from the Katanga mines to the enemy in the previous six months.[2] Schmidt's report, comments his biographer, must have brought relief 'to the few in Washington worriedly convinced there was a desperate race over developing the ultimate weapon first'.[3]

But the uranium mission was far from over. It was still an urgent priority for OSS to make sure that Germany was not getting hold of any of the high quality uranium at Shinkolobwe. It was also of vital importance that the US was able to obtain all the available uranium from this mine.

This created a further imperative—to prevent sabotage by Axis agents. The Allies had themselves used sabotage raids very effectively, to destroy the Germans' source of heavy water—the Vemork Norsk Hydro plant in the county of Telemark in Norway. The heavy water was essential to the operation of a nuclear reactor: and although the development of a reactor did not guarantee the building of an atomic bomb, it increased its possibility. If the

Allies could undermine the Germans' atomic bomb project by commando raids on the Norwegian heavy water plant, so could the Germans wreck the Manhattan Project by sabotaging the mine at Shinkolobwe, the trains and barges taking the uranium ore to Matadi, and even the port itself.

The central importance of uranium created an unusual and tense situation at the US Consulate General in Léopoldville, where invoices for uranium were signed and transportation arrangements were made. This was witnessed by Robert–'Bob'– Laxalt, a fresh-faced and clean-cut 20-old code officer from Nevada, who arrived in Léopoldville to work for the US legation in June 1944.

Laxalt had been disqualified from military service because of a heart murmur, which led to personal and bitter disappointment, in terms of his wish to serve his country. But it also–unfairly–led to accusations of cowardice from the local public, which caused him great anguish. Determined to prove that he was not a coward, Laxalt implored the State Department to assign him to some kind of war service overseas. He finally persuaded them and was accepted for training in their confidential cryptography section in Washington. He was then posted to the Belgian Congo.

After the war he became a newspaper reporter and a well respected author. One of his last books was a memoir about his war service in West Africa, entitled *A Private War: An American Code Officer in the Belgian Congo*. To write the book, he drew heavily on a diary of his daily life which he had kept in Léopoldville.[4] 'This is a record of that time,' he wrote at the start of *A Private War*, 'drawn from a journal I more or less kept, entries expanded upon and memories they triggered.' It has not been possible to trace this journal, even with the assistance of the Special Collections Department at the University of Nevada, which holds his papers.[5] But efforts to check out the information in the memoir demonstrate that it is rooted in actual fact; contemporary sources, such as passenger lists for boats, confirm the accuracy of the details given by Laxalt. The information he gives can therefore be regarded as authoritative and reliable.

The memoir gives a vivid picture of life at the Consulate General, which was located on a street housing other foreign embassies. Coming from a very small town in the USA, Laxalt was impressed at first by the:

> formal manners, polite laughter, serious conversations about world politics, evening dress of tropical white gowns and tuxedos, sultry flirtations and arranged rendez-vous, violin and string instruments playing the background, champagne and Irish whiskey, Scotch and Russian vodka.

But he soon discovered that the polished atmosphere was not what it seemed—and that the legations were busily spying on each other at these 'interminable soirées'.[6]

Laxalt had a strong sense of justice and was appalled by the racism he found in Léopoldville, which he quietly resisted wherever he could. He was aghast at the assumption of whites that blacks were immune to malaria. Whenever he saw someone in the 'native' compound with symptoms of malaria, he would dose him with quinine, 'against all rules'. Just one dose, he reported, would cut the attack short.[7]

In his memoir, Laxalt thinly disguised the legation staff by giving them pseudonyms, which bore a link of some kind to their real names. 'The consul general, whom I will call J. Wesley Hale,' he wrote, 'did not inquire too deeply into the legation's affairs.' This was J. Webb Benton, who had taken over from Mallon in late April, and of whom Laxalt had a low opinion. Benton devoted his time to the social whirl—and 'since most of the legation's society gossip came from him to me for coding', wrote Laxalt, he got to know a lot about him. Benton's chief source was the wife of a Belgian official, with whom he was having an affair. Everybody on Legation Row knew about Benton's 'torrid affair', observed Laxalt, 'but nobody cared. From what I could gather, this kind of relationship was not unusual in the world of diplomacy.' In any case, added Laxalt, the Consul General's reports 'sometimes bore important intelligence inadvertently placed in the context of general gossip'.[8]

Because Benton—or 'Hale'—was frequently away from the office, the legation was largely run by a Vice Consul, to whom Laxalt refers as 'Harry Wolfe'—'a Princeton graduate for whom the Foreign Service had long been a calling'. This was Harry H. Schwartz, who said after the war that his consular role in the Congo involved signing invoices for uranium, which he later learned was destined for the Manhattan Project.[9] Schwartz was 'a tall, rangy man with sandy hair and blue eyes that advertised frankness in diplomatic affairs', who was in love with a woman in Spain called Maria, whom he had met when stationed in Madrid. They had been separated by the war and their plans for marriage interrupted. But they were so much in love that they decided to enact a special ceremony on Christmas Eve 1944 to commit their lives to each other—even though 'Wolfe' was in the Congo and Maria was in Andalucía. Laxalt was a witness to this symbolic marriage, which took place in Léopoldville at a Catholic church. A religious aura was cast over the ceremony by a children's choir practising for High Mass on Christmas Day. 'Even though their native tongue was Swahili', observed Laxalt, 'their accents were in perfect Latin, drummed into them by missionary priests', and their choral hymns were beautiful.

'Two lives separated by war,' observed Laxalt with feeling, 'had been joined at two separate altars in two separate countries.'[10]

The economic attaché to the Consulate General was 'Dan Weathers'—'a burly man who was not an Ivy League product, and showed it. He dealt with his counterparts in business and economics in a bullying manner.' This was Charles Dudley Withers, who was on the staff of the FEA and who had taken Henry Stehli under his wing. Withers, whose father was a car salesman, had been born and raised in Greenville, South Carolina; he had attended university in Greenville and in Lexington, Virginia. Laxalt was pleased that his own work was not concerned with business and economics, so that he was 'mercifully' spared the company of Withers most of the time.

But although Withers was disliked by Laxalt and, as Hogue observed, some others of his male colleagues, he was admired by a very beautiful war widow: Virginia Jane Newkirk, whose husband, Jack was a fighter pilot killed in action in 1942. Jane Newkirk, described by her first husband as a 'willowy blonde', worked in Léopoldville as a stenographer.[11] Later that year—on 16 December 1944, just a week after the symbolic ceremony between Schwartz and Maria—Withers and Newkirk were married by Consul General Benton, at the Office of Civil Administration in Léopoldville.

Of two secretaries in the office, one was a woman, named by Laxalt as 'Joselle', of mixed French and Arab blood. She was 'multilingual, an invaluable asset to anyone working with a handful of nationalists at the same time'. Laxalt suspected that she was in love with Schwartz, who had no time for any woman but Maria.

Another member of staff was 'a barefoot young black whose Swahili name was Mbote'. He had stumbled into the Legation by accident, when he had come into Léopoldville from the bush to look around the city. He was immediately employed as an errand 'boy'. Mbote learned some American ways, but did not 'rid himself of native habits', according to Laxalt. Whenever he was asked to go to the post office for stamps, he would return with them 'at a dog trot, the stamps held to the top of his head by a rock. The system worked. He never lost a stamp.'[12]

An American visitor to the Consulate, wrote Laxalt, was 'Doc Pogue', who 'drifted into the legation only on rare occasion, spent some time with Harry behind closed doors, and nodded to us on his way out.' This was Dock Hogue. Schwartz told Laxalt nothing about Hogue's function in the legation, just saying airily that 'Doc Pogue' was attached to the Office of War Information and that his job was to disseminate American propaganda in the Congo. Laxalt thought this odd; putting out propaganda to a supposedly friendly nation didn't make much sense. Nor, he thought, did the stream of American visitors to the legation make any sense. They all seemed to him to be cut from the same cloth: 'quiet men who didn't bother to exchange more than a greeting to the legation staff'. He wondered why so much attention was being paid to a small consular office in a colony so far from the theatre of war.

But one day in July, his second month of work, he was called in for a meeting, when Hogue introduced him to a man he hadn't seen before. 'Bob,' he said, 'this quiet man here is Paul Cromie. He's attached to the Office of Strategic Services. What the OSS does is no secret in the government. It's the intelligence arm of the United States.' Then he put his cards on the table. 'You might as well know,' he said:

> that I'm with the OSS, too. Both Paul and I trained under Wild Bill Donovan. You might as well know, too, that we are the last living agents in Donovan's first corps of trainees. Our numbers are just about up, I kid you not. But we knew the odds when we signed on.[13]

'Paul Cromie', noted Laxalt, 'was a sturdily built and handsome man cast in a hardened mold', who crossed the room briskly to shake his hand. This was Henry Stehli. The disguise given to him by Laxalt suggests the writer confused Stehli with one of the Vice Consuls, Leonard J. Cromie. This is an understandable confusion, given that Benton had given Leonard Cromie's room to Stehli when he arrived;[14] as well, Laxalt was low down in the hierarchy and could easily have confused the more senior staff.

Hogue and Stehli hadn't wanted or expected to tell Laxalt they worked for OSS, because of the danger involved. 'This place,' warned Schwartz, 'is crawling with Nazi spies.' But they had no choice, because their code man had succumbed to malaria and they needed Laxalt to code for them, until they could smuggle one of their own code men into the Congo operation. He was told not to ask any questions: 'For your own sake, it's better that you don't know.'[15]

Laxalt agreed readily. But as he walked back to the vice-consul quarters that he shared with Schwartz and Withers, he felt bewildered. Two big questions remained unanswered, to which he drew attention in his memoir by writing in italics. 'Why,' he asked, 'is the Congo suddenly important enough to be a hotbed of spies? What was here in a dark corner of darkest Africa that was important enough to set American spies at odds with the Belgian government-in-residence?'[16]

There was 'no shortage of counterspies in Leopoldville,' believed Laxalt. 'Nazi Germany was making sure of that. They revealed themselves often.' Even the cleverest of agents, he noticed, slipped at times into their native language at the endless soirées 'that to me, at least, are a plague upon the diplomatic life.' After enduring a number of these occasions, he used any excuse he could think of to avoid going to any more of them. He was not, he reflected, 'in the business of gathering morsels of information ... The days of Mata Hari and the BIG SECRET were long past.'[17]

But the days of the BIG SECRET were by no means past for Hogue, Stehli and Chidsey. For them, the business of gathering morsels of information was a fundamental part of their work. For the most part, they were looking not so much for Germans who may have clandestinely entered the Congo to spy, as for Belgian and Portuguese people living in the Congo who were Nazi sympathisers and potential collaborators with the Third Reich. Hogue had already learned that Belgian government officials, including the Chief of Police, were suspected of smuggling and collaborating with the Nazis; and he had strong suspicions about prominent businessmen.

British intelligence in London was observing an intense interest on the part of the Abwehr—German military intelligence—in the Belgian Congo, in information derived from its 'Most Secret Sources'. In July 1943, a senior MI5 official, who was responsible for communications with double agents and counter-espionage, wrote a report on 'German Interest in the Belgian Congo'. It observed that the German Secret Service had been taking 'a constant interest' in the Belgian Congo since early 1941 and possibly even earlier, and had attempted to insert agents 'of fairly high calibre', equipped with secret means of communication; in one case, the agent was equipped with W/T (Wireless/Telegraph).[18] Guy Liddell, MI5's Director of Counter-Espionage during the war, discovered from a double agent codenamed WEASEL that he had been asked to go to the Congo by the Germans, but had refused.[19]

A prisoner captured by the British, named Pierre Hermant, revealed under interrogation that he had been trained in December 1940 to work for the Abwehr in the Congo. Hermant was to send information by wireless transmitter, including armament production, military details, departures of ships and their cargoes, imports and exports. It was understood that he had come to the UK, the home of the Belgian government-in-exile, in order to get a visa for the Belgian Congo, as he had made all the necessary arrangements to go there.[20]

Another prisoner, Hans de Meiss-Teuffen, had left for the Belgian Congo on 18 September 1941, to report 'on economic matters'. 'Our branch is interested only in economic research,' he had been instructed by his German handler. They wanted to know:

> if the enemy is developing new industries or sources of raw materials, and where, and what kind. We want to know how he uses them, where he ships them, how he processes them. That's why we want to send you to Rhodesia and the Congo. If our agents see anything of importance—new harbour installations, railroads, airports, dry docks, bridges, factories—they report it to us.

As he was an experienced sailor, the German Navy was looking for a sail-boat for him, so that he could spy on activity on the coast and in the ports. 'On your trip along the African west coast,' he was ordered, 'you'll have many opportunities to observe such matters. You'll probably see convoys and warships, and in the ports you'll find many installations of interest.'[21]

Another German spy captured by the British was Dr Hilaire Westerlinck, an agent of the Abwehr, who had been ordered to proceed to the Belgian Congo. He had arrived in Britain with a comprehensive questionnaire, the answers to which he was 'to transmit to the Germans by means of secret writing'.[22] Before he was caught in London, Westerlinck had been under the management of GRIMM, who had established a network of Abwehr agents in Lisbon, Madeira and Portuguese Africa. One of the agents in Portuguese West Africa controlled agents in the Belgian Congo—but no record of their details is available.[23]

By May 1943, it was obvious to MI5 officials that the Germans were very interested in the Belgian Congo which, they said, seemed 'rather unaccountable to us'. One German agent detained in the UK had said he was supposed to discover the effects of American and British political and economic influence on the Congo, and with what types of production they were concerned. He was also required to find out whether the Americans or British had any plans to detach the Belgian Congo from Belgium. The base of his movements would be Matadi or Boma, a port further up the Congo River.[24] Another agent, Pierre Neukermans, was a Belgian who had been recruited by German Intelligence and arrived in Britain in 1943. He claimed to have escaped from the Nazis and to be eager to help the Allied cause. But he admitted, after interrogation, that he had sent letters to an address in a neutral country, detailing convoy movements from there to the Belgian Congo. He was executed at Pentonville Prison in London in June 1944.[25]

MI5 officials assumed that if the American authorities were told of these cases, they would be 'quite willing' to send an American security official, 'probably FBI', to the Belgian Congo. The reasons for this assumption, explained a note written by a senior official, were that 'American interests are in fact predominant in the Belgian Congo whether from the point of view of supply or military considerations'. This note was written 'simply to place on record the evidence we possess of intense German interest in this area and by inference the necessity of covering the situation in some way'—and whether, if the British were unwilling to force the issue with the Belgian authorities, the Americans would, 'in all probability, be willing to do so'.

Given the reference in this note to the FBI, it appears that its author was unaware of OSS activity in the Congo. But someone in the know added a handwritten comment: 'Donovan not FBI'.[26]

15

FRAMED

As July wore on, Hogue became acutely conscious of the predicament he was in. 'If the officials can ever determine just how much I know,' he warned Boulton, 'they'll throw me out of the Congo. There is no question about that in my mind. They're leery of possible knowledge I may possess right now.'[1] Nevertheless, the Decoster matter went strangely quiet, so Hogue made plans for a two-week trip to Katanga. 'By doing it this way,' he told Boulton, 'I can get into Eville before the Sûreté know I've left Leopoldville, and be gone before they get some Joe on my trail. I will not try to see Decoster personally unless certain people in Eville recommend it.'[2] After Katanga, he would go on to Accra: he was keen to discuss matters with Hunt Harris, who was now in the Gold Coast and head of the OSS operation in West Africa.

'TETON departed this date for Elizabethville to investigate activities there,' reported Stehli on 26 July 1944 to Washington. 'About August 1st he is expected to arrive in Accra to confer with EBERT [Huntington Harris], coming back here August 7th. In accordance with instructions from TETON, I will use this time working out my cover.'[3] These instructions had been set out by Hogue in an informal, but very clear, list:

Spend considerable time developing your cover in textiles, especially silk. Take the ferry to Brazzaville and spend part or most of a day wandering around. Everyone does this when they first come to Leo. Take Mrs. Chidsey with you if you wish as she knows the ropes. Don't forget your Yellow Fever certificate. Have Withers take you to the Police Station an afternoon early this week to get your driver's license. I have already spoken to him about it.

Stehli's sociability, realised Hogue, would be an asset. 'Get acquainted with Wollants,' he advised, referring to a prominent Belgian—'he knows a lot. He has a very nice wife, so if you invite him out, include her.' If Stehli needed any files or newspaper material, he added, ANGELLA would probably be able to dig them up. He also suggested that Stehli take George M. Saks, the Jewish businessman who had been forced to leave France in 1940, out to lunch; Saks, he assured him, would be a good source of information. Finally, he told Stehli to go to the golf club and to play with everyone possible. The fact that Stehli was so eminently clubbable, thought Hogue with satisfaction, could be very useful.

The Decoster affair was a priority. 'Keep your ears open for anything on Decoster on the Eville picture', urged Hogue, adding that he should not be upset by anything unpleasant he might hear. 'Remember,' he cautioned him, 'you and I have no connection as far as the Congo is concerned.'

Hogue's activities were being carefully watched by British officials. On 30 July, Francis M. Shepherd, the British Consul General in Léopoldville, sent a copy of Stephens's earlier report on the Decoster affair to the Permanent Under Secretary of State in the Foreign Office in London. Hogue, observed Shepherd in a covering letter, 'is a very decent sort of chap but he seems to have overreached himself this time'. He wryly noted Hogue's evident reluctance to leave Decoster to get out of the mess—'a piece of tender-heartedness of which I had thought his service would have been innocent'. Hogue was now, he added, thinking of 'fading out' altogether, 'while Stehli remains in Leopoldville with an enquiry into Congo textile stocks as cover'.[4]

Hogue was annoyed to hear that the British were criticising his choice of Decoster. 'All right, if they know so much about the

Congo,' he objected to Boulton, 'why weren't they in here on IDB instead of getting me in it against personal wishes which I expressed to you last fall?' The answer to this, he said, was that the diamond companies, through the Belgian government, had given them orders. In other words, he added, 'it was decided long ago (and we assume up at the top) that the biggest producer of industrial diamonds was *not* to be investigated'.[5]

There are several communications in this period between Léopoldville and Washington that cannot be understood, even after decryption, without the inside knowledge shared by Hogue and Washington. As a result, it is not possible to get a full picture of what was going on. One example is a baffling pouch letter from Hogue to Boulton in August 1944: 'I haven't been able to get any of the iced lobster, but Information Item No. 295 which ANGELLA brewed up will give you a slant on this—perfume or butter?' The reference to lobster is followed by two further obscure sentences: 'Tell the big fellow that I have the ivory salt dishes but have had no way to send them. Will bring them with me if I get out of here all in one piece.'[6]

When Hogue left Léopoldville on 26 August, he made sure that nobody knew he was going unless it was strictly necessary. He was particularly keen to ensure that the Sûreté would not know he was in Elisabethville for at least a few hours after his arrival, so did not wire for a room at the hotel. But fortunately, the cutout Jaubert was staying there already, and had a double room, which would give him somewhere to stay. When Hogue arrived at the hotel, the clerk recognised him, so he just left his luggage and took off: 'Three hours was all I needed,' he reported to Boulton, 'and I got my work done.' But it is impossible to know what this 'work' was: there is no record of it anywhere. Once again, the gaps in information created by the secrecy of the uranium project make it impossible to know exactly what Hogue was doing and the nature of the risks he was taking.

He returned to the hotel at 6:00 p.m. and the Sûreté was waiting for him, 'in the person of Brother Beaudinet himself'. They exchanged greetings—'and for the rest of the evening I was tailed. It made no difference as my work was done. I left early the next morning.' He did not visit Decoster, whom he assumed was being watched. However, he set up a system of communication and signals, in the hope that Decoster would be able to share any information he had. He was relieved to hear from his sources in the city that Decoster was not in too bad a spot.

Then he went on to Accra. Harris invited him to stay with him and Mary in their house, but he chose instead to stay at the Transient Camp.[7] Perhaps, like Schmidt, he was not altogether happy at the idea of mixing domesticity with the serious business of espionage.

While TETON was away, LOCUST diligently followed his instructions. First he took George Saks out for a 'good luncheon' on Thursday 27 July, to see what he could find out from him. For this purpose, he expanded on his cover story: he told Saks that he had offered his services to the government, and that when the State Department had asked him to come out as Benton's assistant, he had accepted. He showed great interest in textiles, which in any case was genuine, and Saks said he would arrange for him to visit the big textile factory, Utexleo. This led to a discussion of diamonds and Saks said he was 'astonished' that Stehli did not know the 'whole diamond story'. From this point, Stehli started to suspect that when Saks was talking about diamonds, he was in fact talking about uranium, which led to a perplexing conversation.

Saks explained that the British had an annual contract with the Congo to purchase their total output of diamonds, which was renewed each September; he was surprised that the State Department did not have a copy of this contract and offered to get hold of it for a few hours 'so that we could either Photostat it or copy it'. When Stehli suggested that a copy of the contract would be worth quite a lot of money, Saks insisted that the US had been good to him and that he would not accept any payment under any circumstances—except perhaps a high priority to return home when the time came. Stehli later discussed this with Benton (without giving away Saks's name), who said that he would give Saks a No. 2 priority on his own responsibility, if he really did provide a true copy of the contract.

Saks advised Stehli to look up 'the North American Purchasing Company, which has been formed in New York City for the purpose of purchasing all USA supplies for both Belgium and the Belgian Congo after the war'. The Board of Directors of this company, Saks told him, represented most of the big commercial interests in the Congo, since Société Générale was on the Board, as well as the Banque de Bruxelles and the Empain Group. Here, Saks was most likely referring to African Metals Corporation, also known as Afrimet, which had been specially set up in New York as the commercial arm of Union Minière to arrange the sale of uranium ore and its transport to the USA.

After lunch, the two men went to Saks's house to have a brandy and Stehli asked Saks what he thought Hogue was doing in Léopoldville; he himself, he said, was mystified. Saks told him that Hogue was working for 'that small organisation in Washington called the "Strategic Services something-or-other" and had to do with valuable raw materials'. 'Finally,' reflected Stehli in a report on the lunch to Washington, 'who fooled who at this luncheon I am not sure.'

A week after this lunch, at 11:30 a.m. on Thursday 4 August, Stehli went with Benton to Ryckmans's office, for an official introduction to the Governor General. Stehli stayed for just a few moments after the introduction had been made, then left Benton alone with Ryckmans.

When Benton emerged, he told Stehli that Ryckmans had received information that a person named Decoster had been arrested by the Sûreté in Elisabethville, and that when Decoster's house was searched, they found 100,000 Belgian Congo francs with a note that all this money was for services in connection with a man called Hogue. The Sûreté also found a list of suspects which Ryckmans believed had been given to Decoster by Hogue, because it was written on Hogue's typewriter. On this list was the name of a magistrate named Etienne De Clerck, based in Elisabethville—and this had offended Ryckmans, since De Clerck was a servant of the government. He wanted to know, he had told Benton in no uncertain terms, how De Clerck's name had got on the list. He did not explain why or how the Sûreté knew anything about Hogue's typewriter.

Benton had then asked Ryckmans if he felt that 'a man named Hogue' was *persona non grata* in the Congo, to which Ryckmans nodded his head vigorously. This 'excited Benton very much' and he told Stehli that he wanted a meeting with Hogue as soon as possible.

The meeting took place at 10:15 on Monday August 7. Hogue had flown back from Accra the day before, to find LOCUST quite upset because, as he put it, 'at last the boom had been lowered' on Hogue. 'I realized of course,' Hogue told Boulton, 'that I must be very careful with Mr. Benton. Having tangled with the Department of State in Liberia, and having come off second best, I did not want to repeat this.' He prepared carefully for the meeting.

Benton repeated to Hogue everything he had told Stehli the day before, following his conversation with Ryckmans. Hogue immediately suspected it was a frame-up. For one thing, Decoster had been given nothing bearing Hogue's name or written on Hogue's typewriter. They had never even been seen together except in public, in a group of people. On top of this, it was impossible that the whole of the sum of 100,000 francs had been found in Decoster's house, since he had already spent a part of it.[8]

Then Benton told Hogue that Ryckmans wanted him to leave the colony immediately. But Hogue resisted. He had been assigned to the Congo by OSS, he reminded him, so could not leave until he was instructed to do so by his superiors. Nor could he leave without being notified in writing by the Governor General that he was *persona non grata*. Then Hogue made a smart move: he offered to give Benton his resignation as Special Assistant to the American Consul, which was his cover, and fall back on his *true* position as OSS station chief. In that way, he pointed out, the Governor General would have to deal with him directly. Benton demurred. He did not want to agree to this, because he had given the Governor General the impression that OSS was under the Department of State.

Hogue then negotiated. He told Benton that he would like to remain in the Congo until the end of his year of service in the Congo, which had started with his departure from Washington on 18 September 1943. If the Governor General would agree to this and take no official action against him, he would prepare for him a confidential and secret report on the industrial diamond situation in the Congo, complete with a list of suspects. Benton agreed to make this proposal to the Governor General, on an unofficial basis.

Ryckmans accepted the plan, but was emphatic that Hogue must be gone by 18 September. 'I can understand his position,' observed Hogue thoughtfully in a report to OSS. 'He is undoubtedly being pressured by a lot of people to get rid of me.' Hogue added that he could also understand the difficulties of Benton's position.[9]

Benton sent a cable to the State Department on 7 August, reporting on the situation that had developed. The Governor General, he said, was especially disturbed by the list of suspects found in Decoster's effects. 'It is most regrettable,' he stated, 'that the name of De Clerck, who is respected everywhere in Elisabethville, was mentioned on this list. Hogue made a poor choice of confidential agent also when he picked De Coster [sic] whom the local police consider very untrustworthy and have been observing for some time.' Consequently, he went on, the Governor General had said that the presence of Hogue was no longer desirable, but was prepared to wait until he had finished his tour of duty on 17 September.

'I know that Stehli is not mired up in this,' added Benton, 'and, as far as I know, he is not suspected.'[10] Evidently, Hogue had been successful in his efforts to ensure that Stehli was not associated with his special mission in the eyes of others.

Hogue was conscious that the difficulties in the Congo were potentially a cause of embarrassment to OSS. He therefore wrote to Boulton to say that he was willing to resign. Making such a decision must have been painful and tough, given that Hogue had dedicated his life to OSS for nearly two and a half years, at great risk to his safety and his health. But he wanted to do the right thing and went ahead: 'You have herewith my resignation from the organization effective upon my arrival in the United States—or, if so desired, can be dated back to August 1, 1944.'[11]

In the midst of these tense developments, an edge was creeping into communications between Hogue and Boulton. 'As far as my admiration for certain personalities blinding me,' wrote Hogue to Boulton, evidently in response to a suggestion that this was so, 'I don't think that's quite true.' There was only one person, he added bluntly, who was more suspicious of the human race than he was: '—that is yourself. There's a difference there, however. I force myself to be that way. For a successful psychologist it comes natural.'[12] At this point, Hogue's enthusiasm for the life of a spy—with its need for suspicion and mistrust—appears to have been wearing thin.

Hogue also defended Stehli against criticism of some cables he had sent, taking full responsibility for them. 'I am sorry that you were upset by 923's cables,' he retorted. 'Until I left here on July 25th, all his cables were sent at my instruction. I was too busy to do much enciphering, and I felt he needed the practice. Please be assured that 923 is very good about conferring with me before he does anything.'[13] As far as Hogue was concerned, Stehli was an excellent agent and colleague. It was sufficient at this point, he observed:

> to merely say that I approve your choice. As for plans for him, now that I am dead and buried, he must carry on as OSS representative in the Congo. I think he would be the first to assure you that I *am* indoctrinating him. Right at the moment he has as his chief a splendid example of what *not* to do to be a successful agent.[14]

But he planned to carry on with his assignment: 'I'll carry this phase on. It can't hurt me now, or us.'[15]

*

Just less than a week after Hogue's awkward and difficult meeting on Sunday 12 August with Benton, the American Consul General, a party was hosted in Léopoldville by A. S. Gerard and his wife for Firmin Van Bree, who had by now succeeded Félicien Cattier as President of Union Minière in Brussels; Gerard was Van Bree's right-hand man. At the party Benton asked Van Bree point blank, reported Stehli, whether or not he had been in England on a recent trip in Europe—and Van Bree said he had not.[16] Benton was evidently following up on the suspicions held by the US pertaining to Van Bree—suspicions that were very much shared by Hogue. Benton and Hogue were both working hard on the same side, even if at this point in time the Consul General was finding it hard to tolerate the OSS station chief.

Hunt Harris flew to Léopoldville for discussions with Hogue—a visit that was greatly appreciated. 'It gave me a boost,' wrote Hogue after he had left, 'which has been of great help. I think that 923 and ANGELLA feel the same way. Hope you'll come again.'[17]

At about 9:00 on Tuesday 22 August, Hogue presented his card to the secretary of Monsieur Brouxhon, the public prosecutor at the Parquet de 1er Instance—the Court of First Instance—in Kalina; he noticed she was black, which was unusual for official staff. He was promptly admitted to Brouxhon's office. After the usual elegant formalities, Brouxhon said he had received some questions from the attorney for the crown at Luluabourg, and wondered if Hogue would be kind enough to answer them, swearing to tell 'the whole truth and nothing but the truth'. Hogue agreed, with the proviso that he could not answer anything of an official nature.

The questions concerned Decoster. 'Do you know Jean Decoster, and how did you meet him?' asked Brouxhon, to which Hogue replied, 'I met him when I went to his office in Elisabethville to subscribe to his newspaper, *L'Echo du Katanga*.'

Then Brouxhon asked, 'Did he ever represent himself in any capacity other than as a newspaper editor?' Hogue answered no.

The other questions concerned the funds supposedly found in Decoster's house, which Hogue refused to answer on the grounds that they involved official activity, which he was not at liberty to discuss. Brouxhon agreed that this was fair enough. But one of the questions was extremely interesting, thought Hogue. This asked for a physical description of the funds that he had apparently given to Decoster: 'Did you give this money to Decoster in the form of large or small bank notes, or by draft?' This supported Hogue's contention that the Sûreté had never found 100,000 francs at all, but merely used the confession forced from Decoster as a basis for their complaint to the Governor General.

After the interrogation was over, Brouxhon commented that Hogue was certainly non-committal. Hogue then offered to have an informal, off- the-record, chat with him, if he would ask his interpreter, who was taking shorthand, to leave the room. Brouxhon agreed. Hogue then asked if it was known that some of his activity was as an American Intelligence Officer. Brouxhon acknowledged that it was, adding that as far as he knew there was no criticism of his conduct. At this point, Hogue said he wished to take an oath that no Belgian in the Congo had ever been paid by him to act as an agent or informer. He repeated this three times in order to convince Brouxhon, pointing out that the prosecution of any Belgian who claimed to have assisted him against their common enemy was something that neither the US government, nor himself, would like at all. Hogue—showing the 'tender-hearted' quality observed by the British Consul General—was determined to protect Decoster to his utmost. But in any case, it was quite true that he had not paid a Belgian in the Congo: he had paid Portuguese informers, but the Belgians had worked voluntarily except for expense money.

Hogue wrote to Harris to report on his 'grand jury summons'. He also said that he was making plans for an imminent departure from the Congo. 'Well,' he wrote, 'a phone call from Matadi this morning tells me that I must go down there on the Friday train. I have had no direct orders from Washington yet, but since we feel it is best to go, I know Washington will understand.'[18] Despite the pressure Hogue was under, he made a point of expressing his gratitude to Harris for his help: 'Give my regards to your charming wife and to the fellows with you. Will write you from Washington. Again let me thank you for your encouragement and support.'[19]

A major concern for Hogue was ANGELLA's position. She had said she was willing to stay on as long as Stehli needed her services, but was ready for a change—she had been in West Africa for nearly two years. Perhaps, too, she did not want to stay on in the Congo without Hogue. Ideally, she wanted to be considered for her old position with OSS in New York. If that was not possible, she was willing to go anywhere, so long as she could have a government rating and, preferably, remain with OSS.

If ANGELLA were to go back to the US, she would need to get a flight with Air Transport Command. This was difficult enough for men, but far more difficult for women—and had prevented Mary Harris from flying with Hunt on the journey from Lourenço Marques to Accra. But Hogue was hopeful that she had a chance. 'After six months service with us,' he thought, 'she should be made eligible for ATC transportation to the United States. ATC is now carrying a limited number of missionary nurses returning to the U.S. I personally feel that her services merit this consideration.'[20] Her work, he said, was very good:

> ANGELLA has tapped a mine of information in Poskin, the news editor of *L'Avenir Colonial Belge*. So, except for the Chief who can't stay out of trouble, things are going along pretty well. I am being snubbed by the 'big shots' now. Rather amusing.[21]

He had paid ANGELLA's August salary, as he wanted to balance up his accounts. But he wanted her to be given a salary or living allowance increase of fifteen dollars a month, as she would have completed six months of service on 30 September. After all, he pointed out, the cost of living was increasing and her income did not equal that of the American women working as secretaries at the FEA. He was planning to take this up in Washington.[22]

On the day after his meeting with Brouxhon, Hogue prepared some further instructions for Stehli, who had been working hard to familiarise himself with the concerns of OSS in the region. He had already visited Brazzaville three times and had been in Matadi between 17 and 19 August. 'You are familiar with my filing system,' wrote Hogue to Stehli, 'which I imagine you will change to meet your particular ideas. ANGELLA knows pretty well what our files contain, and can be of assistance in this respect. Her memory is excellent regarding names of persons on whom we have dossiers, and can save you a lot of time.'[23] But in any case, he felt confident that Stehli was ready to run the station: 'you already have your feet on the ground'.[24]

He handed over to Stehli the funds in his care, including Belgian Congo francs, AEF francs, South African shillings and Gold Coast pounds. He also handed over the diamond fund—'uncounted by myself except for the sums removed. Of the diamond fund, 100,000 francs or $2280.00 were checked out to Jean Decoster at Elisabethville for diamond purchasing.' The balance, he assumed, was either with Decoster or in the hands of the Sûreté. 'Keep your feet on the ground,' he advised Stehli, 'and your chin up.'[25]

On Friday 25 August, Hogue went on a short visit to Matadi, to make preparations for a departure from the Congo—in case that was suddenly to become necessary.

16

COLLABORATING WITH THE NAZIS

One evening in early September 1944, Hogue invited the young code officer, Bob Laxalt, to join him on a walk down the tree-lined boulevard to the centre of Léopoldville, to get a drink at a hotel cafe. Hogue was in 'a rare good humour, talking and chortling'. But his jovial nature, realised Laxalt, 'was only one of the disguises he had learned in OSS training in Washington', in order to throw counter-espionage agents off the track. Hogue had called ahead to reserve a particular table in the middle of the hotel's sidewalk café, in order to avoid the chances of being overheard. He had also chosen a time when they would be less likely to be noticed: people were enjoying pre-dinner drinks, so the sidewalk was crowded.

To Laxalt's horror, Hogue told him that he had just escaped an attempt to stab him in the back, which he assumed was on Nazi orders. This was now the second attempt on his life, following the bomb. But this kind of danger, said Hogue, was the name of the game in his line of work: most of his fellow spies from training had been killed by a rifle, machine pistol, or bomb, and two had been executed.

Laxalt wondered aloud why on earth the Nazis were trying to assassinate Hogue. After all, he said, 'There's no war here.'

'Yes, there is,' responded Hogue. 'But not the battlefield category. We're the solitary soldiers with no supporting fire.'

'What the heck is going on?'

'If you haven't noticed anything particular in the stuff you're coding for us,' said Hogue, 'We're doing okay.'

'I've noticed one thing odd,' said Laxalt. 'Are we in the mining business?'

'We might be.'

'For what? I know there's gold and diamonds in the Congo, but South Africa is a lot better source than here.'

'I think you know enough,' said Hogue—'Let's leave it right there.'

But Laxalt blurted out a word: '*Shinkolobwe*.' In his memoir, he recorded that he said the word 'without thinking'.

Hogue snapped. 'Jesus Christ,' he exclaimed in irritation, as he looked anxiously around the café. 'Don't ever use that word in anybody's presence. Not ever!' It was most unusual for Hogue to lose his cool and calm demeanour, but he was under excessive pressure. Then he leant forward and told Laxalt to stop looking serious and to start smiling, in order to throw off any potential interest in their conversation. The Shinkolobwe mine, he explained, was top secret—'You won't find it in our mining reference reports, so don't bother looking.'

'There's something in that mine that both the United States and Germany want more than anything else in the world,' he said quietly. 'It's in that word I don't want you to repeat, either in Swahili or English. I don't know what it's for. We're not supposed to know. I doubt whether the German agents here know, either.' The Shinkolobwe mine, he went on, 'contains a mineral called uranium. The Congo has the only producing mine.' The Germans, he added, were trying to get all the uranium the Congo could produce. There was 'a deep dark suspicion that King Léopold is waiting to see who's winning the war—Hitler or us. He'll throw all the Congo uranium to us if our side is going to win the war.' Then Hogue explained why the Germans were trying to kill him: 'They think I've discovered something, and they want to squelch it by killing me.' Laxalt was keen to know more. 'Do you really know something they don't?' he asked.

But Hogue refused to answer. That question, he said firmly, 'is what I mean by going too far'. Then his faced closed down into its characteristic 'sphinx cast'.[1]

Hogue had indeed discovered something: he had serious grounds for believing that some Belgian companies operating in the Congo had been collaborating with the Germans, and that Union Minière had sold uranium to Germany.

Before leaving Washington, he had studied a report by Doug Bonner, written when he was chief of the Accra station, of the meeting held shortly after the invasion of Belgium at the home in Elisabethville of Jules Cousin. The men attending the meeting were major industrialists and prominent members of Katanga's white society, who explored ways of supporting Hitler and Léopold III or, at the very least, getting the Congo to take a neutralist position.

When Hogue arrived in the Congo, he had resolved to find out more about the business dealings of 'the gang', as he referred to the men at the meeting.[2] He learned that the meeting had in fact been called by Monsigneur de Hemptinne, at which all the individuals who attended were sworn to secrecy—and that de Hemptinne had proposed that a telegram be sent to the Governor General, advocating that the Congo remain neutral and trade with all the powers. That plan, as Hogue already knew from Bonner's report, had been aborted when one of the men at the meeting reported it to the authorities.

The private sector operating in the Congo, especially in Katanga, had a level of power that easily competed with the colonial administration led by Ryckmans. This was of a pattern with the situation in Belgium after the German invasion on 10 May 1940. Five days later, when the Belgian government—led by Prime Minister Paul Henry Spaak and Finance Minister Camille Gutt—

decided to leave Brussels, they called for the three key men of Belgian finance: the governor of Société Générale, Alexandre Galopin, and the presidents of the Banque de Bruxelles and the Kredietbank. No record was kept of the meeting, but it is clear that the ministers arranged for the bankers to pay civil servants' salaries during the occupation. What is less clear, according to a careful study of bankers and politics in Belgium, is whether the ministers gave the bankers the task of representing big business in dealings with the German occupiers. But in any case, it was a task which they effectively assumed and some Belgian firms boosted their production by obtaining German orders. In 1943 alone, Belgian firms delivered 155 locomotives to Germany.[3]

Galopin's doctrine was 'to carry on with industrial production with the aim of feeding the population and maintaining man-power in Belgium while seeking to avoid supporting the German war effort'. But the government disagreed with this policy of *moindre mal*—lesser evil—conducted by the Belgian business world under the leadership of the committee of prominent financiers and industrialists, headed by Galopin. The policy 'came to a dead end and produced a harsh controversy'.[4] This collaboration with Nazi Germany was criticised by many Belgians, especially in those cases which flouted article 116 of the Penal Code, which forbade the production of arms destined for the enemy.[5]

Hogue believed that similar activities were going on in the Belgian Congo—that some companies were serving the needs of the Axis powers and also smuggling. 'You can now see the end of the mystery,' wrote Hogue to Boulton. 'But we *know* positively that the big boys are in the IDB business.' He had two important sources of information: the De Gesnot brothers. One of them was the Comptroller of Customs in Albertville, and the other was the Comptroller of Customs in Léopoldville; together, they were in a unique position to survey smuggling activity. They told Hogue that Celestin Camus, the Director General of the Compagnie des Chemins de Fer du Congo Supérieur aux Grands Lacs Africains (CFL) at Albertville, which had been founded by Belgian businessman Baron Edouard Empain, had shipped 4–500,000 carats of industrial diamonds to Germany in 1940. The Léopoldville De Gesnot had shown a letter to him from the Albertville De Gesnot, giving details about this. Hogue had gone to Albertville to investigate the matter further. While there, he filmed a CFL train in the railway station, panning back and forth over the name of the train company.

'You know by cable now of my big strike regarding Celestin Camus and the Empain crowd,' wrote Hogue to Boulton on 1 August 1944. 'The gory details will be in my next letter. I'm trying to get the dope organized.'[6] Two weeks later, he sent further details: that there was considerable interlocking among the directors of Empain and Société Générale in the Belgian Congo. 'I hope,' he said, 'you do not take alleged rivalry between the two groups too seriously. It makes a good show on the surface, but there are indications and stories here of parts of each working hand in glove.'

The various lists of company directors had given him an important clue. 'My friend,' he wrote to Boulton, 'the tie-up is astounding. Even our recluse, Jules Cousin of UNION MINIERE, is an Empain director.' Also, he added, 'there has been too much cooperation here among S G mining activity and the Empain mines not to think that these outfits, if not previous to the war, are now enjoying relations if not actually married'.[7]

As always, Hogue never referred explicitly to uranium in his communications with Washington. But he made it clear that his suspicions of collaboration extended to Union Minière and the sale of uranium. These were suspicions that Schmidt, too, had harboured, leading to a request to OSS in Washington in February 1944 for some financial intelligence through the banks 'regarding possible payments in New York to Sengier's African Metals'.

Hogue and Schmidt were right. For Union Minière *did* sell uranium to Germany during the war—which the company, now known as Umicore, is frank about. Umicore opened up its archives to two historians, René Brion and Jean-Louis Moreau, specialists in the history of companies, for the purpose of writing a substantial institutional history. In this history, which was published in 2006 as *De La Mine à Mars: La Genèse d'Umicore*, this sensitive topic is tackled in a detailed section entitled *Les Ambiguités des Fournitures aux Allemands*—'The Ambiguities Surrounding Supplies to the Germans'.[8]

The supply of Congolese uranium to Nazi Germany by Union Minière did not, so far as it appears, involve the shipping of any of the ore directly from the Congo to Germany, but took place within Europe. After the war had started, but before Belgium's invasion by Germany in May 1940, Union Minière executives sold to the Germans about a thousand tons of uranium that had remained in Belgium after refining.[9]

In June 1940, the month after the invasion, Kurt Diebner, a German physicist working for the military, announced that the German authorities intended to buy the company's remaining stocks of refined uranium oxide. Over the next few days, George Velge, the director of Union Minière, responded by saying that the company would not supply uranium products for military purposes. 'We do not require an exact account of how the product will be used,' he stated. 'We simply want to know if on the one hand it will be used for commercial, industrial or scientific purposes, or, on the other hand, if it will be used for military purposes.' Diebner responded that the uranium oxide was destined for industrial purposes. Velge's statement to Diebner is important, since Union Minière claimed after the war that company officials were unaware of the military potential of uranium.[10]

In 1940–42, Union Minière sold 95 metric tons of uranium-bearing finished products to the German companies Auer AG in Berlin, de Boer in Hamburg, and Deutsche Gold-und Silber-Scheideanstalt (Degussa) in Frankfurt. Degussa was a large German firm which supplied the uranium for the Nazis' atomic bomb project; it also specialised in metal refining and chemical production, including the Zyklon-B cyanide tablets used in the gas chambers of the concentration camps.[11] As Brion and Moreau suggest, Union Minière's manner of conducting these and other sales with Germany aroused suspicion and drew criticism: it was frequently the case that the details of these sales agreements were never formally put in writing at the time.[12]

One of General Groves's major fears, all along, had been that Union Minière was selling ore to the Germans—and in January 1944, he discovered that this was indeed the case. Moe Berg, the OSS agent sent to Europe in 1944, reported to headquarters that a consignment of nearly 700 tons of Belgian Congo uranium ore in Belgium had been delivered to Duisburg in Germany.[13] This raised the possibility that Germany had sufficient uranium to build an atomic bomb—especially since reports were also coming in of ore being transported to Berlin from mines in Joachimstal, Czechoslovakia.

Orders were swiftly given to the US air force to bomb Duisburg, and to bomb nearby areas as well, to avert any possible suspicion of the reason for the attack. The aircraft crew were not briefed on any details about their target, in case their plane was shot down and they were interrogated. Duisburg was destroyed.[14]

After Victory in Europe was marked on 8 May 1945, the question of collaboration became highly sensitive in Belgium. There were many areas of activity touched by this question, including those relating to uranium. A Belgian geologist, Professor A. Schoep, who had undertaken various mineralogical investigations on the uranium ores of Katanga, was named as a 'collaborateur' by the Belgian government and suspended from his chair at Ghent.[15]

A decree was passed on 19 September 1945, which 'set the wheels of a purge in motion'. Military auditors investigated the war past of suspects and whoever appeared on the list could lose their civil and political rights. Some 405,000 files were compiled, leading to about 90,000 court cases. Punishment was at its harshest after the return of concentration camp survivors and altogether, 1,202 people were sentenced to death; 242 were actually executed.[16] The concept of economic collaboration was given a restricted interpretation and a list was drawn up of the kinds of trade with the occupier that was a punishable offence. 'Implicitly', explains a political history of Belgium, 'it was recognised that suspects would escape a sentence if it was clear that the company had to trade with the occupying forces to ensure continued employment or food provisions and if it was clear that the suspect had not collaborated for personal gain.'[17]

In November-December 1945, a few months after the bombing of Hiroshima and Nagasaki, an inquiry began into the activities of Union Minière, led by the *Auditorat militaire* (the public prosecutor's office attached to the *Conseil de Guerre*, the Belgian War Council), which ran until April 1946.[18] It heavily criticised the directors of the Études et Traitements Chimiques (ETC), a uranates refinery established in 1929 by the Union Chimique Belge and Union Minière, for having supplied the enemy with strategic materials, likely to be used in the manufacture of an atomic bomb. They also claimed that the capacity of the ETC had been increased for this reason.[19]

This claim appears to be borne out by the history of Union Minière, in which Brion and Moreau analyse the output of the refineries established by, or associated with, Union Minière. It is clear, they note, that an effort was made to increase stocks just prior to the invasion of Belgium. 'It is also clear,' they add, 'that until 1943, production figures were significant, especially if one takes into consideration that the production was intended for the German market alone (before the war, the United States alone consumed 80% of the ETC's production).'[20]

Those concerned protested their innocence: a major plank of their argument was that at the time in question, the military uses of uranates were not yet known. But the military prosecutor did not accept this defence, given the technical expertise of the men involved and the likelihood of their knowing about research into uranium at the time. The prosecutor's argument is supported by Velge's statement to Diebner in June 1940, which distinguished between the military and commercial purposes of the ore. In any case, Edgar Sengier and Union Minière had been in close discussions with General Groves.[21]

On 27 February 1946, *Le Drapeau Rouge*, the daily newspaper of the Belgian Communist Party, ran a shocking headline: 'If the Nazis haven't discovered the atomic bomb, it's no fault of Union Minière!' The directors of Union Minière, it claimed, had freely sold hundreds of metric tons of uranium to the enemy, even propositioning them to this end. 'The matter is clear,' it stated firmly. 'There's no mistaking that Union Minière supplied Hitler's Germany with uranium and radium.'[22]

Sengier was worried. He approached Groves, who was aware of the inquiry that was going on. So long as it was limited to individual employees suspected of collaboration, he told Groves, it could be allowed to run its course. But once it focused on the companies and their directors, he and those companies would no longer feel bound by the terms of confidentiality that had been agreed with the US. The 'upholding of the secret', he argued pointedly, 'would risk casting doubt on the worthiness and patriotism of my colleagues or my team'. He said he would not hesitate, if necessary, to make public the supply of uranium to the Allies; *in extremis*, he would appeal to Spaak, Gutt and De Vleeschauwer to confirm the details.

This was an implicit threat and Groves agreed to help. He said he would give Sengier an official letter addressed to Spaak, drawing the Belgian government's attention to the absolute necessity of ensuring that the ongoing judicial inquiry did not get out of hand—and did not affect the companies and their directors.

On 11 March, the Belgian press learned that the uranium used in the bombs dropped on Japan came from the Belgian Congo. The legal proceedings were dismissed. Brion and Moreau's comment on this takes the form of a simple question: 'Coincidence?'[23]

Edgar Sengier was awarded the Medal for Merit, the highest civilian award by the US government, for his services to the USA. 'As a Belgian,' wrote Groves, 'Sengier fully appreciated the absolute necessity of an Allied victory. It was his broad, statesman-like atti-tude that made it possible for us to reach an agreement satisfac-tory to all.'[24] The award was presented to Sengier by President Truman himself in 1946–at a secret ceremony.[25]

Albert Makelele, a Congolese writer, was outraged when he learned in the 1960s that Edgar Sengier had been awarded the Medal of Merit, as a reward for Union Minière's contribution to the Manhattan Project. 'The bomb won the war for the West against Japan,' he writes in *This is a Good Country: Welcome to the Congo*. 'Bang! What a shock. A Belgian ... stole Congo uranium ... which went into a bomb ... that ended the war ... and I am just learning about it in 1962! How important is my Congo!' Regretting that hardly anyone knows this fact 'easily and publicly', he regards Sengier's medal as a *coup de grâce*. For him, the story of Congo's uranium 'is one of the most heartbreaking events in that country's history, especially when one realises what that metal represents in the matters regarding armament during these mod-ern times'.[26]

17

A DEAD SHOT

Once Bob Laxalt, the code officer, had been told by Hogue about the mine at Shinkolobwe, he started to notice that special arrangements were always made for communications relating to uranium, which went out in a confidential code that the legation 'protected with its life'. After 'uranium entered the picture', he wrote in his memoir, his job was never ordinary again.[1]

One day, Hogue did not turn up for a scheduled meeting at the legation in Léopoldville with Vice Consul Harry Schwartz. They called Hogue's telephone number at his bungalow, but there was no answer; later, they discovered that the line had been cut. Then Schwartz, Laxalt and Withers, the economic attaché, got ready to drive to Hogue's bungalow. Schwartz invited Withers along because he expected trouble—and Withers was 'big and burly'.

They were just about to leave when the Legation secretary called them back to take a phone call from the Belgian gendarmerie. They had been told by Hogue's 'houseboy', who slept in the native quarter, that the front door was open when he arrived. He had made the report three hours earlier, but the gendarmerie had done nothing about it until now.

They drove swiftly to the bungalow and Schwartz 'braked to a squealing stop' in the alleyway that ran next to the bungalow.

They found just one gendarme inside—'no detective squad searching for evidence, dusting for fingerprints, as in the United States or by the French Sûreté'. The living room looked no different from normal, but the bedroom door had been broken down and there was a trail of blood leading out of the kitchen door into the alleyway. Laxalt was horrified, especially since Hogue's bedroom 'looked like a small war had been fought there during the night'. Hanging lamps, a clock, and pottery were in fragments, and the wall beside the bed was pockmarked with bullet holes. 'But what was most curious,' noticed Laxalt, was that the mattress 'had been tipped over toward the wall like a protecting buffer'. Hogue, they assumed, had used this as a shield when the shooting started. To their great relief, they saw there was no blood on the mattress. But they were puzzled: what had happened to Hogue?

Laxalt asked the gendarme if the neighbours had seen or heard anything, at which the gendarme looked at him as if he was an ignorant child. 'Even if they did,' he said, 'Belgians would say nothing. They don't want to be involved with *espions*, which these people obviously are.' He told the three Americans that there had been no dead bodies and no noise. 'Obviously,' he said, 'they used silencers.' He added that he had the shell casings for the bullets that had been dug out of the wall, but they were in his pocket—and he was not going to show them, as they were police evidence. Just then, Laxalt realised he was standing on a shell casing. After the gendarme had left, he picked it up and handed it to Schwartz, who looked at it and passed it to Withers. 'What I figured,' said Withers. 'A machine pistol. Mauser. That spells an SS killer. Machine pistols aren't accurate, but they can spit out a lot of bullets in a hurry.' He gestured to the pockmarked wall to illustrate his point.

Hogue had had a single-shot 45, a gun which had only one chance to hit. But this would have been no problem for Hogue, said Withers. 'Wild Bill Donovan's spy people,' he added darkly, 'had better be dead shots.' He took comfort from the fact that there was so much blood beside the smashed-up bedroom door—because it showed Hogue had 'nailed the sonofabitch'.

They followed the trail of blood left by the killer, which led out of the kitchen door. It was clear that a car had been waiting for him. The trail went to where the driver's seat would have been, if the car had still been parked there; then it went round to the passenger side and stopped.

They looked through Hogue's drawers and closet but found nothing of value; they were familiar with his wardrobe and everything seemed to be in the right place. Then they inspected the desk, but the only item on it of any potential importance was a routine report on the mining activities at Shinkolobwe.

'It was as though Doc Pogue had vanished into thin air,' observed Laxalt in his memoir. 'He was either dead, or he had managed somehow to get away.'

A short time after Hogue's disappearance, Laxalt was forced into bed by a severe case of malaria. He was recovering, but still weak, when—five months later—news came that Hogue was not only alive, but safely back home in the US. The news came in a pouch letter brought by a diplomatic courier from the State Department. Until then, neither Laxalt nor Schwartz had heard anything from Hogue by code or in any other way. They had assumed that either he was dead, or was carrying a 'burdensome' secret. 'We were pretty certain,' wrote Laxalt, 'it had to do with Union Minière's Shinkolobwe mine, where we and the Germans were scrabbling about the uranium for what use nobody seemed to know anything.'

As well as the regular mail and dispatches, the courier had two letters bound by a rubber band: one for Schwartz and one for Laxalt, 'the youngest American in the legation', who by now had turned twenty-one. The letters had been given to the courier in person by Hogue, who had asked that Schwartz and Laxalt burn the letters, once they had read them. The courier added that Hogue 'didn't tell me a damned thing except that he used to work here. Here and at some mine neither he nor anybody else in authority wants to talk about.' Then he muttered, 'I've never seen such a hush-up job. Has to be the best-kept secret in the war.'

Schwartz retreated to his desk to read his letter; and Laxalt pulled a chair to the far corner of the office, to read his. The letters were more or less the same.

Since Laxalt burnt his letter from Hogue, he was not able to refer to it when writing his memoir A *Private War*; and as the letter had to be destroyed on grounds of security, he would not have kept a record in his diary of its contents. His account is therefore a reconstruction of what he recalled; most of it is convincing and fits the historical record, but one aspect is not credible. This is understandable, given that over fifty years had elapsed between Laxalt's experience in the Congo and his decision to write a book about it—and underlines the value of the diary of his daily life which he had kept in Léopoldville.

First of all, said Hogue in the letter, he wanted to apologise for leaving Léopoldville without a proper goodbye. Circumstances, he said, 'made it necessary to make a hasty departure, 'After two attempts on my life, I knew there would be a third.' Then he gave an account of what had happened:

> My leaving in such haste was not without preparation. I set to work the day after the first attempt with the bomb failed. I knew my cover was blown. It would only be a matter of time. As it turned out, I stayed too long after the try with a knife in the back.

But, he went on, 'there was one leak at Shinkolobwe I had to try for before I left. I got it and if it checks out, it was worth the try.' Then he made plans for a quick getaway:

> It took some talking and a bundle of money (always take money), but I found an old French merchant mariner who had retired to a shabby little houseboat on the Congo. He fished for El Capitan mostly to help supplement his income. I made an arrangement with him to take me downriver to the port at Matadi. Short notice and probably at night. I left a handbag with him just in case—change of clothes, toothbrush.

The sailor was clearly a drinker, which was worrying. To scare him away from the bar, Hogue showed him his gun and threatened to kill him if he got drunk.

This arrangement to take Hogue by boat to Matadi is the aspect of Laxalt's recollection which is not credible. For just beyond Kinshasa, the navigation of the Congo River is limited by a series of rapids: the thirty-two cataracts of the Livingstone Falls between the city and the port of Matadi, 200 miles away. It was specifically to bypass these rapids that the railway between Léopoldville and Matadi was built at the end of the nineteenth century. One group of British sailors who *did* manage to navigate the route, with specially developed inflatable boats, were keenly aware of the danger. 'There was a long stretch,' they wrote afterwards, 'with twelve-foot waves pounding over the rocks or large waves and deep holes in an otherwise smooth surface, caused by huge underwater boulders or giant whirlpools. At one whirlpool which was fifty yards across, the boat did a "wall of death" run round the rim.'[2] It is impossible, therefore, that Hogue would have considered, even for one moment, a plan to sail down the Congo River to Matadi in a shabby houseboat skippered by an elderly man with a propensity to drink. It is more likely that Hogue arranged with him to wait at the dock in Léopoldville, ready at any time to provide a safe place to hide.

Laxalt remembered that according to Hogue's letter, he went back to his bungalow after making arrangements with the French sailor. Then he waited for developments:

> That night, I had a hunch they would try (one develops a sixth sense in this game). That's why I locked the bedroom door. I heard their Mercedes drive into the alleyway, pulled the mattress down to protect me from what I was pretty sure would be coming my way. Then I lay down on the floor with my pistol ready.

He didn't have to wait long:

> The SS sonofabitch hit the door like a battering ram. He came through shooting. I took my time. With only one shot, you can get awfully careful. That big .45 slug took him in the belly and threw him back out the door. When he got up, I thought I was done for, but he went down again and started crawling toward the kitchen, grunting like a pig. Sorry I can't be charitable about someone trying to kill me.

195

When he heard the Mercedes take off, he left swiftly. The only thing he took with him was his gun and 'most important, my money belt'. He ran all the way to the dock and found the river-boat and jumped into it.

Laxalt recalled that according to Hogue's letter, the boat then took him to Matadi overnight. What is likely, however, is that Hogue hid safely overnight in the boat and then took the morning train to Matadi. In any case, we know for a fact that he went to Matadi, since his name is included in the passenger list of a boat that left Matadi a few days later.

Once Hogue reached Matadi, according to Laxalt's memory of his letter, he walked down the docks to the room where his second and last contact lived. He had a list ready with the departure dates of Scandinavian freighters heading for the US. His 'luck held up':

> There was a Swedish freighter leaving in two days. The night before, my contact and I went to a bistro where we met with a sailor from the freighter. Some more money changed hands, and I was stowed away on the ship. I lived in a corner of the hold that had been set up with a cot, water, fruit, and bread.

This was Hogue's home for two days. Then he went to find the captain and showed him his papers. He was a Swede—'with no love for the Germans'—and Hogue became a passenger.

Passenger details for the SS *Tarn* confirm that a passenger named Wilbur Owings Hogue, aged thirty-six, from Idaho, left Matadi on the *Tarn* on 27 August 1944, arriving in New York on 24 September.[3] In fact, the freighter SS *Tarn* belonged to the Wilhelmsen Line, which was a Norwegian, not a Swedish, shipping company; most likely, Laxalt had a general recollection that the freighter was Scandinavian. It had in fact previously been used by the Manhattan Project: the Project's records reveal that SS *Tarn* was one of the freighters used to transport uranium from Matadi to the US in 1943; the local agents of the *Tarn* were the Barber Line.[4]

The *Tarn*'s voyage records tell us that it took Hogue to Lobito and then to Takoradi, after which it sailed across the Atlantic to

Brazil and then followed the coastline all the way to New York. The boat trip took just under a month and then he was 'home free.' But he was conscious that Schwartz and Laxalt were still in the Congo. 'Don't ask any questions about Shinkolobwe,' he advised, 'and take money.' He ended his letters with a heartfelt expression of pleasure at coming home: 'I won't be going overseas again this war. No regrets. I will see you next in beautiful, safe Washington, DC. How good it is to be back home.'

Once Hogue had reached North America and landed in New York, he went straight to Washington, arriving on 26 September 1944. It was agreed that he would now join the 'Chairborne' staff of OSS Secret Intelligence, Africa Section, in the Que Building.[5]

Europe was emerging slowly from the war. On 24 August 1944, Paris had been liberated by the Allies. On 2 September, Brussels was also released from Nazi occupation, and most of the rest of Belgium (though not the far eastern region) was liberated by the end of October.

There had also been important developments in relation to the control of Congolese uranium: for the US, with Britain, had finally reached a deal with Belgium. The negotiations had been a major source of concern to General Groves, who was profoundly distrustful of the British. His 'deep-seated Anglophobia', writes one historian, 'only intensified the other reasons he had to be suspicious about Britain's intentions'.[6] But the US needed to reach an agreement with the British, in order to prevent them from taking control of the Congolese uranium for themselves. For the British had an advantage over them: not only did they have long-standing historical contacts with Belgium, but also London had given a home to the Belgian government-in-exile.[7] A further connection of great importance was the British influence on Union Minière, as a result of British representation on the board of directors and British ownership of a significant minority interest in the firm.

A further reason for the US to be dependent on British collaboration was the belief that the greatest potential source of uranium, aside from the Congo, was South Africa, which was part of the British Commonwealth. The then South African Prime Minister, Jan Smuts, was briefed on the atomic bomb programme in London in mid-1944. Washington was therefore once again forced to rely on British assistance to secure access to the mines and to the metal. In effect, observes one scholar, Britain had influence 'as procurator for the new atomic empire'.[8]

The Québec Agreement of 19 August 1943 had already established the Combined Policy Committee, with two representatives from Britain, one from Canada, and three Americans, to oversee and coordinate weapons development. In June 1944 a Combined Development Trust (CDT), with the same membership distribution as the Combined Policy Committee, was created to secure the world's known uranium supplies and to handle the purchase of uranium.

Once the US and Britain had reached agreement on the establishment of the Trust, General Groves and Sir Charles Hambro, acting on behalf of the Trust, began negotiations with Edgar Sengier to expedite arrangements with the African Metals Corporation for the reopening of Shinkolobwe mine. Previously the Trust had dealt only with Sengier, but now the Belgian government-in-exile was brought into discussions, which put pressure on Union Minière to come to terms.

All discussions between and within the different parties were kept tightly secret. In a Top Secret memorandum on 29 August 1944, a senior British official in the Foreign Office told a colleague that the topic should not be discussed over the telephone. 'I attach herewith for your very private eye', he wrote:

> drafts of certain letters which it is proposed to exchange between the [US] Secretary of State, Mr Winant and the Belgian Minister of Foreign Affairs, to which there is annexed a draft Memorandum of Agreement about certain uranium ore.

'Although the Agreement was in form tripartite,' he continued, 'it is in practice really an agreement between HMG [Her Majesty's

Government] and USG [US Government] on the one side and the Belgian Government on the other.' Then the official drew attention to the very secret nature of the discussions and their concerns. 'If you have any views about this,' he advised, 'we might perhaps discuss it, since I gather it is not a subject which can really be talked about on the telephone.'[9]

Special code symbols were prepared by the Combined Development Trust for use in their planned contract with the Africa Metals Corporation: 'S-14' was the code symbol for the Shinkolobwe mine; 'Q-11' was uranium oxide; 'Location A' (the location of the mine) was 'approximately thirty kilometres west of Jadotville, Belgian Congo'; 'Location B' was Lobito in Angola; and 'Location D' was New York.[10]

The negotiations finally culminated in the Belgian, or Tripartite, Agreement of 26 September 1944—the very same day that Hogue arrived back home in Washington. The Agreement was effected by an exchange of letters among Paul H. Spaak, then Belgium's Foreign Minister, Sir John Anderson, the British Chancellor of the Exchequer, and John Gilbert Winant, the US Ambassador to Britain. Under the terms of the agreement, Belgium granted the US and the UK an option on all of its uranium and thorium resources in recognition of the fact that 'the protection of civilisation' required 'effective control of said ores'. The Trust also agreed to furnish Union Minière with the new equipment and materials it would require to reopen and to operate the Shinkolobwe mine. The option was to continue for the period needed to carry out ore contract arrangements as set up under the agreement, as well as for an additional ten-year period.[11] In effect, Union Minière agreed to sell all of its production of uranium ore until 1956.[12]

Belgium reserved the right to retain such ore as might be needed for 'her own scientific research' and 'industrial purposes'. This concession had been granted because the US was concerned that, without it, the Belgians might delay indefinitely the reopening of the Shinkolobwe mine. However, Belgium was not allowed to use Congolese ore for commercial purposes without 'consultation and in agreement with' the US and Britain.[13]

The US sought to give an impression to Britain of a wish for partnership. But in fact, America was seeking to eclipse the British in relation to uranium and the atomic project. Groves, in particular, comments Gregg Herken in *The Winning Weapon*, had been working hard behind the scenes to ensure that real control of atomic raw materials would not be shared with the British.[14] Menzies, the head of MI6, was aware of this and unhappy about it. He said to Guy Liddell that 'the potentialities of uranium as a motive force were enormous and [that] some attempt was being made by the Americans to get control'.[15] He was anxious to restore the pre-war situation, in which the British, rather than the Americans, were close to the Belgian intelligence service.[16]

Given the suspicions held on all sides, the Tripartite Agreement was regarded as a triumph—especially for the US and Britain. But it is arguable that not one of the three countries involved, nor Union Minière, had the moral right to negotiate over future access to Congolese uranium. For the uranium ore was mined in the Congo, the land of the Congolese, and by Congolese hands— at great risk to their health. At the time, Congolese people had no knowledge of the dangers involved, nor of the value of the ore; nor, indeed, of the plans to remove it from their country for purposes that were entirely unrelated to their needs.

The Tripartite Agreement ran counter to the principles of the Atlantic Charter, signed by Roosevelt and Churchill on 14 August 1941, which made a commitment to building a future of self-determination for all peoples. Admittedly, Churchill had signed it cynically, qualifying his position later by saying that it did not apply to the British Empire. But Roosevelt was sincere. Evidently it proved impossible for him to reconcile hopes for America's future atomic project—reaching up to 1956—with support for the colonised peoples of the Belgian Congo.

1. OSS agent Wilbur Owings 'Dock' Hogue in the garden of the US Consulate General in Léopoldville (now Kinshasa) in 1944. He was OSS Station chief in the Belgian Congo and his codename was TETON.

2. Shinkolobwe Mine in 1925. This mine was the source of the uranium used to build the American atomic bombs dropped on Japan in August 1945.

3. A specimen of brightly coloured uraninite from the Shinkolobwe mine. 'Rocks like these,' observed John Gunther, an American writer who saw Shinkolobwe's 'brilliant, hideous ore', 'have fire in them not only figuratively but literally.'

4. General Leslie Groves (left), who in 1942 was appointed to head the Manhattan Project, speaking to Edgar Sengier (middle), the Managing Director of Union Minière du Haut Katanga, the Belgian company which owned Shinkolobwe.

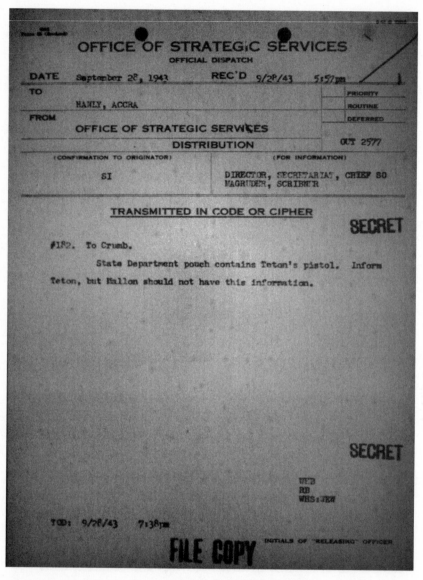

OFFICE OF STRATEGIC SERVICES
OFFICIAL DISPATCH

DATE September 28, 1943   REC'D 9/28/43   5:57pm

TO

HANLY, ACCRA

FROM

OFFICE OF STRATEGIC SERVICES

PRIORITY

ROUTINE

DEFERRED

DISTRIBUTION

OUT 2577

(CONFIRMATION TO ORIGINATOR)	(FOR INFORMATION)
SI	DIRECTOR, SECRETARIAT, CHIEF SO MAGRUDER, SCRIBNER

TRANSMITTED IN CODE OR CIPHER

#182. To Crumb.

State Department pouch contains Teton's pistol. Inform Teton, but Mallon should not have this information.

WEB
RB
WHS:JEW

TOD: 9/28/43   7:38pm

INITIALS OF "RELEASING" OFFICER

5. A cable sent from OSS headquarters in Washington to Accra, Gold Coast (Ghana), on 28 September 1942: 'To Crumb. State Department pouch contains Teton's pistol. Inform Teton, but Mallon should not have this information.' CRUMB was the codename for OSS officer Douglas Bonner, in Accra; Mallon was the US Consul in Léopoldville.

6. The Liberian President's residence and offices in Monrovia. A flag with a swastika—the emblem of Hitler's Third Reich—can be seen at the right. This screenshot was filmed by Hogue on an OSS mission in Liberia in 1942-1943, when Liberia had strong ties with Nazi Germany.

7. Rudyerd Boulton, Divisional Deputy of OSS Secret Intelligence, who was based in the 'Que' Building in Washington and was responsible for espionage activities in Africa. He was an ornithologist who took to intelligence work with ease and flair.

8. Armand Denis, who in early 1942 was sent on an intelligence mission to the Belgian Congo. He was a well known naturalist and his cover was collecting live gorillas, but was unsuccessful as a spy.

9. Dr James Chapin in the Belgian Congo in December 1942, after arriving to work for the OSS. He was a distinguished ornithologist and had previously conducted extensive research in the Congo. He suffered a nervous breakdown during the OSS mission and was sent back to the US, where he was given electric shock treatment.

10. Pierre Ryckmans (at the right), the Governor-General of the Belgian Congo, at the inauguration of the monument to King Albert I in Léopoldville, 1938. After Nazi Germany's invasion of Belgium, Ryckmans rejected calls for neutrality and declared the Congo's support for Britain against Hitler.

11. Major Douglas Bonner (CRUMB), head of the OSS station in Accra, in 1943. After Chapin's breakdown in the Congo, Bonner went to the Belgian colony to recover the situation.

12. Lanier John Violett, OSS agent in Luanda, Angola. His cover was employment by the Texas Oil Company (Texaco) and his codename was HOMER. He died at the age of 39, after returning to New York; his doctors were unable to diagnose the cause of his death.

13. Duane D. Luther, OSS officer in Accra, whose code-name was COACH. After the war he became President of Texaco in the Dominican Republic, where he was accused of bringing in weapons to be used in an assassination of the democratically elected President.

14. A sketch map sent by General Groves to Major General W. D. Styer, Chief of Staff of Army Service Forces, on 13 April 1943: 'Inclosed [sic] herewith is a photostat of a map of a portion of Central Africa showing the location of the mine in which we are interested at Shinkolobwe and the transportation routes by which the ore is carried to the Coast.'

15. A riverboat on the Kasai River at Port-Francqui (now Ilebo). Uranium destined for the US was sent north by train to Port-Francqui, the railhead, where it was loaded onto barges, which sailed on to Léopoldville; at that point the uranium was sent by train to Matadi.

16. A page from the passport of Shirley Armitage Chidsey, who joined the OSS station in Léopoldville in April 1944; her codename was ANGELLA.

17. Before moving to Africa, Shirley Chidsey had worked for OSS in the New York office as a stenographer specialising in French. She signed the OSS Oath of Office in October 1942, swearing to 'support and defend the Constitution of the United States against all enemies, foreign and domestic.'

18. Shirley Chidsey in the Belgian Congo, 1945. Before moving to the Congo she worked in l'Afrique Équatoriale Française for Radio Brazzaville. She was unhappy in Brazzaville and Hogue invited her to move across the Congo River to Léopoldville, to work again for OSS.

19. Lt. Col. Adolph Schmidt in US Army uniform, *c*. 1943. In early 1944 in Accra he received a cable: 'Proceed at once to Léopoldville. Arrange to have all shipments of uranium ore from Katanga mines checked for possible diversions ... Use as your cover investigation of diamond smuggling.'

20. Adolph Schmidt (in cap) as OSS West Africa Station chief in Accra, with a fellow OSS officer and two Ghanaian members of staff. His codename was 'FLARE'.

21. Henry Emil Stehli, who joined the Belgian Congo OSS station in July 1944, aged 41. His codename was LOCUST.

22. The Banque du Congo Belge on the Avenue Hauzeur (now Avenue Wagenia) in Léopoldville. Here Adolph Schmidt arranged for a US army officer to cash cheques into Belgian Congo francs to give to Dock Hogue, to make a purchase on the illegal market.

23. Douglas Bonner (left) and Dock Hogue in the Belgian Congo in a 'home movie' taken with Dock's movie camera in 1943.

24. Major Alexander 'Alec' Binney, British SOE intelligence officer in Accra, who was head of the SOE/SIS combined Mission West Africa. Binney cooperated with OSS officers on an investigation into illicit diamond buying (IDB).

25. Looking upstream at Matadi, the Congolese inland port from where the barrels of uranium from Shinkolobwe were transported by sea to the US. Matadi is 90 miles from the Atlantic Coast.

26. Two *Sapeurs*—members of the SAPE (Société des Ambianceurs et des Personnes Élégantes), which represented a tradition that had evolved in the Congo as a means of resistance to the colonial system, through fashion and dress. Here they are filmed by Hogue in 1944.

27. General de Gaulle addressing the Brazzaville Conference, organised by the Free French in January 1944. Dock Hogue was sent to follow the conference. 'It is essential for us to receive a play by play account of the Brazzaville conference,' instructed OSS Secret Intelligence. 'TETON must supply complete coverage of it.'

28. A postcard with a France Libre stamp, sent from Brazzaville by Shirley Chidsey to her mother: 'But I did have one nice thing happen. I had dinner with a handsome naval officer and sat on his terrace overlooking the Congo and saw the full moon rise big & red out of the dark river and had a tall whisky and soda ... '

29. The front page of *Le Drapeau Rouge*, the daily newspaper of the Belgian Communist Party, 27 February 1946. Below the fold is the headline: 'If the Nazis haven't discovered the atomic bomb, it's no fault of Union Minière'.

Si les Nazis n'ont pas découvert la
BOMBE ATOMIQUE,
ce n'est pas la faute de
l'UNION MINIERE!

Savez-vous que nous avons, en Belgique, une usine équipée pour faire de l'uranium ? Il s'agit de l'usine d'Oolen, près de Hoboken, où du minerai congolais fourni par l'Union Minière, travaillé par la Société Générale Métallurgique de Hoboken, fournissait avant la guerre, le radium d'une part et d'autre part, du sulfate d'uranium, contenant entre 40 et 80 % d'uranium. Et ce dans la proportion de 3 tonnes de sulfate d'uranium pour 1 gramme de radium

Nous disons bien « avant la guerre » parce qu'aujourd'hui, il n'y

a plus d'uranium à trouver sur le marché...

UNE AUBAINE POUR LES NAZIS

Vint 1940. Or, à ce moment, l'Union Minière disposait, à Oolen et chez l'Union Chimique de plusieurs milliers de tonnes de sulfate d'uranium.

Soyons justes : elle essaya de les évacuer La rapidité de la conquête allemande l'en empêcha.

Et que se passa-t-il alors ?

Les Allemands mirent l'embargo sur le stock d'uranium. Il n'est pas douteux qu'ils se rendirent parfaitement compte de l'aubaine.

L'UNION MINIERE

au début de 1942, elle adressait une lettre, signée notamment par M. Robillard à Militärbefehlhaber, section économique, rue de la Loi, lettre dans laquelle elle offrait la vente de 100 tonnes d'uranium !

Cette offre n'eût pas de suite; mais, vers le mois de mai 1942, les Allemands réquisitionnèrent la quantité totale de sulfate d'uranium existant en Belgique.

Les prélèvements allemands s'élevèrent ensuite à 90 millions de francs et furent réglés par le clearing à l'Union Minière, ainsi que quelque 30 millions pour fourniture de radium.

NOUS POSONS UNE QUESTION

Une petite question à M. Robil-

30. A close-up of the headline in *Le Drapeau Rouge* (shown opposite). The article states: 'There's no mistaking that Union Minière supplied Hitler's Germany with uranium and radium.' In 1945, after the bombing of Japan, an inquiry by the Belgian War Council began into the activities of Union Minière; legal proceedings were dismissed in March 1946.

31. The main front entrance of the offices of Union Minière in Elisabethville, Belgian Congo, 1948.

32. Robert Laxalt, who arrived aged twenty in Léopoldville in June 1944, to work for the US legation as a code officer. Laxalt wrote about Hogue's efforts to prevent the smuggling of uranium to Nazi Germany.

33. The centre of Léopoldville shortly after the war, showing pavement cafés on both sides of the street. It was at such a pavement café that Hogue explained to Laxalt the danger of the work he was doing for OSS regarding Shinkolobwe.

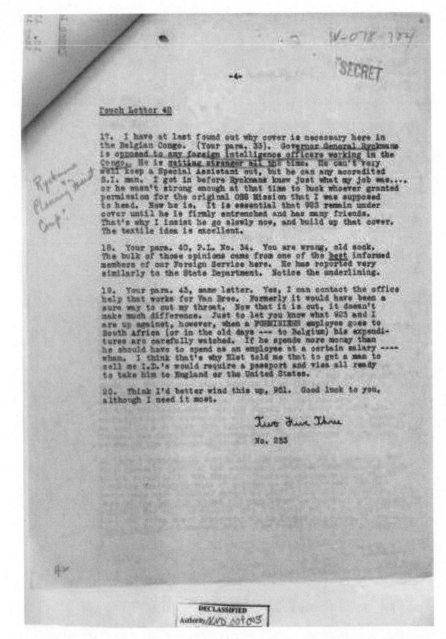

34. An example of pouch letters sent by agents to Washington. This one, sent by Hogue to his superior Boulton on 24 July 1944, reveals the informality of OSS: 'You are wrong, old sock.' It was written at a time of great tensions for Hogue: 'Think I'd better wind this up, 951. Good luck to you, although I need it most.' Boulton's codenumber was 951; Hogue's was 253.

35. The ALSOS team in April 1945 dismantling the German attempt to build a nuclear reactor, in a cave at Haigerloch. Uranium cubes are in the centre. The ALSOS mission established that Germany had not developed an atomic bomb.

36. Dock Hogue left OSS in 1945 and joined UNRRA (the United Nations Relief and Rehabilitation Administration). He ran the Polish Displaced Persons Camp in Germany and was horrified by the suffering in Europe. He described the refugee problem as 'one of the great problems ahead of the World right now'.

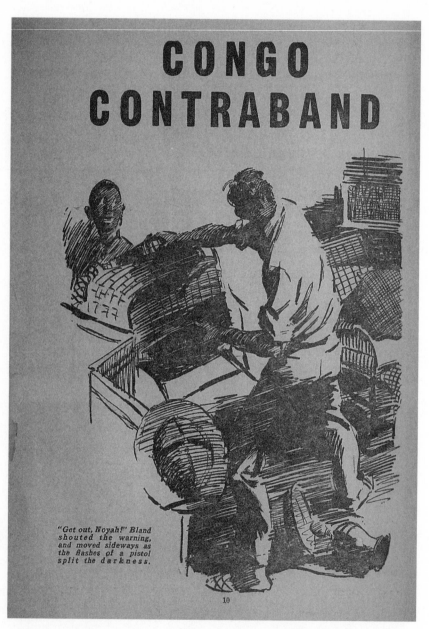

CONGO CONTRABAND

"Get out, Noyah!" Bland shouted the warning, and moved sideways as the flashes of a pistol split the darkness.

10

37. Hogue, a fluent writer of fiction, published a novelette entitled 'Congo Contraband' in *Adventure* in June 1947, which is set in the Belgian Congo in the early Cold War. The themes, characters, and places in the narrative are reminiscent of Hogue's mission in the Congo in 1943–44.

By DOCK HOGUE

ILLUSTRATED BY CHARLES GEER

A VICIOUS Congo sun, stabbing through motionless palms, filtered into the rambling, one-story, stucco building at 74 *Avenue des Etrangers.* Its scorching, mid-day blast had already emptied the streets of Leopoldville. Now, it touched Bland Wayne as he stood on the screened veranda of the combined office and living quarters for South Atlantic Airways, Incorporated. For once, however, the tall American didn't notice the tropical heat. It was no match for the turmoil in his mind.

"What a hellish thing to happen," he said softly, bitterness dripping from each word.

A note from Vice Consul Ken Hardwick, at the United States Consulate, four blocks down the avenue, disintegrated slowly between his strong fingers. A black, khaki-clad M'Betu messenger had delivered it a few minutes before. The four lines were terse. The remains of a white man, removed from the Congo River in Portuguese Angola territory three days before, had been identified as Willard Sutton, an American citizen who was the Angola and Southwest Africa

11

38. Page 2 of 'Congo Contraband'.

39. Congolese miners at Shinkolobwe pushing radioactive uranium ore down a shaft built after the war, 9 September 1960.

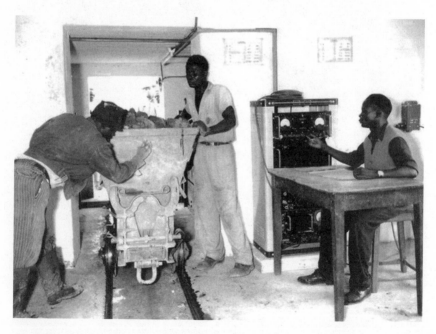

40. Workers after the war at Shinkolobwe, measuring the extracted uranium ore for radioactivity. They have no protective clothing or equipment.

41. A remnant of the former infrastructure at Shinkolobwe. This photograph was taken in the course of a mission to the mine in 2004 instigated by the UN, following the collapse of a mine shaft. The mission established that everyone working at the site is at risk of developing cancer and other health problems because of high radiation levels.

42. A press conference on 6 August 2015 arranged by Congo Square News in Cape Town to focus on the 'missing link' between DR Congo and Japan. Shigeki Furuhata, from the Japanese Consular Agency (left), holds a model of a clock to represent the 70 years that have passed since the bombing of Hiroshima; Fidèle Kalombo from DR Congo (with hat) holds a model of Africa showing the nuclear shadow.

18

STEHLI THE DETECTIVE

Suddenly, about a week before Dock Hogue had arrived in New York, a story broke out in Léopoldville about the smuggling of industrial diamonds from the Congo to Germany in Red Cross packages. It spread like wildfire through the colony. 'Rumors in the street were terrific,' reported Stehli. 'Everyone is talking about the diamond scandal.'[1] Some Congolese newspapers pointed their finger at 'an agent of the Sûreté d'Etat', meaning Jean Beaudinet, the Chef de Sûreté in Léopoldville. Smuggling goods to the enemy was an act of treason and it was being hushed up by prominent officials, claimed some of the press. Le Courrier d'Afrique, a French-language newspaper published in Léopoldville, urged that the guilty parties should be prosecuted. 'Light,' it said, 'is better than darkness.'[2] The story caused considerable anxiety to Governor General Ryckmans, observed the British Consul General, especially because Portuguese vessels were now refusing to load Red Cross and Prisoner of War parcels for transmission to Belgians via Portugal.[3] He arranged for a notice to be put in the papers, telling people with packages not to turn up at the last minute to take a plane, which made it impossible for Customs to check out them out.

'Perhaps the using of Decoster in Elisabethville was one of the smartest things 253 did,' reflected Stehli on Hogue's decision to choose Decoster as a cutout. 'He is a terrific talker and possibly is one of the chief sources of these rumors.' Wouldn't it be wonderful, he mused, 'if by his talking the Red Cross solved the whole matter?' He believed that the Red Cross was 'plenty powerful enough to bring this to a head'.[4] The organisation was better placed than any other group, he thought, to put a spotlight on the problem and stop it dead.

With Hogue gone, Stehli was now in charge of the OSS station in Léopoldville. He was glad to have Shirley Chidsey with him and also the company of Lanier Violett, the agent in Angola working under cover of Texas Oil, who had arrived on a visit. '397 is here keeping ANGELLA busy with very interesting reports', wrote Stehli to Hogue and Boulton in Washington, using Violett's code-number rather than his codename HOMER, in accordance with the recent instructions from Secret Intelligence. 'I am happy,' he added, 'that I have someone helpful to consult with during this possible diamond explosion.'[5] Given that—as we know from Stehli's obituary—he was working to prevent the diversion of uranium to Europe, it is reasonable to assume that this was the chief subject of his consultations with Violett.

But one of his priorities, he decided, was to find out how Hogue's arrangements with Decoster had been discovered—and he resolved to play detective.

He was new to espionage and had appreciated his former boss's guidance on how to gather information. His first move was to set up some dates to play golf with potential sources of information; this was not difficult to arrange, since he had a flair for golf and was an appealing partner on the golf course. On 15 September, he played a round of golf with Mme Gerard, the wife of A. S. Gerard, Van Bree's right-hand man. Next day, she played golf with Alan Williams, who was now the Acting British Consul General in Léopoldville and was 'quite a character, a former stevedore in Dakar'.[6] After this, Stehli and Williams compared notes. It turned out that she had told them both the same thing: that she was in favour of a complete exposure of any possible smuggling in Red Cross packages. She was presumably keen to put herself—and by association, her husband—in the clear.

Alan Williams was proving to be a useful source. He told Stehli that he had had 'two very interesting callers' and gave him the substance of both conversations. It was quite possible, thought Stehli, that Williams didn't tell him everything—but since Williams was very worried that the smuggling exposures might be blamed on the British, 'he is working closely with me to try to ward that off'. Stehli himself was working closely with Williams, to ensure that the Americans did not get blamed. But he was very careful not to give anything away to Williams and to follow to the letter an instruction from Washington: 'Do not discuss any phase of IDB or TETON's activities with anyone, especially British.'[7]

Williams told him that his first caller had arrived on 16 September—the Reverend Père Eugène Wolters, the head of the Congo Red Cross. Wolters told Williams that he intended to tell the Governor General that if Red Cross packages had been used for smuggling industrial diamonds to Germany, he wanted the whole matter out in the open. If not, then he demanded a public apology for the rumours.

Williams's second visitor was completely unexpected—Jean Beaudinet, who asked point blank whether Jacobs, the Chief of Police at Matadi, had been on Hogue's suspect list. Williams told him he had no idea, which prompted Beaudinet to announce that Jacobs had been investigated two years earlier, and had been found to be blameless. Williams asked to see the transcript of this investigation and Beaudinet said he would ask the 'higher-ups' for permission to show it to him.

Stehli played another game of golf on 21 September, in the few hours before sundown—this time, with Governor General Ryckmans. They played slowly, holding up the players behind them, who happened to be Alan Williams and a friend. For the first three or four holes, the conversation was inconsequential. But near the fourth hole, Ryckmans suddenly asked:

'Could you tell me what started the diamond investigation? Was it because you had found evidence of smuggling in the Congo, or was it because you felt that it was astonishing that the Germans had as many industrial diamonds as they seemed to have?'

203

Stehli was evasive—he said he had heard two years before of a British report that Germany must be facing a diamond shortage.

'That is just what I thought,' commented Ryckmans knowingly. Then Ryckmans asked Stehli if he knew that the books of Forminière, the diamond mining company in Kasai, showed that the Germans had captured about 400,000 carats in Belgium.[8] But Stehli, suspecting that Ryckmans was trying to probe how much he knew about uranium, using diamonds as a cover, closed down the subject. 'I have the strictest instructions,' he responded firmly, 'to have nothing more to do with the diamond situation, and I believe the British have the same instructions.' He then asserted his cover—silk. 'My particular diamonds,' he said pleasantly, 'are those two skeins of silk that you promised me at least a month ago.'[9]

On 26 September 1944, Stehli reported to Washington some information he had been given by Peter Stephens, the British Consul in Elisabethville. Stephens had spoken to Decoster, who told him that the Sûreté, in the form of Beaudinet and Scheerlinck, had suddenly descended upon him after Hogue's visit in May. They claimed, Decoster had told him, that the visit was in connection with the recent labour uprising and they examined all his papers—which was when they found the money Hogue had given him, and also the suspect list. But Stehli, listening to Stephens's account, knew this was impossible, as Hogue had not given a list of suspects to Decoster.

Decoster told Stephens that he had told Beaudinet and Scheerlinck the whole story about IDB and Hogue. They apparently thought it was 'a wonderful plan' and advised him to go ahead with his investigation, but not to inform the Parquet—the public prosecutor's department. Decoster followed this instruction. But shortly afterwards, Decoster was picked up by the Sûreté in Luluabourg and a slip of the tongue by the *Procureur du Roi*—the Crown Prosecutor—revealed that Beaudinet had in fact told the Parquet everything.

The 100,000 francs given to him by Hogue, said Decoster to Stephens, were in the hands of the Sûreté, but he believed they should be returned to him.[10] Decoster felt he ought to keep the money, because he had incurred expenses and had also experienced a great deal of unpleasantness, especially since Hogue had now left the Congo and deserted him. Stehli was not impressed. 'If he thinks he rendered us a service,' he noted briskly, thinking about the danger caused to Hogue by Decoster's activities, 'he is certainly wrong.'

Stephens also told Stehli that Mrs Fitch, Scheerlinck's mistress, had called on him with an extraordinary story regarding the diamond suspect list. Scheerlinck, she said, 'had gotten a black girl into the room of an American officer and during that period the list had been taken out of the room for a few hours and copied'.[11] Mrs Fitch claimed that she herself had copied it. And since the list was Hogue's, she appeared to be suggesting that it was Hogue who had been caught in this honey trap. Stehli quickly discounted the story. 'Mrs Fitch,' he reported to Washington, 'is known as unreliable and talks too much anyway.' The British, he added, said they too believed the story was fantastic. But he could well imagine that 'our Congo "Allies" would try to spread the rumor that this list was obtained while one of our men was with a black woman.' Framing another person, he added, was easy.[12]

Hogue and Boulton were following developments as closely as possible from Washington. In their judgement, the OSS station in Léopoldville was vulnerable and they feared that Stehli might have to leave the Congo suddenly—just as Hogue had done. What, they asked him, would he need to do if that happened? Stehli said his first priority was ANGELLA. At the very least, he would want her to be paid her three months' salary. But his preference, if they agreed, was to stop her salary and give her a flat 1000 dollars, because she had been 'a loyal and trusted agent'.[13]

He would hand all the equipment held by OSS to the American Consulate General for safe keeping, including the vehicles, and would pouch the money home. But he was acutely concerned about the contents of the safe. 'Frankly,' he said, 'I would like your permission to destroy all papers in the safe here where copies exist in Washington. I understand I am not allowed to destroy these files without your permission.'

Duane Luther—COACH—was now back on the scene in West Africa, based in Accra. He was instructed to fly to Léopoldville and remove all the files and money relating to IDB. He arrived on Friday 6 October and met with Stehli, explaining his mission— that he planned to take the files and money on the British flying boat that left on Monday for Lagos, the capital of the British colony of Nigeria, where ATC or BOAC ran daily planes to Accra. But he knew that customs inspection at Lagos had become extremely strict, so wanted Alan Williams to seal the envelopes, so that—as British diplomatic items—they would not be opened in Lagos. On Saturday Luther and Stehli went together to see Williams. But he wasn't prepared to help them. This was a bitter disappointment. Having been turned down by Williams, regretted Stehli, '946 and I knew that we had pulled a boner'. The British would now be aware that 'we wanted to sneak something out of the Congo, and, since they are no fools, they must know that it has something to do with IDB, and could notify the Sûreté'.

Stehli and Luther worried all weekend about what to do next. On Monday, Stehli sent a cable to Secret Intelligence in Washington, recommending the burning of the IDB files. Then Luther left on the flying boat.

On Friday 13 October, Stehli received orders from Boulton to burn the files in the presence of Luther. But this was impossible, since Luther had already left, five days earlier. Stehli immediately cabled Accra, asking permission to burn the files in the presence of ANGELLA instead, and to send the money to the Military Observer in Accra. But the message back was unclear; he asked for a repeat but it didn't arrive. As always, poor communications were creating real obstacles for the agents in the field.

On 16 October Howard Dean, the Vice President of Pan Am Africa, arrived in Léopoldville and had lunch with Benton and Stehli; Dean and Stehli had known each other since their shared childhood in Locust Valley. Dean told Stehli that Pan Am was extremely grateful to OSS for helping them get permission to land at the airport in Léopoldville. When Dean asked Stehli if he was with OSS he promptly denied it—but Dean 'knew perfectly well what my denial was'.[14] Since Dean had taken a key role in the shipping of uranium from the Congo to the US, no doubt they talked about this vital strand of the legation's activities.[15] But they both understood the importance of absolute secrecy. In an internal Pan Am document at the highest levels of the organisation, a list of strategic minerals to be transported by air from Léopoldville included uranium, but with an asterisk: '*Uranium'. Next to the list, by hand, was written: '*very confidential'.[16]

There was still the matter of the IDB funds: the $25,000 converted into Belgian Congo francs and given to Hogue for purchases on the illegal market—minus the 100,000 francs that he had given to Decoster for expenses. On Thursday 19 October Stehli planned to pack it up in an envelope marked 'secret', addressed to Luther by name. He would put this into another envelope marked 'secret', addressed to the Military Observer in Accra—Major McCaunahy, who had been a good friend of OSS in the region. This envelope would then be inserted in a package *not* marked 'secret', also addressed to McCaunahy.

Stehli counted the money as he prepared it for shipment. As he did so, he was startled to see that the bills—each one worth 500 francs—had come directly off the printing press in perfect sequence, so that he was able to count out the bills without any effort whatsoever. There were 2,181 bills, going from number 059001 all the way through to number 061182.[17]

The bills had been obtained in April, six months earlier, by Lt. Turk, under the direction of Adolph Schmidt, who had flown from Accra to Léopoldville for the purpose. Neither Stehli nor Hogue had been involved: Stehli had not yet arrived, and Hogue was keeping carefully in the background. Schmidt had noticed that the first set of bills supplied to Turk by the Banque du Congo Belge had been marked, so asked Turk to get them changed; Turk went back to the bank and exchanged the sum for 500 franc bills. In this way, hoped Schmidt, the risk of traceability had been avoided.

But he was wrong: for the sequential nature of the bills meant that the money *was* traceable. This may have been a deliberate move on the part of the cashier, or it may have been an innocent transaction. But in any case, the Banque du Congo Belge would be likely to take notice of a large sum of francs cashed by a US Army officer, who was based in Accra. The bank would also be likely to share such information with the Sûreté or the Belgian Congo administration.

The sequential nature of the notes made it possible to catch Decoster, once he had used some of the money to buy a train ticket to Luluabourg. It looked as if the plan had been scotched from the very start, just as Schmidt had feared it would be: for he had suffered misgivings all the way, as he flew from Accra to the Congo. But it is hard to know what else Schmidt could have done. He had tried to avoid traceability by getting the first set of marked bills replaced, but had no control over the final set of bills that was supplied by the bank.

All those who had been watching the developments of the Decoster affair had been baffled as to how he gave himself away. But now Stehli had worked it out. Life, in this case, had mimicked a standard mystery story—the well-used cliché of sequential bank notes.

Just over a year after Hogue had first arrived in the Congo, Stehli left Léopoldville on 21 November 1944 for a trip into the interior, leaving the OSS station in the care of Shirley Chidsey. The object of his trip was to gather information on the state of affairs in the Congo, and his cover was a plan to inspect the Belgian silk farm at Irumu in the north-east of the Congo, at the request of the State Department.[18] He would be travelling for much of the time with Alan Williams, the British Acting Consul General.

Stehli was determined to continue his detective work into the Decoster affair, especially now that he had discovered, he believed, the reason for Decoster's exposure. His first opportunity came up towards the end of his trip, when he was in Elisabethville. As soon as he arrived on 22 January 1945, he made arrangements to visit Decoster the next day. He went secretly, making sure that Alan Williams was not with him—'nor did he know that I was going. I circled the block twice and I am certain that I was not followed.'[19] He introduced himself to Decoster as the man who had been sent to the Congo to replace Hogue and was greeted with open arms. He was then taken into a private office, where he heard yet another account of what had happened—this time, from Decoster himself.

The day after Hogue had given him 100,000 francs, Decoster said, he went to Scheerlinck, the provincial head of the Sûreté in Katanga, and told him what the Americans wanted—'the whole layout'. Scheerlinck wished him good luck and Decoster believed that at that moment, Scheerlinck meant it, 'feeling as we did that it was a patriotic act'. Then Decoster took the train from Elisabethville for Luluabourg, getting off at a town called Kamina. Here he told the local agents of the Sûreté what he was doing and asked if they could help—but they had nothing to offer.

Decoster then went on to Luluabourg. Here he again went to see the agents of the Sûreté, who carefully went over the suspect list he had brought with him and which, he told Stehli, had been given to him by Hogue. Since Hogue had stated that he had not given such a list to Decoster, Stehli knew he was lying.

The agents at Luluabourg, continued Decoster, had little information to share: in the past, they said, some match-boxes filled with industrial diamonds had been smuggled out, but on a small scale. Decoster then returned to Elisabethville, arriving on Thursday afternoon. Next morning, Beaudinet and Scheerlinck called on him. Beaudinet had come all the way from Léopoldville and they 'really took him apart'. They searched through all the papers in his office and at home. However, they did not find the suspect list because by now, said Decoster to Stehli, he had destroyed it, having memorised all the important names on it. They took samples of the writing of all Decoster's typewriters and then produced another suspect list, which they said they had got from Peter Stephens.

Decoster gave them 80,000 francs, which was in his pocket, and was all that was left of the 100,000 francs Hogue had given him. He told Stehli that he had spent 20,000 francs on the trip to Luluabourg. But Stehli didn't believe him. He had just taken this trip himself—like Hogue, he had travelled on the BCK railroad going north from Katanga, checking out the route used to transport uranium from Shinkolobwe. He therefore knew that the round trip train fare from Elisabethville to Luluabourg was only 1,600 francs. 'So,' observed Stehli drily, 'he must have had a pretty gay time.' Decoster told him that the 80,000 francs had not been returned to him by the Sûreté; if they *were* returned, he said, he proposed to keep them. The whole situation, he complained, had affected his nerves so badly that he had been ill and suffered sleepless nights—so the money would be his compensation.

On two suspect lists—the one allegedly given to Decoster by Hogue, and another one apparently given to Beaudinet and Scheerlinck by Stephens—appeared the name of Etienne De Clerck, the Deputy Crown Prosecutor in Elisabethville. A few days after his interrogation by Beaudinet and Scheerlinck, Decoster was summoned by De Clerck to come and make a deposition on a small difficulty that he had had with one of his 'houseboys'. Since Decoster had been strictly instructed by Scheerlinck and Beaudinet not to say, or do, anything more in relation to diamond buying, he thought he ought to go. De Clerck asked him a few questions about the servant and then leaned back in his chair; the formal part of the meeting, he said, was now over. But informally, he wondered aloud, what did Decoster know about the industrial diamond situation? Decoster said he knew nothing, but asked who had told him about it. De Clerck said it was Scheerlinck—at which point Decoster opened up and told De Clerck everything.

A few days later, Decoster was summoned by a different Deputy Crown Prosecutor and asked to write and sign a full deposition of exactly what had transpired. This he did willingly, as he thought he had the Sûreté on his side.

After this meeting with Decoster, Stehli flew back to Léopoldville on 24 January. He remembered hearing about a letter that Benton had apparently written to the State Department, saying that the Governor General had sent for him and told him that 80,000 francs had been returned to Decoster. He therefore went to the legation to see if he could find the letter, but was unsuccessful. His hunt was all the more difficult because Benton had left Léopoldville by now, and had been replaced by Robert Buell as Consul General.

Later that evening, Stehli had a drink with Alan Williams. In an offhand way, he mentioned that he had seen Decoster. 'Oh', said Williams, 'Beaudinet will know right away.' This made Stehli suspicious. The only reason why Williams could have made such a remark, believed Stehli, was that the British had worked 'very closely' with Beaudinet against Hogue.

Stehli drew two conclusions. The first was that the British had heard of Hogue's activities and had spoken to Ryckmans, to get them stopped. The second was that De Clerck was guilty of smuggling, and Beaudinet knew this. And since De Clerck, given his position, would have known about the collaborationist meeting of 1940, many prominent members of society would not have wanted him to be arrested. For if he was arrested, he might talk.

It also seemed to Stehli that Decoster had seen a good opportunity of getting 100,000 francs, which was a large sum of money in the Congo. By taking it and immediately reporting it to the Sûreté, he could avoid getting into trouble. And if he were now able to get back the 80,000 francs, it would be 'just that much velvet'.[20]

Stehli asked Hogue and Boulton for permission, either by cable or letter, to go to Beaudinet and tell him that the 80,000 francs had not been returned to Decoster—and to ask Beaudinet whether he was going to return the money or not. 'As an individual, not as an agent of the Government,' he added, 'your permission to have this interview would give me enormous pleasure.'[21] He felt highly indignant at the turn of events and a keen sense of loyalty to Hogue. However, it looks as if Stehli may have been disappointed in his wish for this interview with Beaudinet: for no record has been found of permission being granted or of such a meeting taking place.

In West Africa, as in Europe, there was a sense that the war was ending. Radio Brazzaville, the Free French radio station where Shirley Chidsey had worked before moving to the Congo, was closed down permanently in December 1944. In the Congo, the Force Publique had reduced its Congo forces to about 15,000 troops and 1,500 Belgian officers, and the Expeditionary Force had returned from the Middle East. 'The native troops,' reported Stehli, 'were extremely well behaved during debarkation, and no trouble is expected from them in the future. Some of the Force Publique officers are being demobilized and returned to private life.'[22]

The British intelligence organisation in West Africa had closed down by the end of July 1944 and SOE and SIS officials were gradually withdrawn; intelligence work was now in the hands of liaison officers such as Major Birch in Léopoldville and Colonel Russell in Accra. On 9 October 1944 the OSS office in Washington was informed that London had no further interest in IDB.[23] Lord Swinton, Resident Minister in West Africa, left Accra in October to assume the post of Minister of Civil Aviation at home in Britain; he was replaced by Captain Harold Balfour and the post was much diminished.

On 7 November 1944, the American presidential elections were held. Franklin D. Roosevelt, the Democrat nominee, sought his fourth term in office—and won. The lead-up to the election seemed very distant to Stehli, especially since the American community in Léopoldville had received no mail for three weeks. 'This may reach you just before or after you have put an "X" in the wrong square of the ballot,' he wrote jokingly to Boulton and Hogue—as always, addressing both of them equally—in mid-October, 'but since we are winning the war it really doesn't make much difference.'[24]

19

'ONE MINUTE TO MIDNIGHT'

Once Dock Hogue had returned to the US from Africa in September 1944, he wrote a field report on his mission in the Belgian Congo. The report describes his mission as an investigation into the smuggling of industrial diamonds. The evidence available, however, suggests that he was using diamonds as a cover for uranium, as he had done throughout his posting in the Congo—and just as Schmidt and Stehli had done also.

Hogue's report drew attention to the fact that he had expressed misgivings about the IDB investigation before leaving for the Congo—but had nonetheless followed his orders to the letter. The mission had been successful: he had established that 'a full year's supply of industrial diamonds had reached the enemy' through Red Cross parcels in 1942. He had also discovered a diamond smuggling ring 'including a high Belgian cartel official', which used diplomatic pouches; at least one member of the Sûreté was involved (who is not named in the report, but was evidently Jean Beaudinet). Hogue explained that the Sûreté, once they had found out how much he knew, had framed him on a false charge. This was presented to Governor General Ryckmans, who arranged with J. Webb Benton, the American Consul General, that Hogue should leave the Congo. Hogue's report emphasised the failure of Benton to support him and OSS.

Adolph Schmidt was Acting Divisional Deputy in the Africa Section of Secret Intelligence at this time, since Boulton was away. It was therefore Schmidt's job to write a departmental report on Hogue. In fact, there was no one better placed to do this, since he himself had been involved in the early stages of the mission, when he was sent to the Congo from Accra 'to have all shipments of uranium ore from Katanga mines checked for possible diversions to areas other than port of Matadi'. Schmidt backed Hogue vigorously and criticised Benton for not explaining to Ryckmans that Hogue's activities were directed 'against subversive elements who were trading with the common enemy'. It was a shame, said Schmidt, that Benton had not appreciated 'the splendid work which Mr Hogue has performed for this government'; and he added that State officials had told him privately that in their opinion, Benton had been too hasty. 'The timing was particularly unfortunate,' observed Schmidt with feeling, 'in that 253 was in the last stages of resolving many apparently unrelated IDB items into a cohesive pattern.'[1]

The reports by Hogue and Schmidt, along with a memorandum from Benton to the State Department on 26 August, were sent to the Chief of Secret Intelligence, who forwarded them on to Bill Donovan, the Director of OSS, on 12 October. An investigation was conducted, which gave high praise to Hogue's work in the Congo. 'Mr Hogue,' it stated firmly, 'rendered valuable services to the government, and after a thorough review of the facts known to date our confidence in him remains unimpaired.'[2]

Hogue continued to work in the Que Building with the Africa Section of Secret Intelligence and was regarded as an authoritative source on the continent, especially the Congo and Liberia. On 29 December 1944, when a meeting was held at the State Department on Liberia, he was the chief expert present.[3]

Far away in the Congo, the director of customs at the port of Matadi, De Gesnot, accused Jean Beaudinet of smuggling and instigated proceedings against him. Beaudinet lost the case and was forced to step down from his position in the Sûreté.[4] Jean Decoster, meanwhile, returned to life as normal. There is no record of what happened to the remainder of the funds given to him by Hogue to purchase smuggled goods; it was not returned to OSS.

Hogue had gone to extreme lengths to complete his mission and knew he had done his best. Even at the last minute, shortly before his departure, he had taken the dangerous risk of checking out a 'leak' in Elisabethville. But the situation regarding Congolese uranium was starting to change. When Hogue and Schmidt had been given their missions in late 1943, there had been a very real fear among the leaders of the Manhattan Project that Germany was building an atomic bomb—and might even be ahead of the US. It was therefore a matter of acute concern that some of the high quality uranium mined in the Congo might be diverted to Germany. But by November 1944—shortly after Hogue's return to the US—new intelligence was emerging which revealed that Germany had no atom bomb after all, and was not likely to develop one.

This intelligence was gathered by the ALSOS mission, which had been set up by General Groves to learn the progress of German nuclear scientists' efforts to build an atomic bomb.[5] Its codename—'ALSOS'—is the Greek word for 'grove', an allusion to Groves himself, the head of the Manhattan Project. It numbered about thirty personnel, under the scientific direction of Samuel A. Goudsmit, a physicist of Dutch-Jewish descent, whose parents were deported in 1943 to a concentration camp by the Nazi occupiers of The Netherlands and were murdered there. The overall command of ALSOS was under Lt.-Col. Boris Pash. The secrecy of ALSOS was imperative, so Goudsmit took a dim view of its codename—which seemed to him 'a give-away'. To make it 'even more obvious', he objected, 'the Mission's vehicles had license plates bearing the Greek letter Alpha'.[6] But despite this drawback, the mission was highly successful.

After the Allied invasion of Normandy in France—D-Day—on 6 June 1944, the ALSOS team followed closely behind the advancing Allied armies as they pushed into Europe. As soon as Brussels was liberated in September 1944, ALSOS went to the

Belgian capital to interrogate the managers of Union Minière about the uranium from Shinkolobwe.[7]

A priority for ALSOS was to investigate the University of Strasbourg, which had apparently ordered new equipment for nuclear research and had enlarged its staff, recruiting the first-rate theorist, Carl Friedrich Von Weizsacker. This investigation was made possible by the liberation of Strasbourg in late November 1944, following which the ALSOS team rushed immediately to the city. After just 48 hours of study at the university—interviewing scientists, examining documents, and inspecting laboratories—Goudsmit drew a conclusion that afforded him immense relief. 'The evidence at hand,' he stated later, 'proved definitely that Germany had no atom bomb and was not likely to have one in a reasonable time.' The material was sent to Paris and to Washington, where Goudsmit's conclusions were endorsed.[8]

The OSS agents operating in Europe gave considerable assistance to ALSOS, for which Goudsmit was grateful, describing them as 'our O.S.S. friends'.[9] But OSS also set up its own, separate, mission to conduct operations in Europe relating to the German atomic bomb project—AZUSA. Groves was 'so desperate for information about the German programme', comments one historian, that he was willing to back two independent missions to find out what they could. And in 'typical Groves style', he adds, compartmentalisation meant that the two missions—ALSOS and AZUSA—knew nothing of each other.[10]

In late December 1944, AZUSA implemented a plan to kidnap, even to assassinate, Werner Heisenberg, the foremost German atomic theoretician. Heisenberg had stayed in Germany, despite pressure from physicists in the USA to join them, and was leading the German atomic project as director of the Kaiser Wilhelm Institute in Berlin.[11] The OSS mission was given to the baseball player Morris—'Moe'—Berg, the former catcher for the Boston Red Sox, whose codename in OSS was REMUS. He had studied at Princeton and the Sorbonne, was fluent in many languages, and was considered 'the brainiest player in the major leagues'.[12] He was instructed to kill Heisenberg, if evidence emerged that he was helping to build a German atomic bomb: his official assignment was 'to deny Germany his brain'.[13]

Berg wrote notes of the briefing he was given: 'Gun in my pocket. Nothing spelled out, but—Heisenberg must be rendered *hors de combat*.' In December 1944, Berg went to a lecture by Heisenberg in Zurich, carrying in his pocket a small pistol and a cyanide pill, so that he would be able to kill himself if he shot Heisenberg and was unable to escape. But listening to the lecture, he was not persuaded that Heisenberg was an immediate threat, and aborted the mission.[14] Berg's judgement was consistent with the findings of the ALSOS team the month before.

ALSOS went on to find yet more proof of Germany's failure to build an atomic bomb—as well as evidence that Congolese uranium had been obtained by the Germans. In April 1945, the mission discovered several thousand tons of uranium, which had been buried in a hill and then ploughed over.[15] The site of this cache was not far from Hechingen, where part of the Kaiser Wilhelm Institute for Physics had been moved. In a cave nearby, there was also a large chamber with a concrete pit, where the physicists had sought—but failed—to build a reactor.[16] German scientists, observes Jeffrey T. Richelson in *Spying on the Bomb*, 'had not even completed a functioning reactor, and were in no position to *attempt* to build a bomb. There were no German counterparts to Los Alamos, Oak Ridge, or Hanford.' This intelligence confirmed beyond a doubt that Hitler could not avert his imminent defeat by using a superweapon—that the war would not turn against the Allies at 'one minute to midnight', in the words of Lieutenant Colonel Howard Dix, who was head of the Technical Section of OSS's Secret Intelligence Branch.[17]

The confiscation of German uranium ore was of crucial importance to General Groves. An airborne division and two armoured divisions were deployed to achieve this objective. But as it turned out, no military assault was required: the ALSOS team managed to seize the entire stock, which was sent to the US.[18]

*

On Thursday, 12 April 1945, Roosevelt suffered a massive cerebral haemorrhage and died some hours later. His successor was Vice President Harry S. Truman. For the previous few months, Truman had chaired the Senate Special Committee investigating the National Defense Program, which had been investigating the massive discrepancies in military funds allocated to the War Department. Within days of becoming President, he was informed about the Manhattan Project—and now he knew where the missing funds had gone.[19]

On 8 May 1945, in Truman's first few weeks of office, Germany surrendered. Hitler had killed himself on 30 April and it has been said that one of his final acts was to ship 1,235 pounds of uranium ore by U-boat to Japan.[20] Whether or not it was on Hitler's orders, it is indeed the case that a German U-234 boat attempted to sail to Japan with various kinds of weaponry on board, including the uranium. However, the war in Europe ended before the submarine arrived in Japan and the German commander headed to North America, where he surrendered to the US Navy on 19 May 1945. The Japanese officers on board asked for permission to commit suicide, which was granted. A thorough analysis of the doomed voyage has been provided in *Germany's Last Mission to Japan* by Joseph M. Scalia, who concludes that U-234's consignment of uranium oxide was not indicative of any large-scale Axis program. He adds that although Germany and Japan were further advanced in their nuclear programmes than initially suspected, 'it is unlikely that the Axis partners had developed a critical-mass reactor or applicable bomb program by the spring of 1945'.[21] There was no competition of any real kind with the US.

However rudimentary Japanese experimentation with uranium may have been, it appears that no one in America was aware of Japan's atomic programme until after the war. Herbert York, director emeritus of the University of California's Institute on Global Conflict and Cooperation, has said that Manhattan Project scientists appear to have known nothing about it. 'I don't think anybody knew,' said York. 'We didn't think the Japanese were doing anything. We were worried about the Germans.'[22]

Now that Germany was defeated, some of those few people who knew about the Manhattan Project were asking questions about the value, moral and otherwise, of continuing the work—at least, on the same basis as before. In 1939, Albert Einstein had sent a letter to President Roosevelt, warning of the potential of the Nazi regime to develop an atomic bomb and emphasising the need to protect the uranium in the Belgian Congo—'the most important source'. He now said he would never have signed the letter if he had anticipated that the Germans would fail to build a bomb and wrote with a very different message to President Truman. Since Germany's potential had been shown to be unrealised, he urged that the Manhattan Project should be halted or at least scaled back.[23]

But there was no halt and no scaling back. Leo Szilard, the physicist who had been involved with Einstein in persuading Roosevelt to launch the atomic project, started to worry in the spring of 1945 about the use of the bomb. But, he said, it was simply impossible to speak to those who might have influence on President Truman and the military, 'because of the secrecy rules'.[24]

On 16 July 1945, Los Alamos scientists conducted the Trinity test—the first test in history of an atomic bomb—near Alamogordo, New Mexico. The bomb was made from plutonium, a synthetic fissionable element manufactured from uranium.[25] The day before the test, Enrico Fermi, the Italian-American physicist who had built the first nuclear reactor, had wondered aloud whether the test bomb might destroy every living thing on earth. Scientists had conducted various probability analyses—but nobody really knew.[26]

The test was a success and Groves was exuberant—the atomic era had begun.[27] On 25 July, just over a week later, the order was issued to drop an atomic bomb on Japan. The Air Force, it said, 'will deliver its first special bomb as soon as weather will permit visual bombing after about 3 August 1945 on one of its targets: Hiroshima, Kokura, Niigata and Nagasaki.'[28] There is no indication that Japan's efforts to build an atomic bomb contributed to this order, since the Japanese project was not known about by Truman or any other American involved in the decision.[29]

But already, as Gregg Herken observes in *The Winning Weapon*, his account of the atomic bomb in the Cold War, the focus of the atomic mission was being redirected from the wartime to the post-war world—and from Germany and Japan to the Soviet Union. In fact, Groves stated some years after the war that he had had the Soviet Union in his sights from the very start. 'There was never, from about two weeks from the time I took charge of this Project,' he wrote, 'any illusion on my part but that Russia was our enemy. I didn't go along with the attitude of the country as a whole that Russia was a gallant ally.' He had always had his suspicions, he added, 'and the Project was concluded on that basis'. For this reason, the ALSOS mission was tasked not only to investigate the state of German research, but also to keep the scientists and atomic raw materials of the German bomb project out of the hands of the Russians.[30]

The strategic materials mined in Africa, especially uranium, meant that the continent now had an importance for the US that had never existed before the war. This was explored in October 1944 in a report by the Africa Section of OSS Secret Intelligence, which noted the:

> basic lacks in our available strategic materials, which we must compensate. Most other major powers, with perhaps the exception of Russia, also have serious shortages of basic materials and will turn attention to the vast stores in Africa in the hope of gaining ultimate control.

The strongest new power emerging from this war, argued the report, 'is Russia. It has no territory in Africa but does have ties to France which has its colonies on the continent. We must expect some effort by the Russians to gain influence in such an important area. Russian penetration of Africa may be eventually through the French.'[31] It recommended careful planning for the future to resist and prevent this, taking into account the fact that economic warfare was now a very important weapon.

220

France, Italy, Spain, Belgium and Portugal owned vast territories in Africa—'yet each of them', noted the report, 'has deteriorated in real power and prestige as a result of the war. Britain, the only other power of significance, has only a small chance of emerging as a first-rate power.' The final world equilibrium, it predicted, 'will depend on who holds the cards—materials, technology and technologically trained manpower; it now looks as though it would be a balance between USA and Russia. Africa will be one of the largest prizes; its present disequilibrium (due to weakness of its mother countries) will cause it to fall into the orb of one of the other camps.'[32]

Victory in Europe Day was marked in many parts of colonial Africa. From Angola, it was reported to OSS that the Governor General proclaimed a holiday and a torchlight parade was held, with joyful crowds streaming in and out of the consulates of the Allied nations. 'Although the US representative did nothing, except raise the American flag,' it was noted, 'the British, as usual, capitalized on the situation and held a banquet at which the Governor General presided.'[33]

After VE Day, the budget allocated to OSS was drastically reduced and on 5 July 1945 the Africa Division cabled Accra with instructions to terminate operations in the Gold Coast and Liberia, aiming for the end of the month. But the OSS station in the Congo was to stay open—and Rud Boulton's office was working hard to extend OSS coverage in the Belgian colony.[34]

This was by no means an easy task. Henry Stehli had left the Congo in March 1945, suffering from a very serious illness, which was diagnosed as malaria; he returned to the US on 16 April, a thin and exhausted shadow of the fit and healthy man who had left for the Congo the year before. After his departure, Shirley Chidsey became *de facto* chief of station, and she expected to remain until a replacement for Stehli arrived. But this was proving to be a problem, because the Consul General, Robert Buell, was refusing to allow any more members of OSS to be attached to

221

the Consulate. Two men had been recruited in turn for the post, but each one was turned down by Buell.[35]

ANGELLA was now based in the US Consulate. She was giving part time secretarial assistance to Consul Buell, as well as sending reports to OSS. '1080,' noted Secret Intelligence in Washington, 'is developing rapidly into a competent source during this interim period.'[36] After the death of President Roosevelt, she wrote to report on a 'very fine service' in the Protestant Chapel in Léopoldville, which was 'brief and simple', with a large turnout. Many people came up to her 'to say that they were so sorry because to the Belgians Roosevelt truly represented the ideas of democracy and of American friendship'.[37]

Still an enthusiastic railfan, she wrote to *Railroad Magazine* in April 1945 to tell them how much their publication was appreciated in Léopoldville. 'Copies of *Railroad Magazine*,' she wrote, 'sit in proud state on the OWI [Office of War Information] magazine rack here and are very popular.'[38]

But OSS was keen to be represented by a fully trained agent. And since Consul Buell was showing no signs of relenting, it was decided to insert an agent into the Congo who was completely undercover—who would not be disclosed to anyone in the Consulate, not even to Chidsey. The person chosen was CLOCK— John W. Kirkland, who had previously been assigned to Ivory Coast, under cover of working for Texaco. Kirkland, a graduate of Harvard, was 'a hard worker and a keen observer with an analytic mind', in Luther's view.[39] He seemed ideal for the Congo, because he had already worked in Léopoldville for Texaco before going to Ivory Coast and also had wide experience of living in sub-Saharan Africa: as well as working in Ivory Coast and the Congo, he had spent two years prospecting for gold in Tanganyika (now Tanzania), one year selling mining machinery on the Witwatersrand in South Africa, followed by nearly a year of gold prospecting in Swaziland.[40]

Kirkland arrived in the Congo on 2 April 1945, with a new codenumber—1060. His cover in the Congo was again Texaco, as

Senior Representative for the company in Léopoldville, and his chief mission was to watch the Portuguese community in the Congo, with an eye for any smuggling activities. But, as in Ivory Coast, he was plagued by malaria. 'Should you re-read the pouch letters written from my last post,' he wrote to Washington, 'you would doubtlessly find far-too-frequent comments on my health. As ever, the trouble has been and is malaria. During the last month, the office was closed eight days.'[41]

By now, the burly Duane Luther—codenumber 946—was back in Africa as Chief of the Gold Coast station in Accra; he had taken over from Hunt Harris, who had left for Washington in November the year before. On 18 June 1945, Luther flew to the Congo to check out the OSS station in Léopoldville and to arrange cable communications for 1080. There were now '1 secretary at the Léopoldville station, 4 informants regularly used, and 1 undercover agent.'[42]

But Consul Buell continued to refuse to allow an agent to be associated with the Consulate. On 12 July a cable was dispatched to ANGELLA, asking her to put 'subtle pressure' on the Consul to get him to agree. But Buell was obdurate. Instead, he now wanted to employ Chidsey officially as his assistant. He said he would let her send information to OSS, if they made up the difference to her previous salary, since he only had funds available for a secretary's rate of pay.[43] This was agreed by OSS in Washington.

John Kirkland sent reports on the affairs of the colony to Washington. The keynote, he said, was 'one of suspicion, distrust and restlessness and a growing feeling of resentment against the mother country'.[44] The 'colonials', he observed, 'strongly believe that some of the top officials of the Congo were collaborators'. A Major in the Force Publique had been heard to say that a purge 'would have to come; we know who they all are'.[45]

Shirley Chidsey had been touched by the tributes to Roosevelt from Belgians, after the President's death. But Kirkland, as he travelled around the colony, found rather different attitudes: a growing and palpable dislike of Americans by Belgians. There was 'more anti-American sentiment than can reasonably be explained', observed Kirkland, 'unless it is ascribed to the efforts of British propaganda agents'. He was aware, he said, that 'the British have previously fanned anti-American sentiment in the Congo'.[46] Some people believed that 'the United States planned to occupy the Congo' and a representative of an American business firm, who had travelled through the Belgian Congo, said he felt strong anti-American sentiment from Belgians throughout his trip.[47]

Meanwhile, reported Kirkland, the big companies in Katanga were concerned about the steady growth of labour unions during the war. 'Labor has grown strong and united enough,' assessed Kirkland, 'to be able to force representation on government councils. It is obvious, too, that relations between labor and capital in the Congo are not peaceful.' Once Kirkland's report reached Washington, it was sent on to the Department of State.[48] But his information about trade unions related only to white workers in the Congo, since Africans—skilled and unskilled—were not allowed to unionise, by reason of their colour, until 1946 (and even then, the unions were heavily circumscribed).[49]

The people of the Congo were living and working in terrible conditions. In November 1945, 5–6,000 workers in Léopoldville went on strike; and when railway personnel spread the news of the strike to Matadi, the dockworkers joined in. Up to 1,500 strikers marched through the streets of the port and were met with a brutal response: an unknown number, including women and children, were killed by soldiers. A curfew was enforced and the prison at Matadi was so packed that some prisoners died of suffocation.

The moral authority of the struggle against fascism was not applied to the inequalities and injustice in the Congo.[50] There, observes David Van Reybrouck, 'the final days of the war did not feel like liberation. When Brussels was freed, the Congolese danced in the streets of Léopoldville. They hoped that everything was going to be different. But the euphoria did not last for long.'[51]

20

HIROSHIMA

At 8:15 a.m. local time on Monday 6 August 1945, the first atomic bomb used against human beings was dropped by an American plane over the Japanese city of Hiroshima. It was also, in effect, the first test of a bomb built with uranium, rather than plutonium (the synthetic fissionable material manufactured from uranium, which had been used in the Trinity bomb).[1]

'In a blinding, horrifying instant,' records the Hiroshima Peace Memorial Museum, 'that single explosion reduced an entire city to scorched rubble.' The total number of the dead in Hiroshima by the end of December 1945, when deaths from acute conditions had subsided, was approximately 140,000. About 60 per cent are thought to have died of burns from the heat rays and fire, about 20 per cent were killed by blast injuries, and the remaining 20 per cent by radiation. Long after the acute effects of radiation had subsided, radiation damage continued to produce a range of physical problems, including leukaemia and cancer.[2]

The bomb had been built with uranium from the Congo. But the mine workers at Shinkolobwe, comments David Van Reybrouck, 'could never have imagined that the leaden, yellowish ore that was processed into "yellow cake" after they dug it up would lead to such destruction on the other side of the world. No one knew a thing.'[3] Shinji Mikamo, who was left severely injured and burned by the bomb on Hiroshima when he was 19, was astonished when he was told in 2015, at the age of 89, that the bomb had been built with uranium from the Congo. He said it was far from anything he could have imagined. He thought, too, that other survivors—and their descendants—would be surprised to learn of this.[4]

Robert Oppenheimer, the technical director of the Manhattan Project, was remorseful when he was told of the dropping of the bomb in August 1945. 'The physicists,' he commented bleakly, 'have known sin!'[5] President Truman took a very different view. 'This is the greatest thing in history,' he enthused, later saying he had never been happier than when he made the announcement.[6] An account was released of the expense to the US of the atomic energy programme. 'We spent $2,000,000,000 on the greatest scientific gamble in history,' said Truman '—and we won.'[7]

Millions of people across the world were astonished: the secrecy of the Project had been so complete that hardly anyone knew about it. Even among those who had helped to build the bomb in the US, notes the physicist and historian Stanley Goldberg, the fact that the United States possessed an atomic bomb came as a total surprise. This was because very few people had been allowed an overall picture of the project. 'Even though a half-million American citizens worked for the Manhattan Project at some point during the war,' records Goldberg, 'only a handful of people actually understood the purpose of their labor.'[8] Truman trumpeted this fact as a sign of the Project's success: 'Few know what they have been producing.'[9]

Reactions to the atomic bomb were mixed. Across the world, people were worn out by the war and many welcomed the bomb, believing it had brought the conflict to an end. They were told little of the devastation the bomb had caused. When Japan surrendered to the Allies after almost six years of war, there was joyful celebration around the world. The day of surrender, 15 August 1945, was declared Victory in Japan day—VJ Day—and the end of war was marked by two-day holidays in the UK, the USA and Australia.

But many were distressed. 'The news came over the radio,' remembered a British woman then in Berlin, 'and we listened, and we could not believe it. One Army officer—not a softie, a tough soldier—said, "My God, that's not the way to fight a war. *That* is wrong!" There was a feeling that this was beyond the rules of war, a feeling of great shock.'[10] A representative of the Vatican gave a grim warning. 'This war provides a catastrophic conclusion,' he observed. 'Incredibly this destructive weapon remains as a temptation for posterity, which, we know by bitter experience, learns so little from history.'[11] Five senior American commanders criticised the attack, including General Dwight D. Eisenhower, who said, 'The Japanese were ready to surrender, and it wasn't necessary to hit them with that awful thing.'[12]

On the day the bomb was launched, it was headline news on the BBC Home Service in Britain:

> Here is the news. President Truman has announced a tremendous achievement by Allied scientists. They have produced the atomic bomb. One has already been dropped on a Japanese army base. It alone contained as much explosive power as two-thousand of our great ten-tonners.

By quoting Truman's reference to 'a Japanese army base' rather than 'a Japanese city full of civilians', the news was unintentionally misleading—and not as horrifying as the actual truth. Then the newsreader made an awkward shift to the mundane:

> it's been a Bank Holiday of thunderstorms as well as sunshine: a record crowd at Lord's has seen Australia make 265 for 5 wickets.[13]

Prime Minister Attlee had led the Labour Party to a landslide victory in the election of 5 July 1945, which ended Winston Churchill's wartime coalition government. Before leaving government, Churchill had prepared a statement on the atomic bomb, which was now issued by Attlee. It emphasised that the UK had been in partnership with the US and that the scientists had worked together. 'Complete secrecy,' emphasised Churchill, 'guarded all these activities, and no single person was informed whose work was not indispensable to progress.' By 'God's mercy,' he added, 'British and American science outpaced all German efforts. These were on a considerable scale, but far behind.'

He made a point of acknowledging the part played by Canada. 'The Canadian Government, whose contribution was most valuable,' he stated, 'provided both indispensable raw material for the project as a whole and also necessary facilities for the work on one section of the project, which has been carried out in Canada by the three Governments in partnership.'[14] But although he drew attention to the raw material provided by Canada, he made no mention whatsoever of the Congo, which had supplied the essential ingredient.

Next day, *The Times* of London published an article on the bomb, which drew attention to the role of uranium. 'The emergence of the atomic bomb,' it said, 'will undoubtedly stimulate the search for uranium, the principal metal used in the production of the new weapon.' It then went on implicitly to exclude the Congo from the history of the creation of the bomb. 'Canada,' it said, 'leads the Empire and the world in the supply of this metal.'[15] But this was not in any way true. 'Without access to the Shinkolobwe mine,' observes Patrick Marnham in *Snake Dance*, 'it is very unlikely that the bomb would have been built during the Second World War.'[16] The focus on Canada was deliberate disinformation by the British government, in order to draw attention away from Congolese uranium.

Truman made no mention of uranium whatsoever when he announced the use of the 'A-Bomb' on Hiroshima. Secretary of War Henry L. Stimson *did* refer to the centrality of the ore, but did not refer to any country or region of the world as the source. According to the *New York Times*, he simply stated that 'steps have been taken, to assure us of adequate supplies of this mineral'.[17] Both the US and Britain avoided drawing the attention of the Soviet Union to the source of the richest uranium in the world— the Shinkolobwe Mine.

Three days after the bombing of Hiroshima, on 9 August, the US dropped a second atomic bomb on Japan—on the city of Nagasaki. This time the bomb was made with plutonium, like the

Trinity bomb. As at Hiroshima, the results were devastating and tragic. An American news correspondent, who flew over the Nagasaki area 12 hours after the bombing, said the city was still a mass of flames, and that it was 'like looking over the rim of a volcano in process of eruption'.[18]

Leading German physicists were clear that, above all, it was the lack of uranium ore that had impeded German efforts to build a bomb. This judgement was recorded in discussions held among ten German scientists who were taken directly after VE Day to Farm Hall near Godmanchester, 15 miles from Cambridge, which was owned by the British Secret Service. Here they were detained, carefully closed away from the outside world, from July to December 1945. The physicists were: Erich Bagge; Kurt Diebner, who had approached Union Minière in June 1940 on behalf of the Nazi military, stating that the German authorities aimed to buy the company's stocks of refined uranium oxide; Walther Gerlach; Otto Hahn, who had discovered nuclear fission in 1938; Paul Harteck; Heisenberg, whom OSS agent Moe Berg had decided not to kill in Zurich in December 1944; Horst Korsching; Max Theodor Felix Von Laue; Carl Friedrich Von Weizsäcker; and Karl Wirtz.

Their conversations were recorded clandestinely by hidden microphones in an operation called 'Epsilon'; those with intelligence value were sent to London and to the American consulate, from where they were sent directly to Groves. The physicists appear not to have known they were being recorded, judging by an exchange between Diebner and Heisenberg in the presence of their colleagues:

DIEBNER: I wonder whether there are microphones installed here?

HEISENBERG: Microphones installed? (laughing) Oh no, they're not as cute as all that. I don't think they know the real Gestapo methods; they're a bit old-fashioned in that respect.'[19]

When the German physicists imprisoned at Farm Hall learned on 6 August 1945 about Hiroshima, they were staggered. Otto

Hahn was the first to be told and his immediate reaction was to consider suicide. He said that, as the scientist who had discovered the principle of uranium fission in 1938, he felt personally responsible for the deaths of hundreds of thousands of people. After a number of stiff drinks, he calmed down and went to join his colleagues at dinner—where he announced the news to the others.[20] 'At first,' observed a report on the surveillance of their conversations, 'they refused to believe it and felt that it was bluff on our part, to induce the Japanese to surrender. After hearing the official announcement they realised that it was a fact. Their first reaction, which I believe was genuine, was an expression of horror that we should have used this invention for destruction.'

Later in the evening, Hahn left the room. The conversation that followed highlighted Germany's shortage of uranium ore:

WIRTZ: We hadn't got enough uranium.

WEIZSACKER: We would have had to equip long distance aircraft with uranium engines to carry out airborne landings in the Congo or North West Canada. We would have had to have held these areas by military force and produce the stuff from mines. That would have been impossible.[21]

The physicists were right about the importance of Congolese ore, but wrong about Canadian ore. Their mistake reflects the success of the Allies' campaign to spread disinformation about the centrality of ore from Canada.

Ever since September 1945, uranium has been seen by the public at large as less essential to the atomic project than the brilliance of physicists. This view has been cultivated by the official description of the race to build the bomb, such as Truman's announcement that the bombing of Hiroshima marked the end of 'the race of *discovery* against the Germans' (emphasis added).[22] This was deliberate disinformation, argues Stanley Goldberg, which generated 'the widely held belief that there had been *a* secret, some deep hidden principle of nature that had been discovered during the war by physicists in America and that no one else could possibly discover in the short term without assistance from those in the know'. In fact, argues Goldberg, there was no such secret. Groves may have trumpeted the glory of American scientific talent and technical infrastructure, but he knew that the irreplaceable ingredient was high-grade ore: 'No ore, no bomb. Groves was not a stupid man.'[23]

The same lack of sufficient high quality uranium that had impeded the German atomic project had also, as it turned out, obstructed Japanese attempts to make a bomb. The Manhattan Project Intelligence Group arrived in Japan in September 1945 and examined Japan's wartime nuclear weapons programme. The Group concluded that it was the lack of uranium ore, along with low priority, that had doomed the Japanese effort. Contrary to popular belief in the West, they reported, Japan's nuclear physicists were every bit as good as those of other nations.[24]

America had achieved a global hegemony, which was entirely reliant on its monopoly of Congolese uranium—and which had to be maintained at all costs against the Soviet threat. The watchword on everything to do with the atomic project, just as during the years of war, was absolute secrecy. On VJ Day, President Truman issued a memorandum from the White House which set out clearly the parameters of secrecy. The memorandum, which was sent to the Secretary of State, the Secretary of War, the Secretary of the Navy, the Joint Chiefs of Staff, and the Director of the Office of Scientific Research and Development, directed appropriate departments of the Government and the Joint Chiefs of Staff 'to take such steps as are necessary to prevent the release of any information in regard to the development, design or production of the atomic bomb; or in regard to its employment in military or naval warfare, except with the specific approval of the President in each instance'.

On 30 August 1945, the memorandum was slightly modified, but remained substantially the same: the rules prohibited the release of any information of value to any foreign government which that government could not easily obtain without recourse to espionage. This included information about Shinkolobwe. Bill

Donovan, the director of OSS, was sent an early draft of the memorandum, for his signature; and he was sent a copy of the final memorandum on 4 September.[25]

Strict censorship was imposed on Japan by the American occupation forces. Almost no information about the impact of the atomic bombs was revealed to the outside world until 31 August 1946, when John Hersey, an American journalist, published an account of six survivors of the blast in the *New Yorker*.[26]

For several years after the exploding of the A-bombs on Japan, the US and Britain were confident that the Soviet Union did not have sufficient uranium to build an atomic bomb. 'The manufacture of atomic weapons,' observed a report of the British Joint Intelligence Committee in 1948, demands 'the use of large quantities of uranium. The most reliable present estimate that can be made of Russian progress indicates that the limiting factor is their supplies of uranium.'[27] The Committee estimated that the most likely date for the first Soviet test would be January 1954.[28]

But there was anecdotal evidence, at the very least, to suggest that the Soviets were not so very far behind the Americans. According to an entry in October 1945 in the diary of Hugh Dalton, the British Chancellor of the Exchequer, the Foreign Secretary Ernest Bevin told him that at a big reception at the Soviet Embassy, he heard Vyacheslav Molotov, the Soviet Minister of Foreign Affairs, claim that the Soviets already had the bomb:

> he was in the outer hall with Molotov, Gusev [F. T. Gusev, Soviet Ambassador to Britain] and Madame G. Molotov was 'drinking all his toasts as usual' and, Bevin thought, had by now drunk rather much, even for him. Molotov then said, 'Here's to the Atom Bomb!' And then he added, 'We've got it.'

'Gusev, at this point,' Bevin told Dalton, 'put his hand on Molotov' shoulder and hurried him away.'[29]

Perhaps fifty of those who were privy to the Manhattan Project during the war, notes Max Hastings, revealed some of its secrets to the Soviet Union—'which was a major influence on what happened thereafter'.[30] Donald Maclean, a British spy who was to defect to

Moscow in 1951, briefed the Soviets on the uranium ore used by the US. Maclean, who was Second Secretary at the British Embassy in Washington from 1944 to 1948, had top secret security–'Q'–clearance and was responsible for liaison on atomic matters, so was well informed. Another source, according to Svetlana Lokhova, a Russian intelligence expert, was Arthur Aleksandrovich Adams, who by early 1945 had collected ingredient lists for both the Hiroshima and Nagasaki bombs, along with samples of enriched uranium and heavy water. 'One of his couriers, who travelled to Moscow with a uranium sample in his pocket,' according to Lokhova, 'needed blood transfusions on arrival to combat radiation sickness.' He was no James Bond: a description in his MI5 file lists a number of physical defects, including 'two prominent scars, half a missing thumbnail, a broken knuckle and a need for shoes with "built-up arches".'[31] When his cover broke, he fled to the Soviet Union in early January 1946.[32]

Like the Americans, the Soviets were also scouring the world, so far as was possible, for sources of uranium. The American Venona project–which collected and decrypted messages sent in the 1940s by agents of the Soviet military intelligence agency–was later to reveal that a Russian spy with the pseudonym of 'Grisha' was given the task in November 1945 of finding out 'the location of the uranium deposits in SWEDEN: their magnitude: in what form the uranium is found: what percentage of it is contained in the ore: whether these deposits are being worked, etc.'[33]

But in any case, it appears that the Soviets may have obtained Congolese ore, seized by a special Russian military unit which–like ALSOS–followed the Allied troops into Europe at the end of the war to intercept German atomic materials and scientists. This ore may have been the root of the Russian atomic weapon programme, observed Luc Barbé, a Belgian expert on nuclear issues, in 2013.[34]

The shock that was felt across the world at the dropping of the atomic bombs on Japan was shared by the Americans who had been working in West Africa to facilitate or to protect the access of the US to the uranium ore. They appear not to have known the purpose of the ore. 'I don't know what it's for,' Dock Hogue had told Bob Laxalt—'We're not supposed to know.' Edwin Webb Martin and Harry H. Schwartz, two American vice consuls in Léopoldville who organised the shipment of uranium to the USA, did not know what it was for. At the time, said Martin later, he thought it was a 'very expensive' thing to do, but understood the significance after the explosion of the first atomic bomb.[35]

Only after Hiroshima, notes Clarke Thomas, Adolph Schmidt's biographer, 'did Schmidt realize that the spy search and its findings in the Congo had placed him in a significant role in the hidden scramble to invent the most terrifying new weapon in the history of human kind'. It does indeed appear that Schmidt was not informed officially of the purpose of the uranium. Several decades after the war, however, he said that when he was given this mission, he was aware of 'Rumors in Wash[ington]–uranium being diverted to Europe–Germans working on bomb.'[36]

No record is available of Dock Hogue's reaction to the dropping of the bombs on Japan. At that time, he was working in Europe: on 22 June 1945 he had joined UNRRA, the United Nations Relief and Rehabilitation Administration, which had been set up to assist the mass of refugees that was expected. UNRRA sent Hogue to Europe in July, where he ran the Polish Displaced Persons Camp in Germany. As someone who was always sensitive to the sufferings of ordinary people, Hogue was offered by UNRRA a way of directly helping the victims of war.

This period for Hogue was full of a kind of promise. Ruth was expecting their second child—a daughter—in July, and she would be born into a world that was now safer, although the war with Japan was ongoing. As well, he was starting to have some success as a writer: he had had some articles published in the May and June *Atlantic Monthly*, including 'Liberian Road', which drew on his own lived experience. 'Africa was different in 1937,' he observed grimly—'That was before World War II brought men, tanks, guns [and] planes.'[37] *Atlantic Monthly* was impressed with his work and arranged for him to do some writing for them while he was in Germany.[38]

But Hogue was horrified by what he now witnessed in Europe. He travelled in the course of his duties through Germany, where the devastation, he wrote in a letter to his father, 'makes London damage look like child's play. The children would wave at the truck, but most German adults only gave us cold stares. Many of them are still dazed by what has happened.' Hogue also visited Dachau after its liberation, which sickened him. Seeing the SS Troops who had run the camp and were now imprisoned in one section of the camp, he had 'the urge', he wrote in a letter home, 'to turn a machine gun loose'. Vivisection, he discovered, had been practised on the prisoners by medical students and one of the tests, which had a special and chilling significance for Hogue, was for a cure for malaria: 'Dr Schilling, who helped develop atebrin, had 1000 of them [the prisoners] infected with malaria at one time.'[39]

Hogue reflected, appalled, on the fact that many people in the US 'did not believe such horror camps really existed (also thought the pictures were faked)'.[40] He was deeply sympathetic towards those who wished to go to the US to build a new life and was angry at the political resistance to them. In a letter to *Life Magazine*, he pleaded for them to be given special consideration. The refugee problem, he wrote to his father, 'is one of the great problems ahead of the World right now'.[41]

Sickened by 'the greed, stupidity, ignorance, extreme nationalism, and lust for power that breeds war', Hogue was relieved beyond measure by the end of the war.[42] Writing home on 19 August, he said he hoped the family were all 'elated by V-J day'.[43]

Shirley Chidsey had returned to the US by the time the bombs were dropped on Japan. Officially, she had not been briefed on the existence of the Congolese uranium and its purpose. It appears, however, that she knew more than she was supposed to. She was now eager to return to Léopoldville and went to see Rud

Boulton in the Que Building towards the end of 1945, to ask him to send her back. A few days later, she followed up the meeting with a letter. 'I hope,' she said:

> you can arrange something in the matter which we discussed last week. I would be very glad to do it for nothing, because it interests me so much and would be a real stimulus out there where it is easy to slip into a rut. Someday soon when things are reorganised, you will surely be sending someone out there, and I would hope that I could be his assistant.

Then she added in brackets, using the old-fashioned word 'pitch-blende' for uranium: '(since it is, according to the N. Y. Times, one of the two sources of pitchblende, and that source will certainly have to be watched!)'. In fact, the *New York Times* had not identified the Congo as a source of uranium—but in this way Chidsey was able to let Boulton know that she was aware of this vital information relating to the Congo in US affairs.[44]

There is no documentation revealing Henry Stehli's reaction to the bombs dropped on Japan, but he evidently had doubts about atomic weapons. He gave generous financial support to Albert Einstein's movement for World Government, which the physicist advocated as a way of controlling the use of the atom bomb. Einstein envisaged World Government as an alliance of the three great military powers at the time—the US, the Soviet Union, and Great Britain—which would have power over all military matters. Even a tyrannical world government, believed Einstein, was preferable to the far greater evil of war. Henry Stehli, along with other donors including the film star Douglas Fairbanks, Jr, gave a contribution to the movement of $1,000 or more.[45]

Captain Marius Lodeesen, the American captain of a Pan Am flying boat that had carried uranium from the Congo to the US during the war, was troubled when he heard the news. 'I learned,' he said, 'that the unmarked crates put in the Clipper's hold at Leo [sic] contained the uranium ore for the first atomic bomb that was to destroy Hiroshima. Better so. The spring water of the well of knowledge is clear and cold as the truth, but the taste is bitter as tears.'[46]

21

ATOMIC SPIES

On 9 August 1945, the day that the bomb was dropped on Nagasaki, OSS agent Duane Luther was in the process of closing down the OSS station in West Africa. 'Finally,' he wrote to John Kirkland, undercover agent 1060 in the Congo, 'the last pouch from Accra. We have been extremely busy knotting loose odds and ends, but the last are now in the process of being knotted.' If all went well, he said, he would leave on 11 August, and HANLY, who ran the Message Center, would not be far behind: 'And this about winds up Accra.'[1] Two days later, the office was officially closed.

On 11 September 1945 OSS representation ceased in the Congo too, 'with the official closing of the Congo office by 1080. Our undercover agent, 1060, and 1080 both returned to Washington.'[2]

Just over a week later, on 20 September 1945, President Truman signed an Executive Order to abolish OSS, transferring intelligence sections to the army under the title of Strategic Services Unit, and all the research and assessment responsibilities to the Department of State. The wartime activities of OSS, stated Truman in a letter to Donovan, 'will not be needed in time of peace'.[3] The OSS ceased to exist on 1 October 1945.

Rudyerd Boulton—who had come into OSS from the post of Curator of Birds at the Field Museum of Natural History in

Chicago—was horrified. According to Richard Helms, who later became the Director of the Central Intelligence Agency, Boulton shot up from his chair when the news was announced at a meeting. Thrusting 'both arms toward Heaven', he shouted, 'Jesus H. Christ, I suppose this means that it's back to those goddamned birds'. He then stumbled from the room.[4]

But Boulton needn't have worried. The following year, Truman established the Central Intelligence Group. Then, as the Cold War got hotter, he signed the National Security Act of September 1947, which established the Central Intelligence Agency.[5] Many OSS veterans joined the CIA, including four future directors— and also including Boulton. It appears that he held a senior position and in 1953 was on the Steering Group of the CIA Career Service Board.[6]

Boulton's second wife, Inez, died in 1957; the next year he was married again, to Louise. In 1959 he officially retired from the CIA and went with Louise to live in Africa—in Southern Rhodesia, where he founded the Atlantica Ecological Research Station in Salisbury (now Harare), as a research base for naturalists studying African birds. The name Atlantica was intended to signify the connection between Africa and America.[7] A Tennessee newspaper reported that the Boultons landed in Angola and then journeyed to Salisbury 'in a specially fitted truck towing what must be an almost unique mobile laboratory behind them'. Positioned beside the laboratory 'like a small edition of a deep-space radio telescope', added the newspaper:

> is his specially designed, 30-inch parabolic reflector, which can be used to receive and record bird songs for a distance of nearly a quarter-mile. The mobile laboratory was designed by Boulton himself ...Weighing less than an ordinary American sedan, it is equipped with an air-conditioned darkroom, special water-cooling devices and work benches.

Given the extent and range of this equipment, it is possible that Boulton was still more interested in espionage than in 'those goddamned birds'—and that he was continuing his CIA activities. He planned to travel through the Rhodesias in the truck, as well as to

Nyasaland (Malawi), Bechuanaland (Botswana), and Angola, according to the *Washington Post*.[8] He died in 1983, aged 81.

Lanier J. Violett, who had been stationed in Angola under cover as a Texaco inspector and frequently visited the Congo in the course of his work, died before the bombing of Hiroshima and Nagasaki—aged just thirty-nine. He had returned to the USA from Africa in April 1945, suffering from 'general deterioration and debility', and was admitted to the Manhattan Presbyterian Hospital—but nobody, including his doctors, knew what was wrong with him. At the start of July he collapsed, and his sister, Thelma Brewster, called in one of America's best known diagnosticians, who was completely baffled. The doctor spent the whole of 4 July with Violett, to see if he could find some clue, but failed. Violett finally died, after five weeks in hospital, on 5 July.

His sister tried to find out what had happened—she talked to people at Texaco, to see if there was a disease in Africa which could have caused his condition; they said there *was* such a disease, but not much was known about it. Even now, it is not possible to establish the cause of Violett's death: his death certificate, issued by New York City's health department, does not give the reason, stating only that it was due to natural causes; the certificate adds that these natural causes are 'more fully described in the confidential medical report filed with the Department of Health'. A request for a copy of this confidential medical report was submitted in 2016 to the Borough of Manhattan, but they responded that no further records exist on Violett's death.

The invisibility of Violett's war service, as an officer of OSS, is reflected in his death certificate. In response to Question 10, 'Was Deceased [a] War Veteran?', the answer given—written by hand in large capital letters—is 'NONE'.[9]

Dock Hogue returned home from Europe on 24 August 1946, having completed his work for UNRRA. He toyed with the idea of running for Congress, as a way of helping to improve people's lives, but Ruth wasn't keen. He also tried his hand at full-time writing—the dream he had cherished, for as long as he could remember. But it simply wasn't practical; writing was not a reliable, or even a possible, way of supporting a family. Instead, he would have to write in his spare time, a challenge he met with considerable success. He wrote a number of thoughtful articles for journals like *Atlantic Monthly* and added to his repertoire of popular fiction. Under the pseudonym of Carl Shannon, in 1947 he published *Lady, That's My Skull*, and went on to write other mystery stories, such as *Fatal Footsteps* and *Murder Me Never*.[10] Under his own name of Dock Hogue, he published adventure stories and a hugely popular set of 'Bob Clifton' stories for boys, which drew on his experience of West Africa. *Bob Clifton, Elephant Hunter* tells the story of a teenage boy on his father's plantation in the Belgian Congo. By 1949 he was in demand as a public speaker and addressed the Professional Writers Club of Washington DC on the subject of 'Writers and Their Troubles.' He offered advice to his fellow writers:

> Too often the writer does not know where to begin and where to end the story. The advice I give first to any writer is to sit down and cut out the unnecessary words in the work and then polish the opening and conclusion of the story.

'Not bad advice for any writer,' approved the *Salt Lake Tribune* in 1949. 'Idaho has a right to be proud of Dock Hogue.'[11]

In 1947 he followed Boulton into the CIA. He was sent to Lebanon in 1949 as Chief of Station in Beirut, under cover of Labor Attaché to the US Ambassador. Now the war was over, he was able to take his family abroad with him—Ruth, their son Gilbert, and their daughter Kathryn, who had been born while he was in Europe—and they settled in an apartment with a view of the Mediterranean. At last, the Hogues seemed destined for a peaceful life together.

But Dock had frequent bouts of serious illness. His doctors diagnosed it as recurrent malaria, but even with proper medical treatment it would not go away. Then, in 1952, he collapsed on a ship taking him back to the Lebanon after a visit to the US. He was airlifted home and admitted to the Mayo Clinic in Chicago, where he died on 12 April, aged just 42. His diagnosis was stomach cancer, which is far more common in people over 50. Risk factors for this disease include exposure to radiation, which explains why atomic bomb survivors in the Second World War were more likely than most people to get stomach cancer.[12]

Gilbert was nine and Kathryn seven. His death left his family not only painfully grieving, but also broke. 'We never had much money,' recalls his daughter Kathryn, 'and when he died even less, just his death benefit from the government.' Ruth went back to college to get certified to teach in California, so that she could support the family, and they lived in her sister's home until she could get a job.

Henry Stehli, like Hogue, also died young—just 52—on 8 December 1955, from brain cancer. This is a relatively rare cancer, for which the only known risk factor is exposure to radiation.[13] In the years between his return from the Congo and his death, Stehli was head of the New York branch of the Stehli family business. But, again, like Hogue, he suffered from intermittent illness, which was diagnosed as malaria. He was also more interested in global affairs and shortly after the war, he played a role in the drive to defeat the Communists in Italy; for this he was awarded the Star of Solidarity by the Italian government.

Stehli had developed a strong affection for the Congo and in January 1947 he took his wife Grace there for a visit, where she met Shirley Chidsey. 'Arrived in Leo about 11 A.M. wonderful view of the river and town as we came in,' wrote Grace in a lively letter home. She reported that they were 'royally received' by the Pan Am manager; by Henri Cornelis, who was second only to the Governor General; by Chidsey, whom Grace described as 'Henry's ex-Secrt'y'; the American Vice-Consul; and a dozen other people. They were lent a car—'there are lots of new 1946 American cars here.'

Henry 'was greeted by all his old pals' and went off to the golf club, where they all enjoyed cocktails. Their social schedule was 'exhausting' but fun and they managed to see a great deal of the area, including Brazzaville on the other side of the Congo River. It is always possible that the idea for the visit had come from Boulton, who wanted fresh information for the Central Intelligence Group, which had replaced OSS—and would shortly become the CIA. But in any case, Grace loved the trip: 'I'm about the only person in town who thrives on the heat.'[14]

Doug Bonner had moved from Africa to the European Theater in 1943, where he showed outstanding courage and leadership in battle; he was authorised to wear the European Theater ribbon with Battle Awards for Southern France, Western Europe, and Germany.[15] Returning home, he became a senior partner in the stockbroker firm Gregory & Sons and a member of the New York Stock Exchange. Bonner died in New York on 29 December 1960 at the age of 58.[16]

According to the National Center for Health Statistics, the average age of death for white men in 1940 was 66.6, and in 1950 it was 72.2 (no figure is given for the interim).[17] Against this average, the age of death of four OSS agents operating in the field in West Africa—Violett at 39, Hogue at 42, Stehli at 52, and Bonner at 58—can be seen as premature, especially since three of them came from privileged backgrounds. Their early death may have been due to the illnesses they suffered in the field, such as dysentery and malaria, which weakened their systems. But it is also possible that these four men were exposed directly to uranium ore, which may have been a contributing factor.

When President Truman announced the use of the bomb at Hiroshima, sixteen hours after the attack, he emphasised the protection of the health of the workers in the Manhattan Project. 'They have not themselves been in danger,' he assured the public, 'beyond that of many other occupations, for the utmost care has been taken of their safety.'[18] But inevitably this care did not extend to the agents working for OSS.

In comparison with Violett, Hogue, Stehli, and Bonner, Duane Luther had a relatively long life—he reached sixty-five. He and his family left the US after the war. He filed an immigration card with Brazil in September 1945 and next month moved to Rio de Janeiro; they later moved to live in Santo Domingo, Dominican Republic. It is not clear whether or not he worked for the CIA. He continued working for Texaco after the war and became President of Texaco in the Dominican Republic. It was alleged, but never proven, that Texaco conspired with the Dominican Army through Luther to throw out President Juan Bosch, the democratically elected President, in September 1963. Luther was accused of actively supporting Bosch's opponent and of bringing in weapons to be used in an assassination of Bosch; this was looked at in 1975 by the Church Committee on Assassinations.[19] According to one scholar, the Dominican armed forces at the time were dependent on the United States military establishment.[20] Luther died in New York on 9 July 1976, aged 65.

John Kirkland missed reaching the age of 70 by just one year. His cause of death was generalised cerebral encephalopathy—brain disease. It is not clear whether or not he had a brain tumour, for which the causes are unclear; however radiation exposure, including that caused by atomic bombs, produces an increased risk.[21] In September 1945, Kirkland resigned from the Texas Company to take up a position teaching Spanish and French at the Mount Hermon School for Boys in Massachusetts.

Some of the OSS agents in West Africa who were not exposed to uranium went on to live long lives—such as Hunt Harris, who lived until the age of 79. Harris was awarded the Medal of Freedom in 1947 by President Truman for his service in OSS in Africa; special mention was made of his work in Lourenço Marques.[22] After the war, Harris studied for a doctorate in social sciences at Columbia University and then he and his British wife Mary settled down in Leesburg, Virginia, about 60 miles from Washington. He took on the role of business executive and was president of Press Intelligence Inc., which provided a service of news clippings and analysis.[23] In 1967 Harris was one of a number of people, including former Presidents Eisenhower and Truman, who set up the Committee for Peace with Freedom in Vietnam. It set out to offset antiwar propaganda and to convey the idea that, despite the size of the American presence in Vietnam, the conflict remained a Vietnamese rather than an American war.[24] Harris died in 1993; the following year, a Senate Joint Resolution was proclaimed, honouring his memory.

Shirley Chidsey lived until the age of 80. She returned to the Congo in late January 1946 to continue working for the US Consul, Robert Buell.[25] Boulton arranged with the State Department for her to be allowed to send reports back to the Central Intelligence Group, which had replaced OSS. She was given a new code number—987/50—and stayed at La Rotonde, a simple but popular hotel attached to a café and restaurant.[26] 'Anything you hear from me so far,' she wrote to Boulton, 'is completely unofficial and unsponsored. I shall keep it up to whatever extent seems practicable, and meanwhile keep a sort of background file which will be ours ... Best to you all, and I miss hearing from you.'[27]

After finally leaving the Congo in September 1947, Chidsey became editorial assistant on *Railroad Magazine*; by 1951 she had left this position but was still contributing to the magazine. She worked on a number of literary projects as an editor and co-edited a translation of *The Pillow Book* by the Japanese writer Sei Shōnagon. While doing this work in New York, she met Dr William ('Bill') Bridgwater, who was Editor-in-Chief of Columbia University Press. They married in 1955 and Shirley found married happiness for the first time; she and Bill lived peacefully together in Harlem and enjoyed outings to watch the Yankees play baseball. After only nine years, Bill died. Shirley was bereft but resolved within less than ten years to start a new adventure. Though well into middle age, she moved to Austin, Texas, in 1974, where she worked at the state university on literary projects.[28] She died on 27 September 1987.

After his return home from West Africa, Adolph Schmidt was appointed as Boulton's deputy. He then put in a request for a transfer to the European Theater and was sent to occupied

Germany in 1945.[29] He undertook various tasks for William Donovan in Berlin and in late 1945 Donovan called him to the Palace of Justice in Nuremburg, to help him prepare for the trial of twelve prominent Nazis.[30] Donovan, who served as special assistant to Robert H. Jackson, the chief US prosecutor, was unhappy about the conduct of the trial. 'I am going to do it all in German,' he told Schmidt, 'so the men in the box know just why they are being tried. We'll be the laughing stock of the legal profession if we don't show that this war has been criminally conducted... Jackson is saying Hitler and his men lost the war, [so] shoot them...This won't do. Otherwise if we lost a future war, our politicians could be shot too.'[31] Donovan resigned from the prosecution team, whereupon he and Schmidt returned to the USA.

Back in Pennsylvania, Schmidt became president of the A. W. Mellon Educational and Charitable Trust and represented the US at some NATO conventions. President Richard Nixon made him US Ambassador to Canada, a post he held between 1969 and 1974. He died on 17 December 2000, at the age of 96.

Schmidt was honoured with the Legion of Merit in 1947.[32] It was awarded for his service in Africa—most especially for his mission to stop 'diamond smuggling'.

At the end of the war, secrecy about OSS activities in the region was tightly maintained. When Lanier Violett died in 1945, Boulton was concerned that Violett's sister, Thelma Brewster, might be talking about her brother and his work to her family and friends; he sought to keep her quiet. 'Perhaps in your discussions with Mrs Brewster,' he wrote to a colleague in the OSS New York office, 'mention may be made of the Espionage Act .... Undoubtedly the activities of this former employee of our organisation would fall within the category of this act.' Anyone revealing 'information concerning him or his connections with us', he warned, 'would be subject to the terms of the Espionage Act'.[33]

Mrs Brewster complied, but she bitterly resented the order for secrecy and argued that she had met many people from OSS who had talked about their experiences. She never found out what her brother had done in Africa and believed that his services had not been properly valued and used by OSS.[34]

Boulton also silenced James Chapin, the OSS agent who had been forced by a nervous breakdown to leave the Congo in 1943. He had resumed his work at the American Museum of Natural History and was scheduled to give a lecture at the annual dinner of the Explorers Club in New York in January 1946. His topic was the Ascension Islands, where he had conducted a successful mission for OSS before going on to Léopoldville. Boulton, as a fellow ornithologist, planned to attend the dinner. He was worried that Chapin might reveal details of his work for OSS and wrote to him to emphasise the need for secrecy: 'no mention of OSS or of me [should] be made during the course of it'.[35]

But over the years, information about OSS has slowly been made available. When William Casey, himself an OSS veteran, became director of the CIA in 1981, he cleared the way for the transfer of millions of OSS documents to the US National Archives. These included General Donovan's papers, which had been microfilmed in great haste after President Truman terminated OSS in October 1945—a mass of communications between the field and Washington, in the form of cables and pouch letters, as well as reports and memoranda. These were reviewed and sanitised by the CIA and released over the years by the US National Archives. Then, in 2008, the National Archives released more than 35,000 official personnel files of men and women who served in OSS.

In these files, the story of OSS in West Africa can be found, but it is not a full story. It is evident that many documents in the Donovan files are missing and some of the records that do exist are virtually illegible, including many cables, or parts of cables, relating to the Belgian Congo and the Gold Coast. The personnel records are also deficient in relation to West Africa. Although the listing has been described as complete,[36] four names are missing: Wilbur Owings Hogue, John Kirkland, Lanier Violett and Duane Luther.

West Africa has been almost completely neglected in literature on OSS. According to the CIA in an online account, OSS 'was strong and active in North Africa, China, Burma, India, and Europe'[37]—but there is no mention of OSS stations in West Africa, notably Accra and Léopoldville. It is as if the West African stations and their agents never existed. Hunt Harris was awarded the Medal of Honor, but—as the details of the award show—the decoration was explicitly for his service as station chief in Lourenço Marques in Mozambique, not for his work in West Africa. The period of the service was specified as between November 1942 and July 1944, after which he went to Accra.[38]

The sole recognition for service in West Africa between 1943 and 1945 was given to Adolph Schmidt, who was awarded the Legion of Merit for his service in West Africa, notably his mission to stop 'diamond smuggling'—which he had been ordered in late 1943 to use as a cover story for uranium smuggling. 'Colonel Schmidt,' records the recommendation for the award, 'undertook a study of the possibility that industrial diamonds might be smuggled out of the territory under his command to points from which they could be shipped to Germany.' The wording of the recommendation identifies clearly the importance and success of the mission: 'if the diamond traffic to Germany was not entirely stopped, it was at least reduced to a point where [the] German war industry was deprived of most of the supply'.[39]

The OSS agent Moe Berg has been described as 'America's premier atomic spy during World War II'.[40] It is evident that he played a brave role as an atomic spy—but so did Dock Hogue, Henry Stehli, Doug Bonner, Adolph Schmidt, Shirley Chidsey, Duane Luther, Hunt Harris, Lanier Violett, and John Kirkland, in West Africa. In the case of Schmidt, there was at least some recognition, though it was dressed up as an award for a mission against IDB. But in the case of Hogue, Stehli, Bonner, and Violett, there was no acknowledgement of any kind.

It is difficult to measure the success of their mission in the Belgian Congo. But there are important reasons to believe that it had an impact of critical importance to the American war effort. Historians and other sources have shown that Union Minière supplied the Third Reich with some uranium from its supplies in Europe. Given this, there was a real danger that it might seek to supply Germany with additional uranium directly from Shinkolobwe. But this did not happen: none of the Congolese ore, so far as is known, was sent from Africa to Nazi Germany between 1943 and 1945, whether by smuggling or by any other means. And without sufficient uranium ore of that uniquely rich quality, the German atomic project could not succeed.

It is highly likely that Dock Hogue's activities inhibited the illicit removal of uranium ore. His investigations were seen as such a big threat to the Belgian administration and industrialists that he was expelled from the Congo. Indeed, some party or parties were so keen to get rid of him that there were three attempts on his life.

Hogue's sudden return to the US from the Congo was shrouded in mystery. But in the wording of Schmidt's Legion of Merit award, there is a specific reference to Hogue's achievement, without giving his name:

> efforts brought to light the fact that enemy agents, paying fabulous prices, had been able to arrange for smuggling from the Belgian Congo mines of a nearly adequate supply which compliant officials and certain private individuals were forwarding direct through Red Cross parcels or to neutral ports.

'To stop this traffic,' it adds, 'was an exceedingly delicate and difficult task because there were high officials of allied and neutral governments involved.'[41]

When Ruth Hogue was bringing Dock home from Lebanon to the US, shortly before his death, Huntington Harris told her that if she ever needed anything at all, she was just to ask. Over two decades later, in 1967, Ruth *did* need something—help for her daughter Kathryn to get a job. She contacted Harris, who took Kathryn for lunch. Over the meal, he told Kathryn that he wanted to explain the results of her father's work in the Congo.

He said that he had never been able to tell Hogue himself, because of classification restrictions; the information, he added, had only recently been declassified.

Hogue, said Harris, had been sent to determine the source of industrial diamonds that were making their way to the Nazi war manufacturing machine. He had done well, but the information he gathered had implicated some high ranking Belgian officials and he got caught. The information was not acted on because these same officials were supplying uranium for the Manhattan Project, which was highly classified and 'way beyond' Hogue's need to know. Harris regretted that he had been unable to tell Hogue this—and he believed that Hogue had died thinking his work had been ignored.

In his account to Kathryn, Harris fully acknowledged the importance to the US of obtaining Congolese uranium during the war. But he portrayed Hogue's role in the Congo entirely in terms of diamond smuggling—thus maintaining the diamond cover story that had been so successful through the years of war.

Harris did what he could to help Kathryn obtain a job and he also invited her and her brother Gilbert to dinner with himself and Mary whom he had met and married in Lourenço Marques. Kathryn recalls that while she was there, the phone 'rang and rang' in Harris's study and she offered to answer it—but was told to leave it to ring: 'that is Hunt's phone and we don't answer it'. Years later, Kathryn realised that the phone, situated on top of a safe-like box, was a KY-3, a secure voice device developed by the National Security Agency and usually used by high level government officials only, including military Commanders-in-Chief and high level civilians like the President and his close advisors. 'It certainly indicated,' comments Kathryn, 'that Mr Harris had some high level government status.'[42]

Dock Hogue never spoke openly about his mission in the Belgian Congo. But he *did* comment on it indirectly. He frequently drew on his lived experience to write fiction, such as 'Bahnhofstrasse 17', a story about an UNRRA director in early postwar Germany (named Kirk Bonner, possibly a mark of Hogue's respect for Doug Bonner), which was published in *Adventure*, one of America's top pulp magazines. Also in *Adventure*, in June 1947, Hogue published a novelette entitled 'Congo Contraband', which is set in the Belgian Congo in the era of the early Cold War. Although the enemy is no longer Nazi Germany and Japan but the Soviet Union and communism, the themes, characters, and places in the narrative are easily recognisable to those of us who have followed Hogue's mission in the Congo between 1943 and 1944.

The hero himself, Wayne Bland, resembles Hogue: tall and physically fit, with an unyielding concern for the underdog. He is an American intelligence agent working for 'Room X, a well disguised division of a certain United States government department' in Washington—much like the 'Q Building' of OSS. One of the characters, M. Bodart, the head of the Sûreté in Léopoldville, seems much like Jean Beaudinet, with whom Hogue had to deal; and a suspicious man in Angola called Diaz recalls the flamboyant Diaz that Hogue had decided not to use as a cutout. The narrative involves a fictional American Consulate in Léopoldville: the Consul himself, one of the Vice Consuls, and the economic attaché. The worst villain of the piece is a woman, Mme Josette Verhoven—and she recalls Mrs Evelyn Fitch, who was having an affair with François Scheerlinck, the head of the Sûreté in Katanga, and who in Rud Boulton's opinion was 'either a German, Belgian, or British agent'.[43] An important mining company in the story is Confer in Elisabethville, which is reminiscent of Union Minière—and its director and wife are reminiscent of Jules and Madame Cousin.

Bland's mission is to stop the smuggling of diamonds to Communist nations through Portuguese Angola. It is clear that here, just as in real life during the hot war that had recently ended, Hogue—but in the role of author—is using diamonds as a cover for uranium. It is also clear that he is now fully aware of the purpose of uranium: to construct atomic bombs. 'Bland was aware,' writes

Hogue, 'that no satisfactory substitute existed in modern industry for these diamonds.' The lack of them, he goes on:

> had crippled the Nazi war machine, and many US officials had been uneasy during World War II when the American supply had dropped low. Atom bombs could not be produced without them. Now, several Communist nations were not only buying all the industrial diamonds they could commercially, but were creating stock piles by secret methods.

Their purpose, adds Bland, 'was obvious—they meant to have a hard, fast store of such vital materiel in event of war'. This cover is based on a fallacy: the idea that atomic bombs could not be made without industrial diamonds is 'utter nonsense', according to a specialist in nuclear matters.[44]

Like Hogue in 1944, Bland is subject to vicious attacks on his life, including a desperate shoot-out in the bedroom of his house—which he wins, as did Hogue. Bland's mission is a complete success: he 'solves the riddle' and foils the plot of the Communist agents involved in the smuggling ring. Hogue gives Bland the last word in 'Congo Contraband'. At the very end of the story, Monsieur Bodart asks him, 'Why would Diaz, Broussard, and Madame Verhoven try to murder you, Monsieur Wayne?' At this, Bland 'gazed squarely into the eyes of the Sûreté official, a brief smile twisting his lips'; then he answered, 'I guess they didn't like me, Monsieur.'[45] Such dry, self-deprecating humour was the very essence of Dock Hogue.

22

CONCLUSION

THE MISSING LINK

In late 1949 the Soviet Union tested its own atomic bomb, to the profound shock of the US and Britain, neither of which had any idea that the Soviet atomic weapons programme was so well advanced.[1] The US had beaten Germany in the first atomic arms race; and for four years, it had enjoyed an absolute monopoly on atomic weapons. But now, a second atomic arms race was under way—and the Cold War heated up dramatically.

The Shinkolobwe mine in Katanga had been reopened in March 1945 and was fully in operation, supplying America with fresh stocks of high grade uranium ore.[2] As a result, observes Congolese historian Georges Nzongola-Ntalaja, the Congo was 'an important element of Washington's geopolitical strategy in the context of the Cold War'.[3]

Despite strenuous efforts by the US to find alternative sources of rich ore, Shinkolobwe remained its greatest single source in the late 1940s and early 1950s (see Appendix). In 1947, according to figures from the US Atomic Energy Commission, the US obtained 1,440 tons of uranium concentrates from the Belgian Congo; it obtained none from its own territory and only 137 tons from Canada.[4] There was great anxiety that the Shinkolobwe ore would run out. 'You will note,' warned Donald Maclean, the second secretary at the British embassy in Washington (and also a Soviet spy), 'that the amount expected to be available for 1948 is less than one-third of that shipped during 1947. This progressive exhaustion of Congo supplies is expected to continue down to almost zero in about 1951 on present knowledge.'[5]

By 1951, the total quantity of uranium obtained by the US was 3,686 tons: the supply from domestic sources had reached 639 tons, with 255 from Canada, but the largest amount still from the Congo—2,792 tons.[6] A huge amount of money was pumped into the building of a processing plant near Shinkolobwe and the World Bank extended $70 million in loans to Belgium for the improvement of the Congolese transportation infrastructure to facilitate the export of uranium.[7]

The US was vigorously seeking new sources of rich uranium ore. In 1950, with Britain, it came to an agreement with the white minority government of South Africa—which by now had introduced the system of apartheid—for the exclusive purchase of South African ore. In so doing, comments Thomas Borstelmann in *Apartheid's Reluctant Uncle*, America compromised its principle of support for self-determination of all peoples, which had been enshrined in the Atlantic Charter. By the end of the Truman administration in January 1953, observes Borstelmann, these dealings with South Africa had become a political embarrassment to the US in the 'now vociferous Cold War'.[8]

A serious worry, as during the Second World War, was the possibility that the enemy might get hold of Congolese ore. This had been anticipated in 1946 by Ernest Bevin, the British Foreign Secretary. According to an entry in the diary of Hugh Dalton, the Chancellor of the Exchequer, Bevin wanted to build a road 'right across Africa, passing through the top of French Equatorial Africa and enabling us, if need be, to protect the deposits in the Belgian Congo'.[9] Concern about the mine escalated sharply in Washington after the start of the Korean War in

1950. According to Borstelmann, drawing on official documents, the US Joint Chiefs of Staff began making contingency plans for the 'seizure of critical areas in the Congo by force', in case of a Soviet occupation of Western Europe, including Belgium.[10]

Washington also felt threatened by the possibility of Congolese unrest. The Secretary of Defense, records Borstelmann, emphasised that the primary source of danger to American access to the Congolese ore was 'disaffection of the natives employed at the mines' and a possible large-scale uprising. The Joint Chiefs of Staff approved the shipment of $7 million-worth of American military equipment for additional Belgian troops being sent to Katanga, and the CIA, the successor of OSS, planted a 'controlled source' in the area to provide early warning of any problems; it also initiated 'plans and preparations for covert counter-sabotage'.[11]

In 1953, the US acquired 500 tons from South Africa, which was considerably less than it had hoped for. It was increasingly obtaining uranium from its domestic sources, which reached 1,100 tons that year; it also obtained 100 tons from a new source— Portugal. But the Belgian Congo still provided the largest amount of ore: 1,600 tons.[12] John Gunther, an American writer who visited Katanga in the mid-1950s and saw lumps of uranium ore in their 'savage, morbid' colours, was troubled by them. 'The fate of civilisation,' he reflected with concern, 'rests on a more slender thread than at any time in history, because of energies imprisoned in these flamboyant stones. Rock mined from this remote area in the Belgian Congo is capable of burning up the world.'[13]

The American atomic project was ambitious: it would require 9,150 tons of uranium concentrates per year when in full operation. The 1953 receipts, therefore, were less than half the required amount. In fact, it would not be possible to acquire the full amount before 1957, which would be more than a year after the project was programmed for completion.[14] The procurement of ore was a persistent and acute concern for the USA. Meanwhile, the protection and defence of Shinkolobwe was expanded substantially. A vast, 100,000-acre NATO military base was built at

Kamina in Katanga; it had a powerful radio transmitter, and a runway long enough to handle jets.

At Shinkolobwe, a huge garrison was established. 'Today,' wrote an Italian journalist in 1954, 'it is impossible for a white man to move about unobserved in Shinkolobwe ... and for someone to gate-crash the mining zone without the police's knowledge immediately puts the Union Minière in a state of alarm.' Many voices, he added, were raised about Communist espionage, with the result that the barrier was 'moved another mile from the mine and every road, which for one reason or another passed the zone, was sealed off. In addition, a strict check-up was made on all foreigners who came to Jadotville, the town that had to be passed on the way to Shinkolobwe.'[15]

Another visitor in 1954 was astonished when he looked at the local paper to see that:

> Elisabethville's newspapers ... had startling, inch-high headlines. A Government decree, freshly signed, authorized the shooting on sight of any persons found within the boundaries of the Shinkolobwe uranium mine, who had no right to be there.

Reasons for the official action included the discovery of American journalists lurking behind the bushes near the entrance to the mine, and the alleged uncovering of a Communist plot whereby 'red agents' were said to be smuggling away samples of uranium handed over to them by African workers.[16] These agents, according to British files, included Soviets and some Czechs operating under cover of employment by Bata, a Czech shoe company.[17]

The region around Shinkolobwe continued through the 1950s to attract attention from security and intelligence organisations. There are reasonable grounds to speculate that a strange organisation set up in 1953 by Sir Percy Sillitoe, who had recently retired as Director General of MI5 (and, bizarrely, had bought a sweet shop in a British seaside town), aimed to stop smuggling from the uranium mine. This organisation was the International Diamond Security Organization, a private security service operating for De Beers, involving half a dozen former intelligence officers from

MI5. It was allegedly the idea of Sir Ernest Oppenheimer, the founder of De Beers, to stop diamonds from being smuggled to Communist nations.

According to the MI5 website, Sillitoe 'successfully stopped the smuggling of diamonds from Sierra Leone'.[18] But there is no evidence that IDSO did anything of the sort. In three years of apparently intensive work, not more than half a dozen people were charged with smuggling diamonds. In any case, Interpol and the South African diamond police were perfectly capable of dealing with cases of diamond smuggling.[19] What IDSO *did* achieve is not clear. It is possible that the diamond focus was a cover for uranium—replicating the successful cover that had been used in the years of war.

The memoirs of Captain J. H. du Plessis, an IDSO agent, *Diamonds are Dangerous: The Adventures of an Agent of the International Diamond Security Organization* (1960), reveal that many of IDSO's activities took place in Katanga and in the Copperbelt of Northern Rhodesia, just over the border with the Congo. Barely veiled references are made to shadowy meetings with the director of the Rhodesian Federal Intelligence Security Bureau, who had formerly been Britian's intelligence agent for the region, under the leadership in London of Sillitoe.

Whatever its purpose, IDSO became the topic of two books by Ian Fleming—*Diamonds are Forever* (1956) and *The Diamond Smugglers* (1957). IDSO was officially disbanded by Percy Sillitoe in 1957, on the grounds (which many found surprising) that the diamond problem had been solved.[20]

Sillitoe wrote a memoir, *Cloak Without Dagger*, which was extensively censored by the Service when submitted for approval. Other than that, little has been written about him apart from a biography by A. E. Cockerill: *Sir Percy Sillitoe*, which was published in 1975 and raises interesting questions about IDSO's purpose. 'The undue emphasis placed on Communist interest in Western diamonds,' comments Cockerill, 'makes the Fleming and du Plessis accounts suspect and points to an ulterior motive on someone's part.'[21]

*

In 1958, under the aegis of President Eisenhower's Atoms for Peace programme, the US provided the Congo with a 50 kW research nuclear reactor, TRIGA I, which was established at Lovanium University in Léopoldville.[22] This was Africa's first nuclear plant. It was brought about through the vision of Monsigneur Luc Gillon, a Catholic priest who had studied atomic physics at Princeton and wanted to bring the potential for nuclear power to the Congo.[23]

Towards the end of the 1950s the picture regarding Congolese uranium changed. America no longer needed to be worried about supplies of ore, despite its earlier fears. There were two important reasons for this: first, uranium ore had been found in many other parts of the world; and second, new methods of enriching lower grade uranium, to make it fissionable, had been developed. As a result, the US was no longer so dependent on Shinkolobwe, although it continued to be worried about the risk of the Soviets acquiring Congolese ore.

In the same period, the wind of decolonisation was blowing vigorously through the African continent and the people of the Congo demanded independence from Belgium. This became a reality on 30 June 1960. Patrice Lumumba became the Republic of the Congo's prime minister in the nation's first democratic elections.

The year before, Lumumba had been asked by some business-men in New York whether the Americans would still have access to uranium, as they had when the Belgians ran the country. Lumumba's response was clear. 'Belgium doesn't produce any uranium,' he stated firmly, adding that 'it would be to the advantage of both our countries if the Congo and the US worked out their own agreements in the future.'[24] But Union Minière took matters into their own hands and by the time of independence, the company had sealed the Shinkolobwe mine with concrete.

Kwame Nkrumah, the president of newly independent Ghana (formerly the Gold Coast) hoped that Africa could remain above the conflict between the West and the Communist nations. 'My policy,' he said in 1960, 'has always been that at all costs Africa must not be involved in the Cold War.' Ralph Bunche, who had formerly worked for OSS in the Research and Analysis Division and was now a senior official at the United Nations, took the same view, especially in relation to the Congo. The former Belgian colony, he said, 'has quite enough problems without having the cold war added to them'.[25] But it was unavoidable: the Congo's resources, including its uranium, put the newly independent nation at the very heart of Cold War concerns.

Larry Devlin was appointed Chief of Station in the Congo by the CIA, under cover of consul; he arrived in Léopoldville on 10 July 1960, just nine days after independence. 'We regarded Stalin and those who followed him to be just as dangerous as Hitler,' he explained in *Chief of Station, Congo*, a memoir published in 2007. 'We had to defeat the new threat of communism, and we made a considerable contribution to achieving this objective.' In 1960, he added, the Congo had been 'on the front line of the struggle between the Soviet Union and the United States'.[26] One of his fellow soldiers on this front line was Daphne Park, his counterpart in MI6, whose cover was that of first consul at the British embassy. But they were just two of the many spies in Léopoldville at this time; an American businessman gathering intelligence for a mining company described the city as a 'Nest of Vipers', seething with spies.[27]

One of Devlin's instructions was to remove the rods from the atomic reactor at Lovanium. He thought it was a crazy and dangerous idea—as did Monsigneur Gillon. Together, they decided to leave the rods in the reactor. 'I reported his views to Headquarters,' wrote Devlin in his memoir, 'and, happily, never heard another word about the matter.'[28]

Prime Minister Lumumba's rule was challenged by a range of crises, not least of which was the secession of Katanga, led by Moise Tshombe, the province's self-styled president. The secession took place on 11 July, just eleven days after the Congo's independence. Many assumed that the mining corporations, in collaboration with certain Western governments, had planned the secession well before the independence of the Congo. Union Minière, reported a highly connected Belgian to a British diplomat a few months before the independence of the Congo, 'had taken up the position that under no circumstances could they envisage the Katanga being governed by a central native body. (They might accept a provincial puppet government.)'[29]

Lumumba invited the Soviet Union, along with other nations, to assist the Congo. This alarmed the US government and Allen Dulles, the head of the CIA, sent an urgent telegram to Devlin in Léopoldville: 'the removal [of Lumumba] must be an urgent and prime objective ... this should be a high priority of our covert action'.[30] The order had the authorisation of President Eisenhower. Not long after, Devlin was visited by an emissary, codenamed 'Joe from Paris', who brought some deadly poisons to assassinate Lumumba.[31] 'He handed over several poisons,' wrote Devlin. 'One was concealed in a tube of toothpaste. If Lumumba used it, he would appear to die from polio.'[32]

On 17 January 1961, Lumumba was assassinated in Elisabethville, just over 75 miles from Shinkolobwe. A 2001 report by a Belgian Commission of Inquiry has established that Lumumba was murdered by Katangese men, with Belgian involvement.[33]

After Lumumba's death, the UN Security Council passed a resolution authorising the UN mission in the Congo to take all measures to restore order in the country and to prevent civil war; and it called for the withdrawal from the Congo of all foreign advisors and mercenaries, especially those in Katanga. But the UN resolution was difficult to implement, largely because of support by some Western nations for Tshombe's rule. Bitter conflict ensued in Katanga between Tshombe's forces and the UN mission stationed there.

The Shinkolobwe garrison and paracommando training camp near Jadotville was considered of such vital importance to Katanga and its supporters, that the commander put in charge in 1961 was Colonel Roger Faulques, a notorious mercenary. Faulques was a former officer of the *11ième choc*, an elite regiment in the French army which then served as the armed branch of France's external intelligence agency.[34] He was a veteran of Dien Bien Phu and Algeria.[35]

In an effort to bring peace to the Congo and to end the Western-backed secession of Katanga, UN Secretary General Dag Hammarskjöld flew to Ndola, a town in the British colony of Northern Rhodesia, for talks with Tshombe. His plane crashed in circumstances which were highly suspicious, killing all the people on board (there was one survivor but he died from his injuries within a few days). The crash took place on the night of 17–18 September 1961, eight months after Lumumba's assassination—less than 200 miles from Shinkolobwe.[36]

About a week after Hammarskjöld's death, on 27 September 1961, a meeting of the International Atomic Energy Agency in Vienna accepted the Congo as its 77th member. Mr Kahamba, the Congo delegate, announced that his country, 'rich in uranium deposits—was now free to review the agreement which Belgium concluded with the United States and Britain on the supply of this raw material'.[37] Underlying Kahamba's speech was the warning that Shinkolobwe may have been sealed, but the Congolese government had the power to make their own decisions about what to do with the mine.

Some Americans with an interest in Congolese uranium were watching developments carefully. One of these was a businessman named Maurice Tempelsman, who was a middleman for Harry Oppenheimer, the owner-director of Anglo-American and De Beers; Tempelsman was involved in all kinds of intrigue in the Congo.[38] His reputation, and that of his family firm, Leon Tempelsman & Son, rested on diamonds; in the 1950s the firm made a fortune, apparently by convincing the US government to buy industrial diamonds for its stockpile of strategic minerals. But uranium was at the core of his business dealings. On 19 October 1961, Tempelsman wrote a memorandum to President Kennedy, referring to discussions about the purchase of uranium through a barter programme, which had been considered by the President in

January that year. 'Several developments,' wrote Tempelsman to the President, 'reinforce the desirability of the proposal: Atomic weapons testing by the Soviet Union has forced the United States to resume testing in self-defence. Stockpiles of uranium concentrates become more valuable as a matter of prudence.'[39]

In 1965, with instrumental help from the CIA, Joseph Mobutu, a former colonel in the Force Publique, was installed as the leader of the Congo. At the end of 1966, Mobutu's government nationalised Union Minière's Congolese assets, renamed as Gécamines.[40] Befriended by Tempelsman and heavily backed by the US government, Mobutu ruled his country as a dictator; in 1971 he changed the country's name to Zaire and his own name to Mobutu Sese Seko.[41] In 1972, the US supplied the Congo with a second nuclear reactor—TRIGA II, twenty times more powerful than TRIGA I. Its capacity is very low, but the unsafe conditions in which it is kept today are a cause for concern. 'If damaged,' noted the journalist and author Michela Wrong, who visited the installation, 'it could spew radioactivity for kilometres around, leaking contamination into the city's water supply.'[42] It was officially shut down in 2004, but still functions as a research facility.[43]

Mobutu remained President of Zaire until well beyond the end of the Cold War. In 1997 he was expelled by rebel forces led by Laurent-Désiré Kabila, who became President and changed the name Zaire to that of Democratic Republic of Congo (*République Démocratique du Congo*), which had been in use from 1964 to 1971. Kabila was shot at the start of 2001, after which his son, Joseph Kabila, was inaugurated as President; in 2006 Joseph Kabila won the Presidential election.

The uranium mine in Katanga continued to have a resonance for the world, observes Zoë Marriage, a political economist with specialist knowledge of security and development in the Congo. 'There are rumours,' she writes in her 2013 book, *Formal Peace and Informal War*, 'that Mobutu sold uranium to the USA, then to the USSR, and that Laurent Kabila sold it to North Korea and Joseph Kabila [sold it] to Iran.' In interviews she conducted in the course of her research, she found threads of information 'about the power that Congo commands through its access to uranium, and the Congolese leadership defying the USA and being punished'.[44]

Shinkolobwe, noted a 2004 cable from the American Embassy in Kinshasa, released by Wikileaks, 'is definitely a long-term problem, because the Congo's weak state institutions and easily corrupted officials cannot be counted upon to secure the mine site'.[45] A further US cable written in 2007 reported that 15 tons of highly radioactive rock had been obtained by a company in Katanga from freelance diggers at the Shinkolobwe uranium mine; the rock was allowed to be exported. 'All of Katanga Province,' added the cable, 'could be said to be somewhat radioactive. Some areas are more radioactive than others, however, and there have been recent reports that several Katangan mines have abnormally high levels of radiation.'[46]

Concern about the smuggling of uranium—which had brought OSS to the Belgian Congo in the Second World War—has continued to this day. 'A common joke among nuclear policy analysts,' comments Tom Zoellner in Uranium, 'is that the best way to move an atomic bomb across a national border is to hide it inside a truckload of marijuana. In other words, smuggling routes used by average criminals provide good cover for the occasional piece of nuclear merchandise. This appears to have been the case at Shinkolobwe.' A dossier from the government in Kinshasa, he adds, 'reported that radioactive products, with no weights reported, have been sold in Katanga at prices ranging from $300 to $500 to a variety of traffickers from India, China, and Lebanon'.[47]

Théodore Trefon, a Congolese affairs analyst, argues that a real danger for Western governments is 'Congo's minerals, particularly uranium, getting into the wrong hands, such as Iran or the Lebanese Hezbollah'. The United States and regulatory agencies such as the International Atomic Energy Agency appear unable, in his view, to control the illegal trade networks:

Chinese, North Korean, Pakistani, Indian and Lebanese traders are suspected of involvement in trading uranium ore exploited by artisanal

263

diggers in Katanga. Their urine samples reveal abnormally high concentrations of uranium—which proves that they are in contact with the substance.

'It is not improbable,' suggests Trefon, 'that Lebanese Hezbollah groups are involved in uranium exports to Iran which helps explain why the United States Treasury Department has sanctioned a Lebanese businessman active in Congo who is allegedly a Hezbollah financier.' The Italian mafia, he adds, is also known to have been involved in uranium smuggling from Congo.[48]

The doctrine of Mutually Assured Destruction—known as MAD—may have saved the world from a nuclear holocaust at various dangerous flashpoints in history, such as the Korean War and the Cuban Missile Crisis. But it will not apply, comments Amir D. Aczel in *Uranium Wars*, in the disastrous eventuality of terrorists obtaining a nuclear weapon. 'Suicidal behaviour brought on by fanaticism,' he argues, 'cannot be deterred by that old logic.' There is also, he adds, the severe peril of a 'dirty bomb'—one that does not produce a chain reaction but spreads radioactive elements over a large area.[49]

A great deal of attention has been given in the West to health and safety concerns relating to uranium. In 1981, in her book *Blind Faith*, Penny Sanger looked at the devastation wrought by the nuclear industry in the Canadian town of Port Hope, where houses were found to have been built on radioactive rubble salvaged from a demolished radium refinery; runoff from dumps in the countryside was poisoning fields, killing cattle, and polluting the lake. 'Eldorado's wastes have caught up with Port Hope,' she writes, 'and are spreading into the countryside nearby. As industrial wastes they are typical of a problem that has suddenly become acute in the Western world.'[50]

There is also a problem in the US caused by the radioactive waste left by the Shinkolobwe ore that was used in the Manhattan Project. Because the uranium from Shinkolobwe is 'so freakishly powerful', notes Zoellner, its waste has attained the status of legend.

Remnants from typical uranium from the south-western USA, he adds, 'give a radioactive signature of about forty picocuries per gram, about ten times the amount of picocuries per litre of air that is considered safe for humans to breathe'. But the Shinkolobwe remains, by contrast, emit 520,000 picocuries per gram. 'The effect across the register,' he explains, using a vivid image, 'is like comparing a housefly to a moon rocket.' The remains have led to birth defects and an increase in other health problems, such as prostate and breast cancer, causing widespread concern; there is now a project with an annual budget of a half million dollars 'to watch the grave of the Shinkolobwe leftovers'.[51]

But what about the Congo—the home of the Shinkolobwe mine? Astonishingly, hardly any attention has been paid to the Congolese, not one of whom was consulted about plans to make atomic bombs with Shinkolobwe's uranium. What would have been their reaction, on a moral basis, to the building of such a destructive and terrible weapon with a mineral from their own land? What would be their reaction today, if the disinformation, shadows and mirrors were swept aside and the full history was set out?

Nor were the Congolese informed about the terrible health and safety hazards to which they were exposed; they were simply used as workers, as if they had no rights as equal human beings. This was a process for which the US, the UK and Belgium bear a heavy responsibility.

The Shinkolobwe mine has been a battlefield for the last eight decades in successive and very different wars: in the Second World War, in the Cold War, and now—potentially—in a variety of global and local conflicts. The casualties continue. Among these are the workers in the mine and those who transport the ore; but we know little of their conditions and sufferings. By the mid-1960s, notes Gabrielle Hecht in her major study of Africa and the global uranium trade, the Shinkolobwe workers who mined the high grade ore had dropped out of scientific conversations on radiation exposure in mining. 'Not,' she added, 'that they'd been terribly visible in the first place. The invisibility of their exposure cannot be corrected through archival diligence, because the records—assuming they were even kept—do not appear in the inventory of the company's Brussels archives.'[52]

'Congolese minerals are not pure, they are often mixed,' explains Dr Mutombo Nkulu-N'Sengha, a Congolese scholar of religious studies, in 2014. 'There is always a small dose of radio-activity there, cobalt, uranium, etc. What we witness now is genetic mutation. Pollution has been so deep that it has reached the level that we are now giving birth to children without limbs without heads without mouth without legs. This is happening not just in one case but in many cases in Lubumbashi [formerly Elisabethville].'[53] Dr Nkulu-N'Sengha is not able to draw on any statistical data, because they are not available. But people living in Katanga know what they and their families have experienced and suffered.

In 2004, following the collapse of a mine shaft at Shinkolobwe, the International Atomic Energy Agency received a request from the United Nations to investigate conditions at the mine. An investigation was carried out, but it was very limited: it was based on a visit to the Shinkolobwe mine of only ten days, from 25 October to 4 November 2004. A full study was not possible because of time and resource constraints, but also because of issues of physical safety, which made it dangerous to go under-ground. Despite the short period of research, the study found that 6,000 small-scale miners had been digging up coltan and cobalt from the Shinkolobwe uranium mine. It established that every-one working at the site is at risk of developing cancer and other health problems because of high radiation levels.[54]

Oliver Tshinyoka is a Congolese journalist who grew up close to Shinkolobwe, which he describes as a deserted place where vegeta-tion blankets empty homes. He regards the mine as the missing link in the story of events that led to the bombing of Japan: a link that has brought a terrible cost to the Congo. Although the mine has been closed down, he says that freelance miners still go to the site to dig out uranium and cobalt. 'Shinkolobwe has never been commemorated,' he noted sadly in 2015, on the seventieth anniversary of America's atomic bomb attack on Japan. 'The town is dead and is haunted by the ghost of Hiroshima.'[55]

APPENDIX

Sources of US uranium concentrates, 1947–1952 (in tons)

Fiscal year	US	Canada	Belgian Congo	Total
1947 (6 mos)	0	137	1440	1577
1948	116	206	1689	2011
1949	115	217	1909	2241
1950	323	235	2505	3063
1951	639	255	2792	3686
1952	824	210	2623*	3657

*Includes a small amount from the Union of South Africa
Source: Borstelmann, *Apartheid's Reluctant Uncle*, p. 205, adapted from Hewlett and Duncan, A *History of the United States Atomic Energy Commission*, Vol. 2, p. 647.

LIST OF ILLUSTRATIONS

(Photographic acknowledgements are given within parentheses)

Front matter

1. Letter from Albert Einstein to F. D. Roosevelt, President of the United States, 2 August 1939 (*Permission to reproduce the letter granted by the Albert Einstein Archives, The Hebrew University of Jerusalem; Courtesy of the Franklin D. Roosevelt Presidential Library and Museum, Hyde Park, New York*)

Section 1

1. OSS agent Wilbur Owings 'Dock' Hogue, Léopoldville, Belgian Congo, 1944 (*Hogue Film, Hogue Family Papers*)
2. The Shinkolobwe mine in Katanga, Belgian Congo, 1925 (*By Chalux [Public domain], via Wikimedia Commons*)
3. Uraninite from the Shinkolobwe mine (*Attribution: Rob Lavinsky and iRocks.com–CC-BY-SA-3.0*)
4. General Leslie Groves speaking to Edgar Sengier (*Photo courtesy of the Patricia Cox Owen Collection, Atomic Heritage Foundation*)
5. A cable from OSS Washington to OSS Accra, Gold Coast, 28 September 1942 (*NARA, RG 226, A1-180G, Box 153*)
6. The Liberian President's residence in Monrovia, flying a flag with a swastika [1942/43] (*Hogue Film, Hogue Family Papers*)

271

Every effort has been made to contact all copyright holders. The publishers will be happy to make good in future editions any errors or omissions brought to their attention.

NOTES AND SOURCES

The most frequently used abbreviations are:

NARA   National Archives and Records Administration, US
RG   Record Group
TNA   The National Archives, UK

For all other abbreviations see the list at the front of the book.

All quotations in the book follow the form of the original documents. However, the codenames of agents are uniformly printed in small caps, including in the case of those particular quotations where that convention was not applied in the originals.

1. INTRODUCTION: THE MANHATTAN PROJECT AND SHINKOLOBWE

1. Quoted in Brion and Moreau, *De La Mine à Mars*, p. 226.
2. Albert Einstein signed this letter and was instrumental in its composition; however it involved the teamwork of at least four contributors, including the physicists Leo Szilard, Eugene Wigner and Edward Teller. The plan for the letter was initiated by Szilard and it was the idea of the economist Alexander Sachs, advisor to President Roosevelt, for the letter to be sent from Einstein to Roosevelt.
   See http://www.dannen.com/ae-fdr.html
3. A copy of the letter and useful discussion is available at: http://www.dannen.com/ae-fdr.html
4. Arthur L. Gavshon, 'Congo is "Blind" to the Richest Uranium Mine', *Washington Post*, 6 August 1950. The Shinkolobwe mine is also known as the Kasolo mine, Chinkolobwe, and Shainkolobwe.
5. Ibid., pp. 228, 231, 235.
6. The figure of up to 65–75 per cent is given in Hadden (ed.), *Manhattan District History*, commissioned by General Leslie Groves, *Book VII, Feed Materials, Special*

Procurement, and Geographical Exploration, Volume I–Feed Materials and Special Procurement, 12 June 1947, declassified with deletions by Richard G. Hewlett for the US Atomic Energy Commission, 3 June 1970, available online at http://www.osti.gov/includes/opennet/includes/MED_scans/Book%20 VII%20-%20%20Volume%201%20-%20Feed%20Materials%20and%20 Special%20Procurement.pdf. Up to 70 per cent is given in Thomas T. Crenshaw to Colonel J. C. Marshall, 27 April 1943, NARA, RG 77, 5, Box 68; also in Groves, *Now It Can Be Told*, p. 37, note 1.

7. Groves, *Now It Can Be Told*, p. 37, note 1.

8. Lorna Arnold to the author in the course of discussions through 2013. Mark Taylor, Research Director at FAFO Research Foundation in Norway, writing for the International Law and Policy Institute in 2014, gives an account of the steps required to enrich uranium. 'An industrial process,' he explains, 'is applied to separate uranium from the other ores with which it is found naturally.' This is called 'milling'. But for weapons production, 'milled uranium must undergo another industrial process, whereby the two naturally occurring uranium isotopes (U-238 and U-235) are separated from each other. Naturally occurring uranium is over 99 per cent U-238, which is non-fissile, and less than 1 per cent U-235, which is the only naturally occurring fissile nuclide. To create the chain-reaction necessary for weaponization, this ratio needs to be nearly reversed, and the uranium must consist of more than 90 per cent U-235.' To achieve this, writes Taylor, 'the uranium must undergo an isotope separation, or so-called enrichment. In practice this means sending the uranium through centrifuges, where the slightly heavier U-238 is slowly separated from the slightly lighter U-235. If this is repeated enough times, the result will be uranium consisting of more than 90 per cent U-235—so-called weapons-grade or highly enriched uranium (HEU). From 'A rock in hard places', 30 September 2014, which can be found here: http://nwp.ilpi.org/?p=2728. The highly enriched uranium can then be used to make atomic weapons. The isotope U-238 is so numbered because it has 146 neutrons and 92 protons; U-235 has 143 neutrons and 92 protons. Because of its three-neutron deficit, U-235 contains the potential of remarkable power, because its nucleus seeks to achieve internal balance by acquiring the three neutrons it lacks. This means that if the outer wall of the U-235 nucleus is bombarded with a neutron, it ruptures the wall relatively easily and penetrates the nucleus—releasing enormous energy.

9. The letter can be found in full here: http://www.atomicheritage.org/key-documents/einstein-szilard-letter

10. Helmreich, *United States Relations with Belgium and the Congo, 1940–1960*, p. 255, note 4.

11. Brion and Moreau, *De La Mine à Mars*, p. 228.

12. Hadden (ed.), *Manhattan District History*, see note 6 above.

13. Thomas T. Crenshaw to Colonel J. C. Marshall, 27 April 1943, NARA, RG 77, 5, Box 68.

14. Groves, *Now It Can Be Told*, pp. 34–7.

15. Goldschmidt, *Atomic Rivals*, p. 52.
16. Gunther, *Meet the Congo and its Neighbors*, pp. 96–9.
17. Ibid.
18. Rhodes, *The Making of the Atomic Bomb*, p. 379.
19. Brion and Moreau, *De La Mine à Mars*, p. 231.
20. McGrath, *Charles Kenneth Leith*, p. 212.
21. Quoted in Baggott, *Atomic*, p. 152.
22. Hastings, *The Secret War*, pp. 527 and 535.
23. Ziegler and Jacobson, *Spying Without Spies*, p. 22.
24. Rhodes, *The Making of the Atomic Bomb*, p. 697. Conversions author's own using http://www.calculator.net/inflation-calculator.html on 24 January 2016.
25. Marnham, *Snake Dance*, pp. 203–4.
26. Kenneth Nichols interviewed by Stephane Groueff, 4 January 1965. Available online at http://manhattanprojectvoices.org/oral-histories/general-kenneth-nichols-interview-part-2
27. McGrath, *Charles Kenneth Leith*, p. 215.
28. Gavshon, 'Congo is "Blind"'.
28. Discussed in Hecht, *Being Nuclear*, p. 195.
30. Gavshon, 'Congo is "Blind".
31. Marnham, *Snake Dance*, p. 217.
32. Ibid., pp. 217–18.
33. H. K. Calvert to Major John Lansdale, cc General Groves, 5 June 1943, NARA, RG 77, 5, Box 68.
34. John Lansdale to General Groves, 21 May 1943, NARA, RG 77, 5, Box 68.
35. John Ruhoff to General Groves, 25 October 1943, NARA, RG 77, 5, Box 68.
36. Hadden (ed.), *Manhattan District History*.
37. William R. Stanley, 'Trans-South Atlantic Air Link in World War II', *GeoJournal*, August 1944, 33 (4), 459.
38. Lodeesen, *Captain Lodi Speaking*, p. 158; for further information on Howard Brush Dean see http://www.cnac.org/dean01.htm
39. Report by Captain J. W. S. Foster, July 1942, quoted in Ken Lawrence, 'Via Miami 1941–1945', *American Philatelist*, January 2014, p. 38.
40. Goldberg, 'The Secret about Secrets', in Garber and Walkowitz, eds, *Secret Agents*, p. 52.
41. Zoellner, *Uranium*, p. 47.
42. Hewlett and Anderson, *The New World*, p. 285.
43. John R. Ruhoff to General Groves, 27 December 1943, NARA, RG 77, 5, Box 68.
44. Quoted in Casey, *The Secret War Against Hitler*, pp. 49–50.
45. Byrnes, *Speaking Frankly*, pp. 257–8.
46. Sayer and Botting, *America's Secret Army*, pp. 71–6.
47. Statement made in June 1942, quoted in 'Early Government Support', *Atomic Heritage Foundation*. See http://www.atomicheritage.org/history/early-government-support

48. Byrnes, *Speaking Frankly*, pp. 257–8.
49. Helmreich, *United States Relations with Belgium and the Congo, 1940–1960*, p. 29.
50. John R. Ruhoff to General Groves, 23 November 1943, NARA, RG 77, 5, Box 68.
51. Ibid.
52. McGrath, *Charles Kenneth Leith*, p. 215.
53. John R. Ruhoff to General Groves, 23 November 1943, NARA, RG 77, 5, Box 68.
54. John Lansdale to Groves, 21 May 1943, NARA, RG 77, 5, Box 68.

2. TETON

1. This and other details through the book about Dock Hogue were supplied by Kathryn Dinny Hogue to the author between 2014 and 2016.
2. Laxalt, *A Private War*, p. 37.
3. Hogue, *Bob Clifton, Congo Crusader*, p. 117.
4. Kathryn Dinny Hogue to the author, 10 January 2016 (see note 1).
5. Hogue, typescript of 'Liberian Honeymoon', n.d., Hogue Family Papers, p. 3.
6. *Alpha Phi Quarterly*, 52 (3), 1940.
7. The residential area was Harbel Hills, named in memory of the late Harvey S. Firestone and his wife Idabelle.
8. Hogue, typescript of 'Liberian Honeymoon', n.d., Hogue Family Papers, p. 38.
9. Ibid., p. 3.
10. Dock to Ruth, 11 February 1942, Hogue Family Archive.
11. Hogue, typescript of 'Liberian Honeymoon', n.d., Hogue Family Papers, p. 72.
12. Hogue, typescript of 'End of a Liberian Century', n.d., Hogue Family Papers, p. 262.
13. Dr John Whiteclay Chambers, 'Office of Strategic Services Training During World War II', *Studies in Intelligence*, 54 (2), June 2010.
14. Bonner to Howard M. Chapin, 26 April 1943, NARA, RG 226, A1–210, Box 417.
15. As told by Hogue to his wife, reported by Kathryn Hogue to the author, 10 February 2016.
16. See NARA, RG 226, A1–210, Box 405.
17. Hogue, typescript of 'End of a Liberian Century', n.d., Hogue Family Papers, p. 261.
18. 'Liberia–2nd Reel, Dock's Trip 1942–1943'; see Filmography at the end of this book.
19. The author is grateful to Svend Holsoe and Elwood Dunn for their kind assistance in February 2016 in the identification of the building as the Executive Mansion and for their commentary on Liberia's position in the Second World War.
20. Hogue, typescript of 'End of a Liberian Century', n.d., Hogue Family Papers, p. 303.

21. Boulton had an Assistant Divisional Deputy, who acted as his adjutant. Underneath this top layer were an Executive Officer and an Administrative Assistant; a Personnel and Training Liaison; a Reporting Board Liaison; and a Procurement and Security Liaison. See NARA, RG 226, A1-210, Box 367, for relevant documents including flow charts and other figures.

22. There were eighteen altogether, but eleven of these were women in administrative and secretarial posts. O.C. Doering to Whitney H. Shepardson, 27 April 1944, NARA, RG 226, A1-180G, Box 67.

23. Adolph Schmidt to Richard Dunlop, 6 September 1981, AHEC, Richard Dunlop Papers, Box 6.

24. *Tyrone Daily Herald*, 23 April 1930.

25. Conant, *A Covert Affair*, p. 35.

26. Information obtained from a photograph of Boulton in his OSS personnel file, NARA, RG 226, 224, Box 71.

27. David Rockingham-Gill, 'A Talk about Rudyerd Boulton (1901-1983), by Nancy Jacobs (6 October 2011)' in *The Babbler: Newsletter of Bird Life Zimbabwe*, Issue 103 (December 2011/January 2012).

28. Ibid.

29. Ibid.

30. *Chicago Tribune*, 10 April 1942.

31. This book was published under the pseudonym of Mary le Beau by Harper in 1956.

32. Conant, *A Covert Affair*, p. 34.

33. Quigley, *A U.S. Spy in Ireland*, p. 110.

34. Conant, *A Covert Affair*, pp. 34-5.

35. Remarks of General William J. Donovan at final gathering of employees, 28 September 1945. Hogue Family Archive.

36. Laxalt, *A Private War*, p. 53.

37. This and other details about Henry E. Stehli were supplied by Marguerite J. Kelly to the author in 2015.

38. Conant, *A Covert Affair*, pp. 35-6; Ford, *Donovan of OSS*, p. 134.

39. Muggeridge, *The Infernal Grove*, pp. 190-1.

40. McIntosh, *Sisterhood of Spies*, p. xi.

41. Muggeridge, *The Infernal Grove*, pp. 190-1.

42. Information and quotation from Waller, *Wild Bill Donovan*, caption to first photograph on penultimate page of illustrations between pp. 180 and 181.

43. Hastings, *The Secret War*, pp. 299-303.

44. Quoted in Katz, *Foreign Intelligence*, p. 8.

45. Written in 1943; quoted in Price, *Anthropological Intelligence*, pp. 42-3.

46. Statement by Jack Harris in early 1942, quoted in Lawler, *Soldiers, Airmen, Spies, and Whisperers*, p. 135.

47. Adolph Schmidt to Richard Dunlop, 6 September 1981, AHEC, Richard Dunlop Papers, Box 6.

48. Thomas, *A Patrician of Ideas*, p. 40.

49. History Project, Strategic Services Unit, War Department, Washington DC, *The Overseas Targets: War Report of the OSS Vol. 2*, p. 39.

50. Bookman, *Headlines, Deadlines and Lifelines*, p. 40.

51. McIntosh, *Sisterhood of Spies*, p. 19.

52. Thomas, *A Patrician of Ideas*, p. 40.

53. Huntington to Vanderbilt, 2 September 1942, NARA, RG 226, A1–210, Box 405.

54. CIGAR was Harry Watson Starcher, based in Ivory Coast. Information about sightings in Waller, *Wild Bill Donovan*, p. 95.

55. Accra concerned itself with: Cape Verde Islands (now known as Cabo Verde); French West Africa; Portuguese Guinea; Liberia; French Equatorial Africa; Belgian Congo; and Angola.

56. Capetown concerned itself with: Portuguese East Africa; Madagascar; subversive and enemy activity within the Union of South Africa and Southwest Africa; Southern Rhodesia, Northern Rhodesia, Nyasaland, Uganda, Kenya and Tanganyika (although no activities were carried on in British Crown colonies).

57. This base was established in 1943–4, during which time Ethiopia's problems were of primary importance; but went on to be involved in Eritrea, French Somaliland and Italian Somaliland.

58. OSS Planning Group, 'Over-all the Special Programs for Strategic Services Activities in Africa based on Washington', 5 June 1944, PG 77/2, NARA, RG 226, 210, Box 382.

59. Laxalt, *A Private War*, p. 57.

60. Oral History Interview with Edwin W. Martin by Richard D. McKinzie, Washington, DC, 3 June 1975, Harry S. Truman Library, Independence, Missouri. http://www.trumanlibrary.org/oralhist/martinew.htm

61. *Princeton Alumni Weekly*, Obituary for Harry H. Schwartz, 23 October 1991. https://paw.princeton.edu/memorials/70/100/index.xml

62. As recorded by Hogue later in 'Report on Field Conditions in the Belgian Congo', 253 to Executive Office SI, 6 October 1944, NARA, RG 226, A1–180G, Box 71.

63. Boulton to Bonner, 28 July 1943, NARA, RG 226, A1–210, Box 417.

3. CRISP

1. Conversion author's own using http://www.calculator.net/inflation-calculator.html on 24 January 2016.

2. The Belgian Congo at this time included the adjoining Ruanda-Urundi Territories (now Rwanda and Burundi), formerly two districts of German East Africa, which had been entrusted to Belgium in 1925 by the League of Nations; in most respects they were administered as a part of the Belgian Congo, except that they had a separate treasury and it was incumbent on the Congo government to report on their progress to the League of Nations, not only to the Belgian parliament.

3. For the discussion over the next few pages I owe a debt to the excellent article by Bruce Fetter, 'Africa's Role, 1940–41, as seen from Léopoldville', in *African Affairs*, 87 (348), 1988.

4. See W. B. Norton, 'Belgian–French Relations During World War II as seen by Governor General Ryckmans', in *Le Congo Belge durant la Seconde Guerre Mondiale*, pp. 285–311.

5. Pierre Ryckmans, 'The Belgian Congo's War Effort', *Belgian Congo At War*, p. 5.

6. Max Horn, 'The Belgian Congo in the War', *Belgian Congo At War*, p. 7; Fetter, *Colonial Rule and Regional Imbalance in Central Africa*, pp. 162–3; Jean Pierre Sonck, 'Le Congo Belge entre 1940–1945', <http://www.congo-1960.be/Congo_Belge_1940–1945.htm>.

7. Van Reybrouck, *Congo*, p. 182.

8. Conway, *The Sorrows of Belgium*, p. 17.

9. Quoted in Vanthemsche, *Belgium and the Congo*, p. 124. This volume provides a superb account and analysis.

10. Quoted in Vilma R. Hunt, 'Uranium Merchants' ms, Section 5.

11. Ibid., pp. 123–4.

12. Summary biography of Monseigneur de Hemptinne, Acad. Roy. Scienc. D'Outre-Mer, *Biographie Belge d'Outre-Mer*, T. VII-A, 1973, cols 291–299. Online at http://www.kaowarsom.be/documents/bbom/Tome_VIIa/Hemptinne_de.Jean_Felix.pdf

13. Van Reybrouck, *Congo*, p. 168.

14. Bookman, *Headlines, Deadlines, and Lifelines*, p. 40; Van Reybrouck, *Congo*, p. 182; Rudyerd Boulton, Africa Section, to G. W. Cottrell, 'Information from the Belgian Congo', 28 June 1943, NARA, RG 226, 210, Box 81.

15. Van Reybrouck, *Congo*, p. 182; Rudyerd Boulton, Africa Section, to G. W. Cottrell, 'Information from the Belgian Congo', 28 June 1943, NARA, RG 226, 210, Box 81.

16. *New York Times*, 18 December 1940.

17. William J. Donovan to the President, 17 November 1941, NARA, RG 226, 210 Box 348.

18. '1st Report to Coordinator of Information, Washington DC', by Armand Denis, 5 March 1942, NARA, RG 226, 210, Box 338.

19. Denis to Bruce, 17 September 1942, NARA, RG 226, A1–216, Box 2.

20. Quoted in Waller, *Wild Bill Donovan*, p. 922.

21. Monthly Progress Report for October 1942 by Africa Section SI, n.d., NARA, RR6, A1–210, Box 519.

22. Chapin to Boulton, 9 December 1942, NARA, RG 226 A1–210 Box 493.

23. Africa Section Report, SI, 9 October 1943, RG 226, A1–210, Box 519.

24. Craven and Cate, *Army Air Forces in World War II: Services around the world* (Office of Air Force History, 1983). Chapter 2 online at http://www.ibiblio.org/hyperwar/AAF/VII/AAF-VII-2.html; Gordon and Dangerfield, *The Hidden Weapon*, pp. 53–4.

25. George P. Putnam to Boulton, 31 July 1943, NARA, RG 226, 210, Box 382.
26. Chapin to Boulton, 29 November 1942, NARA, RG 226, A1–210, Box 483.
27. Chapin to Boulton, 21 December 1942, NARA, RG 226, A1–210, Box 483.
28. Chapin to Boulton, 5 January 1943, NARA, RG 226, A1–210, Box 493.
29. Ibid.
30. Ibid.
31. Chapin to Boulton, 30 December 1942, NARA, RG 226, A1–210, Box 493.
32. Chapin to Boulton, 13 January 1943, NARA, RG 226, A1–210, Box 493.
33. Chapin to Boulton, 20 December 1942, NARA, RG 226, A1–210, Box 483.
34. Chapin to Boulton, 18 December 1942, NARA, RG 226, A1–210, Box 493.
35. Ibid.
36. Quigley, *A U.S. Spy in Ireland*, p. 38.
37. Boulton to Chapin, 12 January 1943, NARA, RG 226, 210, Box 382.
38. Howard Chapin to James Chapin, 9 February 1943 and 2 March 1943, NARA, RG 226, 210, Box 382.
39. Boulton to Chapin, 31 March 1943, NARA, RG 226, 210, Box 382.
40. Leonard J. Cromie, Léopoldville to Washington, 22 April 1943, NARA, RG 226, 210, Box 383.
41. Chapin to Ruth Chapin, 5 June 1943, NARA, RG 226 210, Box 383.
42. Jerome D. Frank to Ruth Chapin, 28 May 1943, NARA, RG 226 210, Box 383.
43. Jerome D. Frank to Ruth Chapin, 6 May 1943, NARA, RG 226 210, Box 383.
44. Ruth Chapin to Boulton, 20 June 1943, NARA, RG 226 210, Box 383.
45. Ruth Chapin to Boulton, 30 June 1943, NARA, RG 226 210, Box 383.
46. Willard E. Beecher to Director, SI, 9 September 1943, NARA, RG 226 210, Box 383.
47. Chapin to Boulton, 30 December 1943, NARA, RG 226 210, Box 382.

4. CRUMB

1. Monthly Progress Report for October 1942 by Africa Section SI, n.d., NARA, RR6, A1–210, Box 519.
2. 'OSS–Africa', n.d., NARA, RG 226, A1–210, Box 519.
3. Donovan, 'Job Description in the Case of Douglas G. Bonner', 19 March 1943, NARA, RG 226, 224, Box 67; C. B. Briggs to Adjutant General, Washington, 27 November 1943, NARA, RG 226, 224, Box 67.
4. Interview report on Douglas Griswold Bonner, signed H. A. Murray, Major, 28 December 1944, NARA, RG 226, 224, Box 67. Bonner was born on 31 January 1902.
5. Jonathan Crow, 'Private Snafu', in *Open Culture*, 10 February 2014. Online at http://www.openculture.com/2014/02/private-snafu.html; for an example of the Snafu films, see *Private Snafu–Spies* (1943), available at https://www.youtube.com/watch?v=vzIltaAnWFU
6. Bonner to HANLY, 27 July 1943, NARA, RG 226, A1–210, 417.

7. Boulton to Bonner, 7 August 1943, NARA, RG 226, A1–210, Box 417.
8. NORTH to HANLY, 24 June 1943, NARA, RG 226, A1–210, Box 417.
9. Bonner to Hanley, 3 May 1943, NARA, RG 226, A1–210, Box 417.
10. Luther to Boulton, 1 January 1944 [mistakenly written on document as 1943], NARA, RG 226, A1–215, Box 1.
11. Davis to Boulton, 17 September 1943, RG 226, A1–210, Box 417.
12. Bonner to Boulton, 7 June 1943, NARA, RG 226, A1–210, Box 417.
13. Quoted in Hastings, *The Secret War*, pp. 287–8.
14. Bonner to HANLY, 19 July 1943, NARA, RG 226, A1–210, Box 417; Bonner to HANLY, 27 July 1943, RG 226, A1–210, Box 417.
15. Bonner to Boulton, 26 July 1943, NARA, RG 226, A1–210, Box 417.
16. Monthly Progress Report for October 1942 by Africa Section SI, n.d., NARA, RR6, A1–210, Box 519.
17. 'Belgian Congo', 7 January 1943, RG 226, A1–210, Box 210.
18. 'Belgian Congo', 22 February 1943, RG 226, A1–210, Box 210.
19. Thomas T. Crenshaw to Colonel J. C. Marshall, 27 April 1943, NARA, RG 77, 5, Box 68.
20. Harvey H. Bundy, William L. Webster, D.H.F. Rickett, 'Minutes of a Meeting of the Combined Policy Committee,' 8 March 1945, in *FRUS 1945, Vol. II: General: Political and Economic Matters*, p. 8.
21. Groves, *Now It Can Be Told*, p. 179.
22. L. Cahen, 'Contribution à l'histoire du rôle des pouvoirs publics dans l'effort minier de guerre du Congo belge (1940-1945)', in *Le Congo Belge durant la Seconde Guerre Mondiale*, pp. 110–11.
23. John Lansdale, Memorandum for General Groves, 17 July 1943, NARA, RG 77, 5, Box 68.
24. John Lansdale, Memorandum for General Groves, 21 May 1943, NARA, RG 77, 5, Box 68.
25. Vanderlinden, *Pierre Ryckmans 1891–1959*, p. 561.
26. Bonner to Boulton, 26 May 1943, NARA, RG 226, A1–210, Box 417.
27. Bonner to Boulton, 19 May 1943, NARA, RG 226, A1–210, Box 417.
28. Ibid.
29. P. M. Shepherd to Peter Stephens, 7 July 1944, TNA, FO 371/38880.
30. Vilma R. Hunt, 'Uranium Merchants' ms, Section 8.
31. Rudyerd Boulton, Africa Section, to G. W. Cottrell, 'Information from the Belgian Congo', 28 June 1943, NARA, RG 226, E210, Box 81; Bonner to Boulton, 7 June 1943, NARA, RG 226, A1–210, Box 417. Also see Vilma R. Hunt, 'Uranium Merchants' ms, Section 8, with thanks to Dr Hunt's family for allowing the author to read it. Bonner and some other sources suggest it was Cousin who organised the meeting; Dr Hunt suggests it was de Hemptinne. In any case, they were in agreement about the purpose of the meeting and the outcome.
32. See correspondence in NARA, RG 169, 480, Box 2983.
33. Bonner to Boulton, 7 June 1943, NARA, RG 226, A1–210, Box 417.

34. Ibid.
35. Biography of Firmin Van Bree by E. Van der Straeten, 9 October 1970, which can be found here: file:///C:/Users/tedpsaw/Downloads/Doc.1%20 BIOGRAPHIE%20by%20E.%20Van%20der%20Straeten.pdf
36. 'List of Personalities in the Belgian Congo', n.d., produced by the British Consulate in the Congo, TNA FO 371/38880.
37. Rudyerd Boulton, Africa Section, to G. W. Cottrell, 'Information from the Belgian Congo', 28 June 1943. NARA RG 226, E210, Box 81.
38. The author submitted to the UK National Archives a Freedom of Information request for an SOE file on Van Bree that was officially closed for 84 years, until January 2031. The request was approved and the file was made available. TNA, HS 9/1502/3, opened on 24 February 2016.
39. 1 Minute Sheet, 13 December 1943, TNA, HS 9/1502/3.
40. F. M. Shepherd to Eden, 31 August 1944, TNA, FO 371/3888041.
41. Bonner to Boulton, 17 June 1943, NARA, RG 226, A1–210, Box 417.
42. Ibid.
43. Bonner to Boulton, 16 June 1943, NARA, RG 226, A1–210, Box 417.
44. Bonner to Boulton, 26 May 1943, NARA, RG 226, A1–210, Box 417.
45. Bonner to Boulton, 7 June 1943, NARA, RG 226, A1–210, Box 417.
46. Boulton to Bonner, 21 June 1943, NARA, RG 226, A1–210, Box 81.
47. Boulton to Bonner, 30 June 1943, NARA, RG 226, A1–210, Box 417.
48. Boulton to Bonner, 8 June 1943, NARA, RG 226, A1–210, Box 417.
49. Boulton to Bonner, 15 June 1943, NARA, RG 226, A1–210, Box 81.
50. Bonner to Boulton, 26 May 1943, NARA, RG 226, A1–210, Box 417.
51. NORTH to HANLY, 22 June 1943, NARA RG 226, A1–210, Box 417.

5. CHIEF OF STATION, CONGO

1. 253 to 951, 8 August 1944, NARA, RG 226, 215, Box 1.
2. Boulton to Bonner, 7 August 1943, NARA, RG 226, A1–210, 417.
3. Boulton to Bonner, 14 September 1943, NARA, RG 226, A1–210, 417.
4. Boulton to Bonner, 7 September 1943, NARA, RG 226, A1–210, 417.
5. OSS to CRUMB, 28 September 1943, RG 226, A1–180G, Box 153.
6. After its cartridge had been fired, the cartridge case had to be pushed out of the breech with the use of a small stick that came with the pistol.
7. Melton, OSS Special Weapons & Equipment, pp. 34–5.
8. Laxalt, A Private War, p. 62.
9. Boulton to Luther, 11 February 1944, NARA, RG 226, A1–215, Box 1.
10. Boulton to Bonner, 7 August 1943, NARA, RG 226, A1–210, Box 417.
11. 'Special Report. Principal Developments in the Africa Section SI', 1 November 1943–1 February 1944, NARA, RG 226, A1–210, Box 519.
12. Bonner to Boulton, 1 October 1943, NARA, RG 226, A1–210, 417.
13. Bonner to Boulton, 29 September 1943, NARA, RG 226, A1–210, 417.
14. Bonner to Boulton, 7 June 1943, NARA, RG 226, A1–210, Box 417.

15. Laxalt, A *Private War*, p. 31.
16. Jackson Davis to Helen and Ruth, 19 November 1944, Jackson Davis collection, MSS 3072-b, Albert and Shirley Small Special Collections Library, University of Virginia.
17. Pierre Ryckmans, 'The Belgian Congo's War Effort', in The Belgian Information Center, New York, *Belgian Congo At War*, p. 5; and *Belgian Congo At War*, p. 2.
18. The book is held by the Hogue Family.
19. Hogue to Beecher, between 1 and 10 January 1944, NARA, RG 226, A1-215, Box 1.
20. Bonner to Boulton, 7 June 1943, NARA, RG 226, A1-210, Box 417.
21. Young, *Politics in the Congo*, pp. 104-5.
22. Robert L. Buell, 'Daniel', n.d. [1946], Robert L. Buell Papers, Special Collections, University of Oregon Libraries. He says 22:00 but this is an error; it was 21:00 (see for example Njoh, *Planning Power*, p. 217).
23. Laxalt, A *Private War*, pp. 31-2.
24. Hochschild, 'Introduction' to Marchal, *Lord Leverhulme's Ghosts*, p. xiv.
25. Ibid., p. xviii.
26. Ibid., p. xiv.
27. Marchal, *Lord Leverhulme's Ghosts*, pp. 214-15.
28. Hochschild, 'Introduction', p. xiv.
29. 'Belgian Congo', information provided by Rev J. D. R. Allison, 9, 10, October 1942, NARA, RG 226, A1-210, Box 210.
30. Marchal, *Lord Leverhulme's Ghosts*, p. 214.
31. Young, *Politics in the Congo*, p. 223.
32. Van Reybrouck, *Congo*, pp. 191ff.
33. Hochschild, *King Leopold's Ghost*, p. 279.
34. Van Reybrouck, *Congo*, p. 195.
35. Fetter, 'Africa's Role, 1940-41, as seen from Léopoldville', p. 392.
36. Van Reybrouck, *Congo*, p. 198.
37. Latouche, *Congo*, p. 20.
38. Renton et al., *The Congo, Plunder and Resistance*, p. 66.
39. See Fetter, *Colonial Rule and Regional Imbalance in Central Africa*, pp. 162-3.
40. Stephanie McCrummen, 'Nearly Forgotten Forces of WWII', *Washington Post*, 4 August 2009.
41. Van Reybrouck, *Congo*, p. 185.
42. Ibid., p. 189.
43. NARA, RG 226, A1-180G, Box 153.
44. Hogue to Becquet, 2 February 1944, NARA, RG 226, 210, Box 382.
45. 'Belgian Congo', 15 May 1942, NARA, RG 226, A1-210, Box 210.
46. Donald E. Hardy, 'Writes to Ottawa Family of Life in Léopoldville', *Ottawa Citizen*, 8 November 1941.
47. Dock to Ruth, 11 February 1942, Hogue Family Archive.
48. Quoted in Hastings, *The Secret War*, pp. 290-1.
49. As recorded by Hogue later in 'Report on Field Conditions in the Belgian

Congo', 253 to Executive Office SI, 6 October 1944, NARA, RG 226, A1–180G, Box 71.

50. Boulton to Bonner, 14 October 1943, NARA, RG 226, A1–210, Box 417.
51. Bonner to Boulton, 17 June 1943, NARA, RG 226, A1–210, Box 417.
52. Laxalt, *A Private War*, pp. 79–80.
53. Hogue to Beecher, between Jan. 1 & 10, 1944, NARA, RG 226, A1–215, Box 1.
54. Report to Congress On Operations of the Foreign Economic Administration, September 25, 1944, Appendices III and IV, pp. 52–55; https://fraser.stlouisfed.org/docs/historical/martin/54_01_19440925.pdf
55. Bonner to Boulton, 26 May 1943, NARA, RG 226, A1–210, Box 417.
56. Africa Section SI, Monthly Progress Report for December 1943, NARA, RG 226, A1–210, Box 519.
57. CRUMB to Boulton, 14 December 1943, NARA, RG 226, A1–180G, Box 165.
58. 'Coordination of IDB Control Measures in West Africa', sent from Accra to London, 15 December 1943, TNA, HS3/94.

6. 'ATTENTION! BLOC RADIOACTIF!'

1. Newitt, 'The Portuguese African Colonies during the Second World War', in Byfield et al., *Africa and World War II*, p. 220.
2. Gordon and Dangerfield, *The Hidden Weapon*, pp. 3–4.
3. 'Belgian Congo', information from Lanier Violett, 11 April 1942, NARA, RG 226, A1–210, Box 210.
4. 'Angola', 21 December 1942, NARA, RG 226, A1–210, Box 210.
5. Manderstam, with Roy Heron, *From the Red Army to SOE*, pp. 70–74, 79.
6. Ibid., p. 78.
7. The author is grateful to Michelle Kratts for this suggestion.
8. 'Report, West Africa, Project No 1', n.d. [1942/43], NARA, RG 226, A1–210, Box 405.
9. Manderstam, with Roy Heron, *From the Red Army to SOE*, p. 94.
10. Hogue to Willard Beecher, Between Jan 1 & 10, 1944, NARA, RG 226, A1–215, Box 1.
11. The British officer referred to is Alec Binney.
12. OSS, 'Investigation into Diamond Smuggling in Africa', NARA, RG 226, A1–210, Box 358.
13. Bonner to HANLY, 5 November 1943, NARA, RG 226, A1–210, 417.
14. HANLY to OSS, 14 November 1944, NARA, RG 226, A1–180G, Box 153.
15. Sampson, *The Seven Sisters*, pp. 115–17; Sutton, *Wall Street and the Rise of Hitler*, pp. 81–2.
16. 'Belgian Congo', 9, 10, October 1942, NARA, RG 226, A1–210, Box 210.
17. The Sûreté d'Etat was the Belgian Congo colonial state security and information service, which had been set up in 1932 to gather information on foreign

nationals, Communists, Pan-African movements, symptoms of strikes and revolts, and all individuals suspected of espionage or of being hostile to Belgian colonial occupation. See Dominic Emanuel Martin Pistor, 'Developmental Colonialism and Kitawala Policy in 1950s Belgian Congo', p. 29.

18. 'Summary of IDB Case Against Jacobs', written at the request of OSS, Angola, 'Information Item No 140', 21 June 1944, NARA, RG 226, A1–210, Box 489.

19. OSS, 'Investigation into Diamond Smuggling in Africa', NARA, RG 226, A1–210, Box 358.

20. James Chapin to Howard Chapin, 11 January 1943, NARA, RG 226, 210, Box 382.

21. 'List of personalities in the Belgian Congo', TNA, FO 371/38880.

22. Monthly Progress Report for December 1943, 10 January 1944, from Africa Section SI to Chief SI, NARA, RG 226, A1–210, Box 519.

23. Bonner to Boulton, 3 July 1943, NARA, RG 226, A1–210, Box 417.

24. Monthly Progress Report for December 1943, 10 January 1944, from Africa Section SI to Chief SI, NARA, RG 226, A1–210, Box 519.

25. Hogue to Beecher, Between Jan 1 & 10, 1944, NARA, RG 226, A1–215, Box 1.

26. Spellman, *Action This Day*, p. 194.

27. Latouche, *Congo*, p. 178.

28. Hogue to Willard Beecher, Between Jan. 1 & 10, 1944, NARA, RG 226, A1–215, Box 1.

29. For an expert account see Brion and Moreau, *Société Générale de Belgique 1822–1997*.

30. Mommen, *The Belgian Economy in the Twentieth Century*, pp. 114–15.

31. Ibid., p. 115.

32. The intricate relationship between the different companies and their directors had a long history, as Guy Vanthemsche has shown. In 1900, the Compagnie du Katanga and the Congo Free State set up the Comité Spécial du Katanga (CSK), in which they respectively held one-third and two-thirds shares and which proceeded to exploit and manage Katanga's mineral wealth. In 1906 the king, Léopold II, persuaded Société Générale to become involved in the Congo; Société Générale, with the CSK and Tanks, then set up Union Minière du Haut Katanga. Vanthemsche, *Belgium and the Congo, 1885–1980*, pp. 148–50.

33. Helmreich, *Gathering Rare Ores*, p. 6.

34. Vanthemsche, *Belgium and the Congo, 1885–1980*, pp. 148–50.

35. The Sibéka archive in the Belgian state archives in Brussels contains duplicates of telegrams and telexes exchanged in September 1961 between Union Minière in Elisabethville and its headquarters in Brussels. Although this is many years after the Second World War, the fact that Sibéka held these duplicates illustrates the relationship between Sibéka and Union Minière.

36. Gunther, *Meet the Congo and its Neighbors*, p. 88.

37. Laxalt, *A Private War*, pp. 63 and 81.

38. E. Baring to Machtig, 15 October 1944, TNA, FO 371/38880.

39. Gunther, *Inside Africa*, pp. 661–2.
40. Ibid., p. 665.
41. Hogue to Willard Beecher, Between Jan 1 & 10, 1944, NARA, RG 226, A1–215, Box 1.
42. Ibid.
43. Ibid.
44. Ibid.
45. Melton, OSS *Special Weapons & Equipment*, p. 105.
46. Hogue to Willard Beecher, Between Jan. 1 & 10, 1944, NARA, RG 226.

7. ANGELLA

1. Latouche, *Congo*, p. 15.
2. Spellman, *Action This Day*, p. 194.
3. Sichel, 'Germaine Krull and *L'Amitié Noire*', in Hight and Sampson (eds), *Colonialist Photography*, p. 263.
4. Ibid., p. 279, notes 5 and 6.
5. Bookman, *Headlines, Deadlines and Lifelines*, pp. 36–41.
6. 'Dossier Material—People Well Known in the Belgian Congo', 1944. NARA, RG 226, A1–210, Box 4901. After the defeat of France, the Vichy regime organised an intelligence service under the command of Colonel Louis Rivet, who had been head of the Deuxième Bureau since 1936. It was called the Centre d'Information Gouvernemental (CIG). Under de Gaulle, an intelligence service for the Free French was created, known as the Bureau Central de Renseignements et d'Action (BCRA).
7. The film *L'Amitié Noire* was co-directed by François Villiers and Germaine Krull and was completed in 1946.
8. The author is indebted to James Williams and Albertine Fox for the transcription and translation.
9. Although she is not specifically identified in the film as Shirley Chidsey, her appearance conforms to the physical details set out in her OSS personnel file; in addition, the woman in the film resembles Shirley Chidsey's sister, Margaret Armitage.
10. Civilian check-out sheet for Mrs Shirley A. Chidsey, NARA, RG 226, 224, Box 121.
11. Betty Carp to Mr Merrill, 8 December 1943, NARA, RG 226, 224, Box 121.
12. Shirley Chidsey, Application and Personal History Statement, Received 6 October 1942, NARA, RG 226, 224, Box 121.
13. *Saratogian*, Saratoga Springs, New York, 5 January 1943.
14. See ABAA website http://www.abaa.org/book/425626131
15. *Saturday Review of Literature*, 30 November 1940.
16. Shirley Chidsey to Mrs Percival Armitage, n.d. [late 1942], Shirley Armitage (Chidsey) Bridgwater Papers.
17. Schmidt to Geo White, 13 October 1944, NARA, RG 226, 224, Box 121.

18. Beecher to Schmidt, 11 October 1944, NARA, RG 226, 224, Box 121.
19. H. S. Prescott to Willard Beecher, 25 January 1944, NARA, RG 226, 224, Box 121.
20. Shirley Chidsey, Personal History Statement [to OSS], 18 April 1944, NARA, RG 226, 224, Box 121.
21. TETON to Boulton, 19 January 1944, NARA, RG 226, A1–180G, Box 165.
22. H. S. Prescott to Willard Beecher, 25 January 1944, NARA, RG 226, 224, Box 121.
23. W. O. Hogue to Mrs Shirley Chidsey, 16 March 1944, NARA, RG 226, 224, Box 121; Schmidt to Special Funds, Africa SI, 13 October 1944, NARA, RG 226, 224, Box 121.
24. See 'Kinshasa Then and Now' at http://kosubaawate.blogspot.co.uk/2011/05/Léopoldville-1942-us-troops-expand.html
25. Chalou (ed.), *The Secrets War*, p. 24.
26. MacDonald, *Undercover Girl*, p. 246.
27. Chalou (ed.), *The Secrets War*, p. 24.
28. Donovan, Introduction to MacDonald, *Undercover Girl*, p. vii.
29. Davis to Boulton, 17 September 1943, RG 226, A1–210, Box 417.
30. Bonner to Boulton, 29 September 1943, NARA, RG 226, A1–210, 417.
31. Davis to Boulton, 22 August 1943, NARA, RG 226, A1–210, Box 417.
32. CLOCK to Boulton, 14 November 1944, NARA, RG 226, A1–180G, Box 153.
33. HANLY, Accra, 'For Boulton only', 27 November 1944, NARA, RG 226, A1–180G, Box 153.
34. See NARA, RG 226, 224, Box 315.
35. K. Fedorowich, 'British espionage and British counter-intelligence in South Africa and Mozambique, 1939–1944', p. 223.
36. Kevin A. Yelvington, 'A Life In and Out of Anthropology', p. 464.
37. Muggeridge, *The Infernal Grove*, pp. 190–1.
38. Harrison, 'Something Beautiful for "C"', pp. 190–1.
39. Ingrams, *Muggeridge*, pp. 190, 129–33.
40. See http://www.colonialfuneralhome.com/home/index.cfm/obituaries/view/fh_id/11079/id/1355306
41. *Chicago Tribune*, 19 October 1943.
42. EBERT to OSS, 27 January 1944, NARA, RG 226, A1–180G, Box 165.

8. 'BORN SECRET'

1. Thomas Mellon Schmidt to the author, 16 February 2016.
2. Thomas, *A Patrician of Ideas*, p. 43.
3. Adolph Schmidt to Richard Dunlop, 6 September 1981, AHEC, Richard Dunlop Papers, Box 6.
4. Thomas, *A Patrician of Ideas*, pp. 42–3.
5. Ibid.

6. Adolph Schmidt to Richard Dunlop, 6 September 1981, AHEC, Richard Dunlop Papers, Box 6.

7. US War Department, Bern, to Strategic Services Unit, 10 September 1946, NARA, RG 226, A1–216, Box 2.

8. Foreign Relations of the United States, 1949, Volume I, National Security Affairs, Foreign Economic Policy, Document 193.

9. John Lansdale, Memorandum for General Groves, 17 July 1943, NARA, RG 77, 5, Box 68.

10. Report to Congress On Operations of the Foreign Economic Administration, September 25, 1944, chapter II, pp. 18–25; online at https://fraser.stlouisfed.org/docs/historical/martin/54_01_19440925.pdf

11. Helmreich, *United States Relations with Belgium and the Congo, 1940–1960*, p. 29.

12. W. R. Johnson to The Collector of Customs, New York, 21 September 1943, NARA, RG 77, 5, Box 68.

13. Ziegler and Jacobson, *Spying Without Spies*, p. 22.

14. J. C. Marshall to General Groves, 21 April, NARA, RG 77, 5, Box 68.

15. Kaufman et al., *Moe Berg*, pp. 163–4.

16. Nelson, *The Age of Radiance*, p. 154.

17. Sayer and Botting, *America's Secret Army*, p. 71.

18. Ibid., pp. 2–3.

19. Stamped for example on Arthur H. Compton, University of Chicago, to General Groves, 2 September 1943, NARA, RG 77, 5, Box 68.

20. Sayer and Botting, *America's Secret Army*, pp. 71–6.

21. Kai Bird and Martin Sherwin, 'Robert Oppenheimer: A Window on His Life at Los Alamos', in Cynthia C. Kelly (ed.), *Oppenheimer and the Manhattan Project*, p. 73.

22. Sayer and Botting, *America's Secret Army*, pp. 71–6.

23. Powers, *Heisenberg's War*, p. 529, note 45.

24. On the eve of his departure in April 1944, from handwritten notes by Berg, 26 April 1944, 'FURMAN: SECRET'; see Powers, *Heisenberg's War*, p. 297.

25. OSS to EBERT, 18 January 1944, NARA, RG 226, A1–180G, Box 165.

26. Van Reybrouck, *Congo*, pp. 121–2.

27. Gordon and Dangerfield, *The Hidden Weapon*, p. 48. There are several books about the role of diamond smuggling in the war, of which the most widely known are: *Glitter & Greed* (2003) by Janine Roberts; *The Rise and Fall of Diamonds: The Shattering of a Brilliant Illusion* (1982) by Edward Jay Epstein; and *The Last Empire: De Beers, Diamonds and the World* (1993) by Stefan Kanfer.

28. Cockerill, *Sir Percy Sillitoe*, p. 200.

29. Atherton, *Operations in Africa and the Middle East*, pp. 17–18. For actions against diamond smuggling 1942–44, see TNA, HS 3/75, 82, 94.

30. CRUMB to Boulton, 6 December 1943, NARA, RG 226, A1–180G, Box 165.

31. Manderstam, with Roy Heron, *From the Red Army to SOE*, p. 91.

32. OSS, 'Investigation into Diamond Smuggling in Africa', NARA, RG 226, A1–210, Box 358.

33. Gordon and Dangerfield, *The Hidden Weapon*, pp. 48–9.
34. Ibid., p. 50.
35. Ibid., pp. 51–2.
36. Greene, *The Heart of the Matter*, pp. 90–91.
37. Bonner to HANLY, 24 July 1943, NARA, RG 226, A1–210, Box 417.
38. Wilson, *The Life and Times of Sir Alfred Chester Beatty*, p. 238.
39. Quoted in Helmreich, *United States Relations with Belgium and the Congo, 1940–1960*, p. 44.

9. THE MISSION

1. Recommendation for the award of Legion of Merit to A. W. Schmidt, 29 April 1947, NARA, RG 226, 224, Box 684.
2. FLARE to Boulton, 10 February 1944, NARA, RG 226, A1–180G, Box 165.
3. Information in this paragraph is drawn from SOE Personnel file 1939–1946 on Alexander Lindsay Binney, TNA, HS9/153/9.
4. Boulton to Luther, 20 December 1943, NARA, RG 226, A1–215, Box 1. Luther was transferred on 12 December 1944.
5. Luther to Boulton, 1 January 1944 [mistakenly written on document as 1943], NARA, RG 226, A1–215, Box 1.
6. The name of his father-in-law was Colonel Lawrence Mitchell.
7. COACH to Rud, 19 December 1943, NARA, RG 226, A1–215, Box 1.
8. Luther to Boulton, 20 January 1944, NARA, RG 226, A1–215, Box 1.
9. Boulton to Luther, 20 December 1943, NARA, RG 226, A1–215, Box 1.
10. NORTH to Boulton, 16 July 1943, NARA, RG 226, A1–210, 417.
11. Rudyerd Boulton, 'Special Report: Principal Developments in the Africa Section SI, 1 November 1943–1 February 1944', 5 February 1944, NARA, RG 226, A1–210, Box 262.
12. Luther to Boulton, 1 January 1944 [mistakenly written on document as 1943], NARA, RG 226, A1–215, Box 1.
13. Ibid.
14. Cable from Washington to London, 13 February 1944, TNA, HS 9/1502/3.
15. W to WM, 5 January 1944, TNA, HS 9/1502/3.
16. No title, list of allegations and suspicions relating to Firmin Van Brae, n.d., TNA, HS 9/1502/3.
17. D/CE.1 to W., 22 December 1943, TNA, HS 9/1502/3.
18. 'La Roseraie', 29 Avenue Olsen. Address given by Hogue for the FEA and Jaubert on 2 February 1944, NARA, RG 226, 210, Box 382.
19. Luther to Boulton, 20 January 1944, NARA, RG 226, A1–215, Box 1.
20. Hogue to Beecher, Between Jan 1 & 10, 1944, NARA, RG 226, A1–215, Box 1.
21. Bonner to Boulton, 3 July 1943, NARA, RG 226, A1–210, Box 417.
22. Kirkland to Schmidt, 14 May 1944, RG 226, A1–215, Box 1.
23. COACH to Boulton, 28 January 1944, RG 226, A1–180G, Box 165.
24. SI, OSS to HANLY, Accra, 28 January 1944, RG 226, A1–180G, Box 165.

25. SI, OSS to TETON, 26 January 1944 [author's decipherment of faintly printed text] 1944, RG 6, A1–180G, Box 165.
26. Rudyerd Boulton, 'Special Report: Principal Developments in the Africa Section SI, 1 November 1943–1 February 1944', 5 February 1944, 'Copy 4 of 9 copies', NARA, RG 226, A1–210, Box 262.
27. Hogue Film: 'Congo, General de Gaulle' (see Filmography).
28. Quoted in Majhemout Diop et al.,'Tropical and equatorial Africa under French, Portuguese and Spanish domination, 1935–45', in Mazrui with Wondji, *General History of Africa, Vol. VIII*, p. 74.
29. See excellent discussion and analysis of Brazzaville Conference in ibid., pp. 72–4.
30. Rudyerd Boulton, 'Special Report: Principal Developments in the Africa Section, SI, 1 November 1943–1 February 1944', 5 February 1944, NARA, RG 226, A1–210, Box 262.
31. Boulton to Luther, 10 February 1944, NARA, RG 226, A1–215, Box 1.
32. Luther to Boulton, 25 February 1944, NARA, RG 226, A1–215, Box 1.
33. NARA, RG 226, A1–180G, Box 179.
34. OSS, 'Investigation into Diamond Smuggling in Africa', NARA, RG 226, A1–210, Box 358.
35. Conversion achieved by use of http://www.calculator.net/inflation-calculator.html on 24 January 2016.
36. Schmidt to Doc[k], 16 March 1944 [Africa File 2].
37. OSS, 'Investigation into Diamond Smuggling in Africa', NARA, RG 226, A1–210, Box 358.
38. Thomas, *A Patrician of Ideas*, p. 43.
39. Africa Division SI, Monthly Intelligence and Operational Summary, October 1944, NARA, RG 226, A1–210, Box 519.

10. THE BRITISH OPPOSITES

1. Harris, quoted in Price, *Anthropological Intelligence*, p. 245.
2. Yelvington, 'A Life In and Out of Anthropology', p. 463.
3. 'OSS–Africa', n.d., NARA, RG 226, A1–210, Box 519.
4. Quoted by M. R. D. Foot, 'The OSS and SOE: An Equal Partnership?', in Chalou (ed.), *The Secrets War*, p. 295.
5. Foot, ibid.
6. Manderstam, with Heron, *From the Red Army to SOE*, p. 58.
7. Foot, 'The OSS and SOE', p. 299.
8. Manderstam, with Heron, *From the Red Army to SOE*, pp. 116–17.
9. Waller, *Wild Bill Donovan*, p. 235.
10. Frimpong-Ansah, *The Vampire State in Africa*, pp. 29–30.
11. Quoted in Andrew, *The Defence of the Realm*, p. 229.
12. Quoted in Hargreaves, *Decolonization in Africa* (second edn), p. 58.
13. Bonner to Boulton, 7 June 1943, NARA, RG 226, A1–210, Box 417.

14. Ibid.
15. See TNA HS 9/17/8.
16. NORTH to Boulton, 8 June 1943, NARA, RG 226, A1–210, Box 417.
17. Bonner to Boulton, 11 July 1943, NARA, RG 226, A1–210, Box 417.
18. 'Professor Sir Peter Russell', Obituary in *The Telegraph*, 10 July 2006.
19. Boulton to Luther, 12 January 1944, NARA, RG 226, A1–215, Box 1.
20. NORTH to Boulton, 19 May 1943, NARA, RG 226, A1–210, Box 417.
21. NORTH to Boulton, 16 July 1943, NARA, RG 226, A1–210, 417.
22. Bonner to HANLY, 4 October 1943, NARA, RG 226, A1–210, 417.
23. Bonner to Boulton, 9 October 1943, NARA, RG 226, A1–210, 417.
24. Hastings, *The Secret War*, p. 291.
25. Cave Brown, *"C": The Secret Life of Sir Stewart Graham Menzies*, p. 624.
26. Information and quotation from Waller, *Wild Bill Donovan*, p. 205.
27. Winston Churchill, House of Commons, 9 September 1941, Hansard Vol 374, available online at http://hansard.millbanksystems.com/commons/1941/sep/09/war-situation#column_69
28. Quoted in Von Eschen, *Race Against Empire*, pp. 25–8.
29. Boulton to Bonner, 27 October 1943, NARA, RG 226, A1–210, 417.
30. Nechama Janet Cohen Cox, 'The Ministry of Economic Warfare And Britain's Conduct of Economic Warfare, 1939–1945', Kings College London PhD thesis, p. 47.
31. Swinton, *I Remember*, p. 164.
32. http://www.mininghalloffame.org/inductee/beatty. Other members of the Board included J. H. 'Jack' Hambro, the chairman of Hambros Bank, and John Shearer, a Director of Military Intelligence.
33. West (ed.), *The Guy Liddell Diaries Vol. II: 1942–1945*, pp. 223–4.
34. Ibid.
35. Ibid., 29 January 1945, p. 265.
36. Swinton, *I Remember*, p. 194.
37. Maddock, *Nuclear Apartheid*, p. 70; http://www.independent.co.uk/news/people/obituary-lord-sherfield-1351871.html
38. Swinton, *I Remember*, p. 216.
39. Ibid., p. 233.
40. Groves, *Now It Can Be Told*, p. 179.

11. FLARE

1. Schmidt to Hogue, 16 March 1944, NARA, RG 226, 215, Box 1.
2. Ibid.
3. FLARE to OSS, 19 February 1944, NARA, RG 226, A1–180G, Box 165.
4. For more information see the following: http://www.garbagegangstersandgreed.com/blog/love-canal-and-the-manhattan-project; http://issuu.com/fredsakademiet/docs/nuclear_weapon_plants/132; http://www.cdc.gov/niosh/ocas/pdfs/misc/doefacdb090313.pdf; http://projects.wsj.com/waste-lands/site/97-carborundum-company/

5. 'Memo re uranium ore situation', [signature illegible], 26 January 1944, RG 77, 5, Box 68.
6. Jones, *United States Army in World War II*, p. 296.
7. Thomas, *A Patrician of Ideas*, p. 44.
8. Schmidt to Hogue, 16 March 1944, NARA, RG 226, 215, Box 1.
9. SILVA to OSS, 26 February 1944, NARA, RG 226, A1–180G, Box 165.
10. Weaver to Merrill, 25 January 1944, NARA, RG 226, A1–216, Box 10.
11. Merrill to Boulton, 25 April 1944, NARA, RG 226, A1–216, Box 10.
12. Scenes of which he recorded in the short film 'Yellowstone, Bear Tooth Mountain, Congo, Kenya, Rhodesia, Liberty Ship, Gil Baby'. (See Filmography at the end of this book.)
13. OSS, 'Investigation into Diamond Smuggling in Africa', NARA, RG 226, A1–210, Box 358.
14. Schmidt to Boulton, 19 April 1944, NARA, RG 226, 215, Box 1.
15. SOE Accra to London, 18 March 1944, TNA, HS3/94.
16. Schmidt to Boulton, 19 April 1944, NARA, RG 226, 215, Box 1.
17. HANLY to OSS, 31 March 1944, RG 226, A1–180G, Box 179.
18. Schmidt to Boulton, 19 April 1944, NARA, RG 226, 215, Box 1.
19. Charles Elliott to the author, 12 February 2016
20. Ibid.
21. Africa Division SI, Monthly Intelligence and Operational Summary, October 1944, NARA, RG 226, A1–210, Box 519.
22. Beaudinet, Government Intelligence, to Mr Hogue, Special Assistant to the US Consul, 14 April 1944.
23. Rudyerd Boulton, Africa Section, to G. W. Cottrell, 'Information from the Belgian Congo', 28 June 1943, NARA RG 226, 210, Box 81.
24. Schmidt to Boulton, 19 April 1944, NARA, RG 226, 215, Box 1.

12. THE CUTOUT

1. TETON to OSS, 18 April 1944, RG 226, A1–180G, Box 179.
2. TETON to OSS, 17 March 1944, RG 226, A1–180G, Box 179.
3. Hogue to Boulton, 24 July 1944, NARA, RG 226, 215, Box 1.
4. Much of the information given on Jean Decoster is drawn from a biography of his son Albert Decoster, written by J.-L. Vellut, 30 November 1995, in Acad. Roy. Science d'Outre-Mer, *Biographie Belge d'Outre-Mer*, T. VIII, 1998, cols 80–88.
5. This chapter benefits greatly from Bruce Fetter's article, 'The Luluabourg Revolt at Elisabethville', *African Historical Studies*, 2 (2) (1969), 272.
6. P. S. Stephens to A. M. Williams, 29 June 1944, TNA, FO 371/38880.
7. 'List of personalities in the Belgian Congo', TNA, FO 371/38880.
8. Ibid.
9. Quoted in Higginson, *A Working Class in the Making*, p. 197.
10. Quoted and discussed in Elikia M'Bokolo, 'Equatorial West Africa', in Ali A. Mazrui with C. Wondji, *General History of Africa, Vol. VIII*, p. 195.

11. P. S. Stephens to A. M. Williams, 29 June 1944, TNA, FO 371/38880.
12. Fetter, 'The Luluabourg Revolt at Elisabethville,' *African Historical Studies*, 2 (2) (1969), p. 272.
13. Renton et al., *The Congo*, p. 68.
14. Recollection by mine workers quoted in Renton et al., *The Congo*, p. 69.
15. Fetter, *The Creation of Elisabethville 1910–1940*, p. 173; Van Reybrouck, *Congo*, pp. 192–3.
16. Quoted in Van Reybrouck, *Congo*, p. 192.
17. Ibid., pp. 192–3.
18. Africa Section SI, Monthly Progress Report for August 1944, NARA, RG 226, A1–210, Box 519.
19. Fetter, 'The Luluabourg Revolt at Elisabethville', p. 274.
20. Van Reybrouck, *Congo*, p. 193.
21. Bonner to Boulton, 7 June 1943, NARA, RG 226, A1–210, Box 417.
22. 'Opinions Concerning Political and Economic Situation in Belgian Congo', sent from Léopoldville to Washington, dated 10 April 1944, distributed 21 June 1944, NARA, RG 226, A1–210, Box 489.
23. R. Boulton to Chief, SI, 'Consulate in Elizabethville, Belgian Congo', 2 March 1944, NARA, RG 226 A1–210, Box 81,
24. Ibid.
25. Foreign Service List of the United States, Vol. 1944, p 329; see also http://kosubaawate.blogspot.co.uk/2011_01_01_archive.html
26. TETON to OSS, 12 May 1944, NARA, RG 226, A1–180G, Box 179.
27. Hogue Film: 'Congo and the Gold Coast' (See Filmography at the end of this book).
28. TETON to OSS, 12 May 1944, NARA, RG 226, A1–180G, Box 179.
29. Accra to OSS, 3 June 1944, NARA, RG 226, A1–180G, Box 179.
30. TETON to Beecher, OSS, 14 June 1944, NARA, RG 226, A1–180G, Box 179.
31. Hogue to Schmidt, 10 July 1944, NARA, RG 226, 215, Box 1.
32. Schmidt to 'Doc', 30 May 1944, NARA, RG 226, 215, Box 1.
33. HANLY to OSS, [day illegible] June 1944, NARA, RG 226, A1–180G, Box 179.
34. OSS to HANLY, 9 May 1944, NARA, RG 226, A1–180G, Box 179.
35. Newmann in Cordell and Beckerman (eds), *The Versatility of Kinship*, p. xiv.
36. Schmidt to RUFUS, 30 May 1944, NARA, RG 226, 215, Box 1.
37. FLARE to RUFUS, 30 May 1944, NARA, RG 226, 215, Box 1.
38. HANLY to OSS, 24 June 1944, NARA, RG 226, A1–180G, Box 179.
39. HANLY to OSS, [day illegible] June 1944, NARA, RG 226, A1–180G, Box 179.
40. Instruction from 952, 27 June 1944, NARA, RG 226, 215, Box 1.

13. LOCUST

1. Henry Stehli's first wife Sybil Hoching died very young. He later married Grace Hays, the sister of Ethel Sanders Hays, Douglas Bonner's first wife. Douglas Bonner later married Kathleen ('Kay') Curtis. Douglas Bonner's brother (Paul Hyde Bonner) married Lilly Stehli, Henry Stehli's sister.

2. See Chapter 4, entitled 'CRUMB' (Doug Bonner's codename) for more detail on Bonner.

3. R. Boulton to Chief, SI, 'A recommendation by Mr Perry Jester', 2 March 1944, NARA, RG 226 E A1–210 Box 8.

4. Information given in an obituary published by Stehli's school, St Paul's, New Hampshire: *Alumni Horae*, 36 (1), 68, 'Obituaries 4', Spring 1956. http://archives.sps.edu/common/text.asp?Img=4962&Keyword=&Headline=&Author=&SearchMode=0

5. Hogue to Schmidt, 10 July 1944, NARA, RG 226, 215, Box 1.

6. 253 to 951, 17 July 1944, NARA, RG 226, 215, Box 1.

7. Ibid.

8. TETON to Beecher, OSS, 14 June 1944, RG 226, A1–180G, Box 179.

9. 253 to 951, 17 July 1944, NARA, RG 226, 215, Box 1.

10. The list also included Dr John Springer at the Methodist Mission in Elisabethville, Dr John Morrison at the Presbyterian Mission in Luebo, near Luluabourg, and J. L. Campbell at the Seventh-Day Adventist mission in Gitwe, Ruanda-Urundi. In Elisabethville, his sources included Peter Stephens, the British Consul, Ronnie Liddle and L. H. de Plessis of the South African Railroads. At Stanleyville (now Kisangani), he had turned to Patrick Putnam. At Costermansville, the British Vice Consul, Percival R. Morgan, had become a friend, as had Joseph Ide, a Belgian, 'an old S[ecret] I[ntelligence] man from the last war.' 253 to 923, 23 August 1944, NARA, RG 226, 215, Box 1.

11. P. S. Stephens to A. M. Williams, 29 June 1944, TNA, FO 371/38880.

12. Hogue to Schmidt, 10 July 1944, NARA, RG 226, 215, Box 1.

13. OSS to TETON, 2 July 1944, NARA, RG 226, A1–180G, Box 179.

14. Hogue to Schmidt, 10 July 1944, NARA, RG 226, 215, Box 1.

15. Ibid.

16. Ibid.

17. Hogue to Schmidt, 10 July 1944, NARA, RG 226, 215, Box 1.

18. TETON to OSS, 15 [unclear—possibly 13] July 1944, NARA, RG 226, A1–180G, Box 179.

19. Hogue to Schmidt, 10 July 1944, NARA, RG 226, 215, Box 1.

20. Ibid.

21. Ibid.

22. TETON to OSS, 14 July 1944 (but probably a day or so earlier, since it says at bottom, 'Delayed by garble.'), NARA, RG 226, A1–180G, Box 179.

23. TETON to Beecher, OSS, 14 July 1944, NARA, RG 226, A1–180G, Box 179.

24. 253 to 951, 17 July 1944, NARA, RG 226, 215, Box 1.

25. 253 to 951, 24 July 1944, NARA, RG 226, 215, Box 1.

26. Ibid.

27. Africa Division SI, Monthly Intelligence and Operational Summary, February 1945, NARA, RG 226, A1–210, Box 519.

28. Ibid.

29. Ibid.

30. Ibid.
31. Adolph Schmidt to Richard Dunlop, 6 September 1981, AHEC, Richard Dunlop Papers, Box 6.
32. 253 to 951, 24 July 1944, NARA, RG 226, 215, Box 1.
33. Laxalt, A Private War, p. 82.
34. See the discussion of Laxalt's memoir near the beginning of Chapter 13 of this book for an account of Laxalt's reliability as an authoritative source.
35. 253 to 951, 17 July 1944, NARA, RG 226, 215, Box 1.
36. Ibid.
37. See for example New York State archives, Albany, New York, State Population Census Schedules, 1915, Election District 08, Assembly District 01, City: Oyster Bay, County: Nassau, p. 15.
38. TETON to OSS, 15 [unclear, possibly 13] July 1944, NARA, RG 226, A1-180G, Box 179.
39. TETON to OSS, 24 July 1944, NARA, RG 226, A1-180G, Box 179.
40. NYANZA to LOCUST, 25 July 1944, NARA, RG 226, A1-180G, Box 179.
41. 253 to 951, 24 July 1944, NARA, RG 226, 215, Box 1.
42. Ibid.
43. Ibid.

14. 'HOTBED OF SPIES'

1. HANLY to OSS, 24 June 1944, NARA, RG 226, A1-180G, Box 179.
2. Thomas, A Patrician of Ideas, p. 44; Adolph Schmidt to Richard Dunlop, 6 September 1981, AHEC, Richard Dunlop Papers, Box 6.
3. Thomas, A Patrician of Ideas, p. 44.
4. David Río, 'A Clean Writer: An Interview with Robert Laxalt', Revista de Estudios Norteamericanos, 5, 1997, 21-7. See 'http://institucional.us.es/revistas/estudios/5/art_2.pdf
5. Jacquelyn K. Sundstrand to Michelle Kratts by email, 6 October 2015.
6. Laxalt, A Private War, p. 33.
7. Ibid., pp. 65-6.
8. Ibid., p. 35.
9. https://paw.princeton.edu/memorials/70/100/index.xml
10. Laxalt, A Private War, p. 88.
11. Newkirk, The Old Man and the Harley, p. 175.
12. Laxalt, A Private War, p. 37.
13. Ibid., p. 41.
14. 253 to 951, 17 July 1944, NARA, RG 226, 215, Box 1.
15. Laxalt, A Private War, p. 42.
16. Ibid.
17. Ibid., p. 53.
18. H. L. A. Hart, 'German Interest in the Belgian Congo', 24 July 1943, TNA, KV 3/421.

19. West (ed.), *The Guy Liddell Diaries, Volume I: 1939–42*, p. 293.
20. TNA, KV 3/421.
21. de Meiss-Teuffen, *Winds of Adventure*, pp. 204–5.
22. [Illegible] for H. P. Milmo, to Mr Gibbs, [28] October 1942, TNA, KV 3/421.
23. Counter Intelligence War Room London, 'Liquidation Report No 206 A, Aussenstelle Bremen', n.d., Declassified CIA documents under Nazi War Crimes Disclosure Act.
24. H. L. A. Hart, B.I.B., 'German Interest in the Belgian Congo', 24 July 1943. TNA, KV 3/421.
25. http://www.stephen-stratford.co.uk/treachery.htm.
26. [Illegible] for H. p. Milmo, to Mr Gibbs, [28] October 1942. TNA, KV 3/421.

15. FRAMED

1. 253 to 951, 24 July 1944, NARA, RG 226, 215, Box 1.
2. Ibid.
3. LOCUST to OSS, 26 July 1944, NARA, RG 226, A1-180G, Box 179.
4. F. M. Shepherd to p. N. Loxley, 30 July 1944, TNA, FO 371/38880.
5. 253 to 951, 24 July 1944, NARA, RG 226, 215, Box 1.
6. 253 to 951, 14 August 1944, NARA, RG 226, 215, Box 1.
7. 253 to 951, 1 August 1944, NARA, RG 226, 215, Box 1.
8. 253 to 951, 8 August 1944, NARA, RG 226, 215, Box 1.
9. NARA, RG 226, 215, Box 1.
10. Benton to Washington, 7 August 1944, copy in NARA, RG 226, Roll 71, File No. 146.
11. 253 to 951, 8 August 1944, NARA, RG 226, 215, Box 1.
12. 253 to 951, 14 August 1944, NARA, RG 226, 215, Box 1.
13. Ibid.
14. Ibid.
15. Ibid.
16. Ibid.
17. 253 to 185, 22 August 1944, NARA, RG 226, 215, Box 1.
18. Ibid.
19. Ibid.
20. 253 to 951, 14 August 1944, NARA, RG 226, 215, Box 1.
21. Ibid.
22. 253 to 923, 23 August 1944, NARA, RG 226, 215, Box 1.
23. Ibid.
24. Ibid.
25. Ibid.

16. COLLABORATING WITH THE NAZIS

1. Laxalt, *A Private War*, p. 56.
2. 253 to 185, 22 August 1944, NARA, RG 226, 215, Box 1.

3. According to American historian J. Gillingham, quoted in Mommen, *The Belgian Economy in the Twentieth Century*, p. 69.
4. Kurgan-van-Hentenrky, 'Bankers and politics in Belgium in the twentieth century', pp. 97–8; see also Mommen, *The Belgian Economy in the Twentieth Century*, pp. 60–74.
5. Ibid., p. 69.
6. 253 to 951, 1 August 1944, NARA, RG 226, 215, Box 1.
7. 253 to 951, 14 August 1944, NARA, RG 226, 215, Box 1.
8. Brion and Moreau, *De La Mine à Mars*, pp. 246–9. This frank and open approach by the company to its history was welcomed by Luc Barbé, a Belgian expert on nuclear issues, in an interview in 2013. http://www.vrede.be/english/69-news/1347-belgium-and-the-bomb
9. Helmreich, *United States Relations with Belgium and the Congo, 1940–1960*, p. 255, note 4
10. Brion and Moreau, *De La Mine à Mars*, p. 247.
11. Yeadon, *The Nazi Hydra in America*, p. 460.
12. Brion and Moreau, *De La Mine à Mars*, p. 247.
13. Kaufman et al., *Moe Berg*, pp. 169–70.
14. Ibid.
15. C. F. Davidson to Mr Sayers, 22 May 1945, TNA, AB 16/1360.
16. Witte et al., *Political History of Belgium from 1830 Onwards*, pp. 235–6.
17. Ibid., p. 236.
18. See Georg Nolte (ed.), *European Military Law Systems*, p. 223. 'The judgement of collaborators was left to military courts after bad experiences in the wake of the First World War.' Witte et al., *Political History of Belgium from 1830 Onwards*, p. 235.
19. Brion and Moreau, *De La Mine à Mars*, p. 250.
20. Ibid., p. 249. This quotation and all others from *De La Mine à Mars* were translated by Dr Albertine Fox. Her contribution to this chapter has been valuable and important.
21. Ibid., pp. 246–52.
22. Ibid., p. 246.
23. Ibid., p. 252.
24. Groves, *Now It Can Be Told*, p. 178.
25. Gunther, *Inside Africa*, p. 665.
26. Makelele, *This is a Good Country*, pp. 157–62.

17. A DEAD SHOT

1. Laxalt, *A Private War*, p. 34.
2. Kneen and Sutton (comp.), *Craftsmen of the Army*, Vol. II, p. 163.
3. 'New York, New York Passenger and Crew Lists, 1909, 1925–1957', database with images, *FamilySearch* (https://familysearch.org/ark:61903/1:1:2HSV-LRN: accessed 5 November 2015), Wilbur Owings Hogue, 1944; citing immigration,

New York City, New York, United States, NARA microfilm publication T715 (Washington, DC: National Archives and Records Administration, n.d.). The voyage records of the *SS Tarn* are available here: www.warsailors.com/single-ships/tarn.html

4. John Lansdale to General Groves, 21 May 1943, NARA, RG 77, 5, Box 68.
5. Africa Division SI, Monthly Intelligence and Operational Summary, October 1944, NARA, RG 226, A1-210, Box 519.
6. Norris, *Racing for the Bomb*, p. 327.
7. Helmreich, *United States Relations with Belgium and the Congo*, p. 45.
8. Danchev, 'In the back room: Anglo-American defence co-operation', in Aldrich, *British Intelligence, Strategy and the Cold War, 1945–51*, p. 229.
9. P. Dean to Mr Cox, 29 August 1944, TNA, FO 371/38880.
10. CDT to African Metals Corporation, [no day given] August 1944, TNA, AB 1/592.
11. McGrath, *Charles Kenneth Leith*, p. 215.
12. Borstelmann, *Apartheid's Reluctant Uncle*, p. 45.
13. An excellent analysis of this complicated situation can be found in: Justin Tepper, 'The Congo as a Case Study: The Making of Unipolarity', pp. 15–19; see also Jones, *United States Army in World War II*, pp. 300–301.
14. Herken, *The Winning Weapon*, p. 104.
15. West (ed.), *The Guy Liddell Diaries Vol. II: 1942–1945*, pp. 223–4.
16. Cave Brown, *"C" The Secret Life of Sir Stewart Graham Menzies*, p. 626.

18. STEHLI THE DETECTIVE

1. 923 to 253 and 951, 25 September 1944, NARA, RG 226, A1-215, Box 1.
2. *Le Courrier d'Afrique*, 17–18 September 1944.
3. See report for Belgian Congo 30 September 1944, attached to Williams to Eden, 16 October 1944, TNA, FO 371/38880.
4. 923 to 253 and 951, 25 September 1944, NARA, RG 226, A1-215, Box 1.
5. Ibid.
6. Manderstam, with Heron, *From the Red Army to SOE*, p. 78.
7. Quoted in Roberts, *Glitter & Greed*, p. 143.
8. Cf. 700 tons of uranium ore at Duisburg.
9. 923 to 253 and 951, 25 September 1944, NARA, RG 226, A1-215, Box 1.
10. 923 to 253 and 951, 26 September 1944, NARA, RG 226, A1-215, Box 1.
11. Ibid.
12. Ibid.
13. 923 to 253 and 951, 27 September 1944, NARA, RG 226, A1-215, Box 1.
14. 923 to 253 or 951, 17 October 1944, NARA, RG 226, A1-215, Box 1.
15. Howard Dean's role is mentioned in chapter 1, drawing on Lodeesen, *Captain Lodi Speaking*, p. 158.
16. E. Balluder to Vice President Morrison, 4 May 1944, Pan Am-World Airways Inc Records, Accession 2, Box 41, Folder 8.

17. 923 to 253 or 951, 19 October 1944, NARA, RG 226, A1–215, Box 1.
18. Africa Division SI, Monthly Intelligence and Operational Summary, November 1944, NARA, RG 226, A1–210, Box 519.
19. 923 to 253 or 951, 25 January 1945, NARA, RG 226, 215, Box 1.
20. Ibid.
21. Ibid.
22. Africa Division SI, Monthly Intelligence and Operational Summary, November 1944, NARA, RG 226, A1–210, Box 519.
23. Bonner to Boulton, 9 October 1943, NARA, RG 226, A1–210, Box 417.
24. 923 to 253 or 951, 19 October 1944, NARA, RG 226, A1–215, Box 1.

19. 'ONE MINUTE TO MIDNIGHT'

1. Schmidt to Chief SI, 6 October 1944, NARA, RG 226, A1–180G, Box 71.
2. Africa Division SI, Monthly Intelligence and Operational Summary, October 1944, NARA, RG 226, A1–210, Box 519.
3. Africa Division SI, Monthly Intelligence and Operational Summary, December 1944, NARA, RG 226, A1–210, Box 519.
4. Jean-Pierre Sonck, 'Le Congo Belge entre 1940–1945', available online at http://congo-1960.be/Congo_Belge_1940–1945.htm
5. David Cassidy, 'Introduction' in Goudsmit, Alsos, pp. xviii–xix.
6. Goudsmit, Alsos, p. 26.
7. Ibid., p. 56. See Chapter 15 of this book for the connection between Union Minière and German industry.
8. Goudsmit, Alsos, pp. 70–71.
9. Ibid., p. 51.
10. Baggott, Atomic, p. 261.
11. Quotations and discussion in Richelson, Spying on the Bomb, p. 56.
12. Quoted in ibid., p. 39.
13. Norris, Racing For the Bomb, pp. 289–95.
14. Baggott, Atomic, pp. 276–8.
15. Richelson, Spying on the Bomb, p. 58.
16. Quotes and commentary in Richelson, Spying on the Bomb, pp. 58–9.
17. Ibid., p. 62.
18. Ziegler and Jacobson, Spying Without Spies, p. 23.
19. Malloy, Atomic Tragedy, p. 93.
20. Fox, Why We Need Nuclear Power, p. 42.
21. Scalia, Germany's Last Mission to Japan, p. 195.
22. Los Angeles Times, 1 June 1997: http://articles.latimes.com/1997-06-01/news/mn-64618_1_atomic-bomb.
23. For excellent discussion of this see Gimbel, Einstein.
24. 'President Truman Did Not Understand', US News & World Report, 15 August 1960, pp. 68–71.
25. Plutonium is made from U-238. This was easier for the Manhattan Project to

achieve than isolating or concentrating the rare U-235. For a discussion of this, see note 8 of chapter 1.

26. Brooks, *Hitler's Nuclear Weapons*, p. 54.

27. Nichols, *The Road to Trinity*, p. 194.

28. Thos. T. Handy to General Carl Spaatz, 25 July 1945, reproduced in Hiroshima Peace Memorial Museum, *The Outline of Atomic Bomb Damage in Hiroshima*, March 2006.

29. *Los Angeles Times*, 1 June 1997: http://articles.latimes.com/1997-06-01/news/mn-64618_1_atomic-bomb

30. Quoted in Herken, *The Winning Weapon, 1945–1950*, p. 106.

31. Africa Division, SI, 'Intelligence Objectives and Requisitions, Section A, Long Range Intelligence Objectives in Africa', 21 April 1945, NARA, RG 226, A1-210, Box 367.

32. Ibid.

33. Africa Division SI, Monthly Intelligence and Operational Summary, May 1945, NARA, RG 226, A1-210, Box 519.

34. Africa Division SI, 'Resume of Field Stations and Personnel', n.d. [mid-1945], NARA, RG 226, A1-210, Box 183.

35. Africa Division SI, Monthly Intelligence and Operational Summary, April 1945, NARA, RG 226, A1-210, Box 519; Africa Division SI, Monthly Intelligence and Operational Summary, May 1945, NARA, RG 226, A1-210, Box 519.

36. Ibid.

37. ANGELLA to 951, 16 April 1945, NARA, RG 226, 215, Box 1.

38. *Railroad Magazine*, April 1945, 37 (5).

39. Luther to Boulton, 1 February 1944, NARA, RG 226, 215, Box 1.

40. *Harvard Alumni Bulletin*, 49 (6), 276.

41. 1060 to 178, Pouch Letter 1, 5 July 1945, RG 226, A1-215, Box 1.

42. Africa Division SI, Monthly Intelligence and Operational Summary, June 1945, NARA, RG 226, A1-210, Box 519.

43. Ibid.

44. Ibid.

45. Africa Division SI, Monthly Intelligence and Operational Summary, May 1945, NARA, RG 226, A1-210, Box 519.

46. Ibid.

47. Africa Division SI, Monthly Intelligence and Operational Summary, June 1945, NARA, RG 226, A1-210, Box 519.

48. Africa Division SI, Monthly Intelligence and Operational Summary, July 1945, NARA, RG 226, A1-210, Box 519.

49. Renton et al., *The Congo*, p. 70.

50. I have adopted the term 'moral authority', in terms of the war against fascism, as used by Renton et al., *The Congo*, p. 66, which offers a thoughtful discussion of this matter.

51. Van Reybrouck, *Congo*, p. 194.

20. HIROSHIMA

1. For a brief explanation of plutonium, see note 25 of chapter 19; for a discussion of the process of building an atomic bomb with uranium U-235, see note 8 of chapter 1.
2. Hiroshima Peace Memorial Museum, *The Outline of Atomic Bomb Damage in Hiroshima*, p. 23.
3. Van Reybrouck, *Congo*, p. 190.
4. Akiko Mikamo to the author by email, 1 October 2015.
5. Quoted in Jones, *Reflections on Intelligence*, p. 208.
6. Herkel, *The Winning Weapon*, pp. 3–4.
7. *The Times*, 7 August 1945, p. 4.
8. Goldberg, 'The Secret about Secrets', in Garber and Walkowitz (eds), *Secret Agents*, p. 49.
9. Announcement by President Truman, 6 August 1945, in the Harry S. Truman Library—Public Papers of the Presidents. See http://www.pbs.org/wgbh/americanexperience/features/primary-resources/truman-hiroshima/
10. Arnold, *My Short Century*, p. 94.
11. *Osservatore Romano*, 7 August 1945.
12. Quoted in Marnham, *Snake Dance*, p. 253.
13. Quoted in David Irving, *The Virus House*, p. 13.
14. 'First Atomic Bomb Hits Japan', *The Times*, 7 August 1945.
15. 'Damage by New Bomb', *The Times*, 8 August 1945.
16. Marnham, *Snake Dance*, p. 191. This highly intelligent travelogue, which crosses continents in search of the nuclear story, also took the form of a film, written and directed with Manu Riche, 2012.
17. *New York Times*, 6 August 1945.
18. Quoted in 'Nagasaki Like a "Volcano"', *The Times* 13 August 1945.
19. Transcription, Farm Hall Report 1, *Operation Epsilon*, p. 33.
20. Major T. H. Rittner to Mr M. Perrin and Lt.-Cdr Welsh, Farm Hall Report 4, *Operation Epsilon*, p. 70.
21. Transcription, Farm Hall Report 4, *Operation Epsilon*, p. 78.
22. Announcement by President Truman, 6 August 1945. See http://www.pbs.org/wgbh/americanexperience/features/primary-resources/truman-hiroshima/
23. Goldberg, 'The Secret about Secrets', pp. 51–2.
24. Mahoney, 'A History of the War Department Scientific Intelligence Mission (ALSOS), 1943–1945', p. 383.
25. NARA, RG 226, A1–180G, Box 35.
26. As published in book form in Hersey, *Hiroshima*, p. 68.
27. JIC (48) 9 (0) (Final), 'Russian Interests, Intentions and Capabilities', Top Secret, 23 July 1948 in Richard Aldrich (ed.), *Espionage, Security and Intelligence in Britain 1945–1970*, p. 76.
28. Ibid.
29. Dalton, *The Political Diary of Hugh Dalton, 1918–40, 1945–60*, p. 363.

30. Hastings, *The Secret War*, p. 524.
31. *The Times*, 1 March 2014.
32. Quoted in *The Times*, 1 March 2014. In 1999, Boris Yeltsin awarded him the posthumous honour of Hero of Russia.
33. Viktor [iii] in Moscow to Apraksin [i] in Stockholm, 16 November 1945; National Security Administration's Venona Project Top Secret decryption. TNA, HW 15/14. According to notes made on 'Grisha', the agent was probably Jules Nils Marío GUESDE, French Press Attaché in Stockholm: Comments made on decryption of message from Stockholm to Moscow, 25 January 1945; National Security Administration's Venona Project, 'Bride' Top Secret decryption. TNA, HW 15/14.
34. Barbé has said he would like to see this matter investigated in the Russian archives. See http://www.vrede.be/english/69-news/1347-belgium-and-the-bomb
35. Oral History Interview with Edwin W. Martin by Richard D. McKinzie, Washington, DC, 3 June 1975, Harry S. Truman Library, Independence, Missouri. http://www.trumanlibrary.org/oralhist/martinew.htm
36. Thomas, *A Patrician of Ideas*, p. 1; Adolph Schmidt to Richard Dunlop, 6 September 1981, AHEC, Richard Dunlop Papers, Box 6.
37. *Atlantic Monthly*, May 1945.
38. Dock to Dad, 25 June 1945; Dock to Dad, 12 July 1945; Hogue Family Papers.
39. Dock to Ruth, Dad, and family, 4 September 1945, Hogue Family Papers.
40. Dock to Ruth, Dad, family, from Munich, 4 September 1945, Hogue Family Papers.
41. Dock to Dad, 22 August 1945, Hogue Family Papers.
42. For response to war, see Hogue, typescript of 'Liberian Honeymoon', n.d., Hogue Family Papers, p. 72.
43. Dock to Ruth, Dad, family, from Munich, 4 September 1945, Hogue Family Papers.
44. 'Shirley' to Boulton, n.d.[late 1945], NARA, RG 226, 224, Box 121.
45. Kamp, *We Must Abolish the United States*, p. 28.
46. Lodeesen, *Captain Lodi Speaking*, p. 158.

21. ATOMIC SPIES

1. 946 to 953, NARA, RG 226, A1-215, Box 1.
2. Africa Division SI, Monthly Intelligence and Operational Summary, August–September 1945, NARA, RG 226, A1-210, Box 519.
3. Copy of letter in NARA, RG 226, 215, Box 1.
4. Helms, *A Look Over My Shoulder*, p. 65.
5. Liptak, *Office of Strategic Services 1942–45*, p. 5.
6. http://www.foia.cia.gov/sites/default/files/document_conversions/1820853/1953-08-10a.pdf
7. http://www.birdlifezimbabwe.org/Babblers/Babbler%20103.pdf

8. *Washington Post*, 26 August 1959.
9. Ancestry.com, *New York, New York, Death Index, 1862–1948*. Provo, UT, Ancestry.com Operations, Inc., 2014.
10. 'Carl Shannon' was the combination of Hogue's two brothers' first names: Carl (the youngest) and Shannon (the eldest).
11. *The Salt Lake Tribune*, 9 October 1949.
12. http://www.cancerresearchuk.org/about-cancer/type/stomach-cancer/about/stomach-cancer-risks-and-causes
13. http://www.cancerresearchuk.org/about-cancer/type/brain-tumour/about/brain-tumour-risks-and-causes
14. Grace Stehli to family, 13 January 1947, Stehli Family Papers.
15. Interview report on Douglas Griswold Bonner, signed H. A. Murray, Major, 28 December 1944, NARA, RG 226, 224, Box 67.
16. The writing on his death certificate is almost illegible, but may refer to an acute coronary attack as the cause.
17. http://www.infoplease.com/ipa/A0005148.html
18. Statement by President Truman, 6 August 1945, available at http://www.pbs.org/wgbh/americanexperience/features/primary-resources/truman-hiroshima/
19. http://www.dr1.com/forums/dr-debates/19253-us-marines-occupy-haina-embajador-hotel-82nd-airborne-lands-san-isidro-7-print.html
20. Pilisuk, *International Conflict and Social Policy*, pp. 148–9.
21. http://www.mayoclinic.org/diseases-conditions/brain-tumor/symptoms-causes/dxc-20117134
22. Recommendation for the Award of the Medal of Freedom', 29 April 1947, NARA, RG 226, 224, Box 315.
23. *Public Relations Quarterly*, Vols 1–3, 1955.
24. Herring, *LBJ and Vietnam*, pp. 144–5.
25. Bob [?] in Léopoldville to Rud, 15 April 1946, NARA, RG 226, 224, Box 121.
26. See documents in NARA, RG 226, 224, Box 121.
27. ANGELLA to Boulton, April 8 [1945], NARA, RG 226, 224, Box 121.
28. Charles Elliott to the author, 12 February 2016; http://www.utsystem.edu/sites/utsfiles/offices/board-of-regents/board-meetings/dockets/12-78-1967.pdf
29. Casey, *The Secret War against Hitler*, p. 218.
30. Thomas, *A Patrician of Ideas*, p. 45.
31. Discussion and quotation in Salter, *Nazi War Crimes, US Intelligence and Selective Prosecution at Nuremburg*, pp. 376–81.
32. Recommendation for the award of Legion of Merit to A. W. Schmidt, 29 April 1947, NARA, RG 226, 224, Box 684,
33. Boulton to E. K. Merrill, 14 July 1945, NARA, RG 226, A1–216, Box 10.
34. E. K. Merrill to Boulton, 25 April 1944, NARA, RG 226, A1–216, Box 10.
35. Boulton to Chapin, 26 December 1945, NARA, RG 226 210, Box 382.
36. https://opengeography.wordpress.com/2011/09/20/complete-list-of-oss-personnel/

37. https://www.cia.gov/news-information/featured-story-archive/2008-featured-story-archive/office-of-strategic-services.html

38. 'Recommendation for the Award of the Medal of Freedom', 29 April 1947, NARA, RG 226, 224, Box 315. Note: the recommendation lists the period of service as ending on 12 July 1944, when Harris went on to Accra; in fact Harris arrived in Accra on 23 June 1944. Such minor inaccuracies relating to dates are not uncommon in OSS records.

39. 'Recommendation for the Award of the Legion of Merit', 29 April 1947, NARA, RG 226, 224, Box 684.

40. Kaufman et al., *Moe Berg*, p. 163.

41. 'Recommendation for the Award of the Legion of Merit', 29 April 1947, NARA, RG 226, 224, Box 684.

42. Kathryn Hogue to the author, 4 January 2015, by email.

43. Rudyerd Boulton, Africa Section, to G. W. Cottrell, 'Information from the Belgian Congo', 28 June 1943, NARA RG 226, E10, Box 81.

44. Cockerill, *Sir Percy Sillitoe*, p. 200. Cockerill was a consultant to the Canadian nuclear industry and for ten years was a member of the National Technical Committee on Nuclear Quality Assurance.

45. Dock Hogue, 'Congo Contraband', *Adventure*, June 1947.

22. CONCLUSION: THE MISSING LINK

1. Aldrich (ed.), *Espionage, Security and Intelligence in Britain 1945–1970*, p. 76.

2. Report on visit to Shinkolobwe mine by Arthur D. Storke, 8 March 1945, TNA, AB 592.

3. Nzongola-Ntalaja, *The Congo*, p. 259.

4. From Borstelmann, *Apartheid's Reluctant Uncle*, p. 205.

5. Minutes taken by Donald Maclean, 3 December 1947, TNA, FO 1093/514.

6. From Borstelmann, *Apartheid's Reluctant Uncle*, p. 205.

7. Ibid., p. 182.

8. Ibid., p. 4.

9. Entry for Friday 22 March 1946, in Dalton, *The Political Diary of Hugh Dalton, 1918–40, 1945–60*, p. 369.

10. Borstelmann, *Apartheid's Reluctant Uncle*, p. 182.

11. Ibid.

12. Hewlett and Holl, *Atoms for Peace and War: 1953–1961*, p. 159.

13. Gunther, *Inside Africa*, p. 662.

14. Hewlett and Holl, *Atoms for Peace and War: 1953–1961*, p. 159.

15. Bellotti, *Fabulous Congo*, p. 155.

16. Campbell, *The Heart of Africa*, p. 336.

17. See TNA, FO 371/80296, FO 371 90103, FO 371/80298, and FO 371/80337.

18. See brief biography of Sir Percy Sillitoe on the MI5 website: https://www.mi5.gov.uk/home/about-us/who-we-are/staff-and-management/sir-percy-sillitoe.html

19. Cockerill, *Sir Percy Sillitoe*, pp. 199 and 203.

20. Ibid.

21. Cockerill, *Sir Percy Sillitoe*, p. 201.

22. This acronym reflects the fact that it was for Training, Research and Isotope production and was built by General Atomic.

23. See Gillon, *Servir: En actes et en vérité.*

24. Colby and Dennett, *Thy will be done*, pp. 325–6.

25. Press Conference by Dr Ralph J. Bunche at UN HQ, 1 September 1960, quoted in Williams, *Who Killed Hammarskjöld?*, p. 37.

26. Devlin, *Chief of Station, Congo*, p. 271.

27. In reports addressed to Alfred Moeller de Laddersous, drawn up by George Wittman, 1960–61, File 536, Sibéka Papers.

28. Devlin, *Chief of Station, Congo*, pp. 27–8.

29. James [surname illegible], British Embassy, Bogota, to E. B. Boothby, 2 February 1960, TNA, FO 371/146630.

30. Devlin, *Chief of Station, Congo*, p. 63.

31. The Interim Report of the US Senate Select Committee to Study Government Operations with Respect to Intelligence Activities, chaired by Frank Church, 1975.

32. Devlin, *Chief of Station, Congo*, p. 95.

33. 'Report Reproves Belgium in Lumumba's Death', *International New York Times*, 17 November 2001.

34. This agency was the Service de Documentation Extérieure et de Contre-Espionnage (SDECE).

35. *Time*, 22 December 1961.

36. See Williams, *Who Killed Hammarskjöld?* In July 2015, a Panel set up by the UN Secretary General Ban Ki-Moon released a report confirming the existence of new evidence which needs to be investigated, suggesting that the plane may have been shot down. Details may be found here: http://humanrights 2008.org.uk/

37. IAEA, Official Record of the 48th Plenary Meeting, 26 September 1961, 11GC(V)/OR.48, 20 November 1961, which is available here: https://www.iaea.org/About/Policy/GC/GC05/GC05Records/English/gc05or-48_en.pdf

38. Gerald Horne, *From the Barrel of a Gun*, pp. 134–5.

39. Maurice Tempelsman to The President, 19 October 1961, on Leon Tempelsman & Son letterhead paper. Papers of John F. Kennedy, President's Office Files. Tempelsman's memorandum is available digitally on the following website: http://www.jfklibrary.org/Asset-Viewer/Archives/JFKPOF.aspx

40. The full name is La Générale des Carrières et des Mines. See http://gecamines.cd/html/nous.html

41. Weiner, *Legacy of Ashes*, pp. 281–2.

42. Wrong, *In the Footsteps of Mr Kurtz*, pp. 141–2.

43. *London Evening Post*, 7 July 2013, available at http://www.thelondonevening-post.com/features/a-look-inside-the-worlds-least-secure-nuclear-reactor-in-drc/4/

44. Marriage, *Formal Peace and Informal War*, p. 155, note 18.

45. 9 August 2004. The cable as released by Wikileaks is available here: https://www.wikileaks.org/plusd/cables/04KINSHASA1492_a.html

46. 11 July 2007. The cable was released by Wikileaks and is available here: https://wikileaks.org/plusd/cables/07KINSHASA797_a.html

47. Zoellner, *Uranium*, p. 12.

48. Trefon, *Congo's Environmental Paradox*, pp. 122–3.

49. Aczel, *Uranium Wars*, p. 223.

50. Sanger, *Blind Faith*, p. vii.

51. Zoellner, *Uranium*, pp. 289–94.

52. Hecht, *Being Nuclear*, p. 184. Note: Union Minière is now known as Umicore.

53. http://onestruggle.net/2014/05/18/congo-they-play-workers-like-football/

54. International Atomic Energy Agency, 'Radiological Report on an Inter-Agency mission to the Shinkolobwe mine site, Democratic Republic of Congo, 24 October to 4 November 2004', prepared by Peter Waggitt, 16 November 2004, Vienna. http://ochanet.unocha.org/p/Documents/Radiological_Final_Report_161204.pdf

55. Farren Collins, 7 August 2015, *Rand Daily Mail*, available at http://www.rdm.co.za/politics/2015/08/07/hiroshima-s-shadow-over-africa

ARCHIVE REPOSITORIES

BELGIUM

Archives Générales du Royaume de Belgique, Brussels
Papers of Société Minière du Bécéca (Sibéka)

UNITED KINGDOM

The National Archives of the UK, Kew (TNA)
Atomic Energy Authority (AB)
Cabinet Office (CAB)
Colonial Office (CO)
Dominions Office (DO)
Foreign Office (FO)
Foreign and Commonwealth Office (FCO)
Government Communications Headquarters (HW)
Prime Minister's office (PREM)
Security Service—MI5 (KV)
Special Operations Executive and MI6 (HS)

USA

National Archives and Records Administration of the US, Washington, Maryland (NARA)
Records of the Office of Strategic Services (OSS)
Records of the Manhattan Engineer District/Manhattan Project
Records of the Central Intelligence Agency

Albert and Shirley Small Special Collections Library, University of Virginia
Jackson Davis collection

ARCHIVE REPOSITORIES

U.S. Department of Energy OpenNet Database <https://www.osti.gov/opennet/index.jsp>

Foreign Relations of the United States (FRUS)-Historical Documents <https://history.state.gov/historicaldocuments>

Foreign Service List of the United States, 1943, 1944

University of Miami Special Collections, Richter Library
Pan American World Airways, Inc. records, 1902–2005
Captain Marius Lodeesen Files

University of Idaho Library, Special Collections and Archives, Moscow, Idaho
Gilbert H. Hogue Papers

Princeton University Library, Rare Books and Special Collections, New Jersey
Moe Berg Papers

Special Collections, University of Oregon Libraries
Robert L. Buell Papers

US Army Heritage and Education Center, Carlisle, Pennsylvania (AHEC)
Richard Dunlop Papers

Special Collections Research Center, Syracuse University Libraries
Robert Hillyer Papers

PRIVATE COLLECTIONS

Hogue Family Papers
Wilbur Owings Hogue Papers

Vilma R. Hunt Papers
'Uranium Merchants' (unfinished manuscript)

Schmidt Family Papers
Adolph W. Schmidt Papers

Shirley Armitage (Chidsey) Bridgwater Papers

Stehli Family Papers
Henry Emil Stehli Papers

BIBLIOGRAPHY

BOOKS

Aczel, Amir D., *Uranium Wars. The Scientific Rivalry That Created the Nuclear Age* (New York: Palgrave Macmillan, 2009).

Aldrich, Richard J., *British Intelligence, Strategy and the Cold War, 1940–51* (London and New York: Routledge, 1992).

—— (ed.), *Espionage, Security and Intelligence in Britain 1945–1970* (Manchester: Manchester University Press, 1998).

Alvarez, David (ed.), *Allied and Axis Signals Intelligence in World War II* (London: Frank Cass, 1999).

Andrew, Christopher, *The Defence of the Realm: The Authorized History of MI5* (London: Allen Lane, 2009).

Arnold, General H. H., *Global Mission* (London: Hutchinson, 1951).

Arnold, Lorna, *My Short Century: Memoirs of an Accidental Nuclear Historian* (Palo Alto, CA: Cumnor Hill Books, 2012).

Atherton, Louise, *Operations in Africa and the Middle East: A Guide to the Newly Released Records in the Public Record Office* (London: Public Record Office Publications, Crown Copyright, 1994).

Atomic Energy: A General Account of the Development of Methods of Using Atomic Energy for Military Purposes under the Auspices of the United States Government, US Government Printing Office (1945; rpt London: HMSO, 1945).

Baggott, Jim, *Atomic: The First War of Physics and the Secret History of the Atom Bomb: 1939–49* (London: Icon Books, 2009).

Belgian Congo At War (New York: The Belgian Information Center [1942]).

Bellotti, Felice, *Fabulous Congo*, trans. from Italian by Mervyn Savill (London: Andrew Dakers Ltd, 1954).

Birmingham, David and Martin, Phyllis M. (eds), *History of Central Africa Volume 2* (London: Longman, 1983).

Bookman, George B., *Headlines, Deadlines, and Lifelines* (New York: iUniverse, Inc., 2009).

313

Borstelmann, Thomas, *Apartheid's Reluctant Uncle: The United States and Southern Africa in the Early Cold War* (Oxford: Oxford University Press, 1993).

Bothwell, Robert, *Eldorado: Canada's National Uranium Company* (Toronto: University of Toronto Press, 1984).

Bourret, F. M., *Ghana: The Road to Independence, 1919–1957* (London: Oxford University Press, 1960).

Boyce, Fredric and Everett, Douglas, *SOE. The Scientific Secrets* (Stroud: Sutton, 2003).

Brion, René and Moreau, Jean-Louis, *Société Générale de Belgique, 1822–1997* (Belgium: Antwerp, 1998).

——, *De La Mine à Mars: La Genèse d'Umicore* (Tielt, Belgium: Umicore et Editions Lannoo, 2006).

Brooks, Geoffrey, *Hitler's Nuclear Weapons. The Development and Attempted Deployment of Radiological Armaments by Nazi Germany* (London: Leo Cooper, 1992).

Brown, Anthony Cave, *The Last Hero: Wild Bill Donovan* (London: Michael Joseph, 1982).

——, *"C" The Secret Life of Sir Stewart Graham Menzies. Spymaster to Winston Churchill* (New York: Macmillan, 1987).

Byfield, Judith A., Brown, Carolyn A., Parsons, Timothy and Sikainga, Ahmad Alawad (eds), *Africa and World War II* (Cambridge University Press, 2015).

Byrnes, James F., *Speaking Frankly* (London: William Heinemann, 1945).

Calaprice, Alice and Lipscombe, Trevor, *Albert Einstein: A Biography* (Westport, CT: Greenwood Press, 2005).

Campbell, Alexander, *The Heart of Africa* (London: Longmans, Green, 1954).

Canale, Jean-Suret, *French Colonialism in Tropical Africa 1900–1945* (New York: Pica Press, 1971).

Casey, William, *The Secret War Against Hitler* (Washington DC: Regnery Gateway, 1988).

Chalou, George C. (ed.), *The Secrets War: The Office of Strategic Services in World War II* (Washington: National Archives and Records Administration, 1992).

Cobain, Ian, *Cruel Britannia: A Secret History of Torture* (London: Portobello Books, 2012).

Cockerill, A. W., *Sir Percy Sillitoe* (London: W. H. Allen, 1975).

Colby, Gerard and Dennett, Charlotte, *Thy Will Be Done: The Conquest of the Amazon: Nelson Rockefeller and Evangelism in the Age of Oil* (New York: HarperCollins, 1995).

Colvin, Ian, *The Rise and Fall of Moise Tshombe* (London: Leslie Frewin, 1968).

Committee on Africa, the War, and Peace Aims, *The Atlantic Charter and Africa from an American Standpoint* (New York City, 1942).

Conant, Jennet, *A Covert Affair: Julia Child and Paul Child in the OSS* (New York: Simon and Schuster Paperbacks, 2011).

Le Congo Belge durant la Seconde Guerre Mondiale. Recueil d'études (Bruxelles: Académie Royale des Sciences d'Outre-Mer, 1983).

Conway, Martin, *Collaboration in Belgium: Léon Degrelle and the Rexist Movement 1940–1944* (New Haven: Yale University Press, 1993).

——, *The Sorrows of Belgium: Liberation and Political Reconstruction, 1944–1947* (Oxford: Oxford University Press, 2012).

Coon, Carleton S., *A North Africa Story. The Anthropologist as OSS Agent 1941–1943* (Ipswich, MA: Gambit, 1980).

——, *Adventures and Discoveries: The Autobiography of Carleton S. Coon* (Englewood Cliffs, NJ: Prentice-Hall, Inc., 1981).

Cordell, Linda S. and Beckerman, Stephen (eds), *The Versatility of Kinship. Essays Presented to Harry W. Basehart* (New York: Academic Press, 1980).

Craven, Wesley Frank and Cate, James Lea (eds), *Army Air Forces in World War II: Services Around the World* (Office of Air Force History, 1983).

CRISP: Centre de recherche et d'information socio-politiques, *Courrier Hebdomadaire*, Issues 768–785 (Bruxelles: CRISP, 1977).

Dalton, Hugh, *The Political Diary of Hugh Dalton, 1918–40, 1945–60*, ed. Ben Pimlott (London: Jonathan Cape in association with LSE, 1986).

De Coster, Michel, *Séjours insolites au Congo* (Paris: L'Harmattan, 2009).

De Witte, Ludo, trans. Ann Wright and Renée Fenby, *The Assassination of Lumumba* (London: Verso, 2001) [First published as *De Moord op Lumumba*, 1999].

Devlin, Larry, *Chief of Station, Congo: A Memoir of 1960–67* (New York: Public Affairs, 2007).

Dorril, Stephen, *Fifty Years of Special Operations* (London: Fourth Estate, 2000).

Douglas-Home, Charles, *Evelyn Baring: The Last Proconsul* (London: Collins, 1978).

Doyle, David W., *True Men and Traitors: From the OSS to the CIA, My Life in the Shadows* (2000; rpt Chichester: John Wiley & Sons, 2001).

Draitser, Emil, *Stalin's Romeo Spy: The Remarkable Rise and Fall of the KGB's Most Daring Operative: The True Life of Dmitri Bystrolyotov* (Evanston, IL: Northwestern University Press, 2010).

Dulles, Allen, *The Craft of Intelligence* (London: Weidenfeld & Nicolson, 1963).

Dumett, Raymond E., *Mining Tycoons in the Age of Empire, 1870–1945* (Bodmin, Cornwall: Ashgate, 2009).

Dunlop, Richard, *Donovan: America's Master Spy* (1982; rpt New York: Skyhorse Publishing, 2014).

Du Plessis, Captain J.H., *Diamonds are Dangerous: The Adventures of an Agent of the International Diamond Security Organization* (London: Cassell, 1960).

Eckes, Alfred E. Jr., *The United States and the Global Struggle for Minerals* (Austin, TX: University of Texas Press, 1979).

Eichstaedt, Peter, *Consuming the Congo: War and Conflict Minerals in the World's Deadliest Place* (Chicago, IL: Lawrence Hill Books, 2011).

Eisenberg, Dennis, Landau, Eli and Portugali, Menahem, *Operation Uranium Ship* (London: Corgi, 1978).

Epstein, Edward Jay, *The Rise and Fall of Diamonds: The Shattering of a Brilliant Illusion* (New York: Simon and Schuster, 1982).

——, *The Diamond Invention* (London: Hutchinson, 1982).

Fabian, Johannes, *History From Below: The "Vocabulary of Elisabethville"by André Yav. Text, Translations, and Interpretive Essay* (Amsterdam: John Benjamins Publishing Company, 1990).

BIBLIOGRAPHY

Farrell, Joseph P., *Reich of the Black Sun: Nazi Secret Weapons & the Cold War Allied Legend* (Kempton, IL: Adventures Unlimited Press, 2004).

Ferrell, Robert H. and Truman, Harry S., *A Life* (Columbia, MS: University of Missouri Press, 1994).

Fetter, Bruce, *The Creation of Elisabethville, 1910–1940*, Hoover Colonial Studies (Stanford, CA: Hoover Institution Press, 1976).

——, *Colonial Rule and Regional Imbalance in Central Africa* (Boulder, CO: Westview Press, 1983).

Foertsch, Jacqueline, *Reckoning Day: Race, Place, and the Atom Bomb in Postwar America* (Nashville, TN: Vanderbilt University Press, 2013).

Fölsing, Albrecht, *Albert Einstein: A Biography*, trans. from the German by Edwald Osers (London: Viking, 1997).

Foot, M. R. D., *SOE. The Special Operations Executive, 1940–46* (1984; rpt London: Mandarin Paperbacks, 1990).

Ford, Corey, *Donovan of OSS* (London: Robert Hale & Company, 1970).

Fox, Michael H., *Why We Need Nuclear Power. The Environmental Case* (Oxford: Oxford University Press, 2014).

Friedman, Norman, *The Fifty-Year War: Conflict and Strategy in the Cold War* (Annapolis, MD: Naval Institute Press, 2000).

Frimpong-Ansah, Jonathan H., *The Vampire State in Africa: The Political Economy of Decline in Ghana* (Trenton, NJ: Africa World Press Inc., 1992).

Gandt, Robert, *China Clipper: The Age of the Great Flying Boats* (Annapolis, MD: The Naval Institute Press, 1993).

Garber, Marjorie and Walkowitz, Rebecca L. (eds), *Secret Agents: The Rosenberg Case, McCarthyism, and Fifties America* (London: Routledge, 1995).

Gheerbrant, Alain, *Congo noir et blanc* (Paris: Gallimard, 1955).

Gibbs, David N., *The Political Economy of Third World Intervention: Mines, Money, and US Policy in the Congo Crisis* (Chicago: University of Chicago Press, 1991).

Gifford, Prosser and Louis, Wm. Roger (eds), *The Transfer of Power in Africa: Decolonization, 1940–1960* (New Haven, CT: Yale University Press, 1982).

Gillon, Luc, *Servir: En actes et en vérité* (Paris-Gembloux: Editions Duculot, 1988).

Gimbel, Steven, *Einstein. His Space and Times* (New Haven, CT: Yale University Press, 2015).

Gleijeses, Piero, *Conflicting Missions: Havana, Washington, and Africa, 1959–1976* (Chapel Hill, NC and London: The University of North Carolina Press, 2002).

Goldschmidt, Bertrand, *Atomic Rivals*, trans. Georges M. Temmer (New Brunswick, NJ: Rutgers University Press, 1990).

Goldstein, Joshua S., *Winning the War on War: The Decline of Armed Conflict Worldwide* (New York: Dutton Books, 2011).

Goodman, Michael S., *Spying on the Nuclear Bear: Anglo-American Intelligence and the Soviet Bomb* (Stanford, CA: Stanford University Press, 2007).

Gordin, Michael D., *Red Cloud at Dawn: Truman, Stalin, and the End of the Atomic Monopoly* (New York: Farrar, Straus & Giroux, 2009).

Gordon, David L. and Dangerfield, Royden, *The Hidden Weapon: The Story of Economic Warfare* (New York: Harper & Brothers Publishers, 1947).

BIBLIOGRAPHY

Goudsmit, Samuel A., *Alsos, Vol. 1, History of Modern Physics and Astronomy* (1947; rpt Woodbury, New York: American Institute of Physics, 1996).

Gourvish, Terry (ed.), *Business and Politics in Europe, 1900–1970: Essays in Honour of Alice Teichova* (Cambridge: Cambridge University Press, 2003).

Gowing, Margaret, *Britain and Atomic Energy, 1939–1945* (London: Macmillan, 1964).

—— and Slater, A. H. K., *Britain in the Second World War* (Berkeley: University of California Press, 1971).

——, assisted by Arnold, Lorna, *Independence and Deterrence: Britain and Atomic Energy, 1945–1952, Vol. 1, Policy Making* (London: Macmillan, 1974).

——, assisted by Arnold, Lorna, *Independence and Deterrence: Britain and Atomic Energy, 1945–1952, Vol 2, Policy Execution* (London: Macmillan, 1974).

——, 'Reflections on atomic energy history', The Rede Lecture (Cambridge University Press, 1978).

—— and Arnold, Lorna, *The Atomic Bomb* (London: Butterworths, 1979).

Greene, Graham, *The Heart of the Matter* (1948; rpt London: Heinemann 1969).

Greenough, Malcolm W., *Dear Lily: A Love Story* (Dublin, NH: Yankee Publishing, 1987).

Gross, Gerald, *Editors on Editing* (New York: The Universal Library, 1962).

Groves, Leslie R., *Now It Can Be Told: The Story of the Manhattan Project* (London: Andre Deutsch, 1963 [1962]).

Gunther, John, *Inside Africa* (London: Hamish Hamilton, 1955).

——, *Meet the Congo and its Neighbors* (New York: Harper & Brothers, 1959).

Hadden, Gavin (ed.), *Manhattan District History*, commissioned by General Leslie Groves, *Book VII, Feed Materials, Special Procurement, and Geographical Exploration, Volume I–Feed Materials and Special Procurement*, 12 June 1947, declassified with deletions by Richard G. Hewlett for the US Atomic Energy Commission, 3 June 1970, available online at http://www.osti.gov/includes/opennet/includes/MED_scans/Book%20VII%20-%20%20Volume%201%20-%20Feed%20Materials%20and%20Special%20Procuremen.pdf.

Hargreaves, John D., *Decolonization in Africa*. Second Edition (London and New York: Routledge, 2014).

Hastings, Max, *The Secret War: Spies, Codes and Guerrillas, 1939–1945* (London: William Collins, 2015).

Hayes, Paddy, *Queen of Spies: Daphne Park, Britain's Cold War Spy Master* (London: Duckworth Overlook, 2015).

Haynes, John Earl, Klehr, Harvey and Vassiliev, Alexander, *Spies. The Rise and Fall of the KGB in America* (New Haven: Yale UP, 2009).

Hecht, Gabrielle, *The Radiance of France: Nuclear Power and National Identity after World War II* (Cambridge, MA: The MIT Press, 1998).

—— (ed.), *Entangled Geographies: Empire and Technopolitics in the Global Cold War* (Cambridge, MA: The MIT Press, 2011).

——, *Being Nuclear: Africans and the Global Uranium Trade* (Cambridge, MA: The MIT Press, 2012).

BIBLIOGRAPHY

Helmreich, Jonathan E., *Gathering Rare Ores: The Diplomacy of Uranium Acquisition, 1943–1954* (Princeton: Princeton University Press, 1986).

——, *United States Relations With Belgium and the Congo, 1940–1960* (Newark: University of Delaware Press, 1998).

Helms, Richard, with Hood, William, *A Look over My Shoulder: A Life in the Central Intelligence Agency* (2003; rpt New York: Ballantine Books, 2004).

Hempstone, Smith, *The New Africa* (London: Faber & Faber, 1961).

——, *Katanga Report* (London: Faber & Faber, 1962).

——, *Rebels, Mercenaries, and Dividends: The Katanga Story* (New York: Frederick A. Praeger, 1962).

——, *Rogue Ambassador: An African Memoir* (Sewanee, TN: University of the South Press, 1997).

Henry, Charles P., *Ralph Bunche: Model Negro or American Other?* (New York: New York University Press, 1999).

Herken, Gregg, *The Winning Weapon: The Atomic Bomb in the Cold War, 1945–1950* (New York: Alfred A. Knopf, 1980).

Hersey, John, *Hiroshima* (1946; London: Penguin Books, 1985).

Herring, George C., *LBJ and Vietnam: A Different Kind of War* (Austin: University of Texas, 1994).

Herzog, Rudolph, *A Short History of Nuclear Folly: Mad Scientists, Dithering Nazis, Lost Nukes, and Catastrophic Cover-ups* (New York: Melville House, 2013).

Hewlett, Richard G. and Anderson, Oscar E., *A History of the United States Atomic Energy Commission. Volume I: The New World, 1939–1946* (Pennslyvania: The Pennsylvania State University Press, 1962).

Hewlett, Richard G. and Duncan, Francis, *A History of the United States Atomic Energy Commission. Volume II: Atomic Shield, 1947–1952* (Washington, DC: US Atomic Energy Commission, 1972).

Hewlett, Richard G. and Holl, Jack M., *Atoms for Peace and War, 1953–1961. Eisenhower and the Atomic Energy Commission* (Berkeley: University of California Press, 1989).

Heymann, C. David, *American Legacy: The Story of John and Caroline Kennedy* (New York: Atria Books, 2007).

Higginson, John, *A Working Class in the Making: Belgian Colonial Labor Policy, Private Enterprise, and the African Mineworker, 1907–1951* (Madison, WI: University of Wisconsin Press, 1989).

Hight, Eleanor M. and Sampson, Gary D. (eds), *Colonialist Photography: Imag(in)ing Race and Place* (London: Routledge, 2002).

Hillenbrand, Martin J., *Fragments of Our Time: Memoirs of a Diplomat* (Athens and London: The University of Georgia Press, 1998).

Hinsley, F. H. and Simkins, C. A. G., *British Intelligence in the Second World War, Vol. 4, Security and Counter-Intelligence* (London: HMSO, 1990).

Hiroshima Peace Memorial Museum, *The Outline of Atomic Bomb Damage in Hiroshima* (Hiroshima: Hiroshima Peace Memorial Museum, March 2006).

History Project, Strategic Services Unit, War Department, Washington DC, *War*

BIBLIOGRAPHY

Report of the OSS. US War Department Strategic Services Unit History Project (New York: Walker, published with limited redactions, 1976 [completed 1947]) <http://www.ossreborn.com/files/War%20Report%20of%20the%20OSS%20Volume%201.pdf>.

——, *The Overseas Targets. Vol II of War Report of the OSS. US War Department Strategic Services Unit History Project*, with a new introduction by Kermit Roosevelt (New York: Walker, 1976).

Hitler's Uranium Club: The Secret Recordings at Farm Hall, annotated by Jeremy Bernstein, introduced by David Cassidy, 2nd edn (1996; New York: Copernicus Books, imprint of Springer-Verlag, 2001).

Hoare, Oliver (ed.), *Camp 020. MI5 and the Nazi Spies: The Official History of MI5's Wartime Interrogation Centre* (London: Public Record Office, 2000).

Hochschild, Adam, *King Leopold's Ghost: A Story of Greed, Terror and Heroism in Colonial Africa* (1998; rpt London: Pan Macmillan, 1999).

Hodgson, Lynn-Philip, *Inside-Camp X* (Port Perry, Ontario: Blake Book Distribution, 1999).

Hogue, Dock, *Bob Clifton, Elephant Hunter* (New York: Henry Holt and Company, 1949).

——, *Bob Clifton, Jungle Traveler* (New York: Henry Holt and Company, 1950).

——, *Bob Clifton, Congo Crusader* (New York: Henry Holt and Company, 1951).

——, *Bob Clifton, African Planter* (New York: Henry Holt and Company, 1953).

Holloway, David, *Stalin and the Bomb: The Soviet Union and Atomic Energy, 1939–56* (New Haven, CT and London: Yale University Press, 1994).

Horne, Gerald, *From the Barrel of a Gun: The United States and the War Against Zimbabwe, 1965–1980* (Chapel Hill, The University of North Carolina, 2001).

Hyde, H. Montgomery, *The Quiet Canadian: The Secret Service Story of Sir William Stephenson* (London: Constable, 1962).

Hydrick, Carter <http://www.bibliotecapleyades.net/ciencia/atomicbomb/contents.htm.>.

Ingrams, Richard, *Muggeridge: The Biography* (London: HarperCollins, 1995).

International Atomic Energy Agency, *Radiological Report on an Inter-Agency Mission to the Shinkolobwe Mine Site, Democratic Republic of Congo, 24 October to 4 November 2004*, prepared by Peter Waggitt (16 November 2004, Vienna).

Irving, David, *The Virus House* (London: William Kimber, 1967).

Jakub, Jay, *Spies and Saboteurs. Anglo-American Collaboration and Rivalry in Human Intelligence Collection and Special Operations, 1940–45* (Basingstoke: Macmillan, 1999).

Johns, Philip, *Within Two Cloaks: Missions with SIS and SOE* (London: William Kimber, 1979).

Jones, R.V., *Most Secret War* (London: Hamish Hamilton, 1978).

——, *Reflections on Intelligence* (London: Mandarin, 1989).

Jones, Vincent C., *United States Army in World War II: Special Studies. Manhattan: The Army and the Atomic Bomb* (Washington, DC: Center of Military History, United States Army, 1985).

BIBLIOGRAPHY

Kamp, Joseph P., *We Must Abolish the United States: The Hidden Facts Behind the Crusade for World Government* (New York: Hallmark Publishers, 1950).

Kanfer, Stefan, *The Last Empire: De Beers, Diamonds and the World* (1993; rpt London: Hodder & Stoughton, 1994).

Katz, Barry M., *Foreign Intelligence: Research and Analysis in the Office of Strategic Services 1942–1945* (London: Harvard University Press, 1989).

Kaufman, Louis, Fitzgerald, Barbara and Sewell, Tom, *Moe Berg: Athlete, Scholar, Spy* (Boston: Little, Brown and Company, 1974).

Kelly, Cynthia C. (ed.), *Oppenheimer and the Manhattan Project: Insights into J Robert Oppenheimer, "Father of the Atomic Bomb"* (Hackensack, NJ: World Scientific Publishing, 2006).

Kelly, Charles J., *The Sky's the Limit: The History of the Airlines* (1963; rpt New York: Arno Press, 1972).

Kippax, Steven, *The Special Operations Executive and The Office of Strategic Services. A Bibliography* (London, 2004).

Kneen, Brigadier J. M. and Sutton, D. J., compiled by, *Craftsmen of the Army, Vol II: The Story of The Royal Electrical and Mechanical Engineers, 1969–1992* (London: Leo Cooper, 1996).

Kwitny, Jonathon, *Endless Enemies. The Making of an Unfriendly World* (New York: Congdon & Weed, 1984).

La Farge, Oliver, *The Eagle in the Egg* (Boston: Houghton Mifflin Company, 1949).

Lambrecht, Frank L., *In the Shade of an Acacia Tree: Memoirs of a Health Officer in Africa, 1945–1959* (Philadelphia: American Philosophical Society, 1991).

Lankford, Nelson Douglas (ed.), *OSS Against the Reich: The World War II Diaries of Colonel David K. E. Bruce* (Kent, OH: The Kent State University Press, 1991).

Lanouette, William, with Silard, Beth, *Genius in the Shadows: A Biography of Leo Szilard, the Man Behind the Bomb* (New York: Charles Scribner's Sons, 1992).

Latouche, John, photographs by André Cauvin, *Congo* (n.p.: Willow, White & Co., 1945).

Lawler, Nancy, *Soldiers, Airmen, Spies, and Whisperers: The Gold Coast in World War II* (Athens, OH: Ohio University Press, 2002).

Laxalt, Robert, *A Private War: An American Code Officer in the Belgian Congo* (Reno, NV: University of Nevada Press, 1998).

Liddell, Guy, *The Guy Liddell Diaries*—see under West, Nigel.

Lief, Alfred, *The Firestone Story: A History of the Firestone Tire & Rubber Company* (New York: McGraw-Hill Book Company, 1951).

Liptak, Eugene, *Office of Strategic Services, 1942–45: The World War II Origins of the CIA* (Botley, Oxford: Osprey Publishing, 2009).

Lodeesen, Captain Marius, *Captain Lodi Speaking: Saying Goodbye to an Era* (McLean, VA: Paladwr Press, 2004).

MacDonald, Elizabeth P., *Undercover Girl* (New York: The Macmillan Company, 1947).

Mackenzie, W. J. M., *The Secret History of SOE: The Special Operations Executive* (London: St Ermin's Press, 2000).

BIBLIOGRAPHY

MacPherson, Nelson, *American Intelligence in War-Time London: The Story of the OSS* (London: Frank Cass, 2003).

Maddock, Shane J, *Nuclear Apartheid: The Quest for American Atomic Supremacy from World War II to the Present* (Chapel Hill: The University of North Carolina Press, 2010).

Makelele, Albert, *This is a Good Country: Welcome to the Congo* (Bloomington, IN: Authorpress, 2008).

Malloy, Sean L., *Atomic Tragedy: Henry L. Stimson and the Decision to Use the Bomb Against Japan* (Ithaca and New York: Cornell University Press, 2008).

Manderstam, Major L. H., with Heron, Roy, *From the Red Army to SOE* (London: William Kimber, 1985).

Marchal, Jules, *Lord Leverhulme's Ghosts: Colonial Exploitation in the Congo*, trans. Martin Thom (London: Verso, 2008).

Marnham, Patrick, *Snake Dance: Journeys Beneath a Nuclear Sky* (London: Chatto & Windus, 2013).

Marriage, Zoe, *Formal Peace and Informal War: Security and Development in Congo* (London, Routledge, 2013).

Martin, Edwin W., *Divided Counsel: The Anglo-American Response to Communist Victory in China* (Lexington: The University Press of Kentucky, 1986).

Marvel, Tom, *The New Congo* (London: Macdonald,1949).

Maul, Daniel, *Human Rights, Development and Decolonization: The International Labour Organization, 1940–70* (Houndmills, Basingstoke: Palgrave Macmillan, and Geneva: International Labour Office, 2012).

Mazrui, Ali A. with Wondji, C., *General History of Africa, Vol. VIII* (Paris: UNESCO, 1993).

McGrath, Sylvia Wallace, *Charles Kenneth Leith: Scientific Adviser* (Madison, Milwaukee: The University of Wisconsin Press, 1971).

McIntosh, Elizabeth P., *Sisterhood of Spies: The Women of the OSS* (Annapolis, MD: Naval Institute Press, 1998).

Meiss-Teuffen, Hans de, with Rosen, Victor, *Winds of Adventure* (London: Museum Press Ltd, 1953).

Melton, H. Keith, *OSS Special Weapons and Equipment: Spy Devices of WWII* (New York: Sterling Publishing Co, 1991).

Mikamo, Akiko, *Rising from the Ashes: A True Story of Survival and Forgiveness from Hiroshima* (Raleigh, NC: Lulu Publishing, 2013).

Mommen, André, *The Belgian Economy in the Twentieth Century* (London: Routledge, 1994).

Moon, Tom, *This Grim and Savage Game: The OSS and US Covert Operations in World War II* (1991; rpt. Boston, Da Capo Press, 1991).

Muggeridge, Malcolm, *The Infernal Grove: Chronicles of Wasted Time, Vol 2: The Infernal Grove* (New York: William Morris & Co., 1974).

Naimark, Norman M., *The Russians in Germany: A History of the Soviet Zone of Occupation, 1945–1949* (Cambridge, MA: The Belknap Press of Harvard University Press, 1995).

BIBLIOGRAPHY

Namikas, Lise, *Battleground Africa: Cold War in the Congo 1960–1965* (Washington DC: Woodrow Wilson Center Press, 2013).

Nelson, Craig, *The Age of Radiance: The Epic Rise and Dramatic Fall of the Atomic Era* (New York: Scribner, 2014).

Nesbit, Tarashea, *The Wives of Los Alamos* (London: Bloomsbury, 2014).

Newkirk, John, *The Old Man and the Harley: A Last Ride Through Our Fathers' America* (London: HarperCollins, 2008).

Nichols, *The Road to Trinity* (New York, William Morrow & Co, 1987).

Njoh, Ambe J., *Planning Power: Town planning and social control in colonial Africa* (London: UCL Press, 2007).

Nolte, Georg (ed.), *European Military Law Systems* (Berlin: Walter de Gruyter, 2003).

Norris, Robert C., *Racing For the Bomb: The True Story of General Leslie R Groves, the Man Behind the Birth of the Atomic Age* (2002; rpt New York: Skyhorse Publishing, 2014).

Nzongola-Ntalaja, Georges, *The Congo: From Leopold to Kabila* (London: Zed Books, 2002).

——, *Faillite de la gouvernance et crise de la construction nationale au Congo-Kinshasa* (Kinshasa, Montréal, and Washington: ICREDES, 2015).

O'Keefe, Bernard, *Nuclear Hostages* (Boston: Houghton Mifflin Company, 1983).

Osborne, Richard E., *World War II in Colonial Africa: The Death Knell of Colonialism* (Indianapolis, IN: Riebel-Roque Publishing Co.,2001).

O'Toole, G. J. A., *Honorable Treachery* (New York: The Atlantic Monthly Press, 1991).

Pash, Boris T., *The Alsos Mission* (New York: Award House, 1969).

Paterson, Thomas G., *Kennedy's Quest for Victory: American Foreign Policy, 1961–1963* (Oxford: Oxford University Press, 1989).

Patterson, Walter C., *Nuclear Power* (1976; rpt Harmondsworth: Penguin, 1978).

Paul, Septimus H., *Nuclear Rivals: Anglo-American Atomic Relations, 1941–1952* (Columbus: Ohio State University Press, 2000).

Peterson, Neal H. (ed.), *From Hitler's Doorstep: The Wartime Intelligence Reports of Allen Dulles, 1942–1945* (University Park, PA: Pennsylvania State University Press, 1996).

Pilisuk, M., *International Conflict and Social Policy* (Englewood Cliffs, NJ: Prentice-Hall, 1972).

Pinck, Dan C. with Jones, Geoffrey M. T. and Pinck, Charles T., *Stalking the History of the Office of Strategic Services. An OSS Bibliography* (Boston: The OSS/Donovan Press, 2000).

Powers, Thomas, *Heisenberg's War: The Secret History of the German Bomb* (1993; rpt. Boston: Da Capo Press, 2000).

Prados, John, *Lost Crusader: The Secret Wars of CIA Director William Colby* (Oxford: Oxford University Press, 2003).

——, *Safe for Democracy: The Secret Wards of the CIA* (Chicago: Ivan R. Dee, 2006).

Price, David H., *Anthropological Intelligence: The Deployment and Neglect of American*

BIBLIOGRAPHY

Anthropology in the Second World War (Durham, NC and London: Duke University Press, 2008).

Quigley, Martin S., *A U.S. Spy in Ireland: The Truth Behind Irish "Neutrality" During World War II* (Dublin: Marino Books, 1999).

Ray, Ellen, Schaap, William, van Meter, Karl and Wolf, Louis, *Dirty Work 2: The CIA in Africa* (London: Zed Press, 1980).

Renton, David, Seddon, David and Zeilig, Leo, *The Congo: Plunder and Resistance* (London: Zed Books, 2007).

Reves, Emery, *The Anatomy of Peace* (London: George Allen & Unwin, 1946).

Rhodes, Richard, *The Making of the Atomic Bomb* (1998; London, Simon & Schuster, 2012).

——, *Arsenals of Folly: The Making of the Nuclear Arms Race* (New York: Alfred A. Knopf, 2007).

Richelson, Jeffrey T., *Spying on the Bomb: American Nuclear Intelligence from Nazi Germany to Iran and North Korea* (New York: W. W. Norton, 2006).

Roberts, Janine, *Glitter and Greed: The Secret World of the Diamond Cartel* (2003; rpt New York: Disinformation Company, 2007).

Robertson, K. G. (ed.), *War, Resistance and Intelligence: Essays in Honour of M. R. D. Foot* (Barnsley, South Yorkshire: Leo Cooper, 1999).

Russell, Peter, *Prince Henry 'The Navigator': A Life* (New Haven, CT: Yale University Press, 2000).

Salter, Michael, *Nazi War Crimes, US Intelligence and Selective Prosecution at Nuremburg: Controversies regarding the role of the Office of Strategic Service* (Abingdon, Oxon: Routledge-Cavendish, 2007).

Sampson, Anthony, *The Seven Sisters: The Great Oil Companies and the World They Made*. 1975; new edn. (Sevenoaks, Kent: Coronet Books, 1993).

Sanger, Penny, *Blind Faith: The Nuclear Industry in One Small Town* (Toronto: McGraw-Hill Ryerson Ltd, 1981).

Sayer, Ian and Botting, Douglas, *Nazi Gold: The Story of the World's Greatest Robbery–and its Aftermath* (London: Panther Books, 1984).

——, *America's Secret Army: The Untold Story of the Counter Intelligence Corps* (London: Grafton Books, 1989).

Scalia, Joseph M., *Germany's Last Mission to Japan: The Sinister Voyage of U-234* (London: Chatham Publishing, 2000).

Shannon, Carl [pseud. of Wilbur Owings Hogue], *Murder Me Never* (London: T. V. Boardman and Co Ltd, 1951).

——, *Fatal Footsteps* (London: T. V. Boardman and Co Ltd, 1951).

——, *Lady That's My Skull* (Los Angeles, CA: Phoenix Press, 1948).

Shavit, David, *The United States in Africa. A Historical Dictionary* (New York: Greenwood Press, 1989).

Sherwin, Martin J., *A World Destroyed: Hiroshima and Its Legacies* (Stanford, CA: Stanford University Press, 2003).

Smith, Richard Harris, *OSS: The Secret History of America's First Central Intelligence Agency* (1972; rpt Guilford, CT: The Lyons Press, 2005).

BIBLIOGRAPHY

Smyth, H. D., *A General Account of the Development of Methods of Using Atomic Energy for Military Purposes under the Auspices of the United States Government, 1940–1945* (published in the USA by the Government Printing Office, August 1945).

Souchard, Vladi, *Jours de brousse: Congo 1940–1945* (Brussels: Editions de l'Université de Bruxelles, 1983).

Spellman, Francis J., *Action This Day: Letters from the Fighting Fronts* (London: Sheed & Ward, 1944).

Stein, Sarah Abrevaya, *Saharan Jews and the Fate of French Algeria* (Chicago: University of Chicago Press, 2014).

Steinart, Harald, *The Atom Rush: Man's quest for radio-active materials*, translated from the German edition of 1957 by Nicholas Wharton (London: Thames and Hudson, 1958).

Stockwell, John, *In Search of Enemies: A CIA Story* (London: Deutsch, 1978).

——, *The Praetorian Guard: The US Role in the New World Order* (Boston: South End Press, 1991).

Sutton, Antony, *Wall Street and the Rise of Hitler* (Sudbury, Suffolk: Bloomfield Books, 1976).

Swinton, Rt Hon. Viscount, *I Remember* (London: Hutchinson & Co, n.d. [1948]).

Thomas, Clarke M., *A Patrician of Ideas: A Biography of A. W. Schmidt* (Pittsburgh: Pittsburgh History & Landmarks Foundation, 2006).

Thomas, Evan, *The Very Best Men: Four Who Dared: The Early Years of the CIA* (London: Simon & Schuster, 1995).

Thompson, Virginia and Adloff, Richard, *The Emerging States of French Equatorial Africa* (Stanford, CA: Stanford University Press, 1960).

Trefon, Theodore, *Reinventing Order in the Congo: How People Respond to State Failure in Kinshasa* (London: Zed Books, 2004).

——, *Congo Masquerade: The Political Culture of Aid Inefficiency and Reform Failure– African Arguments* (London: Zed Books, 2011).

——, *Congo's Environmental Paradox: Potential and Predation in a Land of Plenty* (London: Zed Books, 2016).

Troy, Thomas F., *Wild Bill and Intrepid: Donovan, Stephenson, and the Origin of CIA* (New Haven, CT: Yale University Press, 1996).

Turner, Thomas, *Congo* (Cambridge: Polity Press, 2013).

Urquhart, Brian, *Ralph Bunche: An American Life* (London: W. W. Norton, 1993).

[US Department of State], *Foreign Relations of the United States (FRUS) 1945, Vol. II: General: Political and Economic Matters* (Washington, DC, 1967).

Van der Bijl, Nick, *Sharing the Secret: The History of the Intelligence Corps 1940–2010* (Barnsley, South Yorkshire: Pen & Sword Books, 2013).

Vanderlinden, Jacques, *Pierre Ryckmans 1891–1959. Coloniser dans l'honneur* (Brussels: DeBoeck Université, 1994).

Van Reybrouck, David, *Congo: The Epic History of a People*, translated from the Dutch by Sam Garrett (2010; London: Fourth Estate, 2014).

Vanthemsche, Guy, *Belgium and the Congo, 1885–1980*, trans. Alice Cameron and

BIBLIOGRAPHY

Stephen Windross, revised by Kate Connelly (Cambridge: Cambridge University Press, 2012).

Von Eschen, Penny, *Race Against Empire: Black Americans and Anticolonialism, 1937–1957* (Ithaca, NY: Cornell University Press, 1997).

Walker, Mark, *German National Socialism and the Quest for Nuclear Power, 1939–1949* (Cambridge University Press, 1989).

Waller, Douglas, *Wild Bill Donovan: The Spymaster Who Created the OSS and Modern American Espionage* (New York: Free Press, 2011).

Wark, Wesley K. (ed.), *Espionage, Past, Present, Future?* (Ilford, Essex: Frank Cass, 1994).

Weiner, Tim, *Legacy of Ashes: The History of the CIA* (London: Allen Lane, 2007).

West, Nigel (ed.), *The Guy Liddell Diaries Vol.II: 1942–1945: MI5's Director of Counter-Espionage in World War II* (London: Taylor & Francis, 2006).

Wevill, Richard, *Britain and America After World War II: Bilateral Relations and the Beginnings of the Cold War* (London: I. B. Tauris, 2012).

Williams, C. Kingsley, *Achimota: The Early Years 1924–1948* (Accra: Longmans, 1962).

Williams, Susan, *Who Killed Hammarskjöld? The UN, the Cold War and White Supremacy in Africa* (London: Hurst, 2011).

Wilson, A. J., *The Life and Times of Sir Alfred Chester Beatty* (London: Cadogan Publications Ltd, 1985).

Winks, Robin W., *Cloak and Gown: Scholars in the Secret War, 1939–1961* (New York: William Morrow and Co, 1987).

Witte, Els, Craeybeckx, Jan and Meynen, Alain, *Political History of Belgium from 1830 Onwards* (Brussels: ASP nv (Academic and Scientific Publishers nv), 2009).

Wright, George, *The Destruction of a Nation: United States' Policy Towards Angola since 1945* (London: Pluto Press, 1997).

Wrong, Michela, *In the Footsteps of Mr Kurtz. Living on the Brink of Disaster in Mobutu's Congo* (London: Fourth Estate, 2000).

Yeadon, Glen, with Hawkins, John, *The Nazi Hydra in America. Suppressed History of a Century: Wall Street and the Rise of the Third Reich* (Joshua Tree, CA: Progressive Press, 2008).

Young, Crawford, *Politics in the Congo: Decolonization and Independence* (Princeton, NJ: University Press, 1967).

Ziegler, Charles A. and Jacobson, David, *Spying Without Spies: Origins of America's Secret Nuclear Surveillance System* (London: Praeger, 1995).

Zoellner, Tom, *Uranium: War, Energy, and the Rock that Shaped the World* (London: Penguin, 2010).

ARTICLES, CHAPTERS IN BOOKS, AND THESES

Avery, Donald, 'Allied Scientific Co-operation and Soviet Espionage in Canada, 1941–45,' in Wesley K. Wark (ed.), *Espionage. Paste, Present, Future?* (Ilford, Essex: Frank Cass, 1994).

Bird, Kai and Sherwin, Martin, 'Robert Oppenheimer: A Window on His Life at

BIBLIOGRAPHY

Los Alamos,' in Kelly, Cynthia C. (ed.), *Oppenheimer and the Manhattan Project: Insights into J Robert Oppenheimer, "Father of the Atomic Bomb"* (Hackensack, NJ: World Scientific Publishing, 2006).

Bundy, Harvey H., Webster, William L. and Rickett, D. H. F., 'Minutes of a Meeting of the Combined Policy Committee,' (8 March 1945), *FRUS 1945, Vol. II: General: Political and Economic Matters*. Washington, DC, 1967).

Cahen, Lucien, 'Contribution à l'histoire du rôle des pouvoirs publics dans l'effort minier de guerre du Congo belge (1940–1945),' in *Le Congo Belge durant la Seconde Guerre mondiale: Recueil d'études* (Bruxelles: Académie Royale des Sciences d'Outre-Mer, 1983).

Chambers, Dr John Whiteclay, 'Office of Strategic Services Training During World War II,' *Studies in Intelligence*, 54 (2) (June 2010).

Chanaiwa, David, 'Southern Africa since 1945,' in Mazrui, Ali A. with Wondji, C., *General History of Africa, Vol. VIII* (Paris: UNESCO, 1993).

Cox, Nechama Janet Cohen, 'The Ministry of Economic Warfare And Britain's Conduct of Economic Warfare, 1939–1945,' 2001, Kings College London PhD thesis.

Danchev, Alex, 'In the back room: Anglo-American defence co-operation,' in Richard J. Aldrich, *British Intelligence, Strategy and the Cold War, 1945–51* (London and New York: Routledge, 1992).

Dumett, Raymond, 'Africa's Strategic Minerals during the Second World War,' *The Journal of African History*, 26 (1985), 381–408.

Fedorowich, Kent, 'British espionage and British counter-intelligence in South Africa and Mozambique, 1939–1944,' *Historical Journal*, 48 (1) (2005), 209–30.

Fetter, Bruce, 'The Luluabourg Revolt at Elisabethville,' *African Historical Studies*, 2 (2) (1969).

——, 'Africa's Role, 1940–41, as seen from Léopoldville,' *African Affairs*, 87 (348) (July 1988), 377–2.

Geraets, Luc H., 'The Fabulous Nuclear Odyssey of Belgium,' *Journal of Pressure Vessel Technology*, 131 (3) (6 April 2009).

Goldberg, Stanley, 'The Secret about Secrets,' in Marjorie Garber and Rebecca L. Walkowitz (eds), *Secret Agents. The Rosenberg Case, McCarthyism, and Fifties America* (London: Routledge, 1995).

Harrison, E. R. D., 'Something Beautiful for "C": Malcolm Muggeridge in Lourenco Marques,' in K. G. Robertson (ed.), *War, Resistance and Intelligence: Essays in Honour of M. R. D. Foot* (Barnsley, South Yorkshire: Leo Cooper, 1999).

Hochschild, Adam, Introduction to Marchal, Jules, *Lord Leverhulme's Ghosts. Colonial Exploitation in the Congo*, trans. Martin Thom (London: Verso, 2008).

Hogue, Dock, 'Congo Contraband,' *Adventure*, June 1947.

——, 'Bahnhofstrasse 17,' *Adventure*, October 1947.

Kurgan-van-Hentenrky, Ginette, 'Bankers and politics in Belgium in the twentieth century,' in Terry Gourvish (ed.), *Business and Politics in Europe, 1900–1970, 1900–1970: Essays in Honour of Alice Teichova* (Cambridge: Cambridge University Press, 2003).

BIBLIOGRAPHY

Lawrence, Ken, 'Via Miami 1941–1945. FAM 22 Trans-Atlantic Air Mail. Part I: To and From Africa,' *American Philatelist* (January 2014), 32–42.

Mahoney, Leo J., 'A History of the War Department Scientific Intelligence Mission (ALSOS), 1943–1945', Kent State University, Ann Arbor, Michigan: PhD thesis, 1981.

Majhemout Diop in collaboration with David Birmingham, Ivan Hrbek, Alfredo Margarido, and Djibril Tamsir Niane,'Tropical and Equatorial Africa Under French, Portuguese and Spanish Domination, 1935-45,' in Ali A. Mazrui with C. Wondji, *General History of Africa, Vol. VIII* op. cit.

M'Bokolo, Elikia, 'Equatorial West Africa,' in Ali A. Mazrui with C. Wondji, *General History of Africa, Vol. VIII* (see above).

Mottoulle, 'The day of the strike, 6 December 1941, at Likasi,' *Greves 1941–42.*

Newitt, Malyn, 'The Portuguese African Colonies during the Second World War,' in Judith A. Byfield, Carolyn A. Brown, Timothy Parsons and Ahmad Alawad Sikainga (eds), *Africa and World War II* (Cambridge University Press, 2015).

Noer, Thomas J., 'New Frontiers and Old Priorities in Africa,' in Thomas G. Paterson, *Kennedy's Quest for Victory: American Foreign Policy, 1961–1963* (Oxford: Oxford University Press, 1989).

Norton, W. B., 'Belgian-French Relations During World War II as seen by Governor General Ryckmans,' in *Le Congo Belge Durant la Seconde Guerre Mondiale*, pp. 285–311.

Pistor, Dominic Emanuel Martin, 'Developmental Colonialism and Kitawala Policy in 1950s Belgian Congo,' MA Thesis in History, 2012, Simon Fraser University.

Río, David, 'A Clean Writer: An Interview with Robert Laxalt,' *Revista de Estudios Norteamericanos*, 5, 1997, 21–7. See http://institucional.us.es/revistas/estudios/5/art_2.pdf

Sichel, Kim, 'Germaine Krull and *L'Amitié Noire*: World War II and French Colonialist Film,' in Eleanor M. Hight and Gary D. Sampson (eds), *Colonialist Photography: Imag(in)ing Race and Place* (London: Routledge, 2002).

Sonck, Jean Pierre, 'Le Congo Belge entre 1940–1945,' <http://www.congo-1960.be/Congo_Belge_1940-1945.htm>

Stanley, William R., 'Trans-South Atlantic Air Link in World War II,' *GeoJournal*, 33 (4), August 1944, 459-63.

——, 'Air Transportation in Liberia,' *The Bulletin. The Journal of the Sierra Leone Geographical Association*, 9 (May 1965), 34-44.

Tepper, Justin, 'The Congo as a Case Study: The Making of Unipolarity,' 2014, *Dissertations and Theses, 2014–Present.* Paper 153. <http://works.gc.cuny.edu/etd/153>.

Thomas, Martin, 'Signals Intelligence and Vichy France, 1940-44: Intelligence in Defeat,' in Alvarez, David (ed.), *Allied and Axis Signals Intelligence in World War II* (London: Frank Cass, 1999).

Yelvington, Kevin A, 'A Life In and Out of Anthropology. An Interview with Jack Sargent Harris,' *Critique of Anthropology*, 28 (4) (2008), 446–76.

FILMOGRAPHY

L'Amitié Noire, co-dir. by François Villiers and Germaine Krull, filmed in 1943, narration added in 1946, written and narrated by Jean Cocteau.

Hogue Films held by Hogue Family

i) Congo and Gold Coast
ii) Liberia 1940–1942, Dock's Trip
iii) Liberia–2nd Reel, Dock's Trip *1942–1943*
iv) Yellowstone, Bear Tooth Mountain, Congo, Kenya, Rhodesia, Liberty Ship, Gil Baby
v) Congo, General de Gaulle

Snake Dance, written and directed by Manu Riche and Patrick Marnham, narrated by Marnham, 2012.

Private Snafu–Spies, 1943, US Army Animated Training Film, available online at: https://www.youtube.com/watch?v=vzIltaAnWFU. There are a number of other Private Snafu films available on Youtube.

Uranium 1 and *Uranium 2*: relatively recent documentary films made at Shinkolobwe and uploaded in 2010–11: https://www.youtube.com/watch?v=3Cu-LH_eM3w and https://www.youtube.com/watch?v=3Cu-LH_eM3w

ACKNOWLEDGEMENTS

The layers of secrecy surrounding the story in this book are thick. It would have been impossible to peel them away without the recent declassification of official records relating to the Office of Strategic Services, the Manhattan Project, and the British intelligence services. There I found the handful of men—and one woman—who are represented in these pages, and who have been my close companions through the years of research. It has been a privilege to get to know these brave and special people.

It has also been an honour to meet some of their descendants. A real breakthrough was making contact with Kathryn Dinny Hogue, the daughter of Dock Hogue, who died when she was only seven years of age. Kathryn knew little about her father's war service in Liberia and the Belgian Congo and was eager to learn more. She and her husband Nicholas Sommese welcomed me into their home and did everything possible to help. Although a fire had destroyed the bulk of her father's papers, Kathryn and her family used considerable ingenuity to find letters, photographs, and a set of six 'home movies' shot by Hogue on his missions in Africa. These unique films were found and digitised just in time, since they were starting to disintegrate.

Marguerite J. Kelly, the daughter of Henry Stehli, was also generous with her help and shared with me some fascinating memories, letters, and photographs; her daughter Mia Walton assisted with logistics. I am grateful as well to Annabel Stehli and to Huntington Stehli.

I was fortunate to make contact with Helen Schmidt, the granddaughter of Adolph Schmidt, who introduced me to Thomas Mellon Schmidt, Adolph Schmidt's son. He gave me much appreciated help with photographs and his recollections.

Making contact with Charles Elliott, a nephew of Shirley Chidsey, was very rewarding: he had been extremely fond of his aunt and his brother, Lewis Elliott, had carefully conserved a box of their aunt's papers, which contained letters, postcards, and photographs. These were generously shared with me and have contributed in significant ways to the book.

Susan Harris Smith was interested to hear about my research into the war service of her father, Huntington Harris. She would have liked to assist me if possible, but unfortunately her father had destroyed all his papers.

This challenge for historians—the destruction and loss of records—highlights the importance of access to information, if we are to have any understanding of the past and the present. I should like to honour the spirit of transparency that led to the release of the records represented in this book, as well as the hard work of campaigners for access to information. The Freedom of Information Acts in the US and the UK have been a significant resource. One of my FOI requests to the UK National Archives was granted just days before the completion of the book. This was a request for an SOE file that had been classified for 84 years: without the FOI release, it would have remained closed until 2031.

I should like to pay tribute to the specialist skills and expertise of Jeremy Bigwood, who conducted essential research for me at the US National Archives and Records Administration in Maryland, near Washington DC. When I met Jeremy for an enjoyable lunch in Washington a few years ago, neither of us had any idea that over the next few years he would research and photograph many thousands of documents for me. In the case of General Donovan's papers, which were microfilmed in haste after

ACKNOWLEDGEMENTS

President Truman terminated OSS in October 1945, some of the cables were difficult to track; many of them had also deteriorated badly. Jeremy went to immense trouble to find what I needed and also to photograph the documents in such a way as to maximise legibility. Jeremy also submitted Freedom of Information Act requests on my behalf to US government departments. I could not have written this book without Jeremy's unique and specialist contribution and I owe him a huge debt of gratitude.

Completing the book required stamina and all kinds of expertise. I was extremely fortunate, therefore, to be superbly assisted in London during the last year by Albertine Fox. Albertine is a postdoctoral specialist in French cinema, whose brilliant analysis of relevant films (including Hogue's 'home movies') and images much enriched my understanding. She helped me beyond measure in many other important ways: research; translation; discussing matters of interpretation and of detail; the finding and presentation of the images; organising endnotes; technical assistance; proofing—the list is long. Her work and her approach are always highly intelligent, tireless, meticulous, and thoughtful. It has been a real privilege to work with Albertine.

I was also fortunate—through the serendipity of a query regarding the Niagara Falls area—to be introduced to Michelle Ann Kratts, a historian, genealogist, and archivist. Michelle was kind enough to take on a series of tasks that were perfectly suited to her special set of skills. Against considerable odds, she unearthed a mass of wonderful information in the US about the OSS agents in this book. No one but Michelle would have been so tenacious, inventive, and thorough, in the search for such information. These gifts, which also inform her own publications, helped me to portray the key people in this book in a meaningful and human way.

Belia Pena conducted some research for me in the archives of Pan American Airways at the University of Miami. This new information pushed the topic forward at a crucial stage and I owe Belia great thanks.

What I have *not* been able to find—because they appear not to exist—are the records of the people of the Belgian Congo

ACKNOWLEDGEMENTS

(Democratic Republic of the Congo) and of the Gold Coast (Ghana) in relation to this story. The grim reality of these Belgian and British colonies meant that the colonised populations were deprived of their agency, power, and voice. Their enforced silence is deafening. It is part of the terrible injustices and cruelties inflicted by European nations on so many people in the nations of Africa.

I never expected to write a book that required an understanding of nuclear physics, even at the most elementary level. For help with this, I was dependent on the kindness—and the clarity—of experts. I owe a tremendous debt of gratitude in particular to Walt Patterson, a nuclear physicist, who is currently writing and campaigning on issues related to energy. Walt went to considerable trouble to explain the basics to me in a straightforward way. His pathbreaking book, *Nuclear Power*, which was first published in 1976 and has been revised and reprinted countless times, has been a key reference work for me and occupies a central spot on my book shelves.

I had a valuable conversation with the late Lorna Arnold, co-author of official histories of Britain's nuclear projects and author of *My Short Century: Memoirs of an Accidental Nuclear Historian*. I was given instruction by Paul Bartlett of the Department of Physics and Astronomy at University College London; thanks are due also to Nick Booth, Curator of the Science and Engineering Collections at the UCL Museums. Robert Standish Norris and William Lanouette also gave me kind help.

I owe debts to many of my colleagues and friends at the Institute for Commonwealth Studies in the School of Advanced Study, University of London: our director Philip Murphy, who was generous with leads and insights and has supported me with kindness in different ways; Mandy Banton, with whom I work closely on a range of projects; James Chiriyankandath; Olga Jimenez; Howard Jones; and Chloe Pieters.

On 16 July 2015, Mandy and I—with our colleague and friend David Wardrop, Chair of the United Nations Association

ACKNOWLEDGEMENTS

Westminster Branch—convened a major international conference at the School of Advanced Study on '"Sowing the Whirlwind": Nuclear Politics and the Historical Record'. I learnt a great deal at this conference from Akiko Mikamo of US-Japan Psychological Services, who gave a moving keynote address about her father Shinji Mikamo, who survived Hiroshima and teaches forgiveness. Other contributors were Knox Chitiyo, Matthew Jones, Bruce Kent, Peter Kuznick, Joe Lauria, Walt Patterson, and Andreas Persbo. The conference took place at a crucial stage of writing this book and it was immensely useful to listen to, and talk with, these distinguished speakers.

An earlier watershed moment took place in Norway on 24 February 2014. I was invited by John Y. Jones, the director of the Dag Hammarskjöld Programme at Voksenåsen near Oslo, to give a lecture, which I entitled 'Silencing and Lies: The death of Hammarskjöld, Congolese uranium, and the annexation of history'. For several intense hours after the lecture, I benefited from a brilliant discussion involving Morten Bøås, Tore Linné Eriksen, Gunnar Garbo, Lars Gule, Bernt Hagtvet, Halle Jørn Hansen, Jahn Otto Johansen, Truls Lie, Arnfinn Nygaard, Arne Ruth, and Randi Solhjell. Also participating were John Jones, Henning Melber, and Hans Kristian Simensen, who deserve a special mention by me for their loyal and wonderful friendship, on both a personal and an intellectual level.

I enjoyed talking on this topic with Théodore Trefon of the Contemporary History Library at the Royal Museum for Central Africa, at Tervuren in Belgium. Théodore also kindly introduced me to the Mémoires du Congo group in Belgium and facilitated a meeting with them on 20 November 2015 at the Royal Museum. I am grateful to the President of the association, Paul Vannès, for welcoming me so warmly to the group meeting. The observations and comments made by Daniel Depreter, Robert Devriese, André de Maere d'Aertrycke, André Schorochoff, Jean-Pierre Sonck, and Paul Vannès, helped me to identify specific locations that were important to my research. I should also like to thank Thierry

ACKNOWLEDGEMENTS

Claeys Bouuaert for the extremely useful resources he gave me and I am grateful to André Schorochoff for supplying information with regard to Shinkolobwe and the railways.

In addition to those people mentioned in the paragraphs above, I have had valuable conversations and communications with Denys Blakeway, Jonathan Bloch, Margaret Bluman, Art Cockerill, Ludo De Witte, Elwood Dunn, Daniel Ellsberg, Bruce Fetter, KG Hammar, Svend Holsoe, Nancy Jacobs, Mama Chibesa Kankasa, Jean-Roger Kaseki, Ken Lawrence, Roger Lipsey, Susan Lipsey, Harvey Minasian, Jonathan Mirsky, Chris Murray, Edward Nahem, Margaret O'Callaghan, Kate Philbrick, Martin Plaut, Declan Power, Beatrice Randall, Andrew Sardanis, Danae Sardanis, Paul Sharkey, Oliver Tshinyoka, Susan Van Gelder, Kevin A. Yelvington, Cynthia Zukas, and Simon Zukas.

On this and related topics I had wonderful conversations with Commander Charles Southall, whose good company and keen insights I greatly miss.

Charles Pinck, President of the OSS Society, facilitated my joining the OSS Society Discussion Group and kindly encouraged my focus on West Africa, identifying it as an important area of study that had so far been neglected. Contact with Mary Curry at the George Washington University National Security Archive has been a genuine pleasure and is always fruitful.

Eliah Meyer generously shared his knowledge about the world of intelligence and business in the relevant years, and his insights led to new discoveries. Margaret Hunt kindly let me read the unfinished manuscript 'Uranium Merchants' written by her mother, Vilma R. Hunt, who was a scientist specialising in radiation. I was also given expert help by Jeremy W. Crampton at the Department of Geography, University of Kentucky, and by Christo Datini and Jim Vehko at the General Motors Heritage Center, Michigan. I am extremely grateful to Daniel Boustead, Volunteer at the US Army Military History Institute, Carlisle Barracks, Pennsylvania, for tracking down and sending to me a key record.

ACKNOWLEDGEMENTS

For his very special assistance I should like to thank Steven Kippax, the founder of the SOE Discussion Group in the UK, whose research project is having the closed H S9 SOE Personal Files at the UK National Archives opened. Steven has been remarkably generous, sharing copies not only of a mass of SOE files, but also his knowledge and insights. I have also been helped with prompt efficiency at the UK National Archives by Robert O'Hara and his team, and by Simon Fowler. Romain Durieux conducted some research for me in Belgium and found an important article in *Le Courrier d'Afrique*. Michael Foedrowitz conducted some background research on German intelligence in Berlin. Jeannette K. Rook and Tanya Parlet in the US were also helpful.

I would like to express my gratitude to a number of other archivists and librarians: Bianka J. Adams at the Office of History, US Army Corps of Engineers, Alexandria, Virginia; Nicolette A. Dobrowolski at the Syracuse University Libraries, New York; Caroline Godet at CRISP, Brussels; Cynthia Harbeson at the Jones Library, Amherst, Massachusetts; Emma E. Hawker at the Bentley Historical Library, University of Michigan, in Ann Arbor; Steve Hersh at the University of Miami Libraries, Florida; Ted Jackson at the Georgetown University Library; Daniel Palmieri at the Library and Public Archives Unit of the International Committee of the Red Cross, Geneva; Jacquelyn Sundstrand at the Mathewson-IGT Knowledge Center, University of Nevada; Bruce Tabb at the University of Oregon Libraries; Amy Thompson at the University of Idaho Library; and Penny White at the University of Virginia.

For much appreciated help with the images used in this book, I would like to thank Barbara Wolff at the Albert Einstein Archives, the Hebrew University of Jerusalem. I was introduced to her by Bryan G. Deziel at the Argonne National Laboratory, Illinois. For his special help and kindness, I should like to express my gratitude to Patrick Fahy at the Franklin D. Roosevelt Presidential Library and Museum in New York. John and Terese Hart very kindly let me use a photograph they found in a signed

ACKNOWLEDGEMENTS

copy of a book they had bought: Dr James Chapin's *Birds of the Belgian Congo*, which he had given to one of his colleagues at the American Museum of Natural History. Stefan Schorn of Mineralienatlas was generous with his knowledge and images of minerals. Sebastian Ballard drew excellent maps.

I should like to express my sincere gratitude to Eric Ezra and Simon Gilchrist for their specialist help.

I owe an immense debt to the considerate and conscientious staff at the British Library in London, where I researched and wrote much of the book—enjoying their remarkable resources and their quiet, peaceful spaces. The National Library of Scotland was another congenial home. I owe Yajun Yang a very special debt. I should also like to thank Lewis Fox, Ray Potgieter, and Stanislav Gerov.

A number of people read drafts of the book at various stages, in some cases more than once: Michael Dwyer, Albertine Fox, Kathryn Hogue, Gervase Hood, Marguerite Kelly, Michelle Kratts, Georges Nzongola-Ntalaja, Jon de Peyer, Clive Priddle, and Myfanwy Williams. All these readers made important suggestions and criticisms.

I am extremely fortunate to have Karolina Sutton at Curtis Brown as my literary agent. Karolina is very perceptive and her insights helped me with the development of the shape of the book.

Michael Dwyer has supported me in various ways during the years of research and it has been valuable and stimulating to discuss the themes of the story with him at key stages. I have enjoyed working with his excellent team at Hurst: Daisy Leitch and Jon de Peyer have worked hard and thoughtfully for the book, with calm efficiency and close attention to detail. Prerana Patel is meticulous and careful. Mary Dalton copyedited the book beautifully and Janet Tyrrell proofread it with kindness and the sharpest of eyes. Sincere thanks to Alex Bell for his hard work on the index.

Clive Priddle at PublicAffairs has shown real interest in the topic, which is very much appreciated. He offered important suggestions, which strengthened the book considerably.

I owe my family special thanks. Tendayi Bloom, my daughter, is an original thinker who explores and creates hopeful possibili-

338

ties for the future; she drew on this gift to offer me valuable insights into my work on the past. She also gave me loyal support. Benedict Wiseman, my stepson, shared with me good music, good sense, and good humour. Josie Jackson, my niece, accompanied me to a museum to look at a block of uranium and listened attentively to my stories about the spies. I greatly enjoyed discussing the book on various occasions with Myfanwy Williams, who is a discerning and judicious reader. James Williams helped in instrumental ways and shared with me his expertise on the French language and cinema. Joan Williams is always a source of lively encouragement.

I have been passionate about writing this book and I will miss it. But it was also a demanding project, because the story is so new and because sleuthing sleuths is inevitably a challenge. At times this was hard. Without my husband and my partner, Gervase Hood, it would have been even harder. With his generosity of spirit, his honesty, his insights, his clarity of mind, his good sense, and his unfailing kindness, he has walked with me all the way, lighting the path.

INDEX

341

INDEX

British Broadcasting Corporation
(BBC), 91, 227
British Overseas Airways
Corporation (BOAC), 130, 145,
206
Brock, Horace, 7
Brooke, Alan, General, 115–16
Brooklyn, New York, 83
Bruce, David Kirkpatrick Este, 23,
29, 34, 50, 93
Brussels, Belgium, 31, 50, 126,
177, 184, 197, 215–16, 224, 289
Brutsaert, Paul, 37, 39
Buell, Robert, 211, 221–3, 244
Buenos Aires, Argentina, 101
Bulawayo, Southern Rhodesia,
129, 143
Bunche, Ralph, 22–4, 52, 259
Bunge Co., 135
Bureau Central de
Renseignements et d'Action
(BCRA) (Free French intel-
ligence service), 290
Bureau de la Population Blanche,
Léopoldville, 59
Bureau de la Population Noire,
Léopoldville, 59
Bureau of Economic Warfare, US
(BEW), 31, 45, 47, 51–2, 122
Burma, 63–4, 247
Burns, Alan, 117
Burundi, 282
Byrnes, James, 10

'C', Head of MI6 (Stewart
Graham Menzies), 108, 122,
200
Cabinda, Angola, 151
Cabo Verde (formerly Cape Verde
Islands), 282
Caltex, see Texaco

Caillavet, Ruth, 90
Cairo, Egypt, 43, 94, 129, 134
California, United States, 52, 87,
107
California Texas Oil Company, see
Texaco
Cambridge University, UK, 120
Campbell, J. L., 298
Camus, Celestin, 50, 184–5
Canada, xxiv, 2, 9, 11, 31, 46, 102,
123–4, 145, 198, 228, 230, 245,
254, 264
cancer, 225, 241, 265–6
Cape Palmas, Liberia, 57, 112
Cape Town, South Africa, 25, 58
Cape Verde Islands (now known as
Cabo Verde), 282
Capone, Alphonse 'Al', 100
Carborundum Company, 126
CARL WEST, see Hogue, Wilbur
Owings
Casey, William, 246
Catholicism, 31, 32, 37, 48, 70,
136–7, 162, 183, 227, 258
Cattier, Félicien, 50, 177
Central Intelligence Agency
(CIA), 238, 243, 246–7, 255,
259, 262
Central Intelligence Group (CIG),
238, 242, 244
Centre d'Information
Gouvernemental (CIG), 290
Cercle Albert, Elisabethville, 32
CFL, see Compagnie des Chemins
de Fer du Congo Supérieur aux
Grands Lacs Africains
Chad, French Equatorial Africa,
84
Chapin, Howard, 38
Chapin, James 'Jim' (CRISP),
34–9, 41, 44, 52, 53, 64, 65, 67,
74, 75, 246

346

INDEX

Chapin, Ruth, 36, 38–9

Chicago, United States, 18, 19, 90, 98, 145, 237–8, 241

Chicago Tribune, 92

chicotte, 59–60

Chidsey, Donald Barr, 86

Chidsey, Shirley Armitage (ANGELLA), 12, 85–90, 132–3, 135, 147, 149, 152, 165, 170, 171, 177, 179–80, 202, 205, 208, 212, 221–3, 235–6, 241, 244, 247, 290

  1935 marries Donald Chidsey, 87

  1940 separation from Donald; moves to New York, 87

  1942 joins OSS in New York, 85–7

  1943 takes job at Radio Brazzaville, 86; hired by Hogue to work for OSS, 88

  1944 becomes *de facto* chief of OSS Congo station, 208, 221

  1945 returns to US; meets with Boulton, 235–6

  1946 returns to Congo to work for US Consul, 244

  1947 meets with Stehli, 241; leaves Congo, 244

  1955 marries William Bridgwater, 244

  1987 death, 244

Chief of Station, Congo (Devlin), 259

Child, Julia, 21

China, 21, 86, 91, 247, 263

Chrysler building, New York, 73

Chungking, China, 21, 91

Church Committee on Assassinations (1975), 243

Churchill, Winston, 1, 9, 121, 122, 123, 200, 227

CIC, *see* Counter-Intelligence Corps

CIGAR, *see* Starcher, Harry Watson

ciphers, 16, 26, 36, 37, 38, 42, 47, 67, 131, 160

de Clerck, Etienne, 174–5, 210–11

Clark, Corporal (HANLY), 144–5, 237

Cloak Without Dagger (Sillitoe), 257

CLOCK, *see* Kirkland, John

Club du Congo Belge, 79

COACH, *see* Luther, Duane

cobalt, 77, 266

Cockerill, A. E., 257

Cocteau, Jean, 85

Cold War, 220, 238, 250–1, 253–62, 264, 265

Collaboration with Nazi Germany, 187–9

College of West Africa, Monrovia, Liberia, 57

colonialism, 22, 32, 43, 47, 59, 60–4, 69, 83–4, 110–11, 118, 120–1, 136–41, 149, 200, 223, 254

Colorado Plateau, 2, 46

coltan, 266

Columbia University, 3, 86, 243, 244

Combined Development Trust (CDT), 198–9

Combined Policy Committee (CPC), 45, 124, 198

Cominière, 76

Comité Spécial du Katanga (CSK), 289

Committee for Peace with Freedom in Vietnam, 244

Commonwealth, British, 198

INDEX

INDEX

INDEX

INDEX

INDEX

Dr. Susan Williams is a historian and a senior fellow in the School of Advanced Study, University of London. Her books draw on a range of previously untapped sources to tell important, original stories. *Who Killed Hammarskjöld?* was instrumental in setting up in 2015 a new UN inquiry into the death of the UN Secretary General in Zambia in 1961. *Colour Bar*, which is a forthcoming major film directed by Amma Asante and starring David Oyelowo and Rosamund Pike titled *A United Kingdom*, is the story of Seretse Khama of Botswana, who was exiled by the British colonial government following his marriage to a white woman. Other recent books include *The People's King*, which is based on declassified records and gives a new perspective on the abdication of Edward VIII and his love for Wallis Simpson.

PublicAffairs is a publishing house founded in 1997. It is a tribute to the standards, values, and flair of three persons who have served as mentors to countless reporters, writers, editors, and book people of all kinds, including me.

I. F. STONE, proprietor of *I. F. Stone's Weekly*, combined a commitment to the First Amendment with entrepreneurial zeal and reporting skill and became one of the great independent journalists in American history. At the age of eighty, Izzy published *The Trial of Socrates*, which was a national bestseller. He wrote the book after he taught himself ancient Greek.

BENJAMIN C. BRADLEE was for nearly thirty years the charismatic editorial leader of *The Washington Post*. It was Ben who gave the *Post* the range and courage to pursue such historic issues as Watergate. He supported his reporters with a tenacity that made them fearless and it is no accident that so many became authors of influential, best-selling books.

ROBERT L. BERNSTEIN, the chief executive of Random House for more than a quarter century, guided one of the nation's premier publishing houses. Bob was personally responsible for many books of political dissent and argument that challenged tyranny around the globe. He is also the founder and longtime chair of Human Rights Watch, one of the most respected human rights organizations in the world.

· · ·

For fifty years, the banner of Public Affairs Press was carried by its owner Morris B. Schnapper, who published Gandhi, Nasser, Toynbee, Truman, and about 1,500 other authors. In 1983, Schnapper was described by *The Washington Post* as "a redoubtable gadfly." His legacy will endure in the books to come.

Peter Osnos, *Founder and Editor-at-Large*